SO-ATL-526

'SCARDED

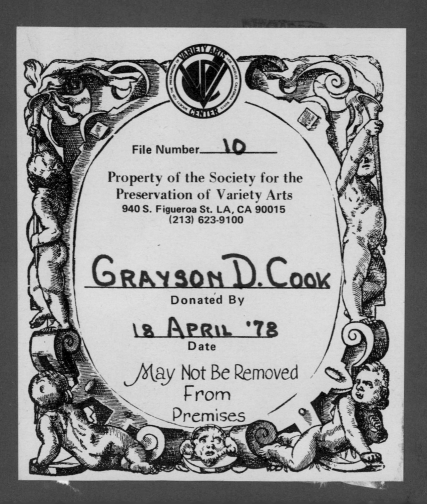

File Number____10____

**Property of the Society for the
Preservation of Variety Arts**
940 S. Figueroa St. LA, CA 90015
(213) 623-9100

GRAYSON D. COOK
Donated By

18 APRIL '78
Date

May Not Be Removed
From
Premises

Books by Pauline Kael

I LOST IT AT THE MOVIES

KISS KISS BANG BANG

Kiss Kiss
Bang Bang

Kiss Kiss Bang Bang

by
PAULINE KAEL

An Atlantic Monthly Press Book

LITTLE, BROWN AND COMPANY · BOSTON · TORONTO

COPYRIGHT © 1965, 1966, 1967, 1968 BY PAULINE KAEL

ALL RIGHTS RESERVED. NO PART OF THIS BOOK MAY BE REPRODUCED
IN ANY FORM OR BY ANY ELECTRONIC OR MECHANICAL MEANS IN-
CLUDING INFORMATION STORAGE AND RETRIEVAL SYSTEMS WITHOUT
PERMISSION IN WRITING FROM THE PUBLISHER, EXCEPT BY A REVIEWER
WHO MAY QUOTE BRIEF PASSAGES IN A REVIEW.

LIBRARY OF CONGRESS CATALOG CARD NO. 68–15561

FIRST EDITION

The articles "Movies on Television" and "Bonnie and Clyde" appeared
originally in the *New Yorker*.

The author wishes to thank the following magazines in whose pages
many of the articles in this book first appeared: *The Atlantic, Holiday,
Life, McCall's, Mademoiselle, The New Republic,* and *Vogue.*

ATLANTIC–LITTLE, BROWN BOOKS
ARE PUBLISHED BY
LITTLE, BROWN AND COMPANY
IN ASSOCIATION WITH
THE ATLANTIC MONTHLY PRESS

*Published simultaneously in Canada
by Little, Brown & Company (Canada) Limited*

PRINTED IN THE UNITED STATES OF AMERICA

A Note on the Title

THE words "Kiss Kiss Bang Bang," which I saw on an Italian movie poster, are perhaps the briefest statement imaginable of the basic appeal of movies. This appeal is what attracts us, and ultimately what makes us despair when we begin to understand how seldom movies are more than this.

Contents

I

Trends

The Creative Business

EARLY this year a producer-writer who began by goading me with lucrative offers — first to ghostwrite a book for him on "a sensational idea" (which turned out to be a denunciation of Method acting), then to work up a treatment for him on "an exciting new idea" (which turned out to be a spy spoof with a female spy), and then to do a quick (three-week) rewrite on a script he'd had sitting around for a decade — became rather hurt that I didn't rise to the bait. Puzzled at my refusals, he asked, "Don't you want to do something creative?"

I think that in his ambivalent way this man liked me and wanted to do something for me, but in show business there's not much point in asking yourself if someone really likes you or if he just thinks you can be useful to him, because there's no difference. In show business the successes are likely to be those whose tastes depend on their projects; after a while they may not know themselves what their tastes are. Besides, success develops a different kind of taste. The men in the movie business who can work regularly and talk publicly about their creative freedom are those whose fundamental aspirations (they really have no convictions) are the same as those of the studio heads — to be successful, to be acclaimed. It's no accident that even producers and exhibitors now talk about their creativity (which has come to mean their ability to make money and get publicity — their becoming celebrities), for they have the same drives and goals as the directors and many of the writers.

I doubt if the man who propositioned me had written a sentence in years: there was always someone (if not me, someone like me) to be hired for that, but these men make a sharp division between being a creative artist and anything else (like a critic) and they're so unselfcritical that they can call themselves and think of themselves as artists — without irony.

Being creative includes knowing how to exploit other people's ideas or earlier work you remember; being creative justifies ignorance and ruthlessness, indifference to and finally even contempt for art. Being creative is having something to sell, or knowing how to sell something, or having sold something. It has taken over what we used to mean by being "wised-up," knowing the tricks, the shortcuts. Television producers "create" a new quiz show; advertising men talk about getting "the creative juices flowing." What they think is *creativity* is simply the excitement of success, the exhilaration of power. It's in this kind of context that picture-making is considered a creative business.

I used to think that those shrewd, energetic (and sometimes even intelligent) men who made lousy big commercial movies must be eaten up by guilt, self-disgust, and the desire to do something good. After all, didn't just about every one of them talk about how as soon as he got in the economic position to do what he really wanted, he was going to make the pictures he couldn't make now; "after two for the public I can afford to make one for myself" was almost a refrain. I thought they wouldn't try so hard to justify their current production of schlock on the basis of the future art this schlock was going to make possible if they weren't ashamed of what they were doing. And although I never believed that they would do what they said, I thought they believed it.

But things have changed in the last few years: the hypocrisy has become merely ritualistic. Yes, they might refer to their new picture as a piece of crap, but they really enjoyed what they were doing. Even before these men embraced McLuhan for turning them into prophets and pioneers of the modern age, it was becoming clear that they dig corruption. Despite their protestations about that future artistic pie in the sky, they enjoy the power of packaging something for the millions and they're contemptuous of something that reaches only a few thousand people — even though what the millions buy may be so readily consumed that it has no more effect than one more candy bar eaten by an adolescent already disfigured by acne, and even though the work that "fails" now because it appeals to only a few thousand or a half million may add a few thousand more year by year, may perhaps be of lasting value.

What makes a man who is producing mass culture believe in it? This is the conversation of a movie mogul, new style: "I'm quite success-oriented. I don't mean artistic success but commercial success. There's nothing I hate more than failure." That isn't some cringing little flunky talking but a rich, powerful multi-Oscared producer — a cringing *big* flunky. And then, after telling me how important it was for him to be a celebrity, he said, in a humble, constricted little voice, "Maybe if I'd grown up in a society with different values, my values would be different. But I exist in a culture which venerates popular success." He went on to tell me about how he was "a suffering person" and how he had avoided reading a review of mine because he knew it would cause him pain; by then my flesh was beginning to crawl and I ended the interview. I am aware of protocol but I figured a man that masochistic is begging to forfeit his prerogatives.

The more powerful these men become, the more they explain themselves as victims of the system. Hollywood is that state of mind where men who make movies about brotherhood and the responsibility of the German people for Hitler and no-man-is-an-island can harass a critic and then ask to be consoled because "you're strong, you don't realize how weak I am."

They don't really accept any responsibility, not even for their own weakness. They use Freud to show they can't help it, just as they reach out for the most specious concepts of social science — "outer-directed," "success-oriented" — in order to justify what they are and do. They grabbed the words out of McLuhan's mouth and now they've got arguments to prove they were right not to care what they threw on the screen or filled television time with. They had been tuned in on the future. They have an instinct for what they can use — like "pop" and "camp" — which for them become ways of discounting any criticism as irrelevant to the "fun" movies they're making. A "fun" movie doesn't mean that you'll have fun seeing it but that you're not expected to think about it one way or another. A lot of the entertainment that is now called "swinging" is what we would once have called stupid. It's "swinging" to accept the worst of mass culture as if it had wonderful "dumb" qualities we weren't previously sophisticated enough to accept. Probably part of the explanation is that people are attempting to "get with" mass culture because it's so omnipresent they feel nothing can be done about it, so they might as well make the best of it by treating it as, after all, "fun." But to buy heavy frolics is to accept the role of consumer of entertainment — to accept, like that producer, the role of victim. But he and his kind only *play* the role. They pollute American life and spread the pollution as far as possible — while buying estates in the least polluted spots in the world, not only for tax purposes but so that they and their children can escape the vulgarity of America.

[October 1966]

A Sense of Disproportion

The Sand Pebbles, Grand Prix, Funeral in Berlin, The Quiller Memorandum

THERE are not — and there never were — any formal principles that can be used to judge movies but there are concepts that are serviceable for a while and so pass for, or are mistaken for, "objective" rules until it becomes obvious that the new work that we respond to violates them. One serviceable notion was the distinction between comedy and mere gag-writing. In comedy, the humor was supposed to be integral, to grow out of a situation and to contribute to a mood or idea and to the development of the structure; in gag-writing, the joke was just brought in for a laugh — and we probably felt mildly contemptuous even when we did laugh. Now we're more likely to respond to surreal suddenness, to the surprises of an "inspired" gag-writer and to be impatient of the too-tame comedic situation with its neat preparations and its air of expectation. The decisive factor, then, is not — or is not any longer — structural preparation but the style of the work and/or the quality of the joke itself.

Good construction used to be considered a formal necessity, but twenty years ago an accident split the seams of the well-constructed Hollywood movie. William Faulkner, Jules Furthman, and their co-writers employed to whip up a screenplay for Howard Hawks out of Raymond Chandler's *The Big Sleep* couldn't figure out the plot, and, probably on the basis that nobody gave a damn anyway, they went ahead with the screenplay. As if determined to blow the plot, somebody even threw in a swatch of "suggestive" dialogue from an old horse-racing comedy, *Straight, Place, and Show,* which hadn't attracted much attention when spoken by Ethel Merman and Richard Arlen but which, out of context, was all innuendo — and with a new high voltage not only because of the Bacall and Bogart delivery but *because* it didn't relate to anything in the movie. Sophisticated sex talk became the link for the movie, and the incidents and talk were so entertaining that audiences didn't care about the solution of the murder plot. More than that, as audience, we enjoyed the joke that (probably partly inadvertently) had been played on us: *The Big Sleep* made us aware how little we often *had* cared about the ridiculously complicated plots of detective thrillers, how fed up with them we were — that we had been going for the riffs for a long time without being aware of it.

Part of the fun of movies is in not believing, and it's often a relief to see a movie that doesn't go through all the clumsy motions of trying to make a situation seem believable. The wits who worked in the movies in the thirties had known it then. In the early Marx Brothers comedies like *Duck Soup,* in the great W. C. Fields–Jack Oakie *Million Dollar Legs,* even in the Crosby-Hope *Road* pictures, part of the pleasure was in the *absence* of solemn preparation. The construction that wasn't there was our referent when we saw these films: we enjoyed its absence as a nose-thumbing at the tediously constructed conventional movies. But those writers had been pressured to pin their wit down in situation comedy and family entertainment.

There was a clue right at the beginning of movies that perhaps dramatic structure wasn't so important: the serials, which were even more primitive — and more flexible — in construction than the simplest stage dramas. They were constructed *serially,* just one incident after another without regard to logic or dramatic coherence. But not even the Hollywood merchants thought that they could get by with that kind of construction in feature films made for metropolitan audiences. The triumph of virtue over vice had to be constructed dramatically: if something was introduced, it had to be related to the whole, if a character appeared we knew there was a reason for his coming on and we waited to find out how he was related to the events. Everything that happened had to be prepared for. The heroine couldn't suddenly be killed in a car accident: we would have to see first that the driver wasn't in condition to drive, that something awful was going to happen. Or as even fairly recently in *Lonely Are the Brave,* the whole movie could be preparation for the final collision. In life there were accidents; in art, it was assumed, there had to be reasons, and fates were explained by character and circumstance. Hack writers and directors showed their hand, forcing each piece of plot creakingly in place; but when a good writer and director were at work, the smooth unfolding was an aesthetic pleasure. Now, this kind of construction can still give pleasure but of a different nature: it appears to be such an *unnecessary* formalism that it is freakishly entertaining — an aesthetic game played for its own sake. In its older form, it can still be viewed weekly on the television series "Peyton Place," which is so full of anxious preparation for each new terrible revelation or calamity that nothing that happens can ever fulfill the dreadful expectations.

When, in the past, movies didn't create expectations, didn't build and prepare for their climaxes, people often referred to them contemptuously as comic strips because they had that dead, flat, one-dimensional quality of narrative without dramatic structure, just one thing after another. That's how we used to be able to tell when a movie director was an amateur who didn't understand the medium. It's only recently, with the success of the James Bond pictures and in the general enthusiasm for pop, that there has been the discovery that for certain kinds of one-dimensional material, this comic-strip style (developed, after all, on one-dimensional material), used intentionally, has a kind of nonreflective immediacy that people enjoy. One of the pleasures of the Bond pictures is in getting away from the mechanics of dramatic construction back to the one-damn-thing-after-another serial; and it's a liberation. The audience doesn't have to watch the characters drag their feet through all those boring, unconvincing motions that used to get them into tricky situations: they start right off in one, and go on to the next.

But even with wit and frenzied invention, how is comic-strip action to hold an audience for a couple of hours — unless the material is somehow deepened and organized dramatically? And that, of course, would destroy the comic-strip simplicity. The demand for one-dimensional entertainment that can fill and sustain an evening is almost impossible to satisfy. But if the Bond pictures and the imitations like *Our Man Flint* and *The Silencers,* or the Richard Lester comic-strip *Help!,* are caught in an aesthetic trap, they are nevertheless lucky because the audience is disposed, by the nature of the entertainment, to accept the brief periods of inaction and the sequences that misfire. It isn't as if the movie laboriously built up to something for an hour: there's always another episode coming up that may be better and even if it isn't, what the hell? It's just a comic-strip anyway.

It's the non-comic-strip movies that are caught in a more serious aesthetic trap which may turn into a box-office problem. The disproportion between the scale of the huge productions and the little that actually goes on in the movies is so staggering that it's not unusual these days to hear people in the lobbies at intermission and afterward saying "I don't get it." They can't comprehend that there isn't any *more* going on in the movie: they think they must be missing something.

And it really is hard to believe that a twelve-million-dollar movie like Robert Wise's *The Sand Pebbles,* which has involved thousands of people in years of labor for the almost incredible task of re-creating ports and waterfronts and villages of China in 1926, is not about anything more than an American sailor (Steve McQueen) who loves engines, and a schoolgirlish American teacher (Candice Bergen) with vague desires for adventure and good work. It's no wonder that Bosley Crowther, searching like the people in the lobby for what he was missing, came up with: "it is not as historical romance that it is likely to grab the audience, but as a weird sort of hint of what has happened and is happening in Vietnam." This weird hint is just that "trying to say something" which so many Hollywood liberals pride themselves on, though what they say is so vague and confused, it's worse than nothing. This movie is just an old-fashioned action-adventure tale. If it had been done twenty years ago, it would have been fast and unpretentious, with some ingeniously faked background shots, or even stock footage, and we would have concentrated our attention on the good moments (like McQueen teaching the Chinese boy about the gunboat engine, or the terrifying instant when McQueen's ax changes from useful implement to lethal weapon) and we would never have asked for larger historical meanings. We probably wouldn't even have looked for deeper characterizations or better acting because we had learned not to expect much from the action genre — although I think even in a modest little adventure melodrama we would have been puzzled by such fumbling exposition. But when a movie is this big (and over three hours long) we sit there thinking, "What's it all for?"

Somebody will probably break through by using disproportion purposefully, or maybe it will accidentally result in some new effects that will cause a breakthrough. Right now going to big movies is like asking for a shot of bourbon and having Niagara come down on your head. You're stoned without ever getting high.

After the first few minutes of *Grand Prix,* my companion leaned over and said, "Now you know what it's like to be run over." Saul Bass had got hold of heavy tires and Cinerama: you don't go to this movie, it comes after you. And you're not rid of Bass after the titles; he keeps coming back with montages — little World's Fair-type documentaries, simpleminded and square, that pad out the three hours. The story of this John Frankenheimer racing-car picture is the same old story with the same types we've seen flying planes and racing horses in dozens of cheap, fast, hour-and-a-quarter movies, and there's even the same kind of cheap, old plot construction that tells us that Yves Montand is going to die in a race (he has to because his bitch of a wife has just informed us she'll never give him a divorce and we know that Eva Marie Saint who loves him is a high-type lady who just can't go on with him like this . . .). The crashes are the best things in the movie, they're really gorgeous, so we don't mind losing a few of the actors, though the picture could more easily have spared James Garner who seems to be taking the whole thing much too seriously, and Miss Saint who is as flat and anxious as a mother in a soap opera.

Though there were lots of women in the audience dozing, I stayed awake and began to enjoy the same sort of silly terrible things that I used to enjoy at bad movies — like Toshiro Mifune who seemed to have a mechanical English voice that needed cranking, and Françoise Hardy who seemed to have wandered in from another picture that was probably more fun, and Brian Bedford who should stay all bandaged up because he has a suffering charm, and Jessica Walter with her Sydney Guilaroff hair that is now, at last, done by Sydney Guilaroff, and Rachel Kempson with her excruciating English mother bit-between-her-teeth, and Genevieve Page curling her upper lip in the role of (honest) "Monique Delvaux Sarti." But there's so much plain and fancy hard work involved in a production like *Grand Prix* that it begins to seem almost cruelly flippant to watch it for the same reasons we'd watch a lousy old movie on television.

The screen is too big for the muddling-through little-spy heroes of *Funeral in Berlin* and *The Quiller Memorandum.* The city of Berlin dominates the movies — not for travelogue purposes and not for atmosphere either but just because the directors had to put *something* on the big wide screens. And the technology that keeps providing panoramic cityscapes is oddly out of scale with the fabricated plots which keep collapsing and are propped up with moralistic lessons about the Nazis or neo-Nazis. When a picture can't make it on its own, the producers pull in a "controversial" message — the way a couple whose marriage is falling apart decide to have a baby.

In *Funeral in Berlin,* which is the more entertaining of the two, Michael Caine is Harry Palmer (of *The Ipcress File*) again but this time he is supposed to gain new humanity when he sees that the Israeli agents really believe in principles. But about the only thing that made Palmer amusing was his shabby small-time "professional's" indifference to the larger stakes: improve his character and you take away the only character he had.

In *The Quiller Memorandum* George Segal is the agent trying to locate the headquarters of the neo-Nazis, and competent and personable actor though he is, it's rather embarrassing to see him the star of a movie in which the assorted spies include Alec Guinness and Max von Sydow. Even the actors are too big for their purposes here: their talents are out of scale with their roles. Von Sydow is reduced to cracking his knuckles for "characterization."

Both Guy Hamilton who directed *Funeral in Berlin* and Michael Anderson who directed *The Quiller Memorandum* were once assistants to Carol Reed, and if it's hard to tell their movies apart, maybe it's because both directors imitate Reed's Vienna-set *The Third Man* and his Berlin-set *The Man Between* (which are clearer in my memory — sharper in outline and in detail — than these movies I saw last week). In Reed's postwar cities, war had changed the survivors, had made them different: they were tired, ravaged opportunists who no longer felt or thought like you and me. So the city was a nightmare city and the simple American (Joseph Cotten in *The Third Man*) or the fresh English girl (Claire Bloom in *The Man Be-*

tween) who stumbled into it was like a tourist in Hell. The intrigues (especially in Graham Greene's script for *The Third Man*) were part of the living rot of postwar corruption, and the melancholy twang of the zither brought evil seductively close.

Hamilton and Anderson show us so much of the impersonal, prosperous modern Berlin that we get the idea that they mean to tell us something about rot under the glitter, though Berlin in their movies looks like pretty pictures of the prettier parts of New York and could as easily be the setting of a comedy. If it's supposed to be sinister just because it's so bland, they could signal us somehow: that's what movie-making is all about. Reed in the forties would have given more meaning to the atmosphere in the first half-dozen establishing shots than they do in two hours. The point is, he had a reason to be quick and economic: if they were, they'd have nothing left to put on the screen. *The Third Man* was disturbingly ambivalent: Greene and Reed made the ruins fascinating and evil attractively baroque, and Orson Welles's sly, puffy, shameless Harry Lime had more life in him than a movie "good" man ever has. These two new thrillers might have been written by the character Joseph Cotten played in *The Third Man* — Holly Martins, who turned out pulp Westerns — though *Quiller* was actually scripted by Harold Pinter. It doesn't have a shred of plausibility, its clichés are not freshened by any original touches, it hasn't a memorable character or a witty line, and yet in some preposterous way it *is* literate. The literacy begins to seem just another expensive element of the empty technology — like Robert Bolt's literacy in *Dr. Zhivago*.

[January 1967]

Movie Brutalists

THE basic ideas among young American film-makers are simple: the big movies we grew up on are corrupt, obsolete or dead, or are beyond our reach (we can't get a chance to make Hollywood films) — so we'll make films of our own, cheap films that we can make in our own way. For some this is an attempt to break into the "industry"; for others it is a different approach to movies, a view of movies not as a popular art or a mass medium but as an art form to be explored.

Much of the movie style of young American film-makers may be explained as a reaction against the banality and luxuriant wastefulness which are so often called the superior "craftsmanship" of Hollywood. In reaction, the young become movie brutalists.

They, and many in their audiences, may prefer the rough messiness — the uneven lighting, awkward editing, flat camera work, the undramatic succession of scenes, unexplained actions, and confusion about what, if anything, is going on — because it makes their movies seem so different from Hollywood movies. This inexpensive, inexperienced, untrained look serves as a kind of testimonial to sincerity, poverty, even purity of intentions. It is like the sackcloth of true believers which they wear in moral revulsion against the rich in their fancy garments. The look of poverty is not necessarily a necessity. I once had the experience, as chairman of the jury at an experimental film festival, of getting on the stage, in the black silk dress I had carefully mended and ironed for the occasion, to present the check to the prizewinner, who came forward in patched, faded dungarees. He got an ovation, of course. I had seen him the night before in a good dark suit, but now he had dressed for his role (deserving artist) as I had dressed for mine (distinguished critic).

Although many of the American experimentalists have developed extraordinary kinds of technique, it is no accident that the virtuoso technicians who can apparently do almost anything with drawing board or camera are not taken up as the heroes of youth in the way that brutalists are. Little is heard about Bruce Baillie or Carroll Ballard whose camera skills expose how inept, inefficient, and unimaginative much of Hollywood's self-praised work is, or about the elegance and grandeur of Jordan Belson's short abstract films, like *Allures,* that demonstrate that one man working in a basement can make Hollywood's vaunted special effects departments look archaic. Craftsmanship and skill don't, in themselves, have much appeal to youth. Rough work looks rebellious and sometimes it is: there's anger and frustration and passion, too, in those scratches and stains and multiple superimpositions that make our eyes swim. The movie brutalists, it's all too apparent, are hurting our eyes to save our souls.

They are basically right, of course, in what they're *against.* Aesthetically and morally, disgust with Hollywood's fabled craftsmanship is long overdue. I say fabled because the "craft" claims of Hollywood, and the notion that the expensiveness of studio-produced movies is necessary for some sort of technical perfection or "finish," are just hucksterism. The reverse is closer to the truth: it's becoming almost impossible to produce a decent-looking movie in a Hollywood studio. In addition to the touched-up corpses of old dramatic ideas, big movies carry the dead weight of immobile cameras, all-purpose light, whorehouse décor. The production values are often ludicrously inappropriate to the subject matter, but studio executives, who charge off roughly 30 percent of a film's budget to studio overhead, are very keen on these production values which they frequently remind us are the hallmark of American movies.

In many foreign countries it is this very luxuriousness that is most envied and admired in American movies: the big cars, the fancy food, the opulent bachelor lairs, the gadget-packed family homes, even the loaded freeways and the noisy big cities. What is not so generally understood is the studio executives' implicit assumption that this is also what American audiences like. The story may not involve more than a few spies and counterspies, but the wide screen will be filled. The set decorator will pack the sides of the image with fruit and flowers and furniture.

When Hollywood cameramen and editors want to show their expertise, they imitate the effects of Japanese or European craftsmen, and then the result is pointed to with cries of "See, we can do anything in Hollywood." The principal demonstration of art and ingenuity among these "craftsmen" is likely to be in getting their sons and nephews into the unions and in resisting any attempt to make Hollywood movie-making flexible enough for artists to work there. If there are no cinematographers in modern Hollywood who can be discussed in the same terms as Henri Decae or Raoul Coutard or the late Gianni di Venanzo, it's because the studio methods and the union restrictions and regulations don't make it possible for talent to function. The talent is strangled in the business bureaucracy, and the best of our cinematographers perform safe, sane academic exercises. If the most that a gifted colorist like Lucien Ballard can hope for is to beautify a John Michael Hayes screenplay — giving an old tart a fresh complexion — why not scratch up the image?

The younger generation doesn't seem much interested in the obstacles to art in Hollywood, however. They don't much care about why the older directors do what they do or whether some of the most talented young directors in Hollywood, like Sam Peckinpah (*Ride the High Country, Major Dundee*) or Irvin Kershner (*The Hoodlum Priest, The Luck of Ginger Coffey, A Fine Madness*), will break through and do the work they should be doing. There is little interest in the work of gifted, intelligent men outside the industry, like James Blue (*The Olive Trees of Justice*) or John Korty (*The Crazy Quilt*), who are attempting to make inexpensive feature films as honestly and independently as they can. These men (and their films) are not flamboyant; they don't issue manifestos, and they don't catch the imagination of youth. Probably, like the students in film courses who often do fresh and lively work, they're not surprising enough, not different enough. The new film enthusiasts are, when it comes down to it, not any more interested in simple, small, inexpensive pictures than Hollywood is. The workmen's clothes and crude movie techniques may cry out, "We're poor and honest. They're rich and rotten." But, of course, you can be poor and not so very honest and, although it's harder to believe, you can even be rich and not so very rotten. What the young seem to be interested in is brutalism. In certain groups, automatic writing with a camera has come to be considered the most creative kind of film-making.

Their hero, Jean-Luc Godard — one of the most original talents ever to work in film and one of the most uneven — is not a brutalist at so simple a level, yet he comprises the attitudes of a new generation. Godard is what is meant by a "film-maker." The concept of a "film-maker" — as distinguished from a director (or even writer-directors like Bergman or Fellini) — is a response and reaction to traditional methods of financing as well as shooting, and to traditional concepts of what a movie is. Godard works with a small crew and shifts ideas and attitudes from movie to movie and even within movies. While Hollywood producers straddle huge fences trying to figure out where the action is supposed to be — and never find out — Godard in himself is where the action is.

There is a disturbing quality in Godard's work that perhaps helps to explain why the young are drawn to his films and identify with them, and why so many older people call him a "coterie" artist and don't think his films are important. *His characters don't seem to have any future.* They are most alive (and most appealing) just because they don't conceive of the day after tomorrow; they have no careers, no plans, only fantasies of roles they could play — of careers, thefts, romance, politics, adventure, pleasure, a life like in the movies. Even his world of the future, *Alphaville,* is, photographically, a documentary of Paris in the present. (All of his films are in that sense documentaries — as were also, and also by necessity, the grade B American gangster films that influenced him.) And even before *Alphaville,* the people in *The Married Woman* were already science fiction — so blank and affectless no mad scientist was required to destroy their souls.

His characters are young, unrelated to families and background. Whether deliberately or unconsciously, he makes his characters orphans who, like the students in the theatres, feel only attachments to friends, to lovers — attachments that will end with a chance word or the close of the semester. They're orphans, by extension, in a larger sense, too, unconnected with the world, feeling out of relationship to it. They're a generation of familiar strangers.

An elderly gentleman recently wrote me, "Oh, they're such a bore, bore, bore, modern youth! All attitudes and nothing behind the attitudes. When I was in my twenties, I didn't just loaf around, being a rebel, I went places and did things. The reason they all hate the squares is because the squares remind them of the one thing they are trying to forget: there *is* a Future and you must build for it."

He's wrong, I think. The young are not "trying to forget": they just don't think in those terms. Godard's power — and possibly his limitation — as an artist is that he so intensely expresses how they do feel and think. His characters don't plan or worry about careers or responsibilities; they just live. Youth makes them natural aristocrats in their indifference to sustenance, security, hard work; and prosperity has turned a whole generation — or at least the middle-class part of it — into aristocrats. And it's astonishing how many places they do go to and how many things they can do. The difference is in how easily they do it all. Even their notion of creativity — as what comes naturally — is surprisingly similar to the aristocratic artist's condescension toward those middle-class plodders who have to labor for a living, for an education, for "culture."

Here, too, Godard is the symbol, exemplar, and proof. He makes it all seem so effortless, so personal — just one movie after another. Because he is so skillful and so incredibly disciplined that he can make his pictures for under a hundred thousand dollars, and because there is enough of a youthful audience in France to support these pictures, he can do almost anything he wants within those budgetary limits. In this achievement of independence, he is almost alone among movie directors: it is a truly heroic achievement. For a younger generation he is the proof that it is possible to make and go on making films your own way. And yet they don't seem aware of how rare he is or how hard it is to get in that position. Even if colleges and foundations make it easier than it has ever been, they will need not only talent but toughness to be independent.

As Godard has been able to solve the problems of economic freedom, his work now poses the problems of artistic freedom — problems that few artists in the history of movies have been fortunate enough to face. The history of great film directors is a history of economic and political obstacles — of compromises, defeats, despair, even disgrace. Griffith, Eisenstein, von Stroheim, von Sternberg, Cocteau, Renoir, Max Ophuls, Orson Welles — they were defeated because they weren't in a position to do what they wanted to do. If Godard fails, it will be because what he wants to do — which is what he *does* — isn't good enough.

Maybe he is attempting to escape from freedom when he makes a beautiful work and then, to all appearances, just throws it away. There is a self-destructive urgency in his treatment of themes, a drive toward a quick finish. Even if it's suicidal for the hero or the work, Godard is impatient for the ending: the mood of his films is that there's no way for things to work out anyway, something must be done even if it's disastrous, no action is intolerable.

It seems likely that many of the young who don't wait for others to call them artists, but simply announce that they are, don't have the patience to make art. A student's idea of a film-maker isn't someone who has to sit home and study and think and work — as in most of the arts — but someone who goes out with friends and shoots — a social activity. It is an extroverted and egotistic image of the genius-creator. It is the Fellini-Guido figure of *8½,* the movie director as star. Few seem to have noticed that by the time of *Juliet of the Spirits* he had turned into a professional party-giver. Film-making, carried out the way a lot of kids do it, is like having a party. And their movie "ideas" are frequently no more than staging and shooting a wild, weird party.

"Creativity" is a quick route to power and celebrity. The pop singer or composer, the mod designer, says of his work, "It's a creative way to make a living" — meaning it didn't take a dull lot of study and planning, that he was able to use his own inventiveness or ingenuity or talent to get to the top without much sweat. I heard a young film-maker put it this way to a teen-age art student: "What do you go to life class for? Either you can draw or you can't. What you should do is have a show. It's important to get exposure." One can imagine their faces if they had to listen to those teachers who used to tell us that you had to be able to do things the traditional ways before you earned the right to break loose and do things *your* way. They simply take shortcuts into other art forms or into pop arts where they can "express themselves" now. Like cool Peter Pans, they just take off and fly.

Godard's conception of technique can be taken as a highly intellectualized rationale for these attitudes. "The ideal for me," he says, "is to obtain right away what will work — and without retakes. If they are necessary, it falls short of the mark. The immediate is chance. At the same time it is definitive. What I want is the definitive by chance." Sometimes, almost magically, he seems to get it — as in many scenes of *Breathless* and *Band of Outsiders* — but often, as in *The Married Woman,* he seems to settle for arbitrary effects.

A caricature of this way of talking is common among young American film-makers. Some of them believe that everything they catch on film is definitive, so they do not edit at all. As proof that they do not mar their instinct with pedantry or judgment, they may retain the blank leader to the roll of film. As proof of their creative sincerity they may leave in the blurred shots.

Preposterous as much of this seems, it is theoretically not so far from Godard's way of working. Although his technical control is superb, so complete that one cannot tell improvisation from planning, the ideas and bits of business are often so arbitrary that they appear to be (and probably are) just things that he chanced to think of that day, or that he came across in a book he happened to be reading. At times there is a disarming, an almost ecstatic innocence about the way he uses quotes as if he had just heard of these beautiful ideas and wanted to share his enthusiasm with the world. After smiling with pleasure as we do when a child's discovery of the beauty of a leaf or a poem enables us to re-experience the wonder of responsiveness, we may sink in spirit right down to incredulity. For this is the rapture with "thoughts" of those whose minds aren't much sullied by thought. These are "thoughts" without thought: they don't come out of a line of thought or a process of thinking, they don't arise from the situation. They're "inspirations" — bright illuminations from nowhere — and this is what kids who think of themselves as poetic or artistic or creative think ideas are: noble sentiments. They decorate a movie and it is easy for viewers to feel that they give it depth, that if followed, these clues lead to understanding of the work. But if those who follow the clues come out with odd and disjunctive interpretations, this is because the "clues" are *not* integral to the movie but are clues to what else the artist was involved in while he was making the movie.

Putting into the work whatever just occurred to the artist is its own rationale and needs no justification for young Americans encouraged from childhood to express themselves creatively and to say whatever came into their heads. Good liberal parents didn't want to push their kids in academic subjects but oohed and aahed with false delight when their children presented them with a baked ashtray or a woven doily. Did anyone guess or foresee what narcissistic confidence this generation would develop in its banal "creativity"? Now we're surrounded, inundated by artists. And a staggering number of them wish to be or already call themselves "film-makers."

A few years ago a young man informed me that he was going to "give up" poetry and avant-garde film (which couldn't have been much of a sacrifice as he hadn't done anything more than talk about them) and devote himself to writing "art songs." I remember asking, "Do you read music?" and not being especially surprised to hear that he didn't. I knew from other young men that the term "art" used as an adjective meant that they were bypassing even the most rudimentary knowledge in the field. Those who said they were going to make art movies not only didn't consider it worth their while to go to see ordinary commercial movies, but usually didn't even know anything much about avant-garde film. I did not pursue the subject of "art songs" with this young man because it was perfectly clear that he wasn't going to do anything. But some of the young who say they're going to make "art movies" are actually beginning to make movies. Kids who can't write, who have never developed any competence in photography, who have never acted in nor directed a play, see no deterrent to making movies. And although most of the results are bad beyond our wildest fears, as if to destroy all our powers of prediction a few, even of the most ignorant, pretentious young men and women, are doing some interesting things.

Yet why are the Hollywood movies, even the worst overstuffed ones, often easier to sit through than the short experimental ones? Because they have actors and a story. Through what is almost a technological fluke, 16 mm movie cameras give the experimental film-maker greater flexibility than the "professional" 35 mm camera user, but he cannot get adequate synchronous sound. And so the experimentalists, as if to convert this liability into an advantage, have asserted that their partial use of the capabilities of the medium is the true art of the cinema, which is said to be purely visual. But their visual explorations of their states of consciousness (with the usual implicit social protest) get boring, the mind begins to wander, and though this lapse in attention can be explained to us as a new kind of experience, as even the purpose of cinema, our desire to see a movie hasn't been satisfied. (There are, of course, some young film-makers who are not interested in movies as we ordinarily think of them, but in film as an art medium like painting or music, and this kind of work must be looked at a different way — without the expectation of story content or meaning.) They probably won't be able to make satisfying *movies* until the problems of sound are solved not only technically but in terms of drama, structure, meaning, relevance.

It is not an answer to toss on a spoofing semi-synchronous sound track as a number of young film-makers do. It can be funny in a cheap sort of way — as in Robert Downey's *Chafed Elbows* where the images and sound are, at least, in the same style; but this isn't fundamentally different from the way George Axelrod works in *Lord Love a Duck* or Blake Edwards in *What Did You Do in the War, Daddy?,* and there's no special reason to congratulate people for doing underground what is driving us down there.

Total satire is opportunistic and easy; what's difficult is to make a movie in which something is taken seriously without making a fool of yourself.

Is Hollywood interested in the young movement? If it attracts customers, Hollywood will eat it up, the way *The Wild Angels* has already fed upon *Scorpio Rising*. At a party combining the commercial and noncommercial worlds of film, a Hollywood screen writer watched as an underground film-maker and his wife entered. The wife was wearing one of those classic film-makers' wives' outfits: a simple sack of burlap in natural brown, with scarecrow sleeves. The screen writer greeted her enthusiastically, "I really dig your dress, honey," he said, "I used to have a dress like that once."

[September 1966]

So Off-beat We Lose the Beat

Georgy Girl, Morgan!, The Red Desert

LIKE just about everything else at the moment, movies seem to be out of control. Is it possible that, as we increasingly hear suggested in discussions of civil rights or air pollution or Vietnam or education, "nobody's minding the store"? At *Georgy Girl* you may find yourself laughing, but intermittently, in discomfort or even stupefaction, asking yourself, "What are they doing in this movie? Do they know what they're doing?" They're obviously very clever, very talented, but what's going on? To get at the peculiar nature of *Georgy Girl,* let me go back a bit to *Morgan!,* which probably just because of the way it's out of control has touched a nerve for this generation.

Thirty years ago in *My Man Godfrey,* when Mischa Auer, as the parasitic left-wing artist, imitated a gorilla to entertain the rich family who kept him as a pet, the meaning and relations were so clear no one had to signal us that it was symbolic. In *Morgan!* David Warner isn't nearly as good at the gorilla act, which is plastered with so many tags and labels that all we can be sure of is that it's meant to be symbolic. He's not just a parasitic left-wing artist with a gorilla act, he's the misfit as hero, and a childlike romantic rebel, anarchist, outsider, nonconformist, etc.; he's also crazy, and in his pop fantasy life he's King Kong. *Morgan!* is Ionesco's *Rhinoceros* turned inside out: the method of *Rhinoceros* may have been absurd but its meaning was the conventional liberal theme — the danger of people becoming conformist-animals. *Morgan!* is a modernized version of an earlier, romantic primitivist notion that people are conformists, animals are instinctively "true" and happy and, of course, "free."

Morgan! was maddening to many older people because of its kids' notion of nonconformity as crazy fun, its way of giving adolescent confusion the borrowed significance of symbols, its maudlin, schizoid mixture of comedy and whimsy and psychopathology and tragedy and pathos. It seemed the ultimate in grotesque pop homogenization: Trotsky's death acted out in farce with a smashed eggshell went even farther than Edward Albee turning a great writer's name into a stupid joke.

I haven't bothered to say that *Morgan!* is a bad movie because although that's implicit in what I'm saying, it's a minor matter. The point is that it's not an ordinary movie and whether it's good or bad is of less interest than why so many young people respond to it the way they do, especially as, in this case, they are probably responding to exactly what we think makes it bad. Sometimes bad movies are more important than good ones just because of those unresolved elements that make them such a mess. They may get at something going on around us that the movie-makers felt or shared and expressed in a confused way. *Rebel Without a Cause* was a pretty terrible movie but it reflected (and possibly caused) more cultural changes than many a good one. And conceivably it's part of the function of a movie critic to know and indicate the difference between a bad movie that doesn't much matter because it's so much like other bad movies and a bad movie that matters (like *The Chase* or *The Wild Angels*) because it affects people strongly in new, different ways. And if it be said that this is sociology, not aesthetics, the answer is that an aesthetician who gave his time to criticism of current movies would have to be an awful fool. Movie criticism to be of any use whatever must go beyond formal analysis — which in movies is generally a disguised form of subjective reaction to meanings and implications, anyway.

Those who made *Morgan!* probably not only share in the confusion of the material but, like the college audience, *accept* the confusion. This indifference to artistic control is new. I think *Morgan!* is so appealing to college students because it shares their self-view: they accept this mess of cute infantilism and obsessions and aberrations without expecting the writer and director to straighten it out or resolve it and without themselves feeling a necessity to sort it out. They didn't squirm as we did: they accepted the grotesque and discordant elements without embarrassment. I'd guess that to varying degrees they felt they *were* Morgan. And that suited them just fine.

They may be shocked when they see that he really is crazy and in pain, but they can quickly accept that, too, because he's mad in a pop way they respond to — madness as the ultimate irresponsibility for the rebel, the only sanity for those who see what the "responsible" people supposedly did to this world, and all that. If flipness is all (as it is in so many of the new movies) the flip-out is just an accepted part of life. Students liberally educated not to regard analysis and breakdowns and treatment as anything shameful refer to their own crack-ups casually, even a little proudly, like battle scars, proof that they've had *experience*. They even talk about breakdowns as "opting-out" — as if it were a preference and a moral choice.

And of course to flip out and then flip back again, that makes you a hero because you've *been* there. It also takes the fear away.

Georgy is a misfit heroine: it isn't that she doesn't want to conform but that she can't because she just about *is* a gorilla. She's a brontosaurus of a girl, with the bizarre problems of a girl who's too big to be treated as a girl, and she's childlike and "natural" and artistic and all the rest of the paraphernalia which now decorate characters designed to be appealing to young audiences. *Georgy Girl* is so shrewdly designed it will probably appeal to older audiences as well. The out-of-control thing is so bad you take it for granted from the beginning. What's offensive about it is that *Georgy Girl* is already a commercialization of what in *Morgan!* seemed a genuine split and confusion. Lack of control is made grotesquely *cute*. Although it's funny, it's tricky and anarchistically chic and on the side of youth (like *The Knack*) — as if the most important thing that the writers and director could imagine was to be "larky."

Georgy Girl is so glib, so clever, so determinedly "kinky" that everything seems to be devalued. It's the cleverness of advertising art, of commercials, of fancy titles — it's as if nothing really meant anything and nothing simple could work any more. It's "touching" one moment and weird the next, and like *The Knack,* it has evaporated before you're outside the theatre.

Even that sense of discomfort, of puzzlement, evaporates, because it is all made trivial — Georgy's pain as well as her bright remarks. For example, without any preparation or explanation, there is a horrifying sequence in which she makes a monstrous fool of herself at a party, and then everything goes on as if it never happened. Will the episode or the lack of reactions to it be upsetting to a younger audience? I doubt it. I recently saw a famous professor make such a spectacle of himself on a public platform that I had one of those great feminine intuitions — a premonition that he would go home and kill himself. As it turned out, he gave a big party for his students later that night, and his students didn't think anything special about how he'd behaved on the platform, because he did it all the time. Maybe they liked him for it; it made him more colorful, more of a character. His lack of control brought him closer to them. And I assume that we're supposed to like Georgy more because she acts out her ludicrous and self-pitying impulses and doesn't think too much about it afterward. She has all the blessings of affect and of affectlessness.

Is *Georgy Girl* a good movie or a bad one? It just isn't that simple. To discuss the cast (Lynn Redgrave, Alan Bates, James Mason) or Narizzano's direction wouldn't help. It's a less important movie than *Morgan!* because it isn't so seriously confused; it doesn't touch a nerve, it only comes teasingly close. It's more enjoyable partly because it doesn't get at anything so fundamental.

These movies are not just symptoms that will go away. I think a pretty good case could be made for including *Lord Love a Duck* and *Who's Afraid of Virginia Woolf?* among the American works that are out of control, and this may suggest that here, as in England, some of the most talented people don't really quite know what they're doing. At best, we may get something that makes a new kind of art out of embarrassment; at worst, lack of control may become what art is taken to mean. There is already a generation for whom art is the domain of the irrational, of whatever can't be clearly expressed or clearly understood, and they have adopted film as their medium, their "religion."

The general public probably cares less about artistic control than has been assumed, or the public is also changing. One of the most surprising box-office successes of last year, *A Thousand Clowns,* laid some claims to being about nonconformity and it, too, went more and more out of control, becoming redundant and embarrassing and gross in that same they-don't-know-what-they're-doing way. It didn't take its hero as far as *Morgan's* romantic insanity but only to romantic crackpotism — harmless American nonconformity. The hero's idea of freedom was to wander in Central Park with a kid and make TV-style jokes about TV before going back to do it for money. Basically, it was about as nonconformist as Mom's apple pie, and it even fudged on that much daring by giving the Madison Avenue spokesman the audience-pulling speech, which the Motion Picture Academy promptly and gratefully honored with an Academy Award.

These movies are full of contradictions. Is part of their appeal the ancient, wheezing plot devices which crank them in motion? The kid is being forcibly taken away from the TV gag-writer; the gorilla is being separated from his mate; Georgy gets a baby to mother only to have the authorities take it away. Underneath all the nonconformity gear are the crooked little skeletons of old Shirley Temple pictures. Heartwarming. *Georgy Girl,* like *The Knack,* is the story of the ugly duckling, and by beating *Funny Girl* to the screen it jumps the gun on the new exploitation of comic pathos. Somehow those who made *Morgan!* managed (instinctively maybe but certainly shrewdly) to alter the original TV play hero from a tired adulterer to a monogamous free spirit — probably the purest-in-heart hero of recent years. The director Karel Reisz's method is so eclectic, in the most blatant sense of that word, that he has taken what he feels will "go" together; the last sequence, which so many people have tried to interpret, is borrowed from the end of Buñuel's *El,* where it made perfect sense. Here it supplies a "larky" finish. The obscenely "happy ending" of *Georgy Girl* is so off-beat we lose the beat.

Because these movies all use and manipulate pop, it's easy for serious critics to attack them for their mixture of conventions, for the infantilism of a Morgan, etc. Yet I think that, for example, the meanings of *The Red Desert* were basically just as confused and uncontrolled.

Those who tried to make sense out of *The Red Desert* as an attack on industrialism had their best efforts quashed by word from the source that nothing of the sort was intended. What *was* intended? No one could be sure, yet the movie did express certain modern emotional states with which we're probably all familiar. I once visited a woman in Beverly Hills who sat in a settee backed by a huge inlaid table covered with a marvelous collection of art books, but when I referred to one of them, her face was blank and confused, as if to say, what are you talking about? She almost quivered with terror whenever anyone came into the room, although God knows the butler had screened them carefully. Her conversation, or rather the phrases she dropped from nowhere into nothing, were about whether she should open an art gallery or give up her marriage or take a trip, but to where? I think she would have been perfectly likely to take a sandwich out of someone's mouth if the idea of food suddenly occurred to her.

Obviously, she couldn't think of anything to do with her life so she did nothing for herself, her husband, or anyone else — and made herself "interesting" by her desolation. Is she fascinating? Well in a way, if you like to observe this kind of post-analytic destroyed consciousness. These ladies who are taken care of and give nothing may be the new heiresses of the ages. They're taken care of presumably because they're so sensitive, so vulnerable. But, of course, who with money and nothing to do can't be sensitive and vulnerable? They're not vulnerable to what the rest of us are; they're indifferent to all that. At worst, they're patronizingly envious of us — of our exhausting jobs, our household chores, our struggle to find time to read and see and think. Their male equivalent is the handsome, rich young man who says, "Sometimes I wish I were Negro or Jewish or something . . ."

Knowing there are people like this, I can understand that *The Red Desert* relates to something. But the title and Ravenna and industrialism, that's all a red herring, and so, I think, is the use of color in the movie. The bored, indolent ladies of Beverly Hills and elsewhere are much more likely to feel that their *clothes* have suddenly gone gray and to rush out to buy others. Their lovers go gray, too, and they try on others. Despite this relationship to the world around us, I found the movie deadly: a hazy poetic illustration of emotional chaos — which was made peculiarly attractive. If I've got to be driven up a wall, I'd rather do it at my own pace — which is considerably faster than Antonioni's. I thought it qualified as the definitive example of art cinema: a movie becomes cinema when it can bore you as much as your worst experiences at lectures, concerts, and ballet; i.e., when it becomes something you feel you shouldn't walk out on. Those who loved the movie, the TV producers' and architects' wives who feel that their lives are wasted and who are too "gifted" to do good, useful work, were likely to say things like, "I loved looking at it, I didn't care what the content was," which probably means not just that they found it visually pleasurable but that they enjoyed drifting away into vague, stylish emotional states — which is about the only way one *can* respond to the frozen rhythms. I think they thought it was the story of their lives: they identified with that crazy sensitive broad the way college students do with Morgan. And as reacting to the movie meant for these women not an interpretation which could be validated by checking it against the meanings and connections in the work, but anything that happened to occur to them as they saw it or thought about it afterward, they didn't necessarily care that it didn't make sense. What it comes down to is which of these bad movies is their movie, or which fantasy of themselves do they adore?

You can wait to see if the high arts will put us in touch with these distortions of experience, or if the social sciences will deal with them in the "fullness of time," or you can go to the key bad movies now.

[November 1966]

Spoofing

Cat Ballou

"I trust ya', Honey — but cut the cards."

Advertising experts look to the future and find — a new breed of sophisticates that will not be so easy to convince.

They're coming. The new generation of young adults. Wise, hip, skeptical — unlike any audience businesses and advertisers have ever known before. A new breed of sophisticates who have been deluged by advertising since they were three. Bred to new wisdom at television's knee. Able to "tune out" automatically at the first sign of advertising puffery. Promising advertisers no problem so great as that of sophisticated disbelief.

    Purveyors of the advertising scene see this coming. The simplest social analysis of the highly educated, worldly American society now emerging indicates it.

THIS is an almost-full-page ad in the New York *Times,* May 11 and June 16, 1965.

    And what is the ad for? *Good Housekeeping* and its Consumers' Guaranty Seal. The ad closes with "Seeing it in *Good Housekeeping* is believing."

    The basic flattery of the customer is familiar, but the *kind* of flattery is new. Advertising, TV commercials, movies are trying to outwit disbelief by including it in the sell.

    Are those who no longer "believe" the advertising they hear and see really "a new breed of sophisticates," part of "the highly educated, worldly American society now emerging"? If disbelief were the result of knowledge, every New York cabdriver would be an educated man. What this generation was bred to at television's knee was not wisdom but cynicism: it is an indication of how self-important and self-congratulatory advertising men have become that they equate the cynical indifference of those wised up to *their* methods with wisdom.

Our society is disastrously utilitarian. We can no longer distinguish the ad from the entertainment, the front cover of the national magazine, in which an actor poses to plug his film, from the back cover, in which an actor sells cigarettes and indirectly also plugs a film. Television shows with groups of celebrities are a series of plugs (for books, records, nightclub appearances, movies) interrupted by commercials. Movies are constructed with product tie-ins worked into their structure: mattresses, stoves, toothpaste, airlines, whiskey, all with their brand names shining. The companies so advertised in turn feature the movie in *their* ads. Even without product tie-ins, modern-dress movies look just like ads and sell the advertising way of life. This is one of the reasons why our movies seem so slickly unreal: they look like the TV commercials that nobody "believes."

The acceleration in the standardization of mass culture since the end of World War II means that we are all hit by the same commodities, personalities, ideas, forces, fashions at the same time, and hit increasingly hard. If you drive across the country you'll find the same movies playing in every town and city, *Fanny Hill* and *Candy* on sale in every drugstore, pop and op in the bank and shop. At roadside restaurants you'll hear the same semi-parodistic songs coming out of jukeboxes; at a motel in the middle of nowhere you'll see the same TV shows, the same commercials you saw at home. The motel itself may be an exact reproduction of other motels, and you'll drive past supermarkets and housing developments that you could swear you'd already passed. The people in the small towns smell, look, read, react like the people in the big cities; there are no sticks anymore.

Only "schtik" — the fraudulent uniqueness that sells when real individuality or difference is risky. Schtik is the special bit, the magic gimmick that makes the old look new, the stale seem fresh; it is what will "grab" the public. It is the desperate hope of an easy solution when the sellers cannot predict what the public, satiated increasingly fast, will buy.

What stories will seem believable, what themes will involve modern audiences, what will interest people? The problem that the "purveyors of the advertising scene" analyze is also being double-faced by the slick magazines and by Hollywood. Like the *Mademoiselle* editor explaining why a piece of Jean Harlow fiction was being printed ("We thought it would be sort of campy and fun"), they clutch at any little schtik.

They're afraid they can't do the same old stuff any more — not straight, anyway — so they do it "tongue in cheek." They pretend they're superior to it. There is a story told about Tennessee Williams at the opening of *The Rose Tattoo*. When a stagehand said in consternation, "Why, Mr. Williams, they're laughing," Williams is supposed to have replied, "If they laugh, it's a comedy." People all over the country were bored with or laughing at advertising, commercials, magazines, movies, so the purveyors found a face-saving device. Now advertising kids advertising, TV commercials kid TV commercials, movies kid movies. They go "way-out," become "send-ups"; they nudge us that what they're doing is just a "put-on." It's as embarrassed and halfhearted a strategy as that of the fat man who makes himself a buffoon so you can't make more fun of him than he has already.

Spoofing has become the safety net for those who are unsure of their footing. Unlike satire, spoofing has no serious objectives: it doesn't attack anything that anyone could take seriously; it has no cleansing power. It's just a technique of ingratiation: the spoof apologizes for its existence, assures us that it's harmless, that it isn't aiming for beauty or expressiveness or meaning or even relevance. To many in the advertising business and to those young artists who often seem to be in the same business, it's a way of life — or, rather, a time killer on the way to the grave.

Still, the purveyors are full of anxieties. In screening rooms, the publicity men and critics can be heard asking nervously, "Will audiences outside the big cities get the joke?" Is it perhaps that they're uncertain whether *they* get it either? What *is* the point? Who is being put-on? Way-out where? Send-up what?

We're sending ourselves up. We are reaching the point at which the purveyors don't care about anything but how to sell and the buyers buy because they don't give a damn. When there is no respect on either side, commerce is a dirty word.

But not all the new generation is buying. Many of them don't just " 'tune out' automatically at the first sign of advertising puffery" because they know there's no place to tune in again. They're surrounded by selling, and they tune out, period. They want some meaning, some honesty, some deeper experience, and they try to find them in romantic ideas of rejection and revolution based on their moral revulsion from the situation in the South, or in folk music, in underground movies, in narcotics.

Even the worst underground movies — the most chaotic, confused, and boring, the most amateurish — may still look more "real," more "sincere" than industrial products like *The Sandpiper* or *Harlow,* which you can't believe, or gigantic spoofs like *The Great Race,* which you're not supposed to believe. But though the desire, the need, the clamor, among college students particularly, for underground movies grows out of important kinds of rejection, the underground movement is infected by what the students are trying to escape.

The underground cinema is largely a fabrication of publicity: the students are put-on by *Film Culture* and the *Village Voice,* and then they're fobbed off with parodies of Maria Montez movies, Andy Warhol spoofs of experimentation, and underground variants of exploitation films. And if these films often spoof old movies, new big movies are already an imitation of the underground. *What's New, Pussycat?* has the kind of jokes associated with underground movies; *The Knack* is already a fashionable, professionally "youthful" treatment of underground attitudes.

A movie that looks amateurish is not necessarily an answer to commercialism — it may be an innocent or a very shrewd form of commercialism; and commercial movies can all too easily imitate the amateurish look. Thus far, underground movies are too easy an answer: they're an illusory solution to a real problem — a commercialized society that nobody believes in.

Cat Ballou is the kind of movie which publicity handouts and all too often even reviews describe as zany romps and frolics, the performers as madcap, piquant, and beguiling. But it's uneven, lumpy, coy, and obvious, a self-consciously cute movie with so many things thrown into it — many of them over and over again — and with so little consistency or sureness of attitude that I was reminded of an architect friend telling me about the prosperous businessman and his wife who came to see him about building a hundred-thousand-dollar house. "You can do anything you want," they told him, "so long as it doesn't have any style."

It's a Western about a girl train robber, Cat Ballou (played by Jane Fonda), a sweet young cattle rustler (played by Michael Callan), his buddy who is whimsically called his uncle (Dwayne Hickman), a lovable old drunken wreck of a gunfighter (Lee Marvin), a darling Indian (Tom Nardini), and assorted killings, robberies, an attempted hanging, etc., mixed with wisecracks, an intermittent ballad, and reminiscences of *Along Came Jones, Destry Rides Again, Seven Brides for Seven Brothers,* etc. Somehow it's all supposed to go together. The producer, Harold Hecht, puts it this way: "It's a delightful spoof, a rib, of the classic Western type characterizations and situations. The film abounds in satire and the hilarious, yet contains great heart. You're moved even as you're laughing. We have everything going for us in the story — lusty, brawling action, fights and gunplay; romance, music, beautiful scenery and wonderful antic comedy à la Mack Sennett. Let me tell you, there's never a dull moment. Something's always happening."

Something's always happening all right, too much is happening, but Hecht is mistaken in thinking there's never a dull moment.

There are some nice things: Nat King Cole singing "They'll Never Make Her Cry"; Lee Marvin's ritual preparations for a gunfight; an almost brilliant bit of graveyard humor — when Marvin mistakes funeral candles for a birthday celebration; occasional good lines. But mainly it is full of sort-of-funny and trying-to-be-funny *ideas;* and a movie is not just ideas. They need to be realized and sustained, they need to be part of a total idea — which is to say a movie needs a *style.* In stage comedy it is timing that separates the first- from the second-rater; in film comedy even the greatest performers, the best scripts may seem second-rate if the director and editor fail in deftness and speed — if they do not give the movie the rhythm of comedy. They must have the supreme discretion to know when a gesture or a repeated bit of business intensifies the humor or destroys it. It is this sureness of touch which is style.

The director Elliot Silverstein and his associates want satire *and* "great heart"; they want to "have everything going" for them. But heavy forced humor and unrealized comic possibilities are not transformed by calling the result a spoof — or to strain it even further, a happening — any more than speeding up a sequence in order to pick up the pace is "à la Mack Sennett." What we are seeing is ineptitude — coyly disguised.

And indecision: the movie tries to keep all possibilities open. The bathtub sequence from the English comedy of twenty years ago, *On Approval,* is soddenly imitated, and then another bathtub scene sinks whatever comedy was left in the first. Two Lee Marvins — playing bad and good gunfighters — may not suffice; perhaps some in the audience may not appreciate parody, may long for a "real" romance — therefore a younger hero is also provided. Youth is supposed to be so attractive that it doesn't require characterization (which might even be considered a deterrent — limiting possible audience appeal), so Callan just cavorts, grinning archly to convey sexiness. And on the chance that he isn't well known enough, there's Hickman of TV "fame" cavorting, and so on. There are even two minstrels. Wasn't Cole enough? Is it perhaps that Stubby Kaye makes it cuter? A black man and a fat man — so nobody can fail to realize that the ballad singing is "for fun."

Cat Ballou isn't a parody — that would mean stylizing the conventions of a genre, not just using them and making jokes about them. It's a spoof, and it spoofs the only safe target — itself. Yet it is so uncertain of its tone that it even tries for a little poignancy or extra depth — something that can pass for meaning or a statement — by having Cat say to the aged robbers who have lost their spirit, "How sad — you got old." It isn't age that's sad, it's wasted lives — like the lives of moviemakers in a commercialized culture who don't know what they want to do or are too fearful to do it. The people who made this movie are in no position to pity others for lacking spirit.

[1965]

Tourist in the City of Youth

Blow-Up

SOME years ago I attended an evening of mime by Marcel Marceau, an elaborate exercise in aesthetic purification during which the audience kept applauding its own appreciation of culture and beauty, i.e., every time they thought they recognized what was supposed to be going on. It had been bad enough when Chaplin or Harpo Marx pulled this beauty-of-pathos stuff, and a whole evening of it was truly intolerable. But afterwards, when friends were acclaiming Marceau's artistry, it just wouldn't do to say something like "I prefer the Ritz Brothers" (though I do, I passionately do). They would think I was being deliberately lowbrow, and if I tried to talk in terms of Marceau's artistry versus Harry Ritz's artistry, it would be stupid, because "artist" is already too pretentious a term for Harry Ritz and so I would be falsifying what I love him for. I don't want to push this quite so far as to say that Marceau is to comedians I like as Antonioni's *Blow-Up* is to movies I like, but the comparison may be suggestive. And it may also be relevant that Antonioni pulls a Marceau-like expressionist finale in this picture, one of those fancy finishes that seems to say so much (but what?) and reminds one of so many naïvely bad experimental films.

Will *Blow-Up* be taken seriously in 1968 only by the same sort of cultural diehards who are still sending out five-page single-spaced letters on their interpretation of *Marienbad?* (No two are alike, no one interesting.) It has some of the *Marienbad* appeal: a friend phones for your opinion and when you tell him you didn't much care for it, he says, "You'd better see it again. I was at a swinging party the other night and it's all anybody talked about!" (Was there ever a good movie that everybody was talking about?) It probably won't blow over because it also has the *Morgan!–Georgy Girl* appeal; people identify with it so strongly, they get *upset* if you don't like it — as if you were rejecting not just the movie but *them*. And in a way they're right, because if you don't accept the peculiarly slugged consciousness of *Blow-Up,* you *are* rejecting something in them. Antonioni's new mixture of suspense with vagueness and confusion seems to have a kind of numbing fascination for them that they associate with art and intellectuality, and they are responding to it as *their* film — and hence as a masterpiece.

Antonioni's off-screen conversation, as reported to us, is full of impeccable literary references, but the white-faced clowns who open and close *Blow-Up* suggest that inside his beautifully fitted dinner jacket he carries — next to his heart — a gilt-edged gift edition of Kahlil Gibran. From the way people talk about the profundity of *Blow-Up,* that's probably what they're responding to. What would we think of a man who stopped at a newsstand to cluck at the cover girls of *Vogue* and *Harper's Bazaar* as tragic symbols of emptiness and sterility, as evidence that modern life isn't "real," and then went ahead and bought the magazines? Or, to be more exact, what would we think of a man who conducted a leisurely tour of "swinging" London, lingering along the flashiest routes and dawdling over a pot party and mini-orgy, while ponderously explaining that although the mod scene appears to be hip and sexy, it represents a condition of spiritual malaise in which people live only for the sensations of the moment? Is he a foolish old hypocrite or is he, despite his tiresome moralizing, a man who knows he's hooked?

It's obvious that there's a new kind of noninvolvement among youth, but we can't get at what that's all about by Antonioni's terms. He is apparently unable to respond to or to convey the new sense of community among youth, or the humor and fervor and astonishing speed in their rejections of older values; he sees only the emptiness of pop culture.

Those who enjoy seeing this turned-on city of youth, those who say of *Blow-Up* that it's the trip, it's where we are now in consciousness and that Antonioni is in it, part of it, ahead of it like Warhol, may have a better sense of what Antonioni is about than the laudatory critics. Despite Antonioni's negativism, the world he presents looks harmless, and for many in the audience, and not just the youthful ones, sex without "connecting" doesn't really seem so bad — naughty, maybe, but nice. Even the smoke at the pot party is enough to turn on some of the audience. And there's all that pretty color which delights the critics, though it undercuts their reasons for praising the movie because it's that bright, cleaned-up big-city color of I-have-seen-the-future-and-it's-fun. Antonioni, like his fashion-photographer hero, is more interested in getting pretty pictures than in what they mean. But for reasons I can't quite fathom, what is taken to be shallow in his hero is taken to be profound in him. Maybe it's because of the symbols: do pretty pictures plus symbols equal art?

There are the revelers who won't make room on the sidewalk for the nuns (spirit? soul? God? love?) and jostle them aside; an old airplane propeller is found in an antique shop; the hero considers buying the antique shop; two homosexuals walk their poodle, etc. Antonioni could point out that the poodle is castrated, and he'd probably be acclaimed for that, too — one more bitter detail of modern existential agony. There is a mock copulation with camera and subject that made me laugh (as the planes fornicating at the beginning of *Strangelove* did). But from the reviews of *Blow-Up* I learn that this was "tragic" and "a superbly realized comment on the values of our time" and all that. People seem awfully eager to abandon sense and perspective and humor and put on the newest fashion in hair shirts; New York critics who are just settling into their upper East Side apartments write as if they're leaving for a monastery in the morning.

Hecht and MacArthur used to write light satirical comedies about shallow people living venal lives that said most of what Antonioni does and more, and were entertaining besides; they even managed to convey that they were in love with the corrupt milieu and were part of it without getting bogged down. And Odets, even in late work like his dialogue for *Sweet Smell of Success,* also managed to convey both hate and infatuation. Love-hate is what makes drama not only exciting but possible, and it certainly isn't necessary for Antonioni to resolve his conflicting feelings. But in *Blow-Up* he smothers this conflict in the kind of platitudes the press loves to designate as proper to "mature," "adult," "sober" art. Who the hell goes to movies for mature, adult, sober art, anyway? Yes, we want more from movies than we get from the usual commercial entertainments, but would anybody use terms like mature, adult, and sober for *The Rules of the Game* or *Breathless* or *Citizen Kane* or *Jules and Jim?*

The best part of *Blow-Up* is a well-conceived and ingeniously edited sequence in which the hero blows up a series of photographs and discovers that he has inadvertently photographed a murder. It's a good murder mystery sequence. But does it symbolize (as one reviewer says) "the futility of seeking the hidden meanings of life through purely technological means"? I thought the hero did rather well in uncovering the murder. But this kind of symbolic interpretation is not irrelevant to the appeal of the picture: Antonioni loads his atmosphere with so much confused symbolism and such a heavy sense of importance that the viewers use the movie as a Disposall for intellectual refuse. We get the stock phrases about "the cold death of the heart," "the eroticism is chilling in its bleakness," a "world so cluttered with synthetic stimulations that natural feelings are overwhelmed," etc., because Antonioni *inspires* this jargon.

When the photographer loses the photographic record of the murder, he loses interest in it. According to *Time,* "Antonioni's anti-hero" — who is said to be a "little snake" and "a grincingly accurate portrait of the sort of squiggly little fungus that is apt to grow in a decaying society" — "holds in his possession, if only for an instant, the alexin of his cure: the saving grace of the spirit." (My Webster doesn't yield a clue to "grincingly"; an "alexin" is "a defensive substance, found normally in the body, capable of destroying bacteria.") In other words, if he did something about the murder, like going to the police, he would be accepting an involvement with the life or death of others, and he would find his humanity and become an OK guy to *Time*. (Would he then not be a representative of a decaying society, or would the society not then decay? Only *Time* can tell.)

This review, and many others, turn the murder into something like what the press and TV did with the Kitty Genovese case: use it as an excuse for another of those what-are-we-coming-to editorials about alienation and indifference to human suffering. What was upsetting about the Genovese case was not those among the "witnesses" who didn't want to get involved even to the degree of calling the police (cowardice is not a new phenomenon), but our recognition that in a big city we don't know when our help is needed, and others may not know when we need help. This isn't a new phenomenon, either; what is new is that it goes against the grain of modern social consciousness, i.e., we feel responsible even though we don't know how to act responsibly. The press turned it into one more chance to cluck, and people went around feeling very superior to those thirty-eight witnesses because they were sure *they* would have called the police.

The moral satisfaction of feeling indignant that people take away from these cases (though I'm not sure that *Time*'s moral is what Antonioni intended; probably not) is simple and offensive. Do all the times that the police are called when they are or aren't needed prove how humanly involved with each other we are? The editorial writers don't tell us. And they couldn't do much with the West Coast case of the young academic beaten, tied to his bed, moaning and crying for help for days before he died. His friends and neighbors heard him all right, but as that's how he customarily took his pleasure, they smiled sympathetically and went about their own affairs, not knowing that this time the rough trade he had picked up to beat him had been insanely earnest.

The quick rise to celebrity status of young fashion photographers, like the quick success of pop singers, makes them ideal "cool" heroes, because they don't come up the slow, backbreaking Horatio Alger route. And the glamour of the rich and famous and beautiful rubs off on the photographer who shoots them, making him one of them. Antonioni uses David Hemmings in the role very prettily — with his Billy Budd hair-do, he's like a Pre-Raphaelite Paul McCartney. But if we're supposed to get upset because this young man got rich quick — the way some people get morally outraged at the salaries movie stars make — that's the moral outrage television personalities specialize in and it's hardly worth the consideration of art-house audiences. Yet a surprising lot of people seem willing to accept assumptions such as: the fashion photographer is symbolic of life in our society and time; he turns to easy sex because his life and ours are empty, etc. Mightn't people like easy sex even if their lives were reasonably full? And is sex necessarily empty just because the people are strangers to each other, or is it just different? And what's so terrible about fast, easy success? Don't most of the people who cluck their condemnation wish they'd had it?

Vanessa Redgrave, despite an odd mod outfit, has a tense and lovely presence, and because she has been allowed to act in this film (in which almost no one else is allowed to project) she stands out. However, someone has arranged her in a wholly gratuitous mood — laughing with her head back and teeth showing in a blatant imitation of Garbo. It's almost a sub-liminal trailer for *Camelot* in which, according to advance publicity, she will be "the Garbo of the sixties." This little deformation does not stick out as it might in another movie because this movie is so ill-formed anyway. The exigencies of the plot force Antonioni to alter his typical "open" construction (famous partly because it was the most painstakingly planned openness in movie history). In *Blow-Up* he prepares for events and plants characters for reappearances when they will be needed, but limply, clumsily; and he finds poor excuses for getting into places like the discotheque and the pot party, which "use" London to tell us about dehumanization. In some terrible way that I suppose could be called Antonioni's genius, he complains of dehumanization in a dehumanized way, and it becomes part of noninvolvement to accept a movie like this as "a chronicle of our time."

Just as *Marienbad* was said to be about "time" and/or "memory," *Blow-Up* is said (by Antonioni and the critics following his lead) to be about "illusion and reality." They seem to think they are really saying something, and something impressive at that, though the same thing can be said about almost any movie. In what sense is a movie "about" an abstract concept? Probably what Antonioni and the approving critics mean is that high fashion, mod celebrity, rock and roll, and drugs are part of a sterile or frenetic existence, and they take this to mean that the life represented in the film is not "real" but illusory. What seems to be implicit in the prattle about illusion and reality is the notion that the photographer's life is based on "illusion" and that when he discovers the murder, he is somehow face to face with "reality." Of course this notion that murder is more real than, say, driving in a Rolls-Royce convertible, is nonsensical (it's more shocking, though, and when combined with a Rolls-Royce it gives a movie a bit of box office — it's practical). They're not talking about a concept of reality but what used to be called "the real things in life," the solid values they approve of versus the "false values" of "the young people today."

Antonioni is the kind of thinker who can say that there are "no social or moral judgments in the picture": he is merely showing us the people who have discarded "all discipline," for whom freedom means "marijuana, sexual perversion, anything," and who live in "decadence without any visible future." I'd hate to be around when he's making judgments. Yet in some sense Antonioni is right: because he doesn't *connect* what he's showing to judgment. And that dislocation of sensibility is probably why kids don't notice the moralizing, why they say *Blow-Up* is hip.

The cultural ambience of a film like this becomes mixed with the experience of the film: one critic says Antonioni's "vision" is that "the further we draw away from reality, the closer we get to the truth," another that Antonioni means "we must learn to live with the invisible." All this can sound great to those who don't mind not knowing what it's about, for whom the ineffable seems most important. "It's about the limits of visual experience. The photographer can't go beyond make-believe," a lady lawyer who loved the movie explained to me. "But," I protested, "visual experience is hardly make-believe any more than your practice is — perhaps less." Without pausing for breath she shifted to, "Why does it have to mean anything?" That's the game that's being played at parties this year at Marienbad. They feel they understand *Blow-Up,* but when they can't explain it, or why they feel as they do, they use that as the grounds for saying the movie is a work of art. *Blow-Up* is the perfect movie for the kind of people who say, "now that films have become an art form . . ." and don't expect to understand art.

Because the hero is a *photographer* and the blow-up sequence tells a story in pictures, the movie is also said to be about Antonioni's view of himself as an artist (though even his worst enemies could hardly accuse him of "telling stories" in pictures). Possibly it is, but those who see *Blow-Up* as Antonioni's version of *8½* — as making a movie about making a movie — seem to value that much more than just making a movie, probably because it puts the film in a class with the self-conscious autobiographical material so many young novelists struggle with (the story that ends with their becoming writers . . .) and is thus easy to mistake for the highest point of the artistic process.

There is the usual post-*Marienbad* arguing about whether the murder is "real" or "hallucinatory." There seems to be an assumption that if a movie can be interpreted as wholly or partially a dream or fantasy, it is more artistic, and I have been hearing that there is no murder, it's all in the photographer's head. But then the movie makes even less sense because there are no indications of anything in his character that relate to such fantasies. Bosley Crowther has come up with the marvelously involuted suggestion that as the little teeny-bopper orgy wasn't "real" but just the hero's "juvenile fantasy," the Production Code people shouldn't have thought they were seeing real titbits on the screen.

What is it about the symbolic use of characters and details that impresses so many educated people? It's not very hard to do: almost any detail or person or event in our lives can be pressed into symbolic service, but to what end? I take my dogs for a walk in New York City in January and see examples of "alienation." An old Negro woman is crooning, "The world out here is lonely and cold." A shuffling old man mutters, "Never did and never will, never again and never will." And there's a crazy lady who glowers at my dogs and shouts, "They're not fit to shine my canary's shoes!" Do they tell us anything about a "decaying society"? No, but if you had some banal polemical, social, or moral point to make, you could turn them into cardboard figures marked with arrows. In so doing I think you would diminish their individuality and their range of meaning, but you would probably increase your chances of being acclaimed as a deep thinker.

When journalistic details are used symbolically — and that is how Antonioni uses "swinging" London — the artist does not create a frame of reference that gives meaning to the details; he simply exploits the ready-made symbolic meanings people attach to certain details and leaves us in a profound mess. (The middlebrow moralists think it's profound and the hippies enjoy the mess.) And when he tosses in a theatrical convention like a mimed tennis game without a ball — which connects with the journalistic data only in that it, too, is symbolic — he throws the movie game away. It becomes ah-sweet-mystery-of-life we-are-all-fools, which, pitched too high for human ears, might seem like great music beyond our grasp.

[February 1967]

¿¿¿¿¿¿¿

Saddle Sore

El Dorado, The War Wagon, The Way West

RECENTLY a young film enthusiast from abroad said, "Someday I'm going to cause a revolution in American movies. I'm going to make a Western that's fair to the Indians." I groaned, because just about every writer and director and star about to make a big Western has explained it that way. And just about every Western one can think of has tried to be "fair" in the sense that the Indians were represented as noble and decent people who were pushed to violence by betrayal — by broken treaties that deprived them of land and food, or, in the usual melodrama, by the treachery of "renegade" whites who sold them guns and whiskey or cheated and manipulated them. In the plot structure, the Indians are almost always the victims, the white men the villains.

Yet that is not how audiences, abroad or here, experience the genre; and each new group of film-makers that sets out to right the movie wrongs done to the Indians probably thinks that they're going to correct a grave injustice — "cause a revolution" — as they make the Western that audiences will experience in the same old way. The mechanism is so simple: King Kong is a lovable creature who, chained and goaded beyond endurance, breaks out into a rampage of indiscriminate destruction; the people in the audience, who are like the people being slaughtered in the movie (Kong even starts his rampage on the theatre audience gathered to look at him), are terrified by the big murderous ape. The fact that they felt sympathy for him only a few minutes before adds to the drama, but does not make them fear him the less. The same mechanism was at work with Karloff as the monster in the original *Frankenstein* — yet producers announce that they're going to make a new kind of monster movie in which the monster will be sympathetic. These movie-makers, too, talking about earlier movies, think only of their fear of the monster; they forget the sympathy built up for him early in the pictures. Yet when they talk about the movies they are going to make, they emphasize the sympathy they are going to build up as if they did not know that this was necessary dramatic preparation for the fear and carnage to follow, which is what dominates their own memories and will dominate memories of their films, too.

As a child, I saw the 1932 movie *Freaks,* in which the circus sideshow attractions — the dwarfs, pinheads, idiots, and maimed creatures — fall upon the beautiful trapeze artist, mutilate her and make her one of themselves; and the sight of any deformity used to bring the movie back to me in nightmares. A few years ago I saw the movie again and was amazed to discover that the freaks were meant to be sympathetic and the trapeze artist was a bitch. But I don't think that the director, Tod Browning, who also directed some of the best of the Lon Chaney pictures — and his horribly maimed phantoms and hunchbacks were also meant-to-be-sympathetic — can have been so naïve. When tiny, deformed creatures are swarming all over the screen on a mission of mutilation, surely the intention is to terrify us. They are good people who have been mistreated and driven to take direct action only in the preparatory dramatic stages, until they are needed for the climactic fearful images.

In the Western, once we are in danger — huddled in the wagon train with the stars and young lovers and old comics, the arrows coming at us, piercing flesh and starting fires that are burning us alive — the Indians circling us are no longer noble victims. Painted, half-naked men who do not speak our language, who do not know that we mean them no harm, might as well be another species. And decent liberal movie-makers will go on congratulating themselves on their sympathetic treatment of the Indians; and new movie-makers will arrive to show us how to do it all over again.

In some Westerns, cruel and mercenary white men torture and kill Indians — as in *Nevada Smith,* where the hero, Steve McQueen, is half Indian. White men raised as Indians (*Hombre*), white men who have married Indians (*Duel at Diablo, The Way West*), and half-Indian heroes may become almost as popular in our Westerns as the half-Jewish heroes of recent American novels, and for the same reason: the authors hope for extra perspective by playing it both ways. (Traditionally, second- and third-generation Jews acted cowboys, first-generation Jews acted Indians; now half-Jews can be half-Indians.) Split in his loyalties, the half-and-half hero can observe the cruelties and misunderstandings of both sides; he's a double loner — an ideally alienated, masochistic modern hero (like Paul Newman in *Hombre*). Typically, his sympathies are with the Indians, though he generally comes through and acts for the whites. In this, the Western has not changed.

But the mechanism of the movie and how we react to it is very different when it is white men torturing Indians. When the murderers are white men, the movie-makers don't feel the guilty necessity to make them sympathetic or to explain them at all; they are simply moral monsters, as in *Nevada Smith,* where the young hero's Indian mother is mutilated — skinned alive — by white degenerates. (This episode is not staged to pleasure the audience or for wanton excitement but rather to make the audience understand the boy's helpless rage. It is violence used to make us hate violence.) And yet their images don't carry the kind of fear that the most meant-to-be-sympathetic Indians do when they turn warlike. We hate the act, but we don't fear the men in the same way. If Hollywood made a movie in which we as audience were involved in the lives of an Indian village which was then attacked by villainous white men, I doubt if we would feel the terror we do when we are attacked by Indians. In general, Wilhelm Reich was probably right when he said that "a horror story has the same effect whether it deals with Ali Baba and the Forty Thieves or with the execution of white spies. The important thing to the reader is the gooseflesh and not whether it is forty thieves or forty counter-revolutionaries who get decapitated." But suppose it is forty frightening men from some strange tribe whose language and customs we don't understand, or forty Dead End Kids. One raises more gooseflesh than the other. It involves primitive fears — of what we don't know.

There is a fairly widespread assumption that no matter how bad American movies in general are, the Westerns are still great. The people who take this for granted probably don't go to them, but they have an idea that Westerns are authentic movie-making — the *real* movies — and are somehow pure (as Western heroes used to be), exempt from the general corruption. They assume that the Westerns are still there, as pristine and "great" as ever for their kids, as if the air of the wide open spaces would have kept the genre clean.

I don't believe that there ever were the great works in this genre that so many people claim for it. There were some good Westerns, of course, and there was a beautiful kind of purity in some of them, and later even the ritual plots and dull action were, at least, set outdoors, and the horses were often good to look at. But all that was a long time ago. The last good Western that had this ritual purity was Sam Peckinpah's *Ride the High Country,* which came out in 1962. (I am not forgetting David Miller's *Lonely Are the Brave,* which came out at the same time: despite the ingenious and entertaining performance by Walter Matthau and the excellent performance by Kirk Douglas, the Dalton Trumbo script gives the film that awful messagey self-righteousness of *High Noon* and *The Gunfighter* and a fake ironic tragedy, an O. Henry finish — the "last" cowboy is run down by a truck loaded with toilets.) Kids may read the same novel by Robert Louis

Stevenson that their parents did, but in movies parents think in terms of the old *Stagecoach* and the kids are going to the new *Stagecoach*. Probably in no art except movies can new practitioners legally eliminate competition from the past. A full-page notice in *Variety* gave warning that Twentieth Century–Fox, which released the 1966 *Stagecoach,* featuring Bing Crosby and Ann-Margret, would "vigorously" prosecute the exhibition of the 1939 original — John Ford's classic Western, one of the most highly regarded and influential movies ever made.

Surely the public should have the right to see the old as well as the new? And not just for its own sake but because that is how we learn about an art. How else do we develop a critical sense about new novels, new paintings, new music, new poetry? If the old is legally retired, we become barbarians (movie barbarians, at least) without a past. The producer of the new version, Martin Rackin, said, "In the process of updating, we can improve on the old films by learning from their mistakes." With equal cynicism, one may reply, "Then why do you remove the old films so that new generations cannot appreciate how much you've improved on them?"

Just about every good Western made since 1939 has imitated *Stagecoach* or has learned something from it. Ironically, the 1966 version merely took the plot and the character stereotypes; and without the simple, clear, epic vision with which John Ford informed them, they are just standard Western equipment. The original *Stagecoach* had a mixture of reverie and reverence about the American past that made the picture seem almost folk art; we *wanted* to believe in it even if we didn't. That is what *Ride the High Country* had, too.

The 1966 *Stagecoach* was undistinguished — a big, brawling action picture that gets audience reactions by brutal fights and narrow escapes photographed right on top of you. The director, Gordon Douglas, doesn't trust you to project yourself imaginatively into his stagecoach; he tries to force you into it — which may make you want to escape to the farthest row in the balcony. Kurosawa (who acknowledges his debt to John Ford) can plunge you into action to make you experience the meaning of action. When the Gordon Douglas crew does it, all it means is they don't want you to get bored. And probably the most that can be said about their movie is that it isn't boring — but then, that could be said of most visits to the dentist.

No one mistakes the 1966 *Stagecoach* for folk art. And though Rackin and company cast Ann-Margret as the prostitute-with-a-heart-of-gold, nobody misunderstands, because Ann-Margret comes through dirty no matter what she plays. She does most of her acting inside her mouth. Julie Andrews could play a promiscuous girl in *The Americanization of Emily* and shine with virtue; Ann-Margret gleams with built-in innuendo. She's like Natalie Wood with sex, a lewd mechanical doll. Men seem to have direct-action responses to Ann-Margret: they want to give her what she seems to be asking for. (A new variation on "star quality"?) This may represent a new polarization of screen types — the good Julie Andrews, the bad Ann-Margret. They're both willing, but for one it's "natural," for the other it's "dirty." Or, as they used to say, it ain't what you do but the way that you do it.

John Ford himself doesn't bother going outdoors much anymore. A few years back I dragged a painter-friend to see *The Man Who Shot Liberty Valance;* it was a John Ford Western, and though I dreaded an evening with James Stewart and John Wayne, I felt I *should* see it. My friend agreed because "the landscapes are always great"; but after about ten minutes of ugly studio sets, he wanted to leave. By the time Edmond O'Brien, as a drunken newspaper editor, was getting beaten up in the offices of the *Star,* which we saw from inside the glass, my friend was fed up: "Star is rats spelled backward; let's get the hell out of here." What those who believe in the perennial greatness of the Western may not have caught on to is that the new big Western is, likely as not, a studio-set job. What makes it a "Western" is no longer the wide open spaces but the presence of men like John Wayne, James Stewart, Henry Fonda, Robert Mitchum, Kirk Douglas, and Burt Lancaster, grinning with their big new choppers, sucking their guts up into their chests, and hauling themselves onto horses. They are the heroes of a new Western mythology: stars who have aged in the business, who have survived and who go on dragging their world-famous, expensive carcasses through the same old motions. That is the essence of their heroism and their legend. The new Western is a joke and the stars play it for laughs, and the young film enthusiasts react to the heroes not because they represent the mythological heroes of the Old West but because they are mythological movie stars. An actor in his forties would be a mere stripling in a Western these days. Nor would he *belong* in these movies which derive their small, broad humor from the fact that the actors have been doing what they're doing so long that they're professional Westerners. Like Queen Victoria, John Wayne has become lovable because he's stayed in the saddle into a new era.

The world has changed since audiences first responded to John Wayne as a simple cowboy thirty-seven years ago; now, when he does the same things and represents the same simple values, he's so archaic it's funny. We used to be frightened of a reactionary becoming "a man on horseback"; now that seems the best place for him.

My father went to a Western just about every night of his life that I remember. He didn't care if it was a good one or a bad one or if he'd seen it before. He said it didn't matter. I have just seen three new Westerns — *The Way West, The War Wagon,* and *El Dorado* — and I think I understand what my father meant. If you're going for *a* Western (the same way you'd sit down to watch *a* television show), it doesn't much matter which one you see. And if you're going for something else, even the best one of these three isn't good enough. The differences between them aren't, finally, very significant — which is what the mass audience probably understands better than film enthusiasts.

The Way West is about as bad an epic Western as I've ever seen. Students in college film departments sometimes say they can learn more from bad movies than from good ones, because they can examine what the director did wrong: to them *The Way West* should serve as a textbook. Everything essential to explain what's going on seems missing. It's a jerk's idea of an epic: big stars, big landscapes, bad jokes, folksy-heroic music by Bronislau Kaper to plug up the holes, and messy hang-ups. In the neurotic-Western mode, the leader of this 1843 caravan of pioneers, Kirk Douglas, goes in for self-flagellation. (He arranges for his Negro servant to whip him; the darkies have the best rhythm?) Richard Widmark's desire to go West seems to be some sort of compulsive behavior; and Robert Mitchum — the scout! — must be cozened out of irrational mourning for his Indian wife. And to make sure that 1967 audiences won't find this pioneering too old-fashioned, the villainess is a frightened virgin and the heroine is a teen-ager so grotesquely avid for sex that at one point her lusty parents tease that if she doesn't get a husband pretty soon they'll have to mate her with an ox — a line which gets a big laugh. (Maybe it should, because oxen don't mate.) Crude as this movie is, audiences seem to enjoy it; it has that stage-Irish comic sentimentality that used to destroy one's pleasure in many of the John Ford epics and was possibly responsible for their box-office success. *The Way West* was directed by Andrew V. McLaglen, a chip off the old block.

Burt Kennedy's *The War Wagon* is classy Western camp with John Wayne, and Kirk Douglas in a black leather shirt, wearing a ring on his black glove. There are pretty little visual divertissements out of von Sternberg's *Shanghai Gesture* and Buñuel's *L'Age d'Or* and Cocteau's *Orpheus,* and hard-edge cinematography (by William H. Clothier, who also did the more conventional shooting of *The Way West*) that makes the actors look like pop cutouts. The delicate decorator colors include fancy salmon pinks; and there's real bougainvillea growing in the sets. There's even a camp version of backlash when the Indians tell John Wayne that they're not asking him to dinner because having a white man at table offends them. Howard Keel turns up playing an Indian named Levi Walking Bear, and old Bruce Cabot (who saved Fay Wray from King Kong) turns up looking like Maurice Chevalier. And *The War Wagon* has an opening song by Dimitri Tiomkin to tell us it's going to be tough and hardheaded — "All men are fightin' for a wagon full of gold. . . ." In Hollywood that's realistic philosophy.

What does all the chic amount to and who is it for? It's a kind of sophisticated exhibitionism. I received a publicity release from the company that represents *The War Wagon* that puts the movie in more accurate perspective. It's entitled "Suggestions for a Feature" and it reads:

John Wayne's Western movies are always made in color. In two colors, to be exact: greenback green and glittering gold.

Not a single one of more than 200 films of the great-outdoorsy genre he's made since 1929 has ever lost money. It's a fact of Hollywood life that John Wayne Westerns always show a profit.

For let's face it: John Wayne *is* the Western movie today. Westerns are a folk phenomenon, the one kind of film which has never really fallen from favor, even temporarily. The cinematic years since *The Great Train Robbery* have seen thousands of Western movies, and hundreds of Western heroes. There are scores of them fully and gainfully occupied right this minute, both on theatre and TV screens.

But among them all, there's only one John Wayne. He looms above the others the way the heroes' heads on Mount Rushmore dominate the surrounding pebbles. He may be a homely, middle-aged, battered, unpretentious, non-Actors Studio guy, but he is *the* Western star. And he is undoubtedly going to remain *the* Western star until he's so old he falls off his horse — which will likely be never.

Big John's next big one, *The War Wagon*, is likely to be an especially lucrative lollapalooza. It has the kind of rugged, roisterous script which is the perfect setting for this human diamond-in-the-rough . . . .

We suggest a story on those three phenomenal W's: Westerns, Wayne and *War Wagon*.

It could turn out to be WWWonderful.

That drool contains the awful germy truth: Westerns are money in the bank. When the big studios were breaking up in the fifties and the big box-office stars were forming their own production companies, the Westerns were the safest investment. The studios tried to get whatever money was left in big-name contract stars like Clark Gable and Robert Taylor; and other stars, like Wayne and Douglas and Lancaster, going into business on their own, wanted to protect their investments. That's how the modern Western with the big old stars took over the genre. Others who went into the "safe" genre in the fifties, like Gregory Peck and Frank Sinatra, dropped out (not, I am afraid, from disgust but from financial failure); but Douglas and Lancaster persisted and were joined later by Robert Mitchum. Soon, because they were so well known anyway and people don't know much about film history, they could pass for real old-time Western heroes, like Wayne.

The structure of this Western-movie business is becoming as feudalistic as the movies themselves: Kirk Douglas has a production company named for his mother (Bryna), another for his son (Joel), yet another for himself and a partner (Douglas-Lewis), etc.; *The War Wagon* is produced by John

Wayne's company, Batjac. These corporate-head Westerners appear in each other's films; there are jobs for their sons and their old buddies and the sons of their old buddies. The next big Batjac production is *The Green Berets,* which Wayne himself will direct and one of his sons will produce.

And so we have Kirk Douglas exposing his fat overmuscled chest in *The War Wagon* and doing a series of parodied leaps onto a horse. And for all the aestheticism of dust and hooves and flowers, after a while it might just as well be *The Way West:* when it's the tired comic spectacle of rich old men degrading themselves for more money and fame and power, does it much matter if it's done poorly or with chic? In some ways the chic is more offensive.

The classic Western theme is the doomed hero — the man without a future because the way of life is changing, the frontier is vanishing, and the sheriff and the schoolteacher are representatives of progress and a new order. The hero is the living antique who represents the best of the old order just as it is disappearing. But star-centered movies and TV gave the Westerner a new future: he's got to keep going to keep the series alive. The toilets won't run him down because that would be flushing away good money. Douglas in *The War Wagon* has metamorphosed back into his post–World War II character — the heel. He's now the too smart Westerner, mercenary and untrustworthy in a way the audience is supposed to like. His Westerner is a swinger — a wisecracking fancy talker with intentionally anachronistic modern attitudes.

El Dorado combines Wayne and Mitchum, both looking exhausted. The director, Howard Hawks, is also tired, and like Ford, he doesn't want to go out on location. The theory of why Westerns are such a great form is that directors can show what they can really do in the framework of a ritualized genre and the beauty of the West. But the directors are old and rich, too. (Ford was born in 1895 and directed his first movie in 1917; Hawks was born in 1896 and has been in films since 1918, directing them since the mid-twenties.) Their recent movies look as if they were made for television. Except for a few opening shots, *El Dorado* is a studio job — and it has the second-worst lighting of any movie in recent years (the worst: *A Countess from Hong Kong*). When the movie starts, you have the sense of having come in on a late episode of a TV serial. Mitchum plays a drunken old sheriff (like Charles Winninger in *Destry Rides Again*), and there are home remedies for alcoholism, vomiting scenes that are supposed to be hilarious, and one of those girls who hide their curls under cowboy hats and are mistaken for boys until the heroes start to wrestle with them. Wayne has a beautiful horse in this one — but when he's hoisted onto it and you hear the thud, you don't know whether to feel sorrier for man or beast.

The Old West was a dream landscape with simple masculine values; the code of the old Western heroes probably wouldn't have much to say to audiences today. But the old stars, battling through stories that have lost their ritual meaning, are part of a new ritual that does have meaning. There's nothing dreamy about it: these men have made themselves movie stars — which impresses audiences all over the world. The fact that they can draw audiences to a genre as empty as the contemporary Western is proof of their power. Writers and painters now act out their fantasies by becoming the superstars of their own movies (and of the mass media); Wayne and Douglas and Mitchum and the rest of them do it on a bigger scale. When it makes money, it's not just their fantasy. The heroes nobody believes in — except as movie stars — are the result of a corrupted art form. Going to a Western these days for simplicity or heroism or grandeur or meaning is about like trying to mate with an ox.

[August 1967]

Bonnie and Clyde

How do you make a good movie in this country without being jumped on? *Bonnie and Clyde* is the most excitingly American American movie since *The Manchurian Candidate*. The audience is alive to it. Our experience as we watch it has some connection with the way we reacted to movies in childhood: with how we came to love them and to feel they were ours — not an art that we learned over the years to appreciate but simply and immediately ours. When an American movie is contemporary in feeling, like this one, it makes a different kind of contact with an American audience from the kind that is made by European films, however contemporary. Yet any movie that is contemporary in feeling is likely to go further than other movies — go too far for some tastes — and *Bonnie and Clyde* divides audiences, as *The Manchurian Candidate* did, and it is being jumped on almost as hard. Though we may dismiss the attacks with "What good movie doesn't give some offense?," the fact that it is generally *only* good movies that provoke attacks by many people suggests that the innocuousness of most of our movies is accepted with such complacence that when an American movie reaches people, when it makes them react, some of them think there must be something the matter with it — perhaps a law should be passed against it. *Bonnie and Clyde* brings into the almost frighteningly public world of movies things that people have been feeling and saying and writing about. And once something is said or done on the screens of the world, once it has entered mass art, it can never again belong to a minority, never again be the private possession of an educated, or "knowing," group. But even for that group there is an excitement in hearing its own private thoughts expressed out loud and in seeing something of its own sensibility become part of our common culture.

Our best movies have always made entertainment out of the anti-heroism of American life; they bring to the surface what, in its newest forms and fashions, is always just below the surface. The romanticism in American movies lies in the cynical tough guy's independence; the sentimentality lies, traditionally, in the falsified finish when the anti-hero turns hero. In 1967, this kind of sentimentality wouldn't work with the audience, and *Bonnie and Clyde* substitutes sexual fulfillment for a change of heart. (This doesn't quite work, either; audiences sophisticated enough to enjoy a movie like this one are too sophisticated for the dramatic uplift of the triumph over impotence.)

Structurally, *Bonnie and Clyde* is a story of love on the run, like the old Clark Gable–Claudette Colbert *It Happened One Night* but turned inside out; the walls of Jericho are psychological this time, but they fall anyway. If the story of Bonnie Parker and Clyde Barrow seemed almost from the start, and even to them while they were living it, to be the material of legend, it's because robbers who are loyal to each other — like the James brothers — are a grade up from garden-variety robbers, and if they're male and female partners in crime and young and attractive they're a rare breed. The Barrow gang had both family loyalty and sex appeal working for their legend. David Newman and Robert Benton, who wrote the script for *Bonnie and Clyde,* were able to use the knowledge that, like many of our other famous outlaws and gangsters, the real Bonnie and Clyde seemed to others to be acting out forbidden roles and to relish their roles. In contrast with secret criminals — the furtive embezzlers and other crooks who lead seemingly honest lives — the known outlaws capture the public imagination, because they take chances, and because, often, they enjoy dramatizing their lives. They know that newspaper readers want all the details they can get about the criminals who do the terrible things they themselves don't dare to do, and also want the satisfaction of reading about the punishment after feasting on the crimes. Outlaws play to this public; they show off their big guns and fancy clothes and their defiance of the law. Bonnie and Clyde established the images for their own legend in the photographs they posed for: the gunman and the gun moll. The naïve, touching doggerel ballad that Bonnie Parker wrote and had published in newspapers is about the roles they play for other people contrasted with the coming end for them. It concludes:

> Someday they'll go down together;
> They'll bury them side by side;
> To few it'll be grief —
> To the law a relief —
> But it's death for Bonnie and Clyde.

That they did capture the public imagination is evidenced by the many movies based on their lives. In the late forties, there were *They Live by Night,* with Farley Granger and Cathy O'Donnell, and *Gun Crazy,* with John Dall and Peggy Cummins. (Alfred Hitchcock, in the same period, cast these two Clyde Barrows, Dall and Granger, as Loeb and Leopold, in *Rope.*) And there was a cheap — in every sense — 1958 exploitation film,

The Bonnie Parker Story, starring Dorothy Provine. But the most important earlier version was Fritz Lang's *You Only Live Once,* starring Sylvia Sidney as "Joan" and Henry Fonda as "Eddie," which was made in 1937; this version, which was one of the best American films of the thirties, as *Bonnie and Clyde* is of the sixties, expressed certain feelings of its time, as this film expresses certain feelings of ours. (*They Live by Night,* produced by John Houseman under the aegis of Dore Schary, and directed by Nicholas Ray, was a very serious and socially significant tragic melodrama, but its attitudes were already dated thirties attitudes: the lovers were very young and pure and frightened and underprivileged; the hardened criminals were sordid; the settings were committedly grim. It made no impact on the postwar audience, though it was a great success in England, where our moldy socially significant movies could pass for courageous.)

Just how contemporary in feeling *Bonnie and Clyde* is may be indicated by contrasting it with *You Only Live Once,* which, though almost totally false to the historical facts, was *told* straight. It is a peculiarity of our times — perhaps it's one of the few specifically modern characteristics — that we don't take our stories straight any more. This isn't necessarily bad. *Bonnie and Clyde* is the first film demonstration that the put-on can be used for the purposes of art. *The Manchurian Candidate almost* succeeded in that, but what was implicitly wild and far-out in the material was nevertheless presented on screen as a straight thriller. *Bonnie and Clyde* keeps the audience in a kind of eager, nervous imbalance — holds our attention by throwing our disbelief back in our faces. To be put on is to be put on the spot, put on the stage, made the stooge in a comedy act. People in the audience at *Bonnie and Clyde* are laughing, demonstrating that they're not stooges — that they appreciate the joke — when they catch the first bullet right in the face. The movie keeps them off balance to the end. During the first part of the picture, a woman in my row was gleefully assuring her companions, "It's a comedy. It's a comedy." After a while, she didn't say anything. Instead of the movie spoof, which tells the audience that it doesn't need to feel or care, that it's all just in fun, that "we were only kidding," *Bonnie and Clyde* disrupts us with "And you thought we were only kidding."

This is the way the story was told in 1937. Eddie (Clyde) is a three-time loser who wants to work for a living, but nobody will give him a chance. Once you get on the wrong side of the law, "they" won't let you get back. Eddie knows it's hopeless — once a loser, always a loser. But his girl, Joan (Bonnie) — the only person who believes in him — thinks that an innocent man has nothing to fear. She marries him, and learns better. Arrested again and sentenced to death for a crime he didn't commit, Eddie asks her to smuggle a gun to him in prison, and she protests, "If I get you a gun, you'll kill somebody." He stares at her sullenly and asks, "What do you think they're going to do to me?" He becomes a murderer while escaping from prison; "society" has made him what it thought he was all along. *You Only Live Once* was an indictment of "society," of the forces of order that will not give Eddie the outcast a chance. "We have a right to live," Joan says as they set out across the country. During the time they are on the run, they become notorious outlaws; they are blamed for a series of crimes they didn't commit. (They do commit holdups, but only to get gas or groceries or medicine.) While the press pictures them as desperadoes robbing and killing and living high on the proceeds of crime, she is having a baby in a shack in a hobo jungle, and Eddie brings her a bouquet of wild flowers. Caught in a police trap, they die in each other's arms; they have been denied the right to live.

Because *You Only Live Once* was so well done, and because the audience in the thirties shared this view of the indifference and cruelty of "society," there were no protests against the sympathetic way the outlaws were pictured — and, indeed, there was no reason for any. In 1958, in *I Want to Live!* (a very popular, though not very good, movie), Barbara Graham, a drug-addict prostitute who had been executed for her share in the bludgeoning to death of an elderly woman, was presented as gallant, wronged, morally superior to everybody else in the movie, in order to strengthen the argument against capital punishment, and the director, Robert Wise, and his associates weren't accused of glorifying criminals, because the "criminals," as in *You Only Live Once,* weren't criminals but innocent victims. Why the protests, why are so many people upset (and not just the people who enjoy indignation), about *Bonnie and Clyde,* in which the criminals *are* criminals — Clyde an ignorant, sly near psychopath who thinks his crimes are accomplishments, and Bonnie a bored, restless waitress-slut who robs for excitement? And why so many accusations of historical inaccuracy, particularly against a work that is far more accurate historically than most and in which historical accuracy hardly matters anyway? There is always an issue of historical accuracy involved in any dramatic or literary work set in the past; indeed, it's fun to read about Richard III vs. Shakespeare's Richard III. The issue is always with us, and will always be with us as long as artists find stimulus in historical figures and want to present their versions of them. But why didn't movie critics attack, for example, *A Man for All Seasons* — which involves material of much more historical importance — for being historically inaccurate? Why attack *Bonnie and Clyde* more than the other movies based on the same pair, or more than the movie treatments of Jesse James or Billy the Kid or Dillinger or Capone or any of our other fictionalized outlaws? I would suggest that when a movie so clearly conceived as a new version of a legend is attacked as historically inaccurate, it's because it shakes people a little. I know this is based on some pretty sneaky psychological suppositions, but I don't see how else to account for the use only against a *good* movie of arguments that could be used against almost all movies. When I asked a nineteen-year-old boy who was raging against the movie as "a cliché-ridden fraud" if he got so worked up about other movies, he informed me that that was an argument *ad hominem.* And it is indeed. To ask why people react so angrily to the best movies and have so little negative reaction to poor ones is to imply that they are so unused to the experience of art in movies that they fight it.

Audiences at *Bonnie and Clyde* are not given a simple, secure basis for identification; they are made to feel but are not told *how* to feel. *Bonnie and Clyde* is not a serious melodrama involving us in the plight of the innocent but a movie that assumes — as William Wellman did in 1931 when he made *The Public Enemy,* with James Cagney as a smart, cocky, mean little crook — that we don't need to pretend we're interested only in the falsely accused, as if real criminals had no connection with us. There wouldn't be the popular excitement there is about outlaws if we didn't all suspect that — in some cases, at least — gangsters must take pleasure in the profits and glory of a life of crime. Outlaws wouldn't become legendary figures if we didn't suspect that there's more to crime than the social workers' case studies may show. And though what we've always been told will happen to them — that they'll come to a bad end — does seem to happen, some part of us wants to believe in the tiny possibility that they can get away with it. Is that really so terrible? Yet when it comes to movies people get nervous about acknowledging that there must be some fun in crime (though the gleam in Cagney's eye told its own story). *Bonnie and Clyde* shows the fun but uses it, too, making comedy out of the banality and conventionality of that fun. What looks ludicrous in this movie isn't *merely* ludicrous, and after we have laughed at ignorance and helplessness and emptiness and stupidity and idiotic deviltry, the laughs keep sticking in our throats, because what's funny isn't only funny.

In 1937, the movie-makers knew that the audience wanted to believe in the innocence of Joan and Eddie, because these two were lovers, and innocent lovers hunted down like animals made a tragic love story. In 1967, the movie-makers know that the audience wants to believe — maybe even prefers to believe — that Bonnie and Clyde were guilty of crimes, all right, but that they were innocent in general; that is, naïve and ignorant *compared with us.* The distancing of the sixties version shows the gangsters in an already legendary period, and part of what makes a legend for Americans is viewing anything that happened in the past as much simpler than what we are involved in now. We tend to find the past funny and the recent past campy-funny. The getaway cars of the early thirties are made to seem hilarious. (Imagine anyone getting away from a bank holdup in a tin lizzie like that!) In *You Only Live Once,* the outlaws existed in the same present as the audience, and there was (and still is, I'm sure) nothing funny about them; in *Bonnie and Clyde* that audience is in the movie, transformed into the poor people, the Depression people, of legend — with faces and poses out of Dorothea Lange and Walker Evans and *Let Us Now Praise Famous Men.* In 1937, the audience felt sympathy for the fugitives because they weren't allowed to lead normal lives; in 1967, the "normality" of the Barrow gang and their individual aspirations toward respectability are the craziest things about them — not just because they're killers but because thirties "normality" is in itself funny to us. The writers and the director of *Bonnie and Clyde* play upon our attitudes toward the American past by making the hats and guns and holdups look as dated as two-reel comedy; emphasizing the absurdity with banjo music, they make the period seem even farther away than it is. The Depression reminiscences are not used for purposes of social consciousness; hard times are not the reason for the Barrows' crimes, just the excuse. "We" didn't make Clyde a killer; the movie deliberately avoids easy sympathy by picking up Clyde when he is already a cheap crook. But Clyde is not the urban sharpster of *The Public Enemy;* he is the hick as bank robber — a countrified gangster, a hillbilly killer who doesn't mean any harm. People so simple that they are alienated from the results of their actions — like the primitives who don't connect babies with copulation — provide a kind of archetypal comedy for us. It may seem like a minor point that Bonnie and Clyde are presented as not mean and sadistic, as having killed only when cornered; but in terms of legend, and particularly movie legend, it's a major one. The "classic" gangster films showed gang members betraying each other and viciously murdering the renegade who left to join another gang; the gang-leader hero no sooner got to the top than he was betrayed by someone he had trusted or someone he had double-crossed. In contrast, the Barrow gang represent family-style crime. And Newman ard Benton have been acute in emphasizing this — not making them victims of society (they are never that, despite Penn's cloudy efforts along these lines) but making them absurdly "just-folks" ordinary. When Bonnie tells Clyde to pull off the road — "I want to talk to you" — they are in a getaway car, leaving the scene of a robbery, with the police right behind them, but they are absorbed in family bickering: the traditional all-American use of the family automobile. In a sense, it is the absence of sadism — it is the violence without sadism — that throws the audience off balance at *Bonnie and Clyde.* The brutality that comes out of this innocence is far more shocking than the calculated brutalities of mean killers.

Playfully posing with their guns, the real Bonnie and Clyde mocked the "Bloody Barrows" of the Hearst press. One photograph shows slim, pretty Bonnie, smiling and impeccably dressed, pointing a huge gun at Clyde's chest as he, a dimpled dude with a cigar, smiles back. The famous picture of Bonnie in the same clothes but looking ugly squinting into the sun, with a foot on the car, a gun on her hip, and a cigar in her mouth, is obviously a joke — her caricature of herself as a gun moll. Probably, since they never meant to kill, they thought the "Bloody Barrows" were a joke — a creation of the lying newspapers.

There's something new working for the Bonnie-and-Clyde legend now: our nostalgia for the thirties — the unpredictable, contrary affection of the prosperous for poverty, or at least for the artifacts, the tokens, of poverty, for Pop culture seen in the dreariest rural settings, where it truly seems to belong. Did people in the cities listen to the Eddie Cantor show? No doubt they did, but the sound of his voice, like the sound of Ed Sullivan now, evokes a primordial, pre-urban existence — the childhood of the race. Our comic-melancholic affection for thirties Pop has become sixties Pop, and those who made *Bonnie and Clyde* are smart enough to use it that way. Being knowing is not an artist's highest gift, but it can make a hell of a lot of difference in a movie. In the American experience, the miseries of the Depression are funny in the way that the Army is funny to draftees — a shared catastrophe, a leveling, forming part of our common background. Those too young to remember the Depression have heard about it from their parents. (When I was at college, we used to top each other's stories about how our families had survived: the fathers who had committed suicide so that their wives and children could live off the insurance; the mothers trying to make a game out of the meals of potatoes cooked on an open fire.) Though the American derision of the past has many offensive aspects, it has some good ones, too, because it's a way of making fun not only of our forebears but of ourselves and our pretensions. The toughness about what we've come out of and what we've been through — the honesty to see ourselves as the Yahoo children of yokels — is a good part of American popular art. There is a kind of American poetry in a stickup gang seen chasing across the bedraggled backdrop of the Depression (as true in its way as Nabokov's vision of Humbert Humbert and Lolita in the cross-country world of motels) — as if crime were the only activity in a country stupefied by poverty. But Arthur Penn doesn't quite have the toughness of mind to know it; it's not what he means by poetry. His squatters'-jungle scene is too "eloquent," like a poster making an appeal, and the Parker-family-reunion sequence is poetic in the gauzy mode. He makes the sequence a fancy lyric interlude, like a number in a musical (*Funny Face,* to be exact); it's too "imaginative" — a literal dust bowl, as thoroughly becalmed as Sleeping Beauty's garden. The movie becomes dreamy-soft where it should be hard (and hard-edged).

If there is such a thing as an American tragedy, it must be funny. O'Neill undoubtedly felt this when he had James Tyrone get up to turn off the lights in *Long Day's Journey Into Night.* We are bumpkins, haunted by the bottle of ketchup on the dining table at San Simeon. We garble our foreign words and phrases and hope that at least we've used them right. Our heroes pick up the wrong fork, and the basic figure of fun in the American theatre and American movies is the man who puts on airs. Children of peddlers and hod carriers don't feel at home in tragedy; we are used to failure. But, because of the quality of American life at the present time, perhaps there can be no real comedy — nothing more than stupidity and "spoof" — without true horror in it. Bonnie and Clyde and their partners in crime are comically bad bank robbers, and the backdrop of poverty makes their holdups seem pathetically tacky, yet they rob banks and kill people; Clyde and his good-natured brother are so shallow they never think much about anything, yet they suffer and die.

If this way of holding more than one attitude toward life is already familiar to us — if we recognize the make-believe robbers whose toy guns produce real blood, and the Keystone cops who shoot them dead, from Truffaut's *Shoot the Piano Player* and Godard's gangster pictures, *Breathless* and *Band of Outsiders* — it's because the young French directors discovered the poetry of crime in American life (from our movies) and showed the Americans how to put it on the screen in a new, "existential" way. Melodramas and gangster movies and comedies were always more our speed than "prestigious," "distinguished" pictures; the French directors who grew up on American pictures found poetry in our fast action, laconic speech, plain gestures. And because they understood that you don't express your love of life by denying the comedy or the horror of it, they brought out the poetry in our tawdry subjects. Now Arthur Penn, working with a script heavily influenced — one might almost say inspired — by Truffaut's *Shoot the Piano Player,* unfortunately imitates Truffaut's artistry instead of going back to its tough American sources. The French may tenderize their American material, but we shouldn't. That turns into another way of making "prestigious," "distinguished" pictures.

Probably part of the discomfort that people feel about *Bonnie and Clyde* grows out of its compromises and its failures. I wish the script hadn't provided the upbeat of the hero's sexual success as a kind of sop to the audience. I think what makes us not believe in it is that it isn't consistent with the intelligence of the rest of the writing — that it isn't on the same level, because it's too manipulatively clever, too much of a gimmick. (The scene that shows the gnomish gang member called C.W. sleeping in the same room with Bonnie and Clyde suggests other possibilities, perhaps discarded, as does C.W.'s reference to Bonnie's liking his tattoo.) Compromises are not new to the Bonnie-and-Clyde story; *You Only Live Once* had a tacked-on coda featuring a Heavenly choir and William Gargan as a dead priest, patronizing Eddie even in the afterlife, welcoming him to Heaven with "You're free, Eddie!" The kind of people who make a movie like *You Only Live Once* are not the kind who write endings like that, and, by the same sort of internal evidence, I'd guess that Newman and Benton, whose Bonnie seems to owe so much to Catherine in *Jules and Jim,* had more interesting ideas originally about Bonnie's and Clyde's (and maybe C.W.'s) sex lives.

But people also feel uncomfortable about the violence, and here I think they're wrong. That is to say, they *should* feel uncomfortable, but this isn't an argument *against* the movie. Only a few years ago, a good director would have suggested the violence obliquely, with reaction shots (like the famous one in *The Golden Coach,* when we see a whole bullfight reflected in Anna Magnani's face), and death might have been symbolized by a light going out, or stylized, with blood and wounds kept to a minimum. In many ways, this method is more effective; we feel the violence more because so much is left to our imaginations. But the whole point of *Bonnie and Clyde* is to rub our noses in it, to make us pay our dues for laughing. The dirty reality of death — not suggestions but blood and holes — is necessary. Though I generally respect a director's skill and intelligence in inverse ratio to the violence he shows on the screen, and though I questioned even the Annie Sullivan–Helen Keller fight scenes in Arthur Penn's *The Miracle Worker,* I think that this time Penn is right. (I think he was also right when he showed violence in his first film, *The Left Handed Gun,* in 1958.) Suddenly, in the last few years, our view of the world has gone beyond "good taste." Tasteful suggestions of violence would at this point be a more grotesque form of comedy than *Bonnie and Clyde* attempts. *Bonnie and Clyde* needs violence; violence is its meaning. When, during a comically botched-up get-away, a man is shot in the face, the image is obviously based on one of the most famous sequences in Eisenstein's *Potemkin,* and the startled face is used the same way it was in *Potemkin* — to convey in an instant how someone who just happens to be in the wrong place at the wrong time, the irrelevant "innocent" bystander, can get it full in the face. And at that instant the meaning of Clyde Barrow's character changes; he's still a clown, but *we've* become the butt of the joke.

It is a kind of violence that says something to us; it is something that movies must be free to use. And it is just because artists must be free to use violence — a legal right that is beginning to come under attack — that we must also defend the legal rights of those film-makers who use violence to sell tickets, for it is not the province of the law to decide that one man is an artist and another man a no-talent. The no-talent has as much right to produce works as the artist has, and not only because he has a surprising way of shifting from one category to the other but also because men have an inalienable right to be untalented, and the law should not discriminate against lousy "artists." I am not saying that the violence in *Bonnie and Clyde* is legally acceptable because the film is a work of art; I think that *Bonnie and Clyde,* though flawed, is a work of art, but I think that the violence in *The Dirty Dozen,* which isn't a work of art, and whose violence offends me *personally,* should also be legally defensible, however morally questionable. Too many people — including some movie reviewers — want the law to take over the job of movie criticism; perhaps what they really want is for their own criticisms to have the force of law. Such people see *Bonnie and Clyde* as a danger to public morality; they think an audience goes to a play or a movie and takes the actions in it as examples for imitation. They look at the world and blame the movies. But if women who are angry with their husbands take it out on the kids, I don't think we can blame *Medea* for it; if, as has been said, we are a nation of mother-lovers, I don't think we can place the blame on *Oedipus Rex*. Part of the power of art lies in showing us what we are *not* capable of. We see that killers are not a different breed but are *us* without the insight or understanding or self-control that works of art strengthen. The tragedy of *Macbeth* is in the fall from nobility to horror; the comic tragedy of *Bonnie and Clyde* is that although you can't fall from the bottom you can reach the same horror. The movies may set styles in dress- or love-making, they may advertise cars or beverages, but art is not examples for imitation — that is not what a work of art does for us — though that is what guardians of morality *think* art is and what they want it to be and why they think a good movie is one that sets "healthy," "cheerful" examples of behavior, like a giant all-purpose commercial for the American way of life. But people don't "buy" what they see in a movie quite so simply; Louis B. Mayer did not turn us into a nation of Andy Hardys, and if, in a film, we see a frightened man wantonly take the life of another, it does not encourage us to do the same, any more than seeing an ivory hunter shoot an elephant makes us want to shoot one. It may, on the contrary, so sensitize us that we get a pang in the gut if we accidentally step on a moth.

Will we, as some people have suggested, be lured into imitating the violent crimes of Clyde and Bonnie because Warren Beatty and Faye Dunaway are "glamorous"? Do they, as some people have charged, confer glamour on violence? It's difficult to see how, since the characters they play are horrified by it and ultimately destroyed by it. Nobody in the movie gets pleasure from violence. Is the charge based on the notion that simply by their presence in the movie Warren Beatty and Faye Dunaway make crime attractive? If movie stars can't play criminals without our all wanting to be criminals, then maybe the only safe roles for them to play are movie stars — which, in this assumption, everybody wants to be anyway. After all, if they played factory workers, the economy might be dislocated by everybody's trying to become a factory worker. (Would having criminals played by dwarfs or fatties discourage crime? It seems rather doubtful.) The accusation that the beauty of movie stars makes the anti-social acts of their characters dangerously attractive is the kind of contrived argument we get from people who are bothered by something and are clutching at straws. Actors and actresses are *usually* more beautiful than ordinary people. And why not? Garbo's beauty notwithstanding, her Anna Christie did not turn us into whores, her Mata Hari did not turn us into spies, her Anna Karenina did not make us suicides.

We did not want her to be ordinary looking. Why should we be deprived of the pleasure of beauty? Garbo could be all women in love because, being more beautiful than life, she could more beautifully express emotions. It is a supreme asset for actors and actresses to be beautiful; it gives them greater range and greater possibilities for expressiveness. The handsomer they are, the more roles they can play; Olivier can be anything, but who would want to see Ralph Richardson, great as he is, play Antony? Actors and actresses who are beautiful start with an enormous advantage, because we love to look at them. The joke in the glamour charge is that Faye Dunaway has the magazine-illustration look of countless uninterestingly pretty girls, and Warren Beatty has the kind of high-school good looks that are generally lost fast. It's the roles that make *them* seem glamorous. Good roles do that for actors.

There is a story told against Beatty in a recent *Esquire* — how during the shooting of *Lilith* he "delayed a scene for three days demanding the line 'I've read *Crime and Punishment* and *The Brothers Karamazov*' be changed to 'I've read *Crime and Punishment* and *half* of *The Brothers Karamazov*.'" Considerations of professional conduct aside, what is odd is why his adversaries waited three days to give in, because, of course, he was right. That's what the character he played *should* say; the other way, the line has no point at all. But this kind of intuition isn't enough to make an actor, and in a number of roles Beatty, probably because he doesn't have the technique to make the most of his lines in the least possible time, has depended too much on intuitive non-acting — holding the screen far too long as he acted out self-preoccupied characters in a lifelike, boringly self-conscious way. He has a gift for slyness, though, as he showed in *The Roman Spring of Mrs. Stone,* and in most of his films he could hold the screen — maybe because there seemed to be something going on in his mind, some kind of calculation. There was something smart about him — something shrewdly private in those squeezed-up little non-actor's eyes — that didn't fit the clean-cut juvenile roles. Beatty was the producer of *Bonnie and Clyde,* responsible for keeping the company on schedule, and he has been quoted as saying, "There's not a scene that we have done that we couldn't do better by taking another day." This is the hell of the expensive way of making movies, but it probably helps to explain why Beatty is more intense than he has been before and why he has picked up his pace. His business sense may have improved his timing. The role of Clyde Barrow seems to have released something in him. As Clyde, Beatty is good with his eyes and mouth and his hat, but his body is still inexpressive; he doesn't have a trained actor's use of his body, and, watching him move, one is never for a minute convinced he's impotent. It is, however, a tribute to his performance that one singles this failure out. His slow timing works perfectly in the sequence in which he offers the dispossessed farmer his gun; there may not be another actor who would have dared to prolong the scene that way, and the prolongation until the final "We rob banks" gives the sequence its comic force. I have suggested elsewhere that one of the reasons that rules are impossible in the arts is that in movies (and in the other arts, too) the new "genius" — the genuine as well as the fraudulent or the dubious — is often the man who has enough audacity, or is simpleminded enough, to do what others had the good taste not to do. Actors before Brando did not mumble and scratch and show their sweat; dramatists before Tennessee Williams did not make explicit a particular substratum of American erotic fantasy; movie directors before Orson Welles did not dramatize the techniques of film-making; directors before Richard Lester did not lay out the whole movie as cleverly as the opening credits; actresses before Marilyn Monroe did not make an asset of their ineptitude by turning faltering misreadings into an appealing style. Each, in a large way, did something that people had always enjoyed and were often embarrassed or ashamed about enjoying. Their "bad taste" shaped a new accepted taste. Beatty's non-actor's "bad" timing may be this kind of "genius"; we seem to be watching him *think out* his next move.

It's difficult to know how Bonnie should have been played, because the character isn't worked out. Here the script seems weak. She is made too warmly sympathetic — and sympathetic in a style that antedates the style of the movie. Being frustrated and moody, she's not funny enough — neither ordinary, which, in the circumstances, would be comic, nor perverse, which might be rather funny, too. Her attitude toward her mother is too loving. There could be something funny about her wanting to run home to her mama, but, as it has been done, her heading home, running off through the fields, is unconvincing — incompletely motivated. And because the element of the ridiculous that makes the others so individual has been left out of her character she doesn't seem to belong to the period as the others do. Faye Dunaway has a sixties look anyway — not just because her eyes are made up in a sixties way and her hair is wrong but because her personal style and her acting are sixties. (This may help to make her popular; she can seem prettier to those who don't recognize prettiness except in the latest styles.) Furthermore, in some difficult-to-define way, Faye Dunaway as Bonnie doesn't keep her distance — that is to say, an *actor's* distance — either from the role or from the audience. She doesn't hold a characterization; she's in and out of emotions all the time, and though she often hits effective ones, the emotions seem *hers,* not the character's. She has some talent, but she comes on too strong; she makes one conscious that she's a willing worker, but she doesn't seem to know what she's doing — rather like Bonnie in her attempts to overcome Clyde's sexual difficulties.

Although many daily movie reviewers judge a movie in isolation, as if the people who made it had no previous history, more serious critics now commonly attempt to judge a movie as an expressive vehicle of the director, and a working out of his personal themes. Auden has written, "Our judgment of an established author is never simply an aesthetic judgment. In addition to any literary merit it may have, a new book by him has a historic interest for us as the act of a person in whom we have long been interested. He is not only a poet . . . he is also a character in our biography." For a while, people went to the newest Bergman and the newest Fellini that way; these movies were greeted like the latest novels of a favorite author. But Arthur Penn is not a writer-director like Bergman or Fellini, both of whom began as writers, and who (even though Fellini employs several collaborators) compose their spiritual autobiographies step by step on film. Penn is far more dependent on the talents of others, and his primary material — what he starts with — does not come out of his own experience. If the popular audience is generally uninterested in the director (unless he is heavily publicized, like DeMille or Hitchcock), the audience that is interested in the art of movies has begun, with many of the critics, to think of movies as a directors' medium to the point where they tend to ignore the contribution of the writers — and the directors may be almost obscenely content to omit mention of the writers. The history of the movies is being rewritten to disregard facts in favor of celebrating the director as the sole "creative" force. One can read Josef von Sternberg's autobiography and the text of the latest books on his movies without ever finding the name of Jules Furthman, the writer who worked on nine of his most famous movies (including *Morocco* and *Shanghai Express*). Yet the appearance of Furthman's name in the credits of such Howard Hawks films as *Only Angels Have Wings, To Have and Have Not, The Big Sleep,* and *Rio Bravo* suggests the reason for the similar qualities of good-bad-girl glamour in the roles played by Dietrich and Bacall and in other von Sternberg and Hawks heroines, and also in the Jean Harlow and Constance Bennett roles in the movies he wrote for *them.* Furthman, who has written about half of the most entertaining movies to come out of Hollywood (Ben Hecht wrote most of the other half), isn't even listed in new encyclopedias of the film. David Newman and Robert Benton may be good enough to join this category of unmentionable men who do what the directors are glorified for. The Hollywood writer is becoming a ghostwriter. The writers who succeed in the struggle to protect their identity and their material by becoming writer-directors or writer-producers soon become too rich and powerful to bother doing their own writing. And they rarely have the visual sense or the training to make good movie directors.

Anyone who goes to big American movies like *Grand Prix* and *The Sand Pebbles* recognizes that movies with scripts like those don't have a chance to be anything more than exercises in technology, and that this is what is meant by the decadence of American movies. In the past, directors used to say that they were no better than their material. (Sometimes they said it when they weren't even up to their material.) A good director can attempt to camouflage poor writing with craftsmanship and style, but ultimately no amount of director's skill can conceal a writer's failure; a poor script, even well directed, results in a stupid movie — as, unfortunately, does a good script poorly directed. Despite the new notion that the direction is everything, Penn can't redeem bad material, nor, as one may surmise from his *Mickey One,* does he necessarily know when it's bad. It is not fair to judge Penn by a film like *The Chase,* because he evidently did not have artistic control over the production, but what happens when he does have control and is working with a poor, pretentious mess of a script is painfully apparent in *Mickey One* — an art film in the worst sense of that term. Though one cannot say of *Bonnie and Clyde* to what degree it shows the work of Newman and Benton and to what degree they merely enabled Penn to "express himself," there are ways of making guesses. As we hear the lines, we can detect the intentions even when the intentions are not quite carried out. Penn is a little clumsy and rather too fancy; he's too much interested in being cinematically creative and artistic to know when to trust the script. *Bonnie and Clyde* could be better if it were simpler. Nevertheless, Penn is a remarkable director when he has something to work with. His most interesting previous work was in his first film, *The Left Handed Gun* (and a few bits of *The Miracle Worker,* a good movie version of the William Gibson play, which he had also directed on the stage and on television). *The Left Handed Gun,* with Paul Newman as an ignorant Billy the Kid in the sex-starved, male-dominated Old West, has the same kind of violent, legendary, nostalgic material as *Bonnie and Clyde;* its script, a rather startling one, was adapted by Leslie Stevens from a Gore Vidal television play. In interviews, Penn makes high, dull sounds — more like a politician than a movie director. But he has a gift for violence, and, despite all the violence in movies, a gift for it is rare. (Eisenstein had it, and Dovzhenko, and Buñuel, but not many others.) There are few memorable violent moments in American movies, but there is one in Penn's first film: Billy's shotgun blasts a man right out of one of his boots; the man falls in the street, but his boot remains upright; a little girl's giggle at the boot is interrupted by her mother's slapping her. The mother's slap — the seal of the awareness of horror — says that even children must learn that some things that look funny are not only funny. That slap, saying that only idiots would laugh at pain and death, that a child must develop sensibility, is the same slap that *Bonnie and Clyde* delivers to the woman saying "It's a comedy." In *The Left Handed Gun,* the slap is itself funny, and yet we suck in our breath; we do not dare to laugh.

Some of the best American movies show the seams of cuts and the confusions of compromises and still hold together, because there is enough energy and spirit to carry the audience over each of the weak episodes to the next good one. The solid intelligence of the writing and Penn's aura of sensitivity help *Bonnie and Clyde* triumph over many poorly directed scenes:

Bonnie posing for the photograph with the Texas Ranger, or — the worst sequence — the Ranger getting information out of Blanche Barrow in the hospital. The attempt to make the Texas Ranger an old-time villain doesn't work. He's in the tradition of the mustachioed heavy who foreclosed mortgages and pursued heroines in turn-of-the-century plays, and this one-dimensional villainy belongs, glaringly, to spoof. In some cases, I think, the writing and the conception of the scenes are better (potentially, that is) than the way the scenes have been directed and acted. If Gene Hackman's Buck Barrow is a beautifully controlled performance, the best in the film, several of the other players — though they are very good — needed a tighter rein. They act too much. But it is in other ways that Penn's limitations show — in his excessive reliance on meaning-laden closeups, for one. And it's no wonder he wasn't able to bring out the character of Bonnie in scenes like the one showing her appreciation of the fingernails on the figurine, for in other scenes his own sense of beauty appears to be only a few rungs farther up that same cultural ladder.

The showpiece sequence, Bonnie's visit to her mother (which is a bit reminiscent of Humphrey Bogart's confrontation with his mother, Marjorie Main, in the movie version of *Dead End*), aims for an effect of alienation, but that effect is confused by all the other things attempted in the sequence: the poetic echoes of childhood (which also echo the child sliding down the hill in *Jules and Jim*) and a general attempt to create a frieze from our national past — a poetry of poverty. Penn isn't quite up to it, though he is at least good enough to communicate what he is trying to do, and it is an attempt that one can respect. In 1939, John Ford attempted a similar poetic evocation of the legendary American past in *Young Mr. Lincoln;* this kind of evocation, by getting at how we *feel* about the past, moves us far more than attempts at historical re-creation. When Ford's Western evocations fail, they become languorous; when they succeed, they are the West of our dreams, and his Lincoln, the man so humane and so smart that he can outwit the unjust and save the innocent, is the Lincoln of our dreams, as the Depression of *Bonnie and Clyde* is the Depression of our dreams — the nation in a kind of trance, as in a dim memory. In this sense, the effect of blur is justified, is "right." Our memories *have* become hazy; this is what the Depression has faded into. But we are too conscious of the technical means used to achieve this blur, of the *attempt* at poetry. We are aware that the filtered effects already include our responses, and it's too easy; the lines are good enough so that the stylization wouldn't have been necessary if the scene had been played right. A simple frozen frame might have been more appropriate.

The editing of this movie is, however, the best editing in an American movie in a long time, and one may assume that Penn deserves credit for it along with the editor, Dede Allen. It's particularly inventive in the robberies and in the comedy sequence of Blanche running through the police barricades with her kitchen spatula in her hand. (There is, however, one bad bit of editing: the end of the hospital scene, when Blanche's voice makes an emotional shift without a corresponding change in her facial position.) The quick panic of Bonnie and Clyde looking at each other's face for the last time is a stunning example of the art of editing.

The end of the picture, the rag-doll dance of death as the gun blasts keep the bodies of Bonnie and Clyde in motion, is brilliant. It is a horror that seems to go on for eternity, and yet it doesn't last a second beyond what it should. The audience leaving the theatre is the quietest audience imaginable.

Still, that woman near me was saying "It's a comedy" for a little too long, and although this could have been, and probably was, a demonstration of plain old-fashioned insensitivity, it suggests that those who have attuned themselves to the "total" comedy of the last few years may not know when to stop laughing. Movie audiences have been getting a steady diet of "black" comedy since 1964 and *Dr. Strangelove, Or: How I Learned to Stop Worrying and Love the Bomb.* Spoof and satire have been entertaining audiences since the two-reelers; because it is so easy to do on film things that are difficult or impossible in nature, movies are ideally suited to exaggerations of heroic prowess and to the kind of lighthearted nonsense we used to get when even the newsreels couldn't resist the kidding finish of the speeded-up athletic competition or the diver flying up from the water. The targets have usually been social and political fads and abuses, together with the heroes and the clichés of the just preceding period of film-making. *Dr. Strangelove* opened a new movie era. It ridiculed *everything* and *everybody* it showed, but concealed its own liberal pieties, thus protecting itself from ridicule. A professor who had told me that *The Manchurian Candidate* was "irresponsible," adding, "I didn't like it — I can suspend disbelief only so far," was overwhelmed by *Dr. Strangelove:* "I've never been so involved. I had to keep reminding myself it was only a movie." *Dr. Strangelove* was clearly intended as a cautionary movie; it meant to jolt us awake to the dangers of the bomb by showing us the insanity of the course we were pursuing. But artists' warnings about war and the dangers of total annihilation never tell us how we are supposed to regain control, and *Dr. Strangelove,* chortling over madness, did not indicate any possibilities for sanity. It was experienced not as satire but as a confirmation of fears. Total laughter carried the day. A new generation enjoyed seeing the world as insane; they *literally* learned to stop worrying and love the bomb. Conceptually, we had already been living with the bomb; now the mass audience of the movies — which is the youth of America — grasped the idea that the threat of extinction can be used to devaluate everything, to turn it all into a joke. And the members of this audience do love the bomb; they love feeling that the worst has happened and the irrational are the sane, because there is the bomb as the proof that the rational are insane. They love the bomb because it intensifies their feelings of hopelessness and powerlessness and innocence. It's only three years since Lewis Mumford was widely acclaimed for saying about *Dr. Strangelove* that "unless the spectator was purged by laughter he would be paralyzed by the unendurable anxiety this policy, once it were honestly appraised, would produce." Far from being purged, the spectators are paralyzed, but they're still laughing. And how odd it is now to read, *"Dr. Strangelove* would be a silly, ineffective picture if its purpose were to ridicule the characters of our military and political leaders by showing them as clownish monsters — stupid, psychotic, obsessed." From *Dr. Strangelove* it's a quick leap to *MacBird* and to a belief in exactly what it was said we weren't meant to find in *Dr. Strangelove.* It is not war that has been laughed to scorn but the possibility of sane action.

Once something enters mass culture, it travels fast. In the spoofs of the last few years, everything is gross, ridiculous, insane; to make sense would be to risk being square. A brutal new melodrama is called *Point Blank* and it is. So are most of the new movies. This is the context in which *Bonnie and Clyde,* an entertaining movie that has some feeling in it, upsets people — people who didn't get upset even by *Mondo Cane.* Maybe it's because *Bonnie and Clyde,* by making us care about the robber lovers, has put the sting back into death.

[October 1967]

II

The Making of *The Group*

The Making of *The Group*

THOSE who get disgusted with American movies may often be heard asking why America isn't producing great film directors — as if we had a shortage of *talent,* as if artists were yet to be attracted to the medium. The more relevant question might be: does the American film industry foster mediocrity and make it almost impossible for artists to work?

What kind of people get to make movies, and what gives a movie its particular shape? I hoped to find some possible answers by observing how Mary McCarthy's novel *The Group* became the movie *The Group.*

THE PACKAGE

By August 28, 1963, when the novel was published, every major American motion picture studio had considered it and turned it down. Charles K. Feldman, an agent turned independent packager of movie properties — a function sometimes described as "executive producer" — bought it for $162,500 (partly in deferred payments) plus 10 percent of the distributor's gross after the break-even point, and proceeded to try to convince the companies that had already rejected the book to finance the production. *The Group* had just reached the bookstores: Feldman hired publicity men to promote it. In addition to the publishers' advertising expenditures, he says he put $50,000 into advertising in the United States, $12,000 in England, and sizable amounts into other countries where the novel was coming out in translation. He claims that it was his money that made the book a best seller. Several reasonably disinterested publishers I have talked with say that *The Group* would have made it without Feldman's money (though it may have helped in keeping the book so high on the lists for so long). Feldman's principal aim was to increase the value of his property so that he could make an advantageous deal with one of the studios. They would need convincing, of course, that the book which they had not thought would make a movie *could* be made into a movie. On the Riviera, he arranged with Sidney Buchman, a veteran Hollywood writer, to adapt the book and serve as producer. Long ago when Buchman had been head of production at Columbia, Feldman had been his agent. Now, Feldman hired Buchman for $180,000, plus a percentage.

Buchman is almost a one-man history of Hollywood. His first screenplay was for Cecil B. DeMille's *The Sign of the Cross* in 1932; his credits as writer or co-writer include such diverse films as *If I Had a Million, Theodora Goes Wild, Mr. Smith Goes to Washington, Holiday, Here Comes Mr. Jordan, Talk of the Town, Jolson Sings Again,* and *A Song to Remember.* Buchman's career fell apart during the House Un-American Activities Committee hearings. He went abroad, made his home at Cannes, and except for the 1961 English film, *The Mark,* which he produced and co-authored, and perhaps a little bootleg job here or there, he was out of work (in a gentlemanly, comfortable way) for fifteen years. He was sixty-three when he took on the labor of *The Group* — a very tired and cynical sixty-three, and yet, curiously enough, determined to turn this new movie into some kind of progressive statement.

It might be asked at this point: why didn't Mary McCarthy adapt her own material for the screen? On the first page of her first book she had used an analogy with movies to describe her writing process, and her fiction — which is reportorial and semi-autobiographical — is peculiarly cinematic. She records characters and relationships from the outside and she details the costumes, furnishings, and locations that give the actions specific meanings. Is there a more completely worked-out scenario in modern fiction than "The Man in the Brooks Brothers Shirt"? It's already a movie. However, there is no indication that she was asked to work on *The Group.* She told Feldman that she didn't think the novel could work as a movie without a lot of invention. But Buchman stayed very close to the book, hardly even inventing any dialogue, although transposing characters' thoughts into speech. She had not asked to see the screenplay. Buchman sent her a copy, anyway. She did not comment on it. Perhaps his fidelity to her material did not please her any more than infidelity might have; she is, notoriously, a writer given to seeing the faults in *any* course of action. And in this case it was obvious that neither inventiveness nor fidelity could be completely satisfactory. There were huge structural gaps in the book that in dramatic terms (and in terms of fiction also) cried out for invention; yet Buchman must have known that he could not invent in her style. He played it safe, preferring narrative holes to inadequate invention.

This was not exactly pleasing to Feldman, who admits publicly that he has no interest in Mary McCarthy's stature as a writer. Feldman's enthusiasm for the project had little to do with the literary qualities or dramatic potential of Miss McCarthy's work, but on the gorgeous possibility of getting options on a group of inexpensive, luscious young nobodies, building them up into stars, and then having them available for his own films and for handsome loan-out deals. He had had a similar intention when he bought *What's New, Pussycat?* — which he had also intended to cast with unknowns and little-knowns. But somehow things got out of hand, in the way movie financing-casting (a peculiarly linked process) often does, and he had wound up with Peter O'Toole, Peter Sellers, Capucine, Ursula Andress, Romy Schneider, and Paula Prentiss. This time, with a property featuring eight young girls, surely he would get his own young Capucines and Andresses; and with a stable of young beauties under option, a modern movie packager-producer could be richer than the greatest whoremasters of history. (There are even directors in Hollywood who make more money from the pieces they own of the stars they gave their first break to than from directing.) Feldman's ideas of casting are rather basic: "You can always teach them to act." He was so confident that this time he would get cheap stars out of the deal that when Buchman had completed a draft of the screenplay, and United Artists became interested, he stipulated as part of the package deal that UA should spend at least $100,000 to exploit the new talent (which he assumed would be *his* new talent).

There was another special interest that Feldman had in the book: a chance to exploit a lesbian theme. He assumed that the screenplay would center on Lakey's affairs — which would, of course, have to be invented for her. Instead, Buchman held so close to the text that waiting for Lakey to reappear in the movie is about like waiting for Godot. And the whole lesbian theme was handled with such discretion that when the movie was finished the United Artists publicity men threw out the campaign they had prepared to exploit it and prepared a new campaign featuring a true-confessions approach to each of the girls.

At the point when the deal was made, Charles K. Feldman became The Man in the background, and Sidney Buchman, more or less in charge of the production, began looking for a director. Most of the men interviewed were television directors who had never made a movie. This partly explains why recent movies are so bad: there is almost no way for young movie directors to get experience or make a reputation except on television (which is very different from movie-making, although movie-making is now becoming like television) or in the theatre (which is even more different). But the older movie directors are dying off or are priced out of the market (they work on huge, slow super-epics). So for a production like this, TV and stage directors are considered and may get their first movie experience. Negotiations and discussions were going on with these men when Sidney Lumet, who has the same agent as Buchman, saw the script and leaped at the job. Lumet had not read the novel; it's doubtful if he'd ever read any Mary McCarthy. What he leaped at, evidently, was Sidney Buchman's screenplay, a job that would pay him $125,000, and a movie with a longer shooting schedule and a larger budget than he had ever had.

Why were they about to start on the cumbersome, tedious process of making a movie out of this novel? Why were they going to all the trouble of construction and reproduction to tell a story that had already been told in a simple, efficient, inexpensive way? Sometimes there are people who really want to bring their vision of a particular novel to life. But the filming of *The Group* was strictly a business proposition. Yet it presented aesthetic problems. In theory, there is little that a novel can do that a movie can't but, practically, American audiences won't sit for the length and detail and complexity of a novel. Almost all the details in this novel — the fads and fashions and chitchat — could be dramatically rendered, but how would the movie re-create the political climate, the sexual morality, the décor of the thirties — the so recent past — for the "large" movie audience? Much distortion and simplification was inevitable; perhaps even more was accidental.

Sidney Lumet had been getting work directing movies for several years because he was cheap, fast, and reliable; but when he was signed for *The Group* he had still never had a box-office hit. And the people who put movie packages together are more concerned with box-office results than with the quality of the films. Lumet was known to critics and perhaps to the art-house audience for his first movie, the one-set, low-budget *Twelve Angry Men,* which, despite critical enthusiasm, hadn't shown a profit; the literate, uneven *Stage Struck;* the spectacular artistic and commercial disaster, the Brando-Magnani *The Fugitive Kind;* the ambitious and financially unsuccessful *A View from the Bridge;* and the superb transcription of O'Neill's *Long Day's Journey into Night,* which had cost less than a half million and still lost money. He had been making some of the most interesting movies coming out of the United States, but without at least one winner he had no standing in the world of big movies, big profits.

He was part of that earlier television-into-movies new generation of directors, but two other members of that generation, John Frankenheimer and Martin Ritt, had already made it into the big time with *hits,* and he was still in the young-promising category, i.e., hustling, taking the quick jobs (like *Fail-Safe*) that bigger directors didn't want. He could get these jobs because of his reputation for staying within budget and maybe even finishing *ahead* of schedule. Lumet wanted to work and he *liked* to work fast. He would not try to reshape the scenario or risk holding up production to do something unscheduled; he wouldn't plead for a few extra days to get something right.

If a director in another country has succeeded financially with an unusual project or approach, he is acclaimed as an artist and the big American companies are anxious to get him, but if a young American director shows any traces of really caring about what he does or how he does it — any signs of artistry — they become uneasy and clamp down on him. Art means risks; to businessmen, taking risks is unprofessional behavior. But by the time a man has made a TV reputation, he knows the score and there's very little he has left of his own to express. He has become a mechanic, and he'll approach making a movie as a job promotion, a step up from television. Businessmen want directors they can trust on the basis of past performance (and this, ironically, may be one of the reasons so many small pictures lose money). Lumet was television-trained; that meant he would do things the obvious ways that producers don't worry about. Or, if he did give them something to worry about, at least it would be something they could understand. And even without any hits on his record, Lumet was trustworthy because, for example, he never considered it a deterrent factor that when he read the novel he hated it. He was no dangerous artist; he was out to do a job.

Sidney Lumet's background was about as far from Mary McCarthy's Vassar as you can get. The son of an actor from Poland who appeared in the Yiddish theatre in New York (the elder Lumet appears as Mr. Schneider in *The Group*), he had himself been an infant actor — indeed the infant Jesus in Max Reinhardt's New York production of *The Eternal Road*. He was Christ again, as a boy, in Maxwell Anderson's *Journey to Jerusalem*, with Arlene Francis as Mary. He was understudy to one of the Dead End Kids on Broadway, and it is not perhaps stretching the point to suggest that both of these roles are still visible in his behavior. He's messianic and driven, but like an understudy to a Dead End Kid, he's in a hurry to get there. Lumet, in the conventional sense, is probably not very well educated. But, in a way, untutored high intelligence may make a person seem even more "creative," as if it came out of nowhere, was "genius." And in show business people love the idea of "genius": it's so much easier to throw the term about than to try to explain why certain people manage to get somewhere. Lumet, despite his almost ostentatious show-business streetboy's manner, is very well self-educated in terms of what he may be able to use. He reads for a purpose. A standard complaint of his earlier producers is: "Sidney doesn't listen." But he hears what he wants to, not what they want him to. In conversation, he doesn't respond to what doesn't immediately relate to his own interests, so the subject soon changes, or he simply changes it — as he is likely to be the dominating force anyway. He seems to have almost no intellectual curiosity of a more generalized or objective nature.

Working on *The Group,* Lumet was not scholarly — to put it mildly — about Mary McCarthy or about Vassar, but as a life-long actor and an experienced TV and movie director, he showed a professional respect for acting and his job. He and Buchman did the casting together, and, with the exception of Candice Bergen, a beauty glorious and young enough to gladden Feldman's and anyone else's heart, they selected for talent. Candy

Bergen was hardly a poor struggling unknown who could be signed up for peanuts and promises and tied up for years of servitude. And the two Sidneys moved so fast in casting and getting underway that by the time Feldman's minions, uncertain and apprehensive about whether Feldman would want the other girls — actresses! — and *which* of them, got around to framing agreements, the girls were already in the picture and didn't need to sign away their futures in order to get this chance.

THE CASTING

The casting of movies is in some ways more important than the casting of plays: in the theatre a competent actor can make many roles his own, but in movies what an actor knows and can do is often less important than what he simply physically *is* — the way he looks, how he photographs, what he inadvertently projects. On stage he may be able to become a whole gallery of characters; but the camera exposes the actor as a man of a certain age, with definite physical assets and liabilities. There he is in close-up, huge on the screen, and if he's trying to play something that is physically different from what he is, he looks like a fool, and only if he is a good and subtle actor can he play something that is psychologically very different from how he is. When a movie is derived from a popular novel, the casting is even more complex: the roles have not been written with certain actors in mind; rather, the actors must somehow fit into the novelist's conception, or at least into a conception the public will accept as a reasonable facsimile. At best, in popular, commercial movies they should be like illustrations to the text — whose cover they will probably adorn in the paperback edition that is timed to the release of the film; or so popular in themselves that they will be stronger than the images in the text. All that was obvious from the outside — I knew it as a critic; these were simply the facts of the situation. But sitting in a little office with the producer and director as they interviewed actors and then discussed them, there were factors I had never really considered as a critic.

Everybody knows and talks about the state of the theatre; we all know there are few jobs, except in TV, which is now almost all in California, but here was the living evidence — actors trying to get a job. Budgeted at $2,600,000, *The Group* was the most expensive movie yet made in New York; there were a lot of parts in it, and perhaps half the out-of-work actors in New York at one time or another must have had hopes. As each actor or actress came in for the prearranged interview, the air in the little room was heavy with strain and embarrassment. Many of them had worked with Lumet in his early days in the theatre or in radio, or had been directed by him in early live TV, so there were the tentative reminders of past association — uneasy good wishes to be conveyed to his father, an uncertainty about how far to press old intimacies with their former associate, now in a

job-giving capacity. Powerlessness made them uncertain of how to deal
with power; desperation made them transparent. The women in turbans or
big, tricky hats all seemed to apologize for their hair; one after another explained how their agents had just notified them of the interview. Asked their
height, most of the men gave the all-purpose five-eleven — wanting to be
considered neither too short nor too tall for whatever the role might be. In
fear of being considered wrong, and not knowing what they were being considered for, they tried to pass themselves off as Everyman. They had been
preceded, of course, by photographs — large, glossy, glamorous photographs
sent in by agents, and as Lumet said, "What's heartbreaking is the pictures
versus the people." We saw them as they *had* looked or *could* look or had
been *doctored* to look, and then we *saw* them. It was like people on TV commercials versus people in subways.

And I was horrified because they were people I knew: I had seen them in
my childhood in the theatre in San Francisco, I had seen them touring with
Katherine Cornell or acting in New York "hits," I had seen them long ago
in the movies as juvenile leads, or in character roles — almost all of them
were familiar names in the theatre, people I thought of as established, secure, honored. And here they were trying to get bit parts, eager for a few
days' work, for a two-line role, and not knowing whether to conceal their
desperation or whether to expose it. You could see them trying to calculate
how much "front" they should put on, or whether a naked appeal would be
preferable. And they spoke in voices I knew so well, the voices that seemed
to belong to their past more than to their present. Some of those familiar
faces were aged, others just burnt-out. I think the worst thing to watch —
because it was the most human, really — was when they tried uncertainly
to play it both ways: to conceal what shape they were in and yet somehow
to appeal. In succession, each applicant threw illumination on the others. It
became like some terrible TV show in which the great, the famous, the
celebrated expose their wrecked careers, their shameful poverty, their
knowledge that they're drifting, waiting for a break, and maybe this show is
it. It's as if they'd never had the breaks, never been famous, because now
they scarcely expect to be remembered. Too many people have obviously
forgotten them; they know how little it means in terms of getting jobs that
they were once stars or almost-stars, that they're "well known."

Why do producers and directors begin to play God? Because they do play
God.

I had only a couple of weeks of observing the casting in May: it had been
going on since late February. (They had looked at over two hundred
"promising" young actresses for the eight leads; I didn't even want to think
about what their pitches must have been like, how eager they must have
been for a chance to make their names, change their fortunes. How cool
they must have tried to appear, perhaps almost as cool as those who got the

roles and then tried to appear indifferent to them. If one believed what they told the papers, several of the girls in the picture really didn't know why they bothered doing it at all.) I found two weeks of it hard to take — like living in a butcher shop with human meat. I had heard plenty of descriptions from actor friends, but I had never seen it from the other side. The casting director had selected the candidates for the meager little roles being cast: mothers or fathers of the girls of *The Group,* a butler, friends — roles that were later cut or reduced to a glimpse, anyway. And so sometimes it went to the actor who had exposed his need more, and then I couldn't help thinking, "Suppose that other one who came on so prosperous and pleasant was really even more desperate and too proud to show it." Most of the middle-aged performers were being considered for the parent roles, and unfortunately those who did not get the parts could not know — and probably they wouldn't have *believed* even if they were told — that they weren't picked because they didn't match up right with their "daughters." After a lifetime in the "theatre" they were being picked not for what they could play, but for their physical types and for chance resemblances. And those who did get these small parts were of course really too good for the roles, which required almost no acting, and whenever they had a line they gave it so much full-throated voice and elegant gesture and presence that the lines generally had to be cut, because all that acting was florid and stagey and ridiculous. They were trying to turn movie bits into rich roles, and the results were generally disastrous: nonprofessionals type-cast might have done as well, or better. But then nonprofessionals probably wouldn't have needed the work so much.

What sustained these people in the most delusionary of all careers — "acting"? There is a great deal written about the rich fantasy life and role playing in the childhood of actors, but actors may have nothing else to sustain them later on, either. Why do they stick with it? Many don't, of course, and I was to meet them shortly. They were the "crew": from the director on down, they were almost all actors who had given up.

THE PLANNING

Under modern production conditions, the key figures in movie-making, who on this film were the producer-writer and the director, are businessmen who claim the prestige and the latitude of the genius-artist role. Buchman and Lumet were already negotiating for their next projects when this one actually got underway. The crucial work for them seemed to be finished before the shooting started: the "deal" and the planning of the production (which, like running a war, involves an almost incredible amount of detail, ledgers full of plans and calculations, including everything from transporting and feeding the actresses to having thirties cars ready at a certain place at a certain date). Like other businessmen, they were already planning their winter line while turning out the summer product. Buchman said he could hardly wait for this to be over so he could "get on to some real work." Eager to get back into his old harness, he was working on a Howard Fast novel. Lumet, while hoping to line up something that "really excited" him — the production of a John Hersey book — was planning his next job, a John LeCarré spy thriller. But, though priding themselves on being good businessmen — which in movie business is what is usually meant by "professionalism" — they did not necessarily recognize how completely they were businessmen, perhaps because they felt that they really believed, if not in this project, at least in those future hoped-for Howard Fast and John Hersey projects.

For Lumet, planning includes the camera position for each shot, the lens to be used, and just about everything the technicians need to know. The camera will rarely move within a shot; "movement" will be accomplished by the actors moving within the frame and by the rapid juxtaposition of shots. During the actual shooting, the director puts the actors through their paces, trying to get some sense of life — mainly by encouraging the actors to come on strong — into this mechanized plan. The director who has enough training and self-confidence to face an army of technicians and experiment or improvise is rare — and what company wants him if his methods lose time, which is money? Tough, bright men like Sidney Lumet can get their effects, not by what we used to think of as the movie director's art, but by "turning on," i.e., turning loose the actors, and by emphasizing certain powerful "big" scenes — emphatic climaxes, shocks, excessive and thus surprising bits of action. Lumet is not so vulgar as most of the new television-trained movie directors who just keep the actors shouting in close-up. And unlike the pretentious ones among them, he knows that he is just shooting a script, that he is not discovering the possibilities in the material and shaping it. Nevertheless, he enthusiastically invited me to observe how the crew would begin to "intermesh" as the shooting went on, and talked often of "the rhythm" that the footage would reveal when it was edited. After observing a few days of shooting, I knew that if the editing would reveal rhythm in the footage, it would be luck; and luck was only likely in bits of sequences, it couldn't be counted on for the total structure.

There *are* movie directors who try to plan out every detail in advance: Hitchcock, for example, conceives the movie visually from the beginning of the script preparation, designing the production like a complicated mousetrap, then building it. His script is a set of plans representing the completed film, including the editing, and if he doesn't need to depart from it, that is because he works for exactly calculated effects of suspense and perversity. He is an ingenious, masterly builder of mousetraps, and more often than not, the audience is caught tight; his techniques, however, probably have more to do with gamesmanship than with art, and they are almost the opposite of the working methods of most great directors for whom making the movie is itself a process of discovery.

That process of discovery is not part of studio movie-making; in Hollywood even Jean Renoir, whose greatest work has been free and improvisatory, was expected to stick to plan, and his American movies showed what happens to an artist in such conditions. If a director is forced to follow a plan, whether another's or even his own, when, at the time of shooting, he wants to do it some other way — to use an idea that occurs to him when he sees the actors together on the set or sees the possibility of using the landscape in a way he hadn't thought of before — the necessity to do it according to specifications is crippling. It means he can't use his wits, he can't be spontaneous or inventive, he can't think and feel as an artist. This is one of the business practices that makes hacks out of American directors. And if the director knows that his being in a position to make movies at all is dependent on sticking to plan, probably after a while he doesn't even think of how he might like to do it; he just does it. These are the men who, in Hollywood, are considered the true pros.

From what I observed, Lumet's planning is based on the hope that he'll come out of the shooting with something he can pull together in the editing room. The precision of his method is illusory: mechanically, the shots are neatly scheduled, but their precise effect in terms of the finished film is not calculated. When he can't match them up properly later, when "the rhythm" isn't revealed, audiences may experience the confusion of not knowing how to react to the action. For example, passages of comedy in *The Group* were often so awkward when assembled that some audiences thought the humor was inadvertent.

That tight schedule looks very businesslike on paper; everything seems to be worked out. But when you watch the shooting, as later when you watch the rushes, and finally when you see the movie, you know he operates on a wing and a prayer — and not just in an emergency but every day. For sheer guts, Lumet is awe-inspiring.

THE NOVEL

Lumet and Buchman had finished their thinking about *The Group;* their minds were already turning on the future. At one level, I was more interested in this film than they were: at the level of what it was all about — how they were interpreting the novel. Except for conversations in which I brought up this subject, I never heard it discussed during the production. Nor did anyone ever talk about Mary McCarthy. Several of the girls (and their stand-ins too) were reading *The Group* during their waiting time at rehearsals — I could not tell whether for the first time. I did not *ask* because, after some early conversations with Lumet, he requested that I not discuss the author or novel with the actresses, and I held to this religiously.

This was astute of him: he sensed some danger in my questioning his interpretations not only with him but with them. The remarks that I had made
which led to this restriction were during a discussion with him in which I
had demurred from Buchman's view of Mary McCarthy and referred to her
autobiographical *Memories of a Catholic Girlhood* — Lumet did not know
the book.

Whenever the subject of the movie came up among the girls or among the
crew it was usually referred to contemptuously as a soap opera — which I
gradually came to understand meant not only that they didn't see more to
the novel than soap opera but that that was how they referred to something
when they felt superior to it, when they considered it commercial rather
than artistic. Was it possible that no one around had any notion of Mary
McCarthy's position in the literary world? She was not only a writer: she
was a culture heroine, with pride in intelligence, and wit that cleaned away
commonplaces. She was direct, a liberator who brought women's experiences out into the open. But her smartness carried a threat to conventionality, and she was often penalized for it. *Time* had expressed what so many
felt, that Mary McCarthy is, "quite possibly the cleverest woman America
has ever produced." This made her a favorite voodoo doll: anyone who
wanted to prove his superiority jabbed at her, and indeed *Time* did it with
the needle of "cleverest" — which, though accurate, is also wounding.
Clever so often means "merely" clever, not profound or truly important,
certainly not "sincere." In the twenty-odd years since the publication of
"The Man in the Brooks Brothers Shirt" she was frequently jabbed in the
wrong places by the sort of people who say, "So she got laid on a train, does
she have to *tell* about it?" — as if she had violated the gentleman's code.
(Those who don't believe in the single standard have no qualms about using
it to reinforce their double standard.)

No one around the movie seemed to connect to *this* Mary McCarthy or
to be aware of how the publication of *The Group* had altered her position,
puzzling her long-time admirers and bringing her a different, a best-seller
audience. In *The Group* she parodies the motives, the aspirations, the styles
in ideas of a group of girls who graduated from Vassar in 1933 into the
midst of the Depression and the New Deal. Her Vassar girls seemed to be
the women as victims so dearly beloved of middle-class fiction. Aggressive,
determined Kay ("Kay was a frightful dancer and always tried to lead")
goes mad; good sweet Polly gets a dear understanding husband to depend
on. It was like a Hollywood movie; the girl who wants "too much" gets
nothing, is destroyed; the girl waiting for the right man gets the Best of
Everything. She wins an undogmatic psychiatrist — the same role so often
filled in movies by a Forward-Looking Architect. This Prince Charming
even sets up a test — that she wouldn't send her loony papa to an institution. It seemed as if *The Group* could almost have been written by a female

equivalent of "The Man in the Brooks Brothers Shirt." Mary McCarthy's attitude to her characters had become embarrassingly like his — from his disapproval of the heroine's suitcase with a missing handle to his final plea: "Forget all this red nonsense and remember that you're just your father's little girl at heart." Her earlier troublemaker-heroine had split into impossible Kay and ludicrous Libby, and "father's little girl at heart" — Polly — had now become the heroine.

Although pieces of the novel had appeared in print almost a decade before book publication, the direction it took was a surprise, and many of her former admirers thought the girls of *The Group* as cold and calculating, and as irrational and defenseless and inept, as if conceived by an anti-feminist male writer. It was depressing to find the book praised by those who thought it showed what happened to girls who "insist on meeting life free from parental protection or guidance" — as if a Victorian training in domestic skills might have equipped them better than their Vassar education and kept them home and out of trouble. This way of reading the book — though naïve — was common, and it was the usual best-seller/Hollywood view of women. And this view, mixed with the idea that it was also a sensational book — "dirty" in places — seemed to be prevalent around the studio.

THE PRODUCER-WRITER

As a screenwriter, Sidney Buchman is known as a good man at "construction" — i.e., clearing through the underbrush of a novel to locate or design a simplified, neat screenplay. This was hardly possible with *The Group;* still, he reduced it without undue vulgarization. But what he had thought or hoped to do was something very different — and rather bewildering.

On our first meeting, Sidney Buchman, courtly and urbane, told me that after his third reading of the novel and after discussion with Granville Hicks, he and Hicks agreed that the theme of *The Group* was: "Higher education does not fit women for life." Not being used to the role of an observer (I never did get used to it), I shot back, "What does? Does higher education fit *men* for life?" He didn't reply and was taken up with another matter: accepting congratulations from someone who had just recently seen *The Mark* in revival and told him how great it was, that there was "not a false note in it." When Buchman had finished shaking hands on this, he turned back to me with a rather belligerent stance and asked, "Just what did you have against *The Mark?*" (He had apparently heard that I had written a less than favorable review but he had not read it). Before I could reply, he went on, "All I was trying to do was get people to feel compassion for the mentally ill."

I said, "But what sort of compassion is necessary when they know that the man is innocent of any wrongdoing?"

"Well," he said, "in the actual case it was based on, the man *did* rape a child, but if I told the truth, I wouldn't have any movie, I couldn't get people to feel compassion for him."

I didn't want to tell him that that was almost a definition of the artist's task, so I just let it drop. But it occurred to me that this preposterous mixture of wanting to do good and yet evading the real problems — not even telling the simple truth if it might prejudice your case — was the basic cheat of Hollywood message movies.

Asked why he'd got involved in this particular project, Buchman said, "I have been interested in the education of the young for many years." And he *had* been: he'd been on the board of Sarah Lawrence when his daughter was there. But I'd have been more reassured if he said he'd been interested in Mary McCarthy's writing for many years; or just said it was a job. He talked a tremendous amount about the problem of contraception; he had somehow convinced himself that the movie would make some sort of contribution to progress and enlightenment. Listening to him, you'd think you were going to get a contraceptive and a birth control pamphlet with your movie ticket. A few days after my abrupt "Does higher education fit *men* for life?", he came over to me and said he'd been giving it a great deal of thought (God knows *why!*) and that, no, it didn't. Still, he went on and on during the production about his favorite theme of education, and how the movie was "about these foolish, shallow girls having their lives wasted." So I put it to him again, a little differently:"Would it have been different for men?" And a few days later, he said he'd thought it over, and "Yes, it could be eight men. You know, Pauline, I don't know what the damn thing's about."

I said that I didn't think Mary McCarthy could resist her impulse to ridicule, that she was driven by the same kind of wicked logic whether she was dealing with the anarchists and socialists of *The Oasis* or the professors of *The Groves of Academe* or the girls of *The Group,* and that I didn't think her concentration on women this time was intended as an attack on education for women — that she herself was a triumphant demonstration that women can and do think without parroting men. He dropped the education-for-women line when we were alone, but I still heard it brought out for public occasions. I would hear him talking about "does not fit women properly" and I would think, is it education or contraception this time? He still wanted the movie to prove something. It wasn't enough for him just to tell a story. He felt guilty that he wasn't doing something *worthwhile,* like getting compassion for the innocent.

I first heard of his next solution to the problem of how he would give the movie "depth" when Lumet announced it to the girls. The girls nodded gravely as he explained it, and indeed, it was one of those superficially plausible ideas that young kids *would* think was brilliant. The idea was that while the girls were going on about their affairs, there would be Depression details in the background — pickets, soup kitchens, apple sellers — *and the girls would never even notice them.* This is just the sort of easy irony that the theatre and movies are full of, those fancy little effects — the products of theatrical training — that are considered "moving" or "deep." Surely anyone who thought about Mary McCarthy's Group would realize that social consciousness was just what Vassar had given them. The novel is not about a bunch of rich girls who don't even notice the Depression; it's about a group of girls who come out of college full of awareness and idealism (mixed with priggishness and pride), and the ways in which their weaknesses and entrapment in ordinary human problems destroy their plans. I said most of this to Buchman and I told him, too, that I was damned tired of movies that made the audience feel so much smarter than the characters. "Gee, look, they didn't even *notice* that poor apple seller. If I'd been there, I would have." After all, what *could* you do except buy an apple? The irony they planned would be particularly grotesque, since the novel had satirized the political activities of the girls, and although the script eliminated much of this, it retained the structure so that the ones who are outside or above it all, the ones who don't get into the political movements of their time come off best — Lakey, Dr. Ridgeley, Polly. Lumet often stressed that Lakey and Polly were "the only ones of the Group who completed themselves. The others are all wrecked by trying to be something else, something they're not."

Later on, I was happy to observe that the "ironic" use of the Depression details was minimized. But the author's curious ambivalence to her material was reflected in these confusions. Although Lumet was delighted with Polly and Lakey for just going on about their own affairs, I don't think he recognized that Mary McCarthy was satirizing the social consciousness of the other girls, not their lack of it. I rather doubt that the author herself intended to do that when she started the book. But in ten years it's all too easy to become an uninvolved, amused aesthete toward even one's own past.

Buchman had another big problem with the material — a central problem. I had been startled to discover on the first day that, according to the producer-writer, "Mary McCarthy is poison. . . . she's competitive." With whom, I wondered? Not Buchman, surely. Although Lumet seemed to share in this view of the author and had frequently said to the press that he would not have done the picture if he'd read the book before seeing the script (which he may have believed, though I didn't), in his case it seemed to be not so much grounded in any specific knowledge as in a general feeling about the *kind* of woman she was. As I got to know him, I concluded that, for Lumet, a woman shouldn't have any problems a real man can't take care of. If she does, she's sick. (Kay wanted to be a director . . .) With Buchman, I felt, it was different. Mary McCarthy, the anti-Communist intellectual, seemed to be a threat he had to fight. He referred to "her vicious attack on Simone de Beauvoir" as something "he would never forgive," as if it were going on right this minute. It was, somehow, as if she were the enemy.

Neither Buchman nor Lumet was comfortable on the subject of Kay, and not just because of the miscasting of a charming giddy blonde who was emotionally too light for the role. The publicity stories all said Lakey was the leader of the group, and even in group photos, the actress who plays Kay seemed to fade away. I think the role was miscast partly because of their discomfort. The discomfort probably went very deep and although they didn't consciously relate Kay to Mary McCarthy, they used the same terms about both. Buchman (who felt that Truffaut's films *Shoot the Piano Player* and *Jules and Jim* were both betrayals of the social point of view for which he had admired Truffaut's first feature, *The 400 Blows*) used exactly the same rancorous terms to describe Catherine of *Jules and Jim*. On this subject, this extraordinarily sophisticated man sounded like a cabdriver or shopgirl — denouncing the movie because he hated the heroine. The cast took the cue: Kay was referred to as "messy and scatterbrained," "a disorderly, disorganized nothing." And when I admired one of Kay's thirties suits, the actress stared in surprise and said, "Of course, Kay was such a schlunk she didn't have any taste." Buchman looked blank at my comment that perhaps Kay could use a little of the self-destructive force that Jeanne Moreau had brought to Catherine. "They were both," he said, "just silly, self-deceived women."

The first day of rehearsals the girls sat around a table — serious, quiet, attentive faces — as Lumet talked. He gave them a little orientation course, not about the screenplay or its point of view or how it was to be interpreted, but about the Depression and Roosevelt and the banks closing and all. He went into his own life during that period as if *The Group* were about The Group Theatre. Then he took up the characters of Gus LeRoy and Mr. Schneider and the antagonism between the Stalinists and Trotskyites. He ended with a description of his only YCL meeting at the age of fourteen, where he asserted that "Soviet artists were a privileged class so the Soviet Union wasn't a classless society" and "I got thrown out."

Buchman spoke up, "You got thrown out? I wasn't. That was my tragedy."

Then he turned and said just to me, qualifying it a bit, "It's not true. I wasn't young enough to be in the YCL."

For the girls, 1933 was obviously as strange as fifth century Rome: they hadn't been born yet.

SIDNEY LUMET, DIRECTOR

Though Sidney Lumet was, at the beginning of *The Group* project, still known as the director producers settled for when they couldn't get the one they wanted — everybody's second choice, the driving little guy who talked himself into jobs and then finished them before the producers even got to know him — by the time *The Group* was finished everybody knew he was going to be a big director. Two pictures he had slammed through opened in New York while he was working on *The Group:* in late April, *The Pawnbroker;* in October, *The Hill. The Pawnbroker,* which ranked high on many best-of-the-year lists, was not only a controversial film (it secured a Production Code Seal only after a group of directors, led by Joseph L. Mankiewicz, put up a fight for it and is still causing embarrassment to the Catholics who proscribed it), it even made some money. *The Hill,* his brutal study of an English military prison camp, made abroad, created considerable excitement before it arrived when word got out that Rex Harrison, on the Cannes Film Festival jury, had wired the Queen about the danger of its getting the grand prize. Lumet was talked about in reviews, even in the not too enthusiastic ones, in a way he hadn't been before.

And yet he is still, in his methods of work, basically a TV director — and it is possible that in the next few years television will wreck movies, not, as was thought possible earlier, by taking the audience away, but by its simplified methods and by killing B movies, which were the training ground for directors, and then inflicting its TV-trained directors on movies. Now that television executives have realized that people prefer old movies to television shows and are going to produce movies for later use on television, this dominance of the TV director may actually convert movies into TV shows, rather than the hoped-for reverse. The difference between the two media is becoming a matter of budget, not technique. The television play type of movie just uses the camera as a recording device for staged action. The director follows a script like a general carrying out a plan who shoots hoping to hit something: he moves the people or the camera around to get some "movement" and hammers some simple points home. And you are cued to react, you're kept so busy reacting you may not even notice that there's *nothing* on the screen for your eye to linger on, no distances, no action in the background, no sense of life or landscape mingling with the foreground action. It's all in the foreground, put there for you to grasp at once. It's all on the surface, it's jumping out of the frame at you. If they want you to notice something, the actor shouts or holds a double-take, and the music accents it further. You don't have to do a thing. You hardly need to look. And if you were deaf, they'd probably shovel it onto your lap.

Lumet, after nine movies — and he is one of the best and most flexible of the TV-trained movie directors — still directs one-dimensionally. He cannot use crowds or details to convey the illusion of life. His backgrounds are always just an empty space; he doesn't even know how to make the principals stand out of a crowd. If he moves the camera, it's just a form of conspicuous expenditure — to prove he can do it. He has only TV foreground action — without intrusions even, and, of course, although this looks fine when the movies later turn up on TV, it basically represents a loss of the whole illusionary delight of movies.

When *The Group* was finished, Lumet told me about some of his plans, and one in particular for a difficult, epic subject, and I said, "But Sidney, you can't *do* that — you can hardly handle more than two people on camera. I saw what happened to the party scenes in *The Group* — they had to be cut down to nothing because nothing was going on in them."

And Lumet, with that surprising boyish honesty which is one of his most engaging qualities, said sheepishly, "I know, but I can learn. I just have to give it some time."

But it's more than just a matter of taking a few weeks or a few months (which I'm convinced he won't do anyway); it's a matter of a different approach to how movies are made, learning to see and compose differently, opening up a movie — in a way that TV just doesn't open up. Lumet can admit this limitation of his technique because he does not recognize its seriousness. It's no accident that he works well with plays; they don't have the texture of novels — so difficult to create on the screen. It makes sense that he preferred the screenplay of *The Group* to the book. That saved him from worrying about problems he didn't want to concern himself with. He'll go on faking it, I think, using the abilities he has to cover up what he doesn't know; he'll go on using space as stage space hyped up with a few tricks, treating movies as just a bigger canvas than TV. For even his honesty about his limitations is probably the result of his not really thinking they are limitations.

The only movie director trained specifically in TV who has at times transcended this limitation has done it in a singular way. Frankenheimer (*The Manchurian Candidate, Seven Days in May*) has converted TV technique into a new look, a new kind of movie style. Lumet's course is a different one. By temperament, he likes the TV speed and the slapdash intensity. He has the temperament to make this system of production work successfully for him because it doesn't frustrate him — he doesn't really want to work any other way. Personally, he's charged. He will take the easiest way to get a powerful effect; in some conventional, terribly obvious way he will be "daring." Chances are, he'll get by with it: he's fearless and dogged, he has a phenomenal memory, and he has an instinct. Lumet surpasses most of the new TV-into-movie directors because he genuinely is not interested in making ordinary movies and because of his energy, his feeling, and, principally, his excesses. What he thinks is emotion is excess. He goes a little farther than others do. Because Lumet can believe in coarse effects, he can bring them off. Sidney Lumet may be one of the next *big* directors because of a basic emotional vulgarity in his work that audiences may respond to. This is a very uncommon man with a common touch. Lumet is a man with a bad ear for dialogue and no eye. Genius? Yes, the genius necessary to convince people he's a genius. Or, to put it more favorably, the determination to convince whoever needs convincing that, whatever it is, he can do it. And that *is* genius, of a kind. You don't get to do much in this world without it. There are a great many sensitive, talented people around who will never do anything but treasure the superiority they feel to people like Lumet, who has pragmatic genius: he'll get it done. It won't be exquisite, it won't be perfect, but it will reflect the energetic, "vulgar" confidence he put into it: it will have some charge or energy which may in some crazy way be more important than perfection anyway.

Lumet made his TV reputation in *live* TV. He's a live wire, he works best under pressure; when it isn't there, he invents it for himself, racing to be *ahead* of schedule. He is happy on the set when everything is going fast, even though the speed may be spurious because the work is slovenly. He isn't reflective, and he doesn't have more to give it if he takes longer. On the contrary, that just makes him impatient and irritable. When directing movies, he re-creates the conditions of live TV — not going back. Other directors plead for retakes; the producer has to force him. He accepts the passable. The advantage is that he gets something live into movies and enjoys what he's doing because of the excitement of the high pressure, the sheer activity of it. Precision seems almost irrelevant to his methods. It's the spirit — or some spirit — that satisfies him, not the exact line of dialogue or careful emphasis on the words. He lets the words fall where they may — which means they must often be post-synchronized because they have been articulated so inaccurately. When you watch scenes being shot and see and hear what's the matter with them, you realize how much bad and negligent work that could be corrected is allowed to pass because of the mystique of movies being the editor's art. There are possibilities for long, fluid scenes in several places in *The Group*. Instead, the scenes will be chopped up with reaction shots and close-ups to conceal the static camera setups and the faults in timing, in acting, in rhythm of performances. Fast editing *can* be done for aesthetic purposes, but too much of it *is* done these days to cover up bad staging and shooting, and the effect is jerky and confusing. But, as it calls so much attention to itself, it is often taken to be brilliant technique. Explaining something he wants done, Lumet will say, "It can be very exciting" — which means what will *work,* not what may relate to any larger conception but simply something that will be effective here and now, in itself. The emphasis on immediate results may explain the almost total absence of nuance, subtlety, and even rhythmic and structural development in his work.

Perhaps because of his live TV approach, his work looks or rather feels somehow *dated* — too derivative, too familiar, too easily accessible as *powerful*. This, in *The Group,* is a commercial advantage, because for a mass audience this material needs some warmth that is not present in the novel. And though the production — and some of the settings in particular — give several of the girls a surprisingly, vulgarly opulent background, this increases the commonplaceness. It is an expression of common fantasies about the rich. And Lumet, by having the girls behave like stenographers or middle-class girls from the Bronx in the midst of this wealth, probably reaches the large audience directly, even if this is not entirely conscious on his part. In watching Lumet work, I was torn between detesting his fundamental tastelessness and opportunism and recognizing the fact that at some level it all *works*. It obviously, too obviously, wants to be moving, but damn it, it is.

Perhaps Lumet does so well with O'Neill (the famous TV production of *The Iceman Cometh,* the movie version of *Long Day's Journey into Night*) because O'Neill's plays don't depend on precision either, but on cumulative emotional power. They're pedestrian, simple, basic, forceful — solid meat and potatoes so honestly served it's great. O'Neill's writing is tenacious, obsessed, determined to get *at* something, to move you. It doesn't depend on a good ear or eye, either. And, of course, Lumet is pedestrian too: what fools you is that he's a fast pedestrian.

During the last week of the shooting, he invited me to his home to see a 16 mm print of the TV *The Iceman Cometh.* The guests were very quiet, very attentive, but Lumet kept laughing. Where O'Neill used comedy to make us more aware of pain, Lumet laughed at the bad jokes. I heard someone near me whisper, "He laughs at places where you have to be insensitive to laugh." Yet he had *directed* it. Probably what we couldn't accept was the crudeness of his enjoyment — he enjoys playing practical jokes on the set, too — a crudeness which, I think, is integral to his strengths as well as his weaknesses as a director. A great many important people now, and throughout history, would probably, up close, seem very crude to the people who admire them from a distance.

The direction of *The Iceman Cometh* showed the same strengths and weaknesses that I had been seeing each day on the set of *The Group.* He hadn't learned, really; he'd just raced ahead. The groupings were stagey, the lines often misread or overemphasized, but there was an overall intensity. And he gave the actors their chance. This was one of the peculiarities of his approach that I had been discovering: he gave his principal thought to the actors during casting. He looked for trained people, and once he'd cast them he expected them to know their business. He directed the actors' readings and interpretations hardly at all. It's as if he couldn't take the time for that, as if it had very little to do with him, it's *their* job — although how they were supposed to learn to work together I couldn't discover nor, obviously, could they. The results are, at worst, amateur theatricals and garbled readings; at average, pressure and excitement; but, at best, an actor who understands his role and can act gets a chance to soar — like Robards in *The Iceman Cometh* and the great family quartet of *Long Day's Journey*. Viewing acting as the responsibility of the actors is an extraordinary attitude for a movie director but not so extraordinary if thought of in terms of live TV, where it's up to them: sink or swim. When they sink — when the lines begin to sound "literary" — he just lets it go, blaming it on their lack of training. But in some cases in *The Group* it's not that simple: they're miscast or they don't understand the roles — which are not necessarily made more comprehensible by Lumet's singularly "instinctive" style of interpretation during the rehearsal period.

LUMET'S REHEARSAL PERIOD

Lumet is rather unusual among movie directors in insisting on a rehearsal period; it was two weeks on *The Group*. This rehearsal period does not serve the same function as rehearsals in the theatre. It is, rather, an attempt to compensate for modern out-of-sequence shooting methods, which are dictated by business considerations, not aesthetic ones. For example, during the actual shooting, sequences involving the same locations or sets will be shot the same day or within a few days, even though they may, as in the case of Kay's wedding and funeral, represent a seven-year interval and will appear at the beginning and end of the finished film. Thrift, Horatio. In movies made in New York, even tiny sets are struck immediately, because space is so precious: all the scenes to be shot in one room are photographed, while another set is constructed right next to it, and the next day that room is dismantled as action shifts to the corner of a restaurant, while workmen try as quietly as possible to construct a doctor's waiting room or a W.P.A. office that will come and go just as fast. In a theatre, the stage goes through the same cycle of transformations each performance of the play. The studio for *The Group* was never the same for two days; construction was always going on. Actors in the same movie may not even meet each other unless they happen to be in the same shot, because their time is scheduled with alarming dexterity, so that they need only be paid for two or three days' work. An actor whose scenes appear to be years apart in the movie may have performed his total duties in a day or two. The elaborate scheduling combines the elements of actors and sets and crew for maximum economy. There is none of that old Hollywood contract-player life of sitting around for weeks in order to pop in and out of a few scenes. Partly because of soaring union costs, it has all been computerized. None of the cast of *The Group* was on salary for the full production: one by one, each said his farewell.

Even the rehearsal period — an attempt to help the actors go through the entire story-action in sequence, so that they can work out the development of their roles — is subject to this calculation. Only the eight girls and a few of the key men were considered essential for the rehearsals. It is at these rehearsals that Lumet explains the movie, as each day it is acted out, and it's here that he is in his element — papa-father, indoctrinator, principal performer, circus ringmaster. Lumet explaining *The Group* to the eight girls who were to embody the roles provided the gloss Mary McCarthy's writing had never had: a thoroughly male, gutsy, folksy, Yiddish interpretation, like the sort of thing one sometimes overhears in buses or restaurants when people are talking about a movie and you think, where did they get that from?

"Dottie is a sweet girl who falls in love. She gets laid and goes home. Bed works for her — first crack out of the box. Dottie thinks Dick Brown did it, and because she thinks so, he becomes the love of her life. . . . Her lack of any self-estimation is so enormous, she thought he did it. Dottie is one of those girls who are so wowed by this orgasm that she doesn't know it would have happened with any man, that she could have done it herself. She doesn't know that she carried this seed of pleasure in her from the beginning."

"Helena uses art for hiding rather than for self-revelation." And then solemnly, as if with insight (indeed, second sight) about the girls way beyond the pages of the book: "She'll drop the newsletter after Kay's death."

"When Helena doesn't scratch Norine's eyes out, that's when she nails her coffin." On this one, I wanted to protest, I wanted to interrupt, "But, Sidney, she scratches Norine's eyes out in her own way, when Norine asks her not to repeat their conversation and she replies that of course she won't, 'But *you* will.' " And I wanted to say that if her "coffin" is "nailed" it's when she lets her father talk her into going to Europe, and that really it's been nailed pretty much from the beginning. Instead I looked at Buchman, who was listening with an amazement akin to my own. Our eyes met: he shrugged.

"Let's talk about one of the winners, Lakey. I think she does marvelously. By the way, the Baroness is going to be beautiful." As it turned out, he was not able to be so generous to Lakey: the beautiful Swedish actress selected to be her lover was out of town when, through a change in the shooting schedule, the Baroness was required.

"Lakey and Polly kid themselves less than the others. They're more true to their own nature. Polly lets herself be used — and as soon as she can use someone, by God, it's great. She takes care of people because she wants to be taken care of. . . . Her strength comes from great sureness. She thinks it's weakness; she doesn't know it's strength . . . I'm thinking of having her play Gus LeRoy's leave-taking scene — the whole thing — with a terrible smile on her face." I looked at the girls as he said this and they seemed to be deeply impressed, and I thought back to how impressed we were in high school when the drama coach used to come up with that "terrible smile" routine. And, of course, Andrea Leeds had actually used it in *Stage Door*. Fortunately, Lumet is prodigal with bad ideas. He seemed to have forgotten all about this one when he shot the scene.

He gave the material his own homey sense of life: rehearsing the graduation sequence, he explained to the actresses that while Helena is giving the valedictory address they should "tell her with their eyes that she's doing great" and some of them should "start applauding when she says 'all shades of opinion are entitled to a hearing.' " Somehow it seems more like a Bronx high school than Vassar.

He was, in other words, a Method director: he looked for the meaning and motivation of everything in himself and his own experience; he thought of the girls in terms of what *he* felt he knew about them. And because most of his experience was in show business, he drew not only upon his own experiences — mostly with show business people — but also upon his second-hand experience, which was, I think, more real to him than his first: all the shored-up memories of old plays, radio, television, old movies. His "experience" was full of terrible smiles. And because his mind lived in all this treasure trove of trash — just as I suspect many Method actors draw upon "theatre" more than they realize — he could use it as if it *were* life. It *is,* in a way, for him. In *The Pawnbroker* he had had Rod Steiger use a soundless scream, and it had *almost* worked — even for those of us with good memories who filled the silence by thinking "Ah, yes, that must be the famous Berliner Ensemble scream. I've heard of it but I've never not heard it before." Terrible smiles and soundless screams, what would show business do without them? Maybe it would do better. When they almost work, they're distracting bits of schtik; when they don't work at all, like Buchman's version of the terrible smile — the "ironic" use of a choral group on the soundtrack to comment on the action (the idea was that the music accelerates to frenzy, getting gayer and gayer as each life goes to pieces) — the idea is totally separable from the result.

Sometimes Lumet's experience worked rather well with the girls: though it had almost no connection with Mary McCarthy's girls, it gave the actresses a sense of how to play, and it was often rather shrewd.

On Libby: "Whatever becomes her bitchiness later on, I want to look for the legitimate reasons for it. I have a friend who everytime you go to a restaurant with her, she orders and then when you do, she feels she's made a mistake. She always feels she's missing something." He has another friend "who can't resist a wisecrack."

On Kay, when asked whether she falls or jumps to her death: "We'll take her as a suicide. . . . I have known four suicides in my life and they all had one thing in common — an increasing isolation."

The flaw in his method is that, as he doesn't look to the original material to try to understand anything but pulls it all out of his *own* background, when the characters are alien to him, when they require some thought or even a little research, he simply neglects them or uses facile explanations of their behavior that just confuse the actors. He never made much sense on the subject of Kay, and then he got more and more impatient with the actress for her inability to become something that was never clearly formulated. This failure caused another failure: because Kay never developed the necessary character, she didn't provide the provocation for her husband, Harald, to beat her up, and the actor kept trying out different readings without any visible clue from the director as to what was wanted. Harald in the movie is, inexplicably, a weakling and a monster. What was the problem of Kay as a character? Well, there are certain kinds of female pushers who arouse more horror than pity: women who push their children to fulfill their own ambitions (stage mothers are perhaps the most glaring example); and women who push their husbands, like those good sacrificial ladies who devote their youth to dull jobs so that their husbands can achieve professional training only to discover that the new M.D. or Ph.D. or LL.B. must abandon them for women to whom they don't feel so horribly indebted. Kay is of this breed, but, a social climber to the Group's standards which she cannot fill so must attempt to overfill — to be ahead of the others — she wants not a mere professional status for her husband but the genius-artist status. And that, given the period and the field — the Depression and the theatre — doesn't even allow for the compromises and shifts of interest which usually enable such ambitions to work themselves out in appropriate ways — like teaching drama in a college or working in radio or television. There's a real pressure for men like Harald — pushed and sacrificed to — to betray, to beat up, to desert the too-helpful little woman.

Kay is not easy to like, and almost impossible to play; it needs a young Katharine Hepburn perhaps, someone who could be intensely wrong about just about everything. Kay is, I think, one of the author's bad dreams of herself, the epitome of all pushing women who are really unsure of themselves and who devote their energies to the careers of "genius" husbands. A difficult role, it is nevertheless the key role, for Kay, with all her delusions and needs to be a leader, is the suffering center of the novel, the poor witch whose story is told from wedding to funeral.

Something went wrong at the start of the casting. Shirley Knight, as the best-known actress in the group and the recipient of two Academy Award nominations, was considered for the two biggest roles, Kay and Polly. Had she been selected for the role of Kay, the picture might have had a center. Shirley Knight has the strength to play Kay. But she was cast as the sweeter character, dear little likable Polly; and this decision, made right at the beginning and not necessarily a wrong one for *her* in terms of her career, was wrong for the story the picture was presumably telling. Joanna Pettet, who got the role, is a perfect type for frivolous, lightheaded comedy roles — a giddy, bouncy girl with naturally bee-stung lips, and a twinkly smile like Stella Stevens.

Watching the eight actresses become the visual embodiment of Mary McCarthy's girls, I began to see that there might be a difference between stage and screen that hasn't been discussed. It's simply that miscasting is not so obvious on screen as on stage. In a play you can see an actor in a role and think of another actor who should have played it; in a movie the physical qualities of the actor dominate the role, he is more vivid than any concept of the role, and he becomes your idea of the role. You're not likely to think of what other actors might have been like in it. In a sense the screen actor *is* his role in a way the stage actor isn't. In a play you separate the two — particularly in a bad performance. These actresses are now the Mary McCarthy girls and will be seen in the mind's eye of those who now read the book.

Questions that might have concerned another director — such as, What had brought these particular girls together and made them a group, or In what ways were Vassar girls different from other college girls and other girls of the period — didn't, I believe, ever exist for Lumet. The answers to questions like these go into the texture of a work, into the nuances, the details. If he'd thought about the milieu and the tastes of these girls, would he have OK'd the set for Libby's bedroom, which is Joan Crawford forties, or for Libby's living room, which is like a Loew's State lounge? In many of the sets, the *art moderne* décor of the thirties, which was such an important part of the novel, had been carefully and often amusingly prepared, and he didn't bother to *use* it. Nor did he observe that the dress designer's unobtrusive good taste was often spoiled by the girls' hair styles. I wondered why Lumet didn't notice that Kay's coiffures in some of the scenes were derived from *My Fair Lady,* and I couldn't imagine why he let Shirley Knight as Polly wear her hair down loose like Alice in Wonderland when she's dressing the corpse. When asked, he says indifferently, "I don't care about things like that" — as if it wouldn't be manly, somehow, as if only nits and nit-pickers noticed things like that.

Lumet carried the Method to extravagance. He found psychological reasons for everything in the script — patterns of behavior and consistent motivation, and even elaborate Freudian relationships between the girls and their parents and each other. He was sometimes remarkably ingenious, like those people who prove that Francis Bacon or Walt Disney wrote Shakespeare's plays. Anything the girls were to say in the movie — even if Buchman had taken it out of someone else's thoughts in the novel — had its origins in their childhood, their repressions, their envy. It was as if God had plotted every detail by a master plan and we must see his mysterious workings. Lumet gave a glorious performance, as Buchman sat staring in wonder, sometimes looking terribly fatigued.

The comedy now became watching the young actresses trying to *find* the motivation in the lines and roles. Actresses of an earlier generation would have *provided* it, but these girls thought it must be there to be found, and Lumet encouraged them in this delusion by seeking and finding whatever he put there. They were as misguided in their "Method" as The Group had been with their thirties ideas — yet what else could they do? They're children of their time, too.

Lumet's great performance as a boring papa full of blather that the impressionable may take for knowledge of life was counterpointed by an appalling performance when the lines were not his own. He cued the girls by reading the roles of almost all the missing actors and actresses; and he read the Mary McCarthy lines with such animal spirits, mixed with ready-made inflections, one might have taken them for radio drama circa 1938. I had asked him during one of our first talks why he had given up acting and he had begun a long explanation about how acting was a faggot's career and how he knew that if he was ever going to give a woman a real human relationship, etc., and I had simply jotted down "too short for acting career." Now, I decided that maybe his style of acting had dated before he had got old enough to face the problem of his height.

Between his own big role and all these other roles, he was "on" all the time. He was "on" even in the coffee breaks, going over charts, designs, schedules. He was indefatigable. And he loved it all.

His approach to speech — so totally at odds with Mary McCarthy's dialogue — was to cause trouble throughout the production. The girls, and many of the young men, were, like him, indifferent and insensitive to the value of words, the shadings of language. They produced sounds — as American Indians seem to — without real articulation; they did not time their dialogue for comprehension. They gave it some kind of emotional birth, during which they were quite likely to use their own words, which contrasted feebly with the author's. They did not seem to hear the difference. During casting, Lumet had asked one Method actor, "Does your experience with improvisation get in the way when you're working with a script?" The actor's answer — worthy of the Sphinx — was, "Only when the writing is bad. When it's good, your instinct should work with the dialogue."

Because of actors' instinct, much of the dialogue had to be postsynchronized. Several of the girls took so long gestating their lines before delivery that good moments had to be cut because it was too absurd to switch from the potential speaker to reaction shots of the listener, and deathly dull just waiting on the speaker's face. The talk had to become faster in the editing room and, as a result, the movie became choppy and frenetic.

By the second week of rehearsals, the girls were whizzing through the whole movie, with the seedy old ballroom that had been rented for rehearsals turned into a maze of markings and charts, and chairs and tables and old mattresses simulating graduation exercises, church, restaurant, hotel, etc. They would do a complete run-through, quick, from sequence to sequence, hopping from one "set" to the next. And I was puzzled: as the action covered seven years, why compress it to something like the running time of the movie in rehearsal? Why not do it scene by scene in sequence but allow them to think about it in between? They were so worn down from chasing around the markings, they didn't have time to think. Their anxieties about making their right positions took precedence over what the rehearsals were *for*. The rehearsals might have suggested movie conditions better and been much simpler if the actresses could have just stayed in one area and *imagined* that it was now a restaurant or a hotel — which actually is much closer to how a movie is shot, because the same space becomes one thing or another. Less strain and tension about where they had to get to for the next scene and more concentration on how to read the lines would have served them better in the movie. But it was great training for live TV where the actors need to move around and get into different positions fast — if anybody was still doing live TV.

THE CREW

A caricaturist, Mary McCarthy is funny at the expense of the girls: she records their pratfalls. But she does not even try to suggest what they may gain in humanity and experience, or what they may truly lose by defeat. The actresses of *The Group* are "on their way up." The crew, most of them failed actors, had had some pratfalls; they knew that they weren't going to do much, and certainly not what they'd hoped to do when they were younger. Only once did I hear one say he was considering going back to acting, and nobody believed him.

The crew were cool and ironic in their evaluation of the performers; they gave measured praise when it was due. The grips, carpenters, makeup men, disbursers, controllers, the little white-haired wardrobe mistress who had been in a sister-act in vaudeville were not the sort of people to be impressed by young actresses who might come on like starlets. Youth and beauty are not in short supply in the theatre, and many of the stand-ins and women who worked in one job or another on the sets — preparing Baked Alaska for the wedding breakfast or the hors d'oeuvres for Libby's party — were as beautiful, and often livelier and more interesting. When one of the flat-chested actresses exposed more of herself than was necessary for a scene, a member of the crew gave a W. C. Fields snarl: "Two aspirin on an ironing board." There were so many short scenes that took so long to set up; if nothing really came off in the performance, there was a blank, dull feeling on the set. For, of course, it was all up to the performers, everything else was mechanized — and though there might be mechanical failures, there was no such thing as a mechanical success.

The person on the set who was talked about with unfailing respect was Boris Kaufman, the almost legendary Boris Kaufman, who was the cinematographer for *The Group*. In the early thirties, as the cameraman for Jean Vigo's *Zero for Conduct* and *L'Atalante,* Kaufman had brought new poetic lyricism to the screen. Many on the crew had had long experience with him; they were known as "Kazan's crew" because they had first worked together with Kaufman on Elia Kazan's films (*On the Waterfront, Baby Doll, Splendor in the Grass*), and they had worked with him on most of Lumet's pictures. They worked quickly and respectfully. For the technicians and actors in the East, Boris Kaufman has been a godsend; he has been the cinematographer for *most* of the important pictures made in New York in the past decade. Without him, it is safe to say, New York would not have attracted even the few productions it had.

When Kaufman came into the rehearsal hall to announce the happy news that the budget had been increased to shoot in color, several of the girls reacted with disdain. Color, for them, was "commercial." They thought the picture would be more "artistic" in black and white, but Joan Hackett said it should be in brown and white to suggest a faded old photograph album. Shirley Knight topped this by the lofty, definitive information that she had seen only one film that justified the use of color, *The Red Desert*. In that moment I hated those actresses for behaving just like The Group. And although I'm sure that Kaufman, a modest, sensitive, quietly efficient man, would be the first to admit that on this kind of production he is a craftsman, not an artist, I think I can guess a little of how he may have felt when even his craftsmanship was destroyed. The beautiful, modulated color he worked so hard to achieve was turned into even worse-than-standard American movie color in the prints that reached theatres, as simply and carelessly as turning the knob on color TV.

As the cinematographer is responsible for the lighting, he is in charge of most of the work that goes on on the set, which is preparation for the brief periods of shooting. While he works — and he is the hardest working person on the set — the director waits. I wondered why Lumet did not use this waiting time to work with the actors, but he seemed too impatient to get going, to get it shot. There were no rehearsals after that first two-week period (which meant that there were no rehearsals at all for most of the cast), only the run-throughs for the camera and lights before the take.

It would be difficult for people who have seen some of these pictures to believe that they were shot where they were — in spaces so small you can hardly move the camera. People think of movies being made in beautiful luxurious studios with the stars emerging from big dressing rooms. Even Hollywood studios don't look the way they do in movies about Hollywood; in New York, most of *The Group* was shot in the old Fox Movietone building on West 54th Street and Tenth Avenue, where "the stars' " dressing rooms were known as the cellblock, which is what they looked like. And when things got too crowded at Movietone, there'd be a few days' shooting in a building in the fur district where, if you didn't watch your step, you might stumble over Kay's coffin. Wherever the shooting was going on, at the St. Regis or St. Marks in the Bouwerie or Connecticut or Long Island, the technicians, the carpenters, the visitors, all froze during takes — as in *Marienbad*. And in those moments, and perhaps only in those moments, did there seem to be some magic in this movie-making.

For those who were interested in movie-making, this was just a job until they could get a chance at the real thing. The crew wanted to do a good job; they enjoyed the work and each other, but they were indifferent to the material they were working on. They didn't respect this way of working. But they were negative — like regular army men bitching about the army — with no real alternative in mind. The "real thing" was a day dream — an idea of creative work somewhere, which, when it was expressed more definitely, usually turned out to be either "something honest" — i.e., a documentary; or something "experimental" — i.e., TV commercials and the Richard Lester kind of movie-making; or, something poetic, something strange. Yet if they wanted to try to do something of their own, there was equipment they could scrounge, there was no shortage of actors; why didn't they try something in 16 mm or in 35 mm instead of griping about the crap they were working on? Except for a very few — three or four, I think — who were writing or shooting on weekends, I don't think most of them had the drive. They wanted to get paid for work; and their idea of making movies was the same old megalomaniac-genius racket of power, fame, big profits, etc. — only they wanted it to be "creative" too.

Their contempt for what they were working on was intensified by the general knowledge that despite the superficially democratic spirit on the set — pet names and lots of kisses — they couldn't even make suggestions, which Lumet took as implied criticism. As Adlai Stevenson pointed out, "Absolute powerlessness corrupts absolutely." Probably not even the experienced and tactful assistant director Dan Eriksen felt that he could make any recommendations. Of course, there is nothing surprising in this. It is part of the paranoia of power that men at the top who have stolen from everyone and everywhere to get there can't accept anything that's freely offered.

Could the crew have helped? On specific matters, yes. There were very few of the errors or careless stupidities or miscalculations that had to be cut out, or that, remaining, mar the film, which were not remarked on and sometimes widely commented on by the people on the set. But I think it would be a mistake to think that the director cared that much. And there was the producer, Buchman, the only person with authority to challenge Lumet's judgment, sitting by, watching, and lifting his eyes to heaven. If he didn't care enough to prevent Kay's twirling around the walls of her hospital room like a trapped animal (another "terrible smile" — and an effect which made the hospital room look large as a salon) or to raise hell about Kay's ludicrous purple sunset of a black eye, why should the actors or the crew members risk a put-down and disfavor by pointing it out except to each other?

How little the Sidneys cared about accuracy in terms of the meaning of the material may be indicated by citing a simple error which I naïvely and diligently tried to get corrected. In the scene between Helena and Norine, Helena is supposed to reply to Norine's charge that The Group were "the aesthetes" as distinguished from "the politicals" by saying, "The whole group was for Roosevelt in the college poll — except Poke who forgot to vote." But the actress said, "The whole class was for Roosevelt . . ." I heard the error during the shooting, but mindful of my agreement with the director not to discuss the material with the girls, I didn't mention it to the actress — who, I am sure, would have consulted her script and discovered that she was making a mistake. Instead, I mentioned it as casually as possible to each of the Sidneys, and as the sound on this sequence was badly recorded and was obviously going to need looping (i.e., post-synchronization), I assumed the word would then be corrected. During the first screenings of the film — without the music and with some editing still to be done — I noted the error again, and this time pointed it out somewhat more forcefully to the Sidneys. Each assured me I must be hearing it wrong. Neither apparently took the trouble to check or listen, because when the film was screened for the press, there it was again. By then, Lumet was in London working on his next film, Buchman was back on the Riviera.

Thinking that *someone* might care about the blooper, I called around, and after three people involved in the production assured me that if the Sidneys had had Helena say "class" that must have been what they wanted, I finally got hold of the editor Ralph Rosenblum, who realized at once that it was an error. But he had enough other problems to worry about: in the absence of the Sidneys, he was left to argue the cuts the National Catholic Office for Motion Pictures (a new euphemism for the Legion of Decency) wanted.

These negotiations are more ambivalent than is generally known. Because, of course, the distributing company may benefit from the publicity that accrues to a film if it is having Legion trouble. But at the same time, the company will certainly want the public to think that the "dirty" parts haven't really been altered. Frequently scenes are put in a picture just for the purpose of mollifying the Legion by agreeing to remove them, and as a bargaining weapon to retain other crucial scenes. And ironically, the Legion sometimes passes over these deliberately flagrant scenes and insists on removing others essential to the material. On its side of the bargaining counter the Legion traditionally demands major, even thematic changes, and then settles for small excisions, usually of semi-nude scenes. The negotiations involve horse-trading, low cunning, and general hypocrisy. On *The Group* the National Catholic Office objected to "eight or nine elements" and settled for two bits of flesh, and United Artists was able to defy "anyone to discern any appreciable difference . . . even after three screenings . . ." — which nobody was likely to go to anyway.

THE RESULTS

Mary McCarthy has always satirized women. We all do, and men are happy to join us in it, and this is, I think, a terrible feminine weakness — our coquettish way of ridiculing ourselves, hoping perhaps that we can thus be accepted as feminine, that we will not be lumped with those imaginary gorgons who are always held up as horrible examples of competitive, castrating women. We try to protect ourselves as women by betraying other women. And, of course, women who are good writers succeed in betrayal but fail to save themselves.

The most condescending, most sanctimonious, the phoniest dialogue in the movie (and it's right out of the book) is uttered by dear little Polly and is intended to show what a fine girl she is. She tells Gus LeRoy that she set out to be a doctor. And he says, "Too late now?" and she says, "Well, not if I had Libby's drive, I suppose — or Kay's." Gus says, "You think you haven't?" and she answers, "Worse. In college, I never cared particularly for people with drive — or those most likely to succeed. The truth is, the only way I could like assured, aggressive girls was to feel sorry for them." This dreadful nonsense — which would be called Uncle Tomism if uttered by a Negro — is very appealing to men and, of course, men like the Sidneys (rightly) include the author in the category she is condemning. I don't think there's any doubt that Polly is here speaking for the author because the structure of the book says the same thing: that the quiet girls who don't come on strong come off best as human beings. Although at the time she was writing *The Group,* she may have believed in this quietism and imagined that as the author of *Venice Observed* and *The Stones of Florence* she had become an elegant aesthete like Lakey, it is her inability to endow Polly and Lakey with the hideous believability of the others that gives the lie to the structure of the book. It is only when Polly is asking clear questions — like earlier Mary McCarthy heroines — that she has some stature as a character: Mary McCarthy can bring Polly to life when she's seeing through Dr. Bijur but not when she's selling blood — or feeling "sorry" for the other girls. That comes easier to Buchman and Lumet than to Mary McCarthy. If *The Group* had had a woman script-writer and director, it might have been much more satirical. But, ultimately, Buchman and Lumet have betrayed women in a more basic way: by treating the girls as poor, weak creatures, as insignificant "little women." For this, of course, is their way of being sympathetic, of making the movie more compassionate than the novel. (They don't feel the same condescending need to soften the men's roles, so these men seem like even worse bastards than the men in the novel, now that the women are so much more sympathetic.)

Mary McCarthy has said, "What I really do is take real plums and put them in an imaginary cake." In the movie, they have baked a different cake, using ready-mix, but the plums are still there — good juicy plums of real experience — recognizably real and familiar, so that we laugh with the pleasure of recognition. In a sense, the girls and crew in calling it a soap opera were more instinctively accurate than the Sidneys, with their meanings and interpretations. But, it isn't soap opera just because it deals with tangled lives and loves (almost all novels do — good as well as bad ones). The quality of observation, though at times at a soap-opera level, is generally much higher. Actually, the Sidneys' *ideas* are closer to soap opera than the material they're working with. When they "think," they dish out soap-opera interpretations, but what they worked with is interesting enough to make their interpretations seem silly and phony — which they are. Life — to the degree that Mary McCarthy catches it and they use her material — is not reducible to their ideas, which, oddly, they seem to feel are higher, more important than giving us something of the life of a period. They really are products of the thirties, using fashionable, liberal "ideas" to explain and falsify what they're doing, which is what Mary McCarthy was exposing in the girls.

What gives the movie its vitality — and despite its carelessness and sloppy style, it is one of the few interesting American movies of recent years — is that the talented, fresh young performers are given some material to work with. There's solid observation in Mary McCarthy's writing, and the movie is a considerably more realistic and sophisticated account of modern male-female relationships and what goes wrong in them than we've had on the screen. It deals with the specific experiences of women in our time that Mary McCarthy has always specialized in: how a girl (Dottie) may want to lose her virginity but then feel unwanted and deserted when a casual affair doesn't turn into "love"; how scared virgins may come on as the sexiest teasers (Libby); how a woman's life can be made a ridiculous martyrdom to theories of child care (Priss); how people now "use" analysis in their relationships (Polly and Gus).

After his part of the editing was finished, a few days before he left for England, Sidney Lumet asked me to a ritual lunch — at the same restaurant where we had had our first. The United Artists executives had just seen the picture, and Sidney was chuckling in triumph. "You know," he said, "at first they were afraid I couldn't do this picture, that I wasn't a woman's director." In Hollywood that is generally a euphemism for a fussy, effeminate director. Although Lumet has given *The Group* something the usual woman's director wouldn't, I miss the clarity and detail a *good* woman's director might have given it. I have an awful feeling that in the movie when Libby protects her virginity by kneeing Nils in the groin, and Nils says, "Did your lady teachers teach you that?" Sidney Lumet thinks they did. But if his sense of the material is a little primitive, some of its reality got to him, too. "Funny thing" he said, "you remember that day you mentioned the actor Harold that Mary McCarthy was married to, dying in a hotel fire. I didn't remember until later: I knew Harold Johnsrud. When I was a kid starring on Broadway in *My Heart's in the Highlands,* he had a small part in it."

He asked if I had gotten what I wanted from following the course of the production and I didn't know what to answer because I had really got more than I wanted. When you see a movie, it has a certain inevitability; but when you see a movie being made, you see how it might be, how it could be, how it should be. The worst thing about movie-making is that it's like life: nobody can go back to correct the mistakes. I think now I know the answer to one question that always comes up when people discuss what has happened to novels when they become movies, and ask why did they leave out so and so? The obvious answers were: for length or unnecessary complication, because they couldn't include everything; for propriety, and to please church or pressure groups. To these I can add: because they didn't shoot it very well, and when the sets have been struck and the actors and technicians have gone on to other commitments, it's almost impossible to go back and redo it. They just hack it out. This problem of no return also explains why so many obviously bad things are in it. They were too integral to the story to be left out, so they just had to be used, no matter how bad. If an actor's reading is too awful, he may be dubbed. If performances are so disastrous that editing can't save them, the roles may be almost eliminated. They generally can't be totally eliminated because then sequences involving large numbers of people or sequences essential to the story line would have to be cut. When I asked what had happened to some particularly nice little scenes, Lumet tried out the gaudy explanation that he had learned not to be self-indulgent about retaining too many unusually good moments. But either he's too honest or my face gave me away because he began to laugh. When important material is cut — even crucial material — the justification is always that the movie is too long anyway. But when one persists and says why this rather than that, the plain truth generally comes out that because of negligence or some error in planning, the bit couldn't be properly made to fit. The editor takes the pieces for a jigsaw puzzle and, if they don't quite fit, forces them into place. We're supposed to ignore little holes as unimportant — as even more modern and jazzy. If a director is more concerned to get something on film than to get it right, the editing is going to be very tricky. The beginning of this movie is too fast and confusing for the simple reason that the big scenes of the graduation and Kay's announcement of her engagement to Harald were a shambles and were chopped to fragments. When asked how the audience would get its bearings, how they would be able to tell who the girls were and what was going on, Lumet said it didn't matter. The problem of the time transitions and how to link the episodes so that the audience might get some sense of the girls' lives didn't matter either. The material flying by so fast may even help Lumet's reputation as an "artistic" director. This, more and more, is the way movies are going to be made, because it is more businesslike. Lumet has had the "genius" to be a pioneer: he doesn't think "the little things" matter.

Economy represents the decisive factor in the working arrangements, yet because of these working arrangements, there is one large area of waste. After watching a few weeks of shooting, I sat down with the script and calculated I could save close to a quarter of a million dollars in production costs just by cutting out, before it was shot, what I assumed would have to be cut out after it was shot. *The Group,* like most movies these days, began with a script for an unconscionably long movie — over three hours (many four-hour movies are shot). I gradually came to see that, given the working methods, they needed this extra footage because they were never sure of what would work out and what wouldn't. My calculations were posited on a coherent story line and the retention of the best material; the actual final cut removed much that I would have cut, but also a great deal I considered essential. And I realized that they had shot an over-three-hour script so that they could pull some kind of two-and-a-half-hour movie out of it. Economy, speed, nervousness, and desperation produce the final wasteful, semi-incoherent movies we see.

Carried much further, this pioneering could mean the death of what we now still know as the art of the film. The key word in that sentence is that little shrinking "we." Lumet has the right chemistry for the new kind of picture-making and the genius to know that for the really big audience, "the little things" don't count. If vast audiences are indifferent to the absence of beauty on television, if they do not object to the loss of visual detail when they see old movies on television, if they do not object that the shape of the image destroys much of what remains of the compositions, if they do not object to the cuts which make the story line and characterization incoherent and to the interruptions for commercials which destroy the intensity, the suspense, the whole dramatic construction, then why not give them what, apparently, is all they really want: the immediacy of foreground action and as many climaxes as possible?

I would not have written this lengthy analysis if I did not feel that there are basic, crucially important reasons for not making movies in this way. I discovered that my subject was not so much what happens when a book becomes a movie but what happens when movies become television.

[Spring 1966]

III

Reviews, 1965–1967

Night Games

Now we see his head, now hers, and over and over they turn, rolling and writing in bed. Have the movies invented a new position? Or has the phrase "a roll in the hay" been taken literally? Kids who learn about sex at the movies are in for a miserable time if they try the roll. And that seems to be the trouble with the hero of *Night Games,* one of a number of movies in which the rotating slows down enough for us to see anguished faces. Then we know that although the lovers have certainly been trying their calisthenic best, they have not succeeded. As these are all too likely to be serious movies, we can't very well dismiss all that grim activity with the cheerful hope that maybe next time they'll try something a little more . . . classical.

Night Games is a Gothic tale about decadence and impotence, combining the worst of Fellini with the worst of Bergman, and featuring the kind of depraved upper-class partying at which the question "Don't you wish you were dead?" is answered by "I'm dead already." As a truly terrible idea, the party sequence in which Ingrid Thulin gives birth (to a dead child, of course), to the accompaniment of a jazz ensemble and a recitation on the birth of Christ, beats even the most baroque castrations and assorted excesses in Tennessee Williams's plays. Less flamboyantly bad, and so, in a way, even worse, is the wedding night party: the poor hero who can't make it gets out of bed, lets the birds out of their fancy cage and puts the cage on himself. And he vomits great gushing torrents, i.e. his whole past life. (But it's the kind of movie effect that destroys its purpose because all we can think of is "How did he do it?") He gives yet another party at which he dynamites the ancestral castle which, because it is where his childhood took place, is presumably the block to his potency. He literally blasts through.

It seems like a huge joke — part Freudian, part Marxist — but it isn't played for comedy. Mai Zetterling directs in the grand manner, with elaborate shifts between past and present, and the kind of visual style that is usually described as "stark," and she is more than competent. The movie isn't dead, but it's ludicrous. (How should we react to lines like "You won't find the truth in a brandy bottle"?) I've never seen a movie with such a sophisticated technique joined to such bizarrely naïve content. But there are good moments. There is a startling, dramatically effective sequence of a child caught masturbating. There are the look-alikes of mother and wife — the wicked bitch mother (excitingly played by Thulin as a fierce despot), the wife (Lena Brundin) as a Reformation madonna with sad eyes and heavy breasts. And while the wanly virtuous young couple are having their ghastly wedding-night roll, the "degenerates" are having what looks like a pretty good time — running a porny home movie they've made. That porny movie is so much wittier and more entertaining than the rest of *Night Games* that one can only wish Miss Zetterling wouldn't strain for seriousness.

The Comedy of Depravity

Accident

"Isn't the moonlight *terrible!*" cried the young girl in *Our Town,* and we in the audience laughed at the comedy of sensual innocence, at the desires that made her fear the excitement of beauty. The images say it in *Accident:* the sunlight is terrible, it's *rotten,* because it makes the characters feel sexy. Joseph Losey uses sexual desperation and the beauty of Oxford in summertime to make our flesh crawl. It's a comedy of depravity, and we laugh all right, maybe not out loud but at least to ourselves. It's hard not to: Losey and his scenarist, Harold Pinter, are so knowingly sensual and we are so alerted to look for their knowingness. We laugh, also, at Pinter's barbed, mannered dialogue as a sign of recognition, a demonstration of our knowingness. We see how clever it all is. And I mean "clever" pejoratively — meaning *limited, thin,* meaning without the imagination of innocence. We're all "in the know" and corrupt together in the sheer physicality of it all — the triangular compositions of legs and crotch, the lines of dialogue that ooze out of sweating faces. But, at least, it *is* clever. *Accident* is nasty fun — a fascinating, rather preposterous movie, uneven, unsatisfying, but with virtuoso passages of calculated meanness.

Separately, Pinter and Losey have similar weaknesses (of organization, purpose, dramatic clarity) and they share an inability to achieve a dramatic climax. They have almost the same specialty: Pinter can create scenes that are loaded with unspecified anxieties and emotions; Losey is a master of sloth, and he can make the atmosphere of a scene thick with loathsome erotic overtones. As Losey's target is often the middle or upper classes, his erotophobia is often taken to be an expression of social consciousness, but his purposes are often so opaque that, for example, in *King and Country* the homoeroticism took over and the military argument got lost. The union of Pinter and Losey is almost incestuous: it produces a doubling of their defects and their specialties. *Accident* is so full of ambience and the director and writer seem to have so little sense of what to do with it that they just use it for its own sake. Their work is full of "suggestions" and "implications" about marriage and class and education and violence; they use malice and cruelty as if to speak volumes of truth. The movie is saturated with "meaning," it drips attitudes.

Accident is effective because it's almost all set within their specialty, but although what they do is a formidable accomplishment in terms of current movies (and *Accident* is the best new movie around), it's too easy for art. It's too easy to get audience response by pointing up the enervation and bestiality of educated and/or rich people. Are they muckraking for us or for themselves? Maybe they really dig that muck.

Albee gave us Maggie and Jiggs at the old U; Losey and Pinter give us a black sudser — Oxford as Peyton Place, full of lust, hatred, promiscuity ("Three men in love with the same girl . . . who is this strange seductress who has disrupted the peaceful lives of the respected citizens of Peyton Place? Can Stephen and Rosalind go on as before? Will Charley's wife Laura recover her wits and come in out of the rain?"). It's good theatrical gimmickry — not, however, to be confused with a masterpiece, as the mixed media of reviews and advertising might suggest. We now have generations of moviegoers who have never been to a burlesque show and who react to jokes about age and potency as if they were the latest invention of art movies. And as they didn't go to the theatre much either, they don't know that the comedy of manners was almost always the comedy of bad manners, and that dirty gamesmanship is the staple of melodrama. But critics are supposed to have been born at least the day before yesterday and to be able to sort out what's new in a work from what's old. And to know that schtik is an anagram of kitsch.

The protagonist of *Accident* is the nothing-heart, not-much-of-a-man at work and play. As the philosophy-don husband, Dirk Bogarde is just about perfect: he acts like a man who's had a spinal tap. He's a virtuoso at this civilized, stifled anguish racket, better even than Ralph Richardson used to be at suppressed emotion because he's so much more ambiguous that we can't even be sure what he's suppressing. He aches all the time all over, like an all-purpose sufferer for a television commercial — locked in, with a claustrophobia of his own body and sensibility. Bogarde looks rather marvelous going through his middle-aged frustration routines, gripping his jaw to stop a stutter or folding his arms to keep his hands out of trouble. The Ralph Richardson civilized sufferer was trying to spare others pain, but Bogarde isn't noble: he goes through the decent motions because of training and because of an image of himself, but he's exquisitely guilty in thought — a mouse with the soul of a rat. He compulsively tells little half-lies that he intends to make true and hesitates before each bit of truth he calculatingly parts with. If only Losey and Pinter would let him out now and then! A man can stay in a continual, acute state of suppression and humiliation only so long. If Bogarde plays this role again, he may wind up his career touring backwaters of the Commonwealth countries in *The Browning Version.*

So often men like Pinter and Losey who are acclaimed on the "less is more" principle are really giving us much too much — but all of the same kind. Pinter is indirect and Losey provides treatises on how rolling green fields and beautiful buildings can be made ominous. They sustain interest by portent, but portent without any clear intent. In this, too, *Accident* resembles sudsers, as it does in its manufactured incidents (the visit to the television studio), the worked-up parallels (Laura with Rosalind).

It also has many resemblances to Pinter's play *The Homecoming:* each has its philosophy professor; each has its enigmatic female — the respectable whore to whom all the important male characters are attracted. Each is a satire of home, and in both movie and play Pinter's peculiar talent for dislocating family life and social and sexual relations to a kind of banal horror has some recognizable truth in it, and his cadences are funny and reverberating. He's a new — hideously sophisticated — kind of cliché expert. He deals with characters who give each other nothing willingly, who defend their privacy against attack with evasions, repetitions, silences. And we laugh to show that we appreciate what is unsaid — the underside of what is said. The focus in *Accident* is on the men, who are trying to get one up on each other; the women (Jacqueline Sassard as the love object, Anna, and Vivien Merchant as the wife, Rosalind) are passive and sly. (We must partly guess at this from Miss Sassard's inept performance.) We laugh because of the absence of goodwill. In the theatre and movies, truly dedicated selfishness is amusing; and it is somehow liberating to laugh at a family of monsters. Isn't that the secret of the success of plays like *Tobacco Road* and *The Little Foxes* and the comic mechanism of the recent *A Lion in Winter?* The monsters of a melodramatist like Lillian Hellman are rich and decadent white Southerners or Nazis, and these people who *lust* are contrasted with the good, straight, affirmative people who are for civil rights and Life and who have healthy, decent impulses.

Pinter (in *The Servant,* in his play *The Homecoming,* and now in *Accident*) carries this traditional device further by omitting any sympathetic characters. What makes for all the lust in his works is that his people have no tender or compassionate feelings; if they're not decent enough for love, then any sex impulses they feel can only be lust. Elizabeth Hardwick has written that in *The Homecoming* Pinter "avoids exposition in the ordinary sense and is not seduced by affection for pieties." True enough, but perhaps we are seduced by his disaffection for pieties? Pinter is so consistent that there's not a single likable character in any of these three works: what happens, on screen as on stage, is that in a competition of monsters the most fiendish and obscene are the most amusingly theatrical and become the favorites of the audience — the belligerent, lecherous father and his son, the pimp, in *The Homecoming;* Stanley Baker's swinish Charley in *Accident.* Charley's best line is the vile (in context), "What room is everybody in?" This is fine with me. I enjoy it because I enjoy fancy kitsch. But I don't think Pinter's device — which is ingeniously theatrical but nothing more — should be overrated or confused with an *artistic* solution. (I don't mean to suggest that Pinter has claimed to discover new forms; but that claim has been made for him.) We are so aware of the absence of goodness and of the usual melo- dramatic conflict that we wait eagerly to see what he will provide in its place. So far he hasn't come up with anything, and that's why one leaves *Accident* as one left *The Homecoming* — dissatisfied and perhaps a little indignant. Like Albee, Pinter is good at dialogue with a sense of drama in it. For the rest of what makes drama, Albee provides explanations which don't explain the charge of the dialogue; Pinter is cagier. But though he's smart enough to avoid the adversary approach to good and evil, he rattles some very dry bones from the theatre basement: woman as eternal, mysterious whore-wife- mother; the man of thought who is cut off from the instinctual; etc. Those old bones aren't going to grow any meat.

In movies Pinter doesn't avoid exposition — he's just no good at it. His talent is for cryptic, "suggestive" dialogue and for ghastly scenes; in *Accident,* as in *The Pumpkin Eater* and *The Servant,* when he tries to use dra- matic narrative methods, he uses them so badly that the movies fall apart. In *Accident,* it shouldn't be that difficult to make at least the accident itself relate to the characters and plot. Nothing in the movie would be much changed if there were no accident (the only revelation — that the philoso- phy don would "take advantage" of a girl in shock — isn't convincing any- way).

Off screen Losey and Pinter, perhaps following a course set for them by the enthusiasts for *The Homecoming,* have taken the position that (as Pinter said when queried about the movie) "I have no explanation for any- thing I do at all." This might give the impression that the movie has been written out of the unconscious, but it is so carefully plotted that you can watch the preparations being made and chart how each event or reaction was led up to. And in some cases — as when the don is raping the girl while the phone is ringing to tell him his wife is having a baby — even those construction men who lay out Sodom and Gomorrah in weekly segments might be ashamed to be so crude. But although it can be charted by a viewer (and, no doubt, was cunningly planned), the plotting often doesn't work dramatically — the viewer can only piece it together *afterward.* (For example, when Stephen returns from London and finds Charley and Anna in his home, it takes too long to figure out what's going on, and the obfuscation of Anna's face and her appearance in Rosalind's clothes are merely chic.)

Losey and Pinter work best close-in, and their smaller version of the Antonioni-Fellini terrible party — the long, drunken Sunday house party, with people sitting down to supper when they're too drunk to eat — is perhaps the most shocking of movie parties because it's so exactly, familiarly horrible. They're less successful at show pieces — like the affectation of their reprise of *Marienbad,* with Delphine Seyrig as a dumb blonde (with what sounds like Vivien Merchant on the voice-over dialogue). And the big exhibition piece — "aristocrats" playing some nasty game in the great hall of a castle — tells less than a flushed face in close-up. The final crash — a fancy, ambiguous finish — is a cheat.

I enjoyed *Accident,* but I don't really *like* it. It has an archness which I associate with a kind of well-written but fundamentally empty novel. *Accident* is, despite what Losey and Pinter say in it, for and of "the upper classes." They use a lot of craftsmanship and technique to pave the old dirt roads.

The Shameless Old Lady

The Shameless Old Lady is pleasant enough, and though the material is thin, it's stretched out rather deftly, and I wouldn't have minded the picture too much if the audience hadn't been so audibly pleased with its capacity to respond. I can hear someone saying, "What snobbery! She didn't like the picture because the audience enjoyed it." And that's not too far wrong. I wished the audience wasn't chuckling so comfortably at the exhibitions of French miserliness: there was something so mean about feeling pleasurably superior to those little signs of meanness. I experienced a groan of recognition when the man behind me said happily, "It's so French!" People used to say that in the forties about those synthetic rural comedies like *The Well-Digger's Daughter:* I remember that one particularly because the man who took me *had* said it and I *had* groaned, and the next night he went back to see it with another girl.

As it's a sort of parable, it is, rather refreshingly, a-Freudian: the wise little old lady has no responsibility for the selfish, niggardly monsters she has produced (this, too, makes it easier for the audience to respond). Has this Bertolt Brecht story been done before or is it just that the details are familiar from countless "so French" movies, and that Sylvie, expert as she is, has gone through this bag before? I used to admire her in her mean obsessive old lady roles: goodness sits too lightly on her, as on Bette Davis humbly saying "God bless." René Allio's direction is clean but the script is undernourished: the old lady's discovery of the modern world doesn't have the texture or imaginative substance to sustain a full-length film, nor does the script suggest the ironies or ambiguities that are possible in her delight.

But the critics! Give them a newly made antique and a good clean old peasant and a name like Brecht to patronize, and they'll give you everything they've got. There hasn't been a set of reviews with so much self-congratulatory virtue and such beautiful condescension since *The Shop on Main Street* (and before that, *David and Lisa* and *Ballad of a Soldier*). Yes, I know there's a danger of going to extremes of disaffection when a movie has been as overpraised as this one, and probably if I'd seen it unheralded I would have thought it a decent enough little try at something. But what I'm objecting to is not so much the movie as what it represents for the audience — an urban version of pseudo-folk that lulls them back to what they think of as the wonderful old French movies. The critics are always asking of movies that they be again as they were, and then when you hear what they thought they were —!

Is this the alternative to the harshness and chaos of so many movies — heartwarming little well-made Q.E.D. pictures? After we've watched the director loading the dice, it's not really much fun watching him roll them. The sentimental gratifications of the well-turned plot that fulfills our expectations belong to the old movies we don't watch on TV.

Band of Outsiders

JEAN-LUC GODARD intended to give the public what it wanted. His next film was going to be about a girl and a gun — "A sure-fire story which will sell a lot of tickets." And so, like Henry James's hero in "The Next Time," he proceeded to make a work of art that sold fewer tickets than ever. What was to be a simple commercial movie about a robbery became *Band of Outsiders*.*

The two heroes of *Band of Outsiders* begin by playacting crime and violence movies, then really act them out in their lives. Their girl, wanting to be accepted, tells them there is money in the villa where she lives. And we watch, apprehensive and puzzled, as the three of them act out the robbery they're committing as if it were something going on in a movie — or a fairy tale. The crime does not fit the daydreamers nor their milieu: we half expect to be told it's all a joke, that they can't really be committing an armed robbery. *Band of Outsiders* is like a reverie of a gangster movie as students in an espresso bar might remember it or plan it — a mixture of the gangster film virtues (loyalty, daring) with innocence, amorality, lack of equilibrium.

It's as if a French poet took a banal American crime novel and told it to us in terms of the romance and beauty he read between the lines; that is to say, Godard gives it *his* imagination, re-creating the gangsters and the moll with his world of associations—seeing them as people in a Paris café, mixing them with Rimbaud, Kafka, Alice in Wonderland. Silly? But we know how alien to our lives were those movies that fed our imaginations and have now become part of us. And don't we — as children and perhaps even later — romanticize cheap movie stereotypes, endowing them with the attributes of those figures in the other arts who touch us imaginatively? Don't all our experiences in the arts and popular arts that have more intensity than our ordinary lives tend to merge in another imaginative world? And movies,

* *Band of Outsiders* (with Anna Karina, Sami Frey, Claude Brasseur) opened and closed in New York in a single week of March 1966.

because they are such an encompassing, eclectic art, are an ideal medium for combining our experiences and fantasies from life, from all the arts, and from our jumbled memories of both. The men who made the stereotypes drew them from their own scrambled experience of history and art — as Howard Hawks and Ben Hecht drew *Scarface* from the Capone family "as if they were the Borgias set down in Chicago."

The distancing of Godard's imagination induces feelings of tenderness and despair which bring us closer to the movie-inspired heroes and to the wide-eyed ingenue than to the more naturalistic characters of ordinary movies. They recall so many other movie lives that flickered for us; and the quick rhythms and shifting moods emphasize transience, impermanence. The fragile existence of the characters becomes poignant, upsetting, nostalgic; we care *more*.

This nostalgia that permeates *Band of Outsiders* may also derive from Godard's sense of the lost possibilities in movies. He has said, "As soon as you can make films, you can no longer make films like the ones that made you want to make them." This we may guess is not merely because the possibilities of making big expensive movies on the American model are almost nonexistent for the French but also because as the youthful film enthusiast grows up, if he grows in intelligence, he can see that the big expensive movies now being made are not worth making. And perhaps they never were: the luxury and wastefulness, that when you are young seem as magical as peeping into the world of the Arabian Nights, become ugly and suffocating when you're older and see what a cheat they really were. The tawdry American Nights of gangster movies that were the magic of Godard's childhood formed his style—the urban poetry of speed and no afterthoughts, fast living and quick death, no padding, no explanations — but the meaning had to change.

An artist may regret that he can no longer experience the artistic pleasures of his childhood and youth, the very pleasures that formed him as an artist. Godard is not, like Hollywood's product producers, naïve (or cynical) enough to remake the movies he grew up on. But, loving the movies that formed his tastes, he uses this nostalgia for old movies as an active element in his own movies. He doesn't, like many artists, deny the past he has outgrown; perhaps he is assured enough not to deny it, perhaps he hasn't quite outgrown it. He reintroduces it, giving it a different quality, using it as shared experience, shared joke. He plays with his belief and disbelief, and this playfulness may make his work seem inconsequential and slighter than it is: it is as if the artist himself were deprecating any large intentions and just playing around in the medium. Reviewers often complain that they can't take him seriously; when you consider what they do manage to take seriously, this is not a serious objection.

Because Godard's movies do not let us forget that we're watching a movie, it's easy to think he's just kidding. Yet his reminders serve an opposite purpose. They tell us that his aim is not simple realism, that the lives of his characters are continuously altered by their fantasies. If I may be deliberately fancy: he aims for the poetry of reality and the reality of poetry. I have put it that way to be either irritatingly pretentious or lyrical — depending on your mood and frame of reference — in order to provide a critical equivalent to Godard's phrases. When the narrator in *Band of Outsiders* says, "Franz did not know whether the world was becoming a dream or a dream becoming the world," we may think that that's too self-consciously loaded with mythic fringe benefits and too rich an echo of the narrators of *Orphée* and *Les Enfants Terribles,* or we may catch our breath at the beauty of it. I think those most responsive to Godard's approach probably do both simultaneously. We do something similar when reading Cervantes. Quixote, his mind confused by tales of Knight Errantry, going out to do battle with imaginary villains, is an ancestor of Godard's heroes, dreaming away at American movies, seeing life in terms of cops and robbers. Perhaps a crucial difference between Cervantes' mock romances and Godard's mock melodramas is that Godard may (as in *Alphaville*) share some of his characters' delusions.

It's the tension between his hard, swift, cool style and the romantic meaning that style has for him — and for other lovers of "unsentimental" (!) American gangster movies — that is peculiarly modern and exciting in his work. It's the casual way he omits mechanical scenes that don't interest him so that the movie is all high points and marvelous "little things." Godard's style, with its nonchalance about the fates of the characters — a style drawn from American movies and refined to an intellectual edge in postwar French philosophy and attitudes — is an American teen-ager's ideal. To be hard and cool as a movie gangster yet not stupid or gross like a gangster — that's the cool grace of the privileged, smart young.

It's always been relatively respectable and sometimes fashionable to respond to our own experience in terms drawn from the arts: to relate a circus scene to Picasso, or to describe the people in a Broadway delicatessen as an Ensor. But until recently people were rather shamefaced or terribly arch about relating their reactions in terms of movies. That was more a confession than a description. Godard brought this way of reacting out into the open of *new* movies at the same time that the pop art movement was giving this kind of experience precedence over responsiveness to the traditional arts. By now — so accelerated has cultural history become — we have those students at colleges who when asked what they're interested in say, "I go to a lot of movies." And some of them are so proud of how compulsively they see everything in terms of movies and how many times they've seen certain movies that there is nothing left for them to relate movies *to*. They have been soaked up by the screen.

Godard's sense of the present is dominated by his movie past. This is what makes his movies (and, to a lesser degree, the movies of Jacques Demy) seem so new: for they are movies made by a generation bred on movies. I don't mean that there haven't been earlier generations of directors who grew up on movies, but that it took the peculiar post-World War II atmosphere to make love of movies a new and semi-intellectualized romanticism. To say it flatly, Godard is the Scott Fitzgerald of the movie world, and movies are for the sixties a synthesis of what the arts were for the post-World War I generation — rebellion, romance, a new style of life.

The world of *Band of Outsiders* is both "real" — the protagonists feel, they may even die — and yet "unreal" because they don't take their own feelings or death very seriously, as if they weren't important to anybody, really. Their only identity is in their relationship with each other. This, however we may feel about it, is a contemporary mood; and Godard, who expresses it, is part of it. At times it seems as if the movie had no points of reference outside itself. When this imagined world is as exquisite as in *Band of Outsiders,* we may begin to feel that this indifference or inability to connect with other worlds is a kind of aesthetic expression and a preference. The sadness that pervades the work is romantic regret that you can no longer believe in the kind of movie you once wanted to be enfolded in, becoming part of that marvelous world of beauty and danger with its gangsters who trusted their friends and its whores who never really sold themselves. It's the sadness in frivolity — in the abandonment of efforts to make sense out of life in art. Godard in his films seems to say: only this kind of impossible romance is possible. You play at cops and robbers but the bullets can kill you. His movies themselves become playful gestures, games in which you succeed or fail with a shrug, a smile.

The penalty of Godard's fixation on the movie past is that, as *Alphaville* reveals, old movies may not provide an adequate frame of reference for a view of *this* world. Then we regret that Godard is not the kind of artist who can provide an intellectual structure commensurate with the brilliance of his style and the quality of his details. Because, of course, we think in terms of masterpieces and we feel that here is a man who has the gifts for masterpieces. But maybe he hasn't; maybe he has artistry of a different kind.

It's a Great Technique, but What Can You Do with It?

The Knack and *Help!*

FOR some time, the "smart boys" had been saying that the future of movies was in TV commercials, that that's where the real experimentation was going on, where the real talents were working. They didn't mean it cynically: it was possible to try tricky shots and fast cutting — which looked like an advance over the sluggish big-studio methods. And then Richard Lester came along and demonstrated that movies could be made that were just like TV commercials; not too surprisingly, he was quickly acclaimed as a cinematic genius. He and other directors fill their time between movies by making commercials; as Lester puts it, "It's a year's free testing of tricks."

There's just one thing the matter with his genius, but it's a big thing: the content of his 1965 movies, *The Knack* and *Help!,* is the same as the content of TV commercials. At first, in *A Hard Day's Night,* it seemed to be different, because the Beatles were exhibited as joyful, anarchic, witty — that is to say, mildly rebellious. It almost looked as if the techniques of TV could be separated from and used against what was being sold.

The Beatles were thought to be anti-Establishment; but with astonishing speed, the advertising establishment has incorporated rebellion. Only the consumption patterns, the tokens remain: the long hair, the tight pants, the leather jackets, the motorcycles, the attitudes of indifference to adult values, contempt for adult hypocrisy. The outer forms of fantasy and rebellion become the new conformity. Youth is encouraged to be narcissistically youthful: it is cool not to let anything interfere with having a good time. Anarchism becomes just another teen-age pop fad, another pitch.

In the two-dimensional comic-strip world of *Help!,* everybody's in a rush. The movie can't slow down any more than TV commercials can. It (deliberately) has no depth. It is *nothing* but a chase, turning a structural device of early movies into the total substance, and without anywhere to go. *Help!* is all climax, but nothing is prepared for; finally it just exhausts itself and stops. In *The Knack,* the running jokes and gags never come off. In Mack Sennett comedies (to which Lester's work is often compared), an idea would be developed, and there would be the audience delight in watching it build, and as the two-reel format provided a quick cutoff point, the audience was quickly released from the surreal and restored, refreshed, to ordinary viewing. Lester doesn't build ideas; he picks up a gag and goes on to another. If there are enough gags, perhaps the audience, panting to keep after them, will not worry about why they don't go anywhere. The ingenuity becomes as tiresome as the pace; nothing is more fatiguing than things whizzing by too fast; after a while, you don't care how clever it all is.

Despite all the activity, or perhaps because of it, the main figures are rather flat. The more spurious the spontaneity around them, the more lacking in spontaneity they seem. Lester, perhaps aware of this problem, tries to manufacture sympathy by placing a Ringo Starr or a Rita Tushingham at the center; but the center will not hold. In this advertising context, in which the first principle is that everything can be made beautiful, they are awkward survivors from an earlier kind of comedy who give the lie to the format. There really isn't any such thing as character in the world of TV commercials; there is only anonymous popularity: we are all models.

If there were an idea, if there were characters, the movie would risk being "square." In the current world of popular entertainment, the more pointless and nonsensical the plot, the more cool and sophisticated the movie may seem — an indication, perhaps, that the advertising world has made all feeling seem false. It's commercially safer to be deliberately foolish than to attempt something and be thought foolish.

These impersonal makeshift movies — inoffensive, pleasant-enough nonsense while you're seeing them — are all over with the seeing. The product is completely consumed. There is not even any roughage. By the time you're outside the theatre, you've already forgotten the movie. You're hungry again. There is nothing to take home, no memory, hardly even an aftertaste.

꠹꠹꠹꠹꠹

The Moment of Truth

I SAW *The Moment of Truth* at the opening night of the Montreal Film Festival where the audience reacted with shock and admiration to the bloody
brilliance of the work. It was an audience of people who knew the left-wing
Italian author-director Francesco Rosi from such earlier films as *Salvatore
Giuliano* and *Hands Across the City;* some of them probably knew that his
working title for this film had been simply *Spain*. In any case his intentions
were overwhelmingly achieved, and the savagery of his view of that bullfighting culture was so strong that several times I gripped the arm of my
companion — a film director — for support, and he, although he had been
a doctor before becoming a director and had assisted at the bloodiest kinds
of surgery, half rose from his seat when the bulls attacked helplessly suffering horses (the first victims of the bull ring, customarily sacrificed before
the matador goes to work).

Rosi takes the conventional *Blood and Sand* story and, stripping it of
romance and sentiment and melodrama, makes it the classic organic story
of Spanish society. In Hollywood's versions it has always been the rags-to-
riches story of the rise and fall of a hero; in Rosi's view the individual story
is part of the great neorealist theme of migration from rural poverty to
urban poverty, dislocation and corruption — a hopelessness that is like a
plague that never lifts. The Spain of this film is the Spain of that earlier
great documentary, Buñuel's *Land Without Bread*.

The boy leaves the Andalusian farm so that he won't have to live an
animal's life like his father, but the city is no better. The lure of bullfighting
is the money to be made at it: "For a million I'd wait for the bull with open
arms." Those who talk about "sacred art" are just bull-slingers; it's an "art"
like prizefighting for an ambitious American Negro boy with no capital but
his body and nerve, and what's "sacred" about it is the risk of death. The
bravado of "courage" is your trade, it's the self you sell. What you keep for
yourself is fear.

Rosi and his great cinematographer Gianni di Venanzo used documentary techniques, following the young bullfighter Miguelin from city to city, shooting silent with hand-held cameras, in color. The approach is a kind of dramatic journalism: apparently objective and impersonal, the movie treats fact as fiction, fiction as fact, combining them into a concept of truth. The footage has the looseness and freedom of unstaged reality, the immediacy and speed of decisive moments — images that persist in the memory out of all proportion to their duration on the screen.

Near the end there is a special one of the boy alone on the screen with the large head of a bull. It is like a time between wars, and the mind races for concepts that will express the emotions called up — waste, doom, empathy, epiphany? They suggest but don't encompass it. In that instant and in the struggle to comprehend it, and the uncertainty about why it seems to mean so much, there is more of a sense of being suspended in time than in all the juggler's tricks of *Last Year at Marienbad*. The beauty of *The Moment of Truth* is not in bullfighting (Goya did not love war because he made great etchings of it) but in the beauty of rage, masterfully rendered in art.

In Montreal the film had not had English subtitles, so when *Life* asked me to review it, I went to see it again in a New York theatre. I had, of course, read some of the New York reviewers and had noted that several recommended it as a film celebrating "the sport" of bullfighting. Although I have in the past observed that audiences frequently seem to incorporate what they have read about a movie in what they see — sometimes to the point of accepting reviewers' interpretations based on obvious mistakes as part of their experience of the film — still I was not prepared for this New York audience which, from audible indications, had come to see a bullfight picture.

Before the movie started there was chatter about the blue-jeaned El Cordobes which might have sounded very "inside" if I too hadn't read the *Life* article on him a few weeks before, and then from several voices, "They say that this bullfighter in the picture is third in rank." And I knew who the "they" were: the movie reviewers who had gotten it from a publicity handout. Where else would "they" have heard of Miguelin's apocryphal rank?

A black comedy was running contrapuntally to Rosi's tragedy. "Oh, I'd love to see that!" said the woman next to me, as the movie opened upon an ornate golden altarpiece held high, with ragged feet below. This woman was not alone in applauding when Miguelin killed his first bull. But when a beast poured blood, she said, "This is unnecessary," in disapproving tones. She — and who knows how many others like her? — had come for the pure rites of bullfighting, myth and spiritual release and all. They rejected the blood as in "bad taste" — as if the movie were suddenly turning commercial and sensational, displaying poor sportsmanship. They wanted it nice — *The Brave Bulls,* not these poor great maddened beasts with such bad manners that they bleed and slaver in pain and hold on to life. And the distributor, to protect such delicate sensibilities, had cut the picture, had cleaned up the blood. He had removed a moment of another kind of truth — the spurting, dripping horror that made bullfighting in Rosi's view unmistakably a slaughterhouse attraction for a charnel-house civilization.

And so for those who can limit what they see to the skill and grace of a bullfighter, an artist's attack on the business of blood and death becomes another movie about the poetry of blood and death. The advertising says, "The passion, danger and loves of a matador . . ." and, of course, it's all set in the colorful Spain of the tourist folders. Those who can look at *The Moment of Truth* and respond to it in that way can read Swift's *A Modest Proposal* as gourmets.

Madame X

THERE has been much praise of the originality of William Dozier, producer of the new "Batman" television series, in insisting that the performers keep straight faces; but really Ross Hunter pioneered in this field. In his latest production *Madame X* there is little danger of the performers' breaking up, because they are so masked and taped they couldn't laugh if they wanted to. Anyway, I doubt if those connected with this movie will have much to laugh about for a while, though audiences may.

Madame X has one of the "classic" (which, in Hollywood, means perennial) pop-movie themes: a woman is forced to abandon her baby and, years later, having committed a murder, is defended by . . . her very own son, who does not know that . . . she is his very own mother. It jerked tears in silent-movie houses in 1916 and again when Pauline Frederick played the role in 1920; and in 1929, with the great Ruth Chatterton, directed by Lionel Barrymore, it was one of the most celebrated of the early talkie courtroom dramas. In 1937, Gladys George gave it the benefit of her superb technique and her gin-and-tears voice that seemed to have found new lower octaves at the bottom of a glass. These were actresses who knew how to carry a load. And they could get into a broken-down old vehicle and get some mileage out of it.

Lana Turner hasn't the power or the technique.* She's not Madame X, she's Brand X; she's not an actress, she's a commodity. And instead of attempting to update the story so it might make some sense to modern audiences, the Hunter production just buries it under layers of other commodities. The idea is you're supposed to go see it for the gowns, the furs, the jewels and the furnishings, and the sumptuous "production values." That would make sense if, for example, you were going to see Capucine in some breathtaking clothes (that may not be movie art, but it's another kind

---

* In her alcoholic sequence she projects a lewd, grinning depravity that is the most interesting thing about her, but she does not use it as an actress.

of art and, in its own way, satisfying). But Miss Turner does not wear clothes well: she wears them as expensively dressed, aging women without much style wear them. Which is not a treat to the eye or the imagination. Her "lavish wardrobe" and the "lush surroundings" are merely gross, and the production values consist of atrocious color and pathetically obvious camera setups.

At the opening of the film, a matronly-looking woman and a man of indefinite age get out of a car in front of a mansion, and we realize they are supposed to be young newlyweds. She seems to be wearing a Lana Turner mask, but before we have time to react, they are greeted by what seems to be a young girl, waiting at the door of the house to welcome them. The groom calls out, "Hello, Mother," and then the youthful apparition comes close, and we see, with horror, that she is wearing a Constance Bennett mask. There were gasps in the audience.

Upper-class mother Bennett and bride Turner are supposed to be a social world apart, but they are alike as two frozen peas in a pod. The dialogue came out of cold storage, too: "Oh, Clay, I don't share your life — I only exist in a cubbyhole of it." The bride and groom are named Holly and Clay. Holly greets Clay with lines like "Oh, Clay, it's so good to have you home." And he musters up the energy to respond, "I'm so happy to *be* here." Holly is lonely when he's away: "I guess I needed to feel needed." She doesn't really even want to go to that dinner party that leads to her ruin, and she wouldn't have except that the hostess says, "You'll throw my seating off."

The average age of the cast must be at least fifty. As Turner is supposed to be a ravishing young beauty, the production is designed like a cocoon to protect her. There isn't a *young* actress in the cast, not even among the bit players. This *Madame X* isn't about mother love; it's about mummy love.

It isn't even imitation of life; it's just imitation of movies. This movie is in love with the glamour of old movies. It turns Holly (short for Hollywood?) into a Flying Dutchman, just to get her into more clothes, more décor. To compensate for all those swell clothes, she keeps suffering: not one moment of fun in twenty years. The dialogue begins to comment on the movie itself: "You couldn't cope." "She's worn out in spirit as well as in body. She can't endure much more." "Life has long ceased to have meaning for me."

How can we react to experiences like this film? At the screening where I saw it, some of the same people who were laughing at it also cried in the sad places. Later, I heard that the company was looking for the "instigators" of the laughter: in true paranoid Hollywood style, they can account for it only by a conspiracy.

Madame X presents, in an intensified form, a common problem of movie interpretation. Children sometimes interpret movies in terms of what they actually see on the screen, and the adults with them often try to explain what they are *supposed* to see, so that the children will be able to follow the plot. We would be in the midst of some gigantic confusions if the themes and story lines of all those movies with pouting marshmallows like Lana Turner or iron maidens like Joan Crawford were to be interpreted at the level of what we actually see. No Hollywood plot can really encompass *that* many layers of ambiguity. And so we try to separate out the intentional from the unintentional, what we are supposed to see from what we see. In general, the wider the gap, the less connection the movie has with art or talent or any forms of honesty.

The conventions of the period protect us, to some degree, from seeing what we're not supposed to. It is this lack of protection when we see old movies on television that often makes them seem so absurd: what audiences of the movie's period were willing to ignore is now nakedly exposed.

Madame X is so excruciating not only because the actors and actresses do not embody what they're supposed to, but because the movie depends on the conventions of the MGM style of the forties. It is spiritually dedicated to the worst of old Hollywood — the Hollys and the Clays. How small an aspiration — to want to make a glossy forties' woman's picture — too piddling even to be called decadent; but the clock can't be turned back, even to that. File your regrets at the nearest five-and-dime.

Before the Revolution

THERE have been few young prodigies in the history of movies: not only must one grasp a complex medium but also perform the more difficult task of finding cash. In 1941 the twenty-five-year-old Orson Welles startled the studios and the moviegoing public with the impious, high-spirited wit of *Citizen Kane*. A few years ago a group of miraculously talented young Frenchmen shook up their country's paralytic film industry. Now from Parma — the most unlikely and yet poetically perfect place, the place where Stendhal set his great, ironic paean to youth, *The Charterhouse of Parma* — has come *Before the Revolution,* written and directed by Bernardo Bertolucci, at the preposterous age of twenty-two.

It is a richly romantic work which makes us realize that most moviemakers are never so far away from youth as when they condescendingly try to deal with those cardboard kids next door — as if youth were a kind of simplicity that will be outgrown. This movie expresses what it means to be young with the lyricism and narcissism and self-consciousness of the intelligent young. (What young artist isn't self-conscious? It's a stage in learning to express yourself.) Bertolucci, a prizewinning poet at twenty-one, deals with the experience of so many young poets and novelists — rebellion against bourgeois life, an egocentric dedication to Communism, disillusion. The movie is set in the 1960s. It is the story of a boy who discovers that he is not singleminded enough to be a revolutionary, that he is too deeply involved in the beauty of life as it is *before* the revolution. He has "a nostalgia for the present."

Not too surprisingly, the love affair between Fabrizio and his young aunt Gina, though the characters are derived from Stendhal, is closer to the seventeen-year-old Raymond Radiguet's *Devil in the Flesh*. However, Bertolucci, trying to discover his feelings and attitudes in movie terms — in image and sound — is much less precise than Radiguet was. This lack of precision, which may be characteristic of modern youth, may also be a factor in their involvement in movies — an art in which so much can be responded to without forming definite attitudes.

I would not insist so much upon Bertolucci's youth if it were not integral to the romantic profusion of this movie, which is most extravagantly beautiful in its excesses—in the manner of supremely gifted children. He has the kind of talent that breaks one's heart: where can it go, what will happen to it? In this country we encourage "creativity" among the mediocre, but real bursting creativity appalls us. We put it down as undisciplined, as somehow "too much." Well, *Before the Revolution is* too much and that is what is great about it. Art doesn't come in measured quantities: it's got to be too much or it's not enough.

When Fabrizio is told that he speaks like a book, it is apparent that Bertolucci is aware that he too is pretentiously literary. But trying to say too much, and saying it too exquisitely, and not always saying it clearly are not the worst crimes in an artist. No doubt the greatest sequences — a Chekhovian lament for the river and forest that the landed gentry are about to lose, and a brilliant night at the opera with the social classes layered in their tiers — stand out "too much"; nevertheless they *are* great.

The worst mechanical defect is that the editing, particularly at the beginning, is too obtrusive, and it takes us a while to get our bearings — to understand, for example, that Fabrizio, who is callowly doctrinaire, is quarrelling with his friend Agostino for failing to accept the Communist party as the answer to all human troubles. And the continuity is confusing. We do not always know where or why the action is taking place. But Bertolucci's defects would make the reputation of a dozen lesser directors. And his use of various kinds of music (the most imaginative score since *Jules and Jim*) to fuse the emotions suggests new operatic possibilities in movie-making.

The greatest achievement is that you come out of the theater, not dull and depressed the way you feel after movies that insult your intelligence, but *elated* — restored to that youthful ardor when all hopes are raised at once.

A Man and a Woman

THE worst thing about *A Man and a Woman* is that its director, Claude Lelouch, is so young. His assurance and facility are indications that he's already found his style, and, no doubt, he will take this financial and prestigious success as encouragement. Lelouch is his own cinematographer and he never lets us forget it. He uses a "delicate" palette and he shoots through rain and snow and ice and into sunsets; he blurs for romantic softness, and he tints for mood and variety. With swinging graphics and a teasing score, *A Man and a Woman* is designed and rhythmed more like a trailer than a movie. It's all promises.

Lelouch conveys young tender love by cutting to gamboling lovers among gamboling horses, and then lambs, and then dogs. The people have exciting photogenic occupations: stuntman, script girl, racing-car driver. They take their kids on photogenic boats, for walks on wintry beaches. The actors don't have to do anything because the gamboling camera supplies all the moods for them. Anouk Aimée is blankly mysterious and glamorous, like Joan Crawford as the Mona Lisa. Both the men, Jean-Louis Trintignant and Pierre Barouh, are oddly like a teen-age girl's dream boyfriend— he may be a daredevil to the world but with her he's real sweet. Lelouch throws a nimbus of mist around everything: he makes everything pretty. Maybe *A Man and a Woman* is drawing such long lines of customers because all this gauzy enchantment makes it a good make-out movie — which is the best thing to be said for it.

Masculine Feminine

Masculine Feminine is that rare movie achievement: a work of grace and beauty in a contemporary setting. Godard has liberated his feeling for modern youth from the American gangster-movie framework which limited his expressiveness and his relevance to the non-movie centered world. He has taken up the strands of what was most original in his best films — the life of the uncomprehending heroine, the blank-eyed career-happy little opportunist-betrayer from *Breathless,* and the hully-gully, the dance of sexual isolation, from *Band of Outsiders.* Using neither crime nor the romance of crime but a simple romance for a kind of interwoven story line, Godard has, at last, created the form he needed. It is a combination of essay, journalistic sketches, news and portraiture, love lyric and satire.

What fuses it? The line "This film could be called The Children of Marx and Coca-Cola." The theme is the fresh beauty of youth amidst the flimsiness of pop culture and pop politics. The boy (Jean-Pierre Léaud) is full of doubts and questions, but a pop revolutionary; the girl (Chantal Goya) is a yé-yé singer making her way.

It is fused by the differing attitudes of the sexes to love and war even in this atmosphere of total and easy disbelief, of government policies accepted with the same contempt as TV commercials. The romance is punctuated with aimless acts of aggression and martyrdom: this is young love in a time of irreverence and hopelessness. These lovers and their friends, united by indifference and disdain toward the adult world, have a new kind of community in their shared disbelief. Politically they are anti-American enough to be American.

They are also Americanized. This community of unbelievers has a style of life by which they recognize each other; it is made up of everything adults attack as the worst and shoddiest forms of Americanization and dehumanization. It is the variety of forms of "Coca-Cola" — the synthetic life they were born to and which they love, and which they make human, and more beautiful and more "real" than the old just-barely-hanging-on adult culture. Membership is automatic and natural for the creatures from inner space. The signals are jukebox songs, forms of dress, and, above all, what they do with their hair. Americanization makes them an international society; they have the beauty of youth which can endow pop with poetry, and they have their feeling for each other and all those shared products and responses by which they know each other.

There are all sorts of episodes and details and jokes in the film that may be extraneous, but they seem to fit, to be part of the climate, the mood, the journalistic approach to this new breed between teen-agers and people. Even if you don't really like some pieces or can't understand why they're there, even if you think they're not well done (the episode out of LeRoi Jones, or the German boy and prostitute bit, or the brief appearance of Bardot, or the parody of *The Silence* which isn't as ludicrously pretentious as *The Silence* itself, or the ambiguous death of the hero — the end of him like a form of syntax marking the end of the movie), they're not too jarring. The rhythms, and the general sense, and the emotion that builds up can carry you past what you don't understand: you don't need to understand every detail in order to experience the beauty of the work as it's going on. An Elizabethan love song is no less beautiful because we don't catch all the words; and when we look up the words, some of the meanings, the references, the idiom may still elude us. Perhaps the ache of painful, transient beauty is that we never can completely understand, and that, emotionally, we more than understand. *Masculine Feminine* has that ache, and its subject is a modern young lover's lament at the separateness of the sexes.

Godard has caught the girl now in demand (and in full supply) as no one else has. Chantal Goya, like Sylvie Vartan (whose face on a billboard dominates some of the scenes), is incredibly pretty but not beautiful, because there is nothing behind the eyes. Chantal Goya's face is haunting just because it's so empty: she doesn't look back. Her face becomes alive only when she's looking in the mirror, toying with her hair. Her thin, reedy little singing voice is just as pleasantly, perfectly empty, and it is the new sound. There's nothing behind it musically or emotionally. The young girls in the movie are soulless — as pretty and lost and soulless as girls appear to a lover who can make physical contact and yet cannot make the full contact he longs for, the contact that would heal. The girl he loves sleeps with him and is forever lost to him. She is the ideal — the girl in the fashion magazines she buys.

Possibly what flawed the conception of Godard's *My Life to Live* was the notion of the prostitute giving her body but keeping her soul to herself, because there was no evidence of what she was said to be holding back. Now, in *Masculine Feminine,* Godard is no longer trying to tell just the girl's story but the story of how a lover may feel about his girl, and we can see that it's not because she's a prostitute that he gets the sense that she isn't giving everything but because she's a girl and (as the camera of *My Life to Live* revealed though it wasn't the story being told) a love object. A lover may penetrate her body but there is still an opaque, impenetrable surface that he can never get through. He can have her and have her and she is never his.

The attraction of this little singer is that she isn't known, can't be known, and worst of all, probably there's nothing to know (which is what we may have suspected in *My Life to Live*). The ache of love is reaching out to a blank, which in this case smiles back. This male view of the eternal feminine mystery is set in the childlike simplicity of modern relations: before they go out on their first date, the boy and girl discuss going to bed. Easy sex is like a new idiom, but their talk of the pill is not the same as having it, and the spectre of pregnancy hovers over them. The old sexual morality is gone, but the mysteries of love and isolation remain; availability cancels out the pleasurable torments of anticipation, but not the sadness afterward.

With the new breed, Godard is able to define the romantic problem precisely and essentially. This approachable girl who adores Pepsi — the French cousin of Jean Seberg in *Breathless* — is as mysterious as a princess seen from afar, *more* mysterious because the princess might change if we got close. The boy's friend says, what's in "masculine" — mask and ass, what's in "feminine" — nothing. And that's what defeats the boy. Worse than losing a love is holding it in your arms and not finding it. At the close of the movie the word the boys failed to see in "feminine" is revealed — *fin*.

In *Masculine Feminine* Godard asks questions of youth and sketches a portrait in a series of question-answer episodes that are the dramatic substance of the movie. The method was prefigured by the psychiatric interview in Truffaut's *The 400 Blows* (Léaud, now the questioning hero, was the child-hero who was quizzed), the celebrity interview in *Breathless,* and cinema vérité movies by Jean Rouch and Chris Marker. It is most like Chris Marker's rapturous inquiry of the young Japanese girl in *The Koumiko Mystery*. There are informal boy-to-boy conversations about women and politics; there is a phenomenal six-minute single-take parody-interview conducted by the hero with a Miss Nineteen, who might be talking while posing for the cover of *Glamour;* and there are two boy-girl sessions which define the contemporary meaning of masculine and feminine. These dialogues are dating talk as a form of preliminary sex play — verbal courtship rites. The boy thrusts with leading questions, the girl parries, backs away, touches her hair. Godard captures the awkwardnesses that reveal, the pauses, the pretensions, the mannerisms — the rhythms of the dance — as no one has before. *Masculine Feminine* is the dance of the sexes drawing together and remaining separate. He gets the little things that people who have to follow scripts can't get: the differences in the way girls are with each other and with boys, and boys with each other and with girls. Not just what they do but how they smile or look away.

What can a boy believe that a girl says, what can she believe of what he says? We watch them telling lies and half truths to each other and we can't tell which are which. But, smiling in the darkness because we know we've all been there, we recognize the truth of Godard's art. He must have discovered his subject as he worked on it (as a man working on a big-budget movie with a fixed shooting schedule cannot). And because he did, we do, too. We can read all those special fat issues of magazines devoted to youth and not know any more than we do after watching big TV specials on youth. But even in the ladies' lounge right after the movie, there were the girls, so pretty they hardly seemed real, standing in a reverie at the mirror, toying with their shiny hair. And because Godard uses people (as he uses ideas) for suggestiveness, echoes, romantic overtones — for resonance — we see them differently now.

There is a question that remains, however: why haven't more people responded to this movie? Maybe because *Masculine Feminine* is not only partial to youth but partial as a view, and movie hucksterism has accustomed people to big claims (and movie experience to big flops). Maybe because Godard has made so many films and critics have often urged the worst upon the public. I would not recommend *The Married Woman* or *Pierrot le Fou:* Godard loves the games and style of youth but does not have the same warm feeling for older characters. He presents them as failed youth: they don't grow up, they just deteriorate, and those movies in which they figure become cold and empty. But there's life in *Masculine Feminine,* which shows the most dazzlingly inventive and audacious artist in movies today at a new peak.

Epics

The Bible, Hawaii, Dr. Zhivago

WHEN the announcement was made that Norman Mailer's *An American Dream* was to be made into a movie, my reaction was that John Huston was the only man who could do it. And what a script it could be for him! But Huston was working on *The Bible.* A quarter of a century had passed since *The Maltese Falcon,* it was a long time since *San Pietro* and *The Treasure of Sierra Madre* and *The Red Badge of Courage* and *The African Queen.* It was a decade since the stirring, often brilliant, but misconceived *Moby Dick,* and Huston had gone a different route — away from the immediacy of men testing themselves and the feel and smell of American experience. He had become a director of spectacles. Possibly, because of the way that big movie stars and directors live in a world of their own, insulated and out of touch, he might not even recognize that *An American Dream* was the spectacle of our time; was, even, his spectacle.

It turns out he was, at least, testing himself — as, earlier, he had attempted to do in *Moby Dick,* and, even after that, in parts of *The Roots of Heaven.* If, in making *The Treasure of Sierra Madre* he risked comparison with *Greed,* and if with *The Red Badge of Courage,* he risked comparison with *The Birth of a Nation, The Bible* risks comparison with *Intolerance.* It is a huge sprawling epic — an attempt to use the medium to its fullest, to overwhelm the senses and feelings, for gigantic mythmaking, for a poetry of size and scope.

In recent years the spectacle form has become so vulgarized that probably most educated moviegoers have just about given it up. They don't think of movies in those terms anymore because in general the only way for artists to work in the medium is frugally. Though there might occasionally be great sequences in big pictures, like the retreat from Russia in King Vidor's *War and Peace,* those who knew the novel had probably left by then. If, however, you will admit that you went to see *Lawrence of Arabia* under the delusion that it was going to be about T. E. Lawrence, but you stayed to enjoy the vastness of the desert and the pleasures of the senses that a huge movie epic can provide — the pleasures of largeness and distances — then you may be willing to override your prejudices and too-narrow theories about what the art of the film is, and go to see *The Bible*.

For John Huston is an infinitely more complex screen artist than David Lean. He can be far worse than Lean because he's careless and sloppy and doesn't have all those safety nets of solid craftsmanship spread under him. What makes a David Lean spectacle uninteresting finally is that it's in such goddamn good taste. It's all so ploddingly intelligent and controlled, so "distinguished." The hero may stick his arm in blood up to the elbow but you can be assured that the composition will be academically, impeccably composed. Lean plays the mad game of superspectacles like a sane man. Huston (like Mailer) tests himself, plays the crazy game crazy — to beat it, to win.

The worst problem of recent movie epics is that they usually start with an epic in another form and so the director must try to make a masterpiece to compete with an already existing one. This is enough to petrify most directors but it probably delights Huston. What more perverse challenge than to test himself against the Book? It's a flashy demonic gesture, like Nimrod shooting his arrow into God's heaven.

Huston shoots arrows all over the place; he pushes himself too hard, he tries to do too many different things. The movie is episodic not merely because the original material is episodic but also because, like Griffith in *Intolerance,* he can find no way to rhythm together everything that he's trying to do. Yet the grandeur of this kind of crazy, sinfully extravagant movie-making is in trying to do too much. We tend, now, to think of the art of the film in terms of depth, but there has always been something about the eclectic medium of movies that, like opera, attracts artists of Promethean temperament who want to use the medium for scale, and for a scale that will appeal to multitudes. I don't mean men like DeMille who made small-minded pictures on a big scale — they're about as Promethean as a cash register. I mean men like Griffith and von Stroheim and Abel Gance and Eisenstein and Fritz Lang and Orson Welles who thought *big,* men whose prodigious failures could make other people's successes look puny. This is the tradition in which Huston's *The Bible* belongs. Huston's triumph is that despite the insanity of the attempt and the grandiosity of the project, the technology doesn't dominate the material: when you respond to the beauty of such scenes in *The Bible* as the dispersal of the animals after the landing of the Ark, it is not merely the beauty of photography but the beauty of conception.

The stories of Genesis are, of course, free of that wretched masochistic piety that makes movies about Christ so sickly. Pasolini's *The Gospel According to St. Matthew* was so static that I could hardly wait for that loathsome prissy young man to get crucified. Why do movie-makers think that's such a good story, anyway? The only thing that gives it plausibility is, psychologically, not very attractive. And whether it's told the DeMille way, loaded with hypocritic sanctity, or the Pasolini way, drabness supposedly guaranteeing purity and truth, it's got a bad ending that doesn't make sense after those neat miracles.

The legends that Huston uses are, fortunately, more remote in time, are, indeed, all "miracles," and we are spared sanctity. The God who orders these events is so primitive and inexplicable that we may indeed wonder and perhaps be appalled. From Eve, whose crime scarcely seems commensurate with her punishment, on through to Hagar cast into the wilderness, and the cruel proof of obedience demanded of Abraham, it is a series of horror stories, alleviated only by the sweet and hopeful story of the Ark, where, for once, God seems to be smiling — no doubt, because we are taken inside the boat rather than left outside to suffer in the Flood. Huston retains that angry God, and Eve as the source of mischief, and phrases disquieting to modern ears, like "Fair are the angels of God." He hasn't taken the fashionable way out of trying to turn it all into charming metaphors and he hasn't "modernized" it into something comfortable and comforting. He doesn't, in the standard show business way, twist the story to make the hero sympathetic. Only with Peter O'Toole's three angels do we get the stale breath of the New Testament with the familiar skinny figure and that suffering-for-our-sins look.

The movie may present a problem for religious people who have learned not to think of the Bible stories like this: it is commonly understood now that although the childish take the stories for truth, they are then educated to know that the stories are "metaphorical." The movie undercuts this liberal view by showing the power (and terror) of these cryptic, primitive tribal tales and fantasies of the origins of life on earth and why we are as we are. This God of wrath who frightens men to worship ain't no pretty metaphor.

One of the worst failures of the movie is, implicitly, a rather comic modern predicament. Huston obviously can't make anything acceptable out of the Bible's accounts of sinfulness and he falls back upon the silliest stereotypes of evil: the barbaric monsters who jeer at Noah's preparations for the Flood look like leftovers from a Steve Reeves Hercules epic, and the posing, prancing faggots of Sodom seem as negligible as in *La Dolce Vita*. God couldn't have had much sense of humor if He went to the trouble of destroying them. Even their worship of the Golden Calf seems like a nightclub act, absurd all right, but not nearly as horrible as the animal sacrifices that God accepts of Abel and orders of Abraham. It is a measure of the strength of Huston's vision that we are constantly shocked by the barbarism of this primitive religion with its self-serving myths; it is a measure of weakness that he goes along with its strange notions of evil without either making them believable or treating them as barbaric. Only in the rare moments when the Bible's ideas of wrong and our ideas of wrong coincide — as in Cain's murder of his brother — can Huston make sin convincing.

This movie has more things wrong with it than his *Moby Dick,* but they're not so catastrophic. Though Huston might conceivably have made a great Ahab himself, Gregory Peck could not: that nice man did not belong in the whirling center of Melville's vision. In *The Bible* it's questionable if that Ahab-character Huston belongs in Noah's homespun on the Ark. He plays it in the crowd-pleasing vein of his cute, shrewd Archbishop in *The Cardinal:* his Noah is a puckish, weathered old innocent, a wise fool. He indulged his father Walter Huston in one scene of *The Treasure of Sierra Madre,* when the grizzled, toothless old prospector, tended by native love-lies, cocked an eye at the audience. Huston's Noah keeps asking the audience's indulgence, and Huston as director extends it. What was a momentary weakness in Huston Senior is the whole acting style of Huston Junior. His air of humility and wonder isn't so much acted as assumed, like a trick of personality — a double-take that has taken over the man.

The early part of the Abraham and Sarah story is poor: it looks and sounds like acted-out Bible stories on television. But then it begins to unfold, and we see Abraham raised to nobility by suffering. George C. Scott has the look of a prophet, and he gives the character an Old Testament fervor. It's a subdued, magnificent performance.

Probably the most seriously flawed sequence is the Tower of Babel, and as it is one of the most brilliant conceptions in the work, it is difficult to know why it is so badly structured and edited. The ideas remain latent: we can see what was intended, but the sequence is over before the dramatic point has been developed. And in this sequence, as in several others, Huston seems unable to maneuver the groups of people in the foreground; this clumsiness of staging and the dubbing of many of the actors in minor roles produce occasional dead scenes and dead sounds. It would be better if the musical score *were* dead: it is obtrusively alive, and at war with the imagery.

And what of *An American Dream?* It has been written and directed by some fellows from television. The first fifteen minutes of Eleanor Parker in and out of bed can be recommended to connoisseurs of the tawdry, though the movie as a whole doesn't rank with *The Oscar. The Oscar* is the modern classic of the genre. The Joseph E. Levine beds and draperies were already deluxe in *The Carpetbaggers* and *Harlow.* In *The Oscar* he added Harlan Ellison's incomparable bedroom conversations, and it's such a perfect commingling the words might have sprouted from the coverlets.

The overture to *Hawaii* prepares us to expect the worst: it's that kind of all-purpose pastiche with excruciating claims to authenticity that sells (six hundred thousand albums of *Dr. Zhivago* have already been sold) and inevitably gets nominated for an Academy Award. The photography confirms our fears: it is bad picture-postcard art, with not more than two or three shots worth looking at in the entire movie.

Hawaii is an epic in the tradition of best-seller adaptations like *Gone with the Wind,* with love and rape and incest and childbirth and storms at sea and battles and fires and epidemics; it's based on an 1130-page book with eight extra pages of genealogical charts of the principal characters — who have names like Abner and Jerusha and Captain Rafer Hoxworth. During the seven years that it has been in various stages of preparation, *Hawaii* has worn out a succession of screen writers, and a succession of directors, and if you look at the book they were attempting to transfer to film, you can see why.

What I am describing sounds like a stinker. And by formal aesthetic standards it is. But it's a surprisingly absorbing movie, just the same.

Conventional movie forms can sometimes be brought to life by unconventional material or unconventional characters. *Gone with the Wind* (which was not a work of movie art, either) was entertaining largely because of that scheming little vixen Scarlett who cared more for land than for love. The theme of *Hawaii* is the destruction of the Hawaiian culture and its people; the movie opens in 1819, roughly forty years after Captain Cook landed, and covers the influx of missionaries and land grabbers. At the center of the action (and, fortunately, he is rarely off screen) is Max von Sydow as, undoubtedly, the most unlikely hero who ever dominated an expensive American movie. It's hard to guess if those who backed the movie were courageous or just foolhardy, but this central character is an insufferable, tactless man who antagonizes everybody, a Calvinist minister frighteningly strong in his narrow views. He's not human in the way we expect movie heroes to be, he's even an unjust man — a racist who believes in the superiority of his God and his skin and his traditions. Von Sydow accomplishes the almost impossible: he makes us give the ghastly, ludicrous minister our grudging admiration. Julie Andrews, pleasing enough in her early scenes, doesn't have the range or depth to develop a character. By the end, when she talks to her husband of love, she sounds quietly superior, like a schoolmistress teaching him little lessons in humanity. It isn't acting, it's condescension, in the ladylike manner of Miss Greer Garson. Richard Harris, however, provides the romantic strength that his swashbuckling role requires. And a nonprofessional Tahitian named Jocelyne La Garde is sublime as Malama, the sacred queen of the island, a warm mountain of flesh that is balanced against von Sydow's scarecrow of spirit.

Unlike earlier generations of movie directors, the television and stage-trained directors who now make movies (and who rarely attempt spectacles) are not able to use a historical novel as source material to give their movies richness of atmosphere and detail. But George Roy Hill compensates for his inexperience in the medium by developing strong characterizations that succeed in binding the material. And the editing is astute: the movie keeps picking up its pace, moving ahead like an impatient storyteller, so that we rarely get too much of anything.

Even the things done badly are interesting because we can see what those who made the film were trying to get at, and why, and how hard it was to get as much as they did. It would be a loss if people couldn't respond to a movie like *Hawaii* for its characters and subject matter. As they say in the South about a meal of beans and rice, this movie sticks to your bones.

The recent huge films of David Lean suggest that even solid, well-trained film craftsmen can't bind together the protagonists and the story material with the spectacular effects now considered obligatory in "big" pictures. *The Bridge on the River Kwai* was good only in pieces; *Lawrence of Arabia,* though perhaps the most literate and tasteful and exciting of the modern expensive spectacles, failed to give an acceptable interpretation of Lawrence and failed to keep its action clear and intelligible. The scenarist, Robert Bolt, had turned the central figure into such a poetic enigma that he was displaced in the film by a simpler hero — Ali, the handsome sheik with liquid brown eyes and conventionally sympathetic lines to speak. Ali, an old-fashioned kind of movie hero, was more at home in what, despite all the literacy, was a big action movie. And as it became apparent that audiences hadn't the remotest idea of what the Arabs and Turks were doing in World War I, or which was which, or why the English cared, the critical question the movie raised was: can complicated historical events and a complex hero function in an expensive spectacle? Fortunately for *Lawrence of Arabia,* audiences seemed to be satisfied with the explanation that the Turks were more cruel than the Arabs, and although the movie Lawrence became cruel, too, there was warmhearted Ali to take over.

The unresolved question, however, is the same one that *Dr. Zhivago* answers negatively. Ali, Omar Sharif, is now at the center as Bolt's new poetic enigma, and Lean, a very literal-minded director, surrounds him with enormous historical reconstructions of the Russian Revolution. Neither the contemplative character nor the flux of events is intelligible, and what is worse, they seem unrelated to each other. It's difficult to imagine what kind of hero or even group of protagonists *could* be interesting enough to hold all these events together.

Are the events and all the pageantry necessary? Only in one sense. This kind of historical reconstruction is usually not very interesting artistically, and good designers and directors can provide the illusion of being in Moscow without rebuilding the city; but then, the movie wouldn't be, in commercial terms, an "epic," and it loses its principal selling point — expensive technology. Despite the technology involved in building all this and photographing it, the method is basically primitive, admired by the same sort of people who are delighted when a stage set has running water or a painted horse looks real enough to ride. When a city street or a village is built for a movie, even though it's real, it may look more false than a sketchy set because it calls so much attention to itself. In this movie, so full of "realism," nothing really grows, not the performances, not the ideas, not even the daffodils, which are also so "real" they have obviously been planted for us, just as the buildings have been built for us.

After the first half hour you don't expect *Dr. Zhivago* to breathe and live; you just sit there. It isn't shoddy (except for the music), it isn't soap opera; it's stately, respectable and dead: the photography static, the comings and goings without rhythm. It's like watching a gigantic task of stone masonry, executed by unmoved movers. It's not art, it's heavy labor — which, of course, many people respect more than art.

Dr. Zhivago is not in itself a disgraceful failure. It does, however, have one disgraceful effect: the final shot of a rainbow over the huge dam where Zhivago's lost daughter is working. This banal suggestion that it has all been for the best, that tomorrow will be brighter, etc., is not only an insult to us, it is a coarse gesture of condescension and appeasement to the Russians. Would Lean and Bolt place a rainbow over the future of England?

A Funny Thing Happened on the Way to the Forum

There is a sequence of a girl dancing in *A Funny Thing Happened on the Way to the Forum* but the director, Richard Lester, breaks it up so much with camera and editing that we can't see the dance, only flashes of parts of her body, and we can't even tell if the girl *can* dance because the movement is almost totally supplied by *his* means. This technique is a good one for concealing the ineptitude of performers, but Lester's short-term camera magic keeps cutting into and away from the comedians (Zero Mostel, Phil Silvers, Jack Gilford, Michael Hordern), who never get a chance to develop a routine or to bring off a number. What are we being distracted from?

There was probably no way to predict that Lester's style would be at war with the form, which in Plautus, as in the musical comedy adaptation by Burt Shevelove and Larry Gelbart, with Stephen Sondheim's songs, seemed the least strict imaginable; one might have thought it open enough for almost any kind of improvisation. But, seeing the result, we get the sense that Lester thinks it would be too banal just to let us see a dance or a pair of comedians singing a duet. Yet if they're good, they're a lot less banal than camera movement designed to cover emptiness. We go to see great clowns precisely for the way they move, for the grace and lightness of their style. The marvel of burlesque is that those lewd men become beautiful: their timing and skill transform the lowest forms of comedy. When Lester supplies the rhythms for them by film editing he takes away the one great asset of burlesque: that triumph of style which converts leering into art. He takes away their beauty and they become ugly and gross; he turns artists back into mugging low comics. (He also uses the women execrably: they are blank-faced bodies or witless viragos.) Some of the best moments are the least doctored: Hordern's vocal inflections, a satirical entrance song by Leon Greene. Lester's technique works successfully intermittently — as in the parody recap of the love duet which is lovely, like the song in the snow in *Help!*

It's difficult to make dance and song "work" on screen, and it's understandable that a talented, inventive director should fall back upon what looks so "cinematic" — the nervous camera, the restless splicing, the succession of "visual" jokes. But the sight gags of television commercials have a purpose: they are there to sell something and they make their point and they're over. In *Forum* as in *The Knack,* when Lester strings these gags together, they're just pointless agitation — just "clever" and "imaginative." He proceeds by fits and starts and leaves jokes suspended in mid-air: it's as if he'd forgotten what it's all for. And for an audience the experience becomes one of impatience and irritation — like coitus interruptus going on forever.

︶︶︶︶

A Shaggy-Man Story

Boudu Saved from Drowning

JEAN RENOIR'S *Boudu Saved from Drowning* was made in France in 1931*
when talkies were new and subtitling had not yet become a standard procedure, and so, like many other films of the early sound period, it was not
imported. Some of those talkies waited a few years, some a few decades;
others are still waiting — and may go on waiting because of the New York
press response to *Boudu.*

The four New York dailies agreed: to the *Times* it is "a second-rate
antique"; the *Post* found that it "is easily dismissed"; the *World Journal
Tribune* said it should not have been rescued; and the *Daily News* gave it
two stars — an event which should have alerted everyone that *Boudu* was a
movie of unusual quality, because the *Daily News* plasters almost every
Hollywood dud with four stars. They fall harder that way.

One may suspect that many early classics of the screen would be given
the same short shrift by the daily reviewers if they opened now — the 1931
À Nous La Liberté, for example, or Vigo's *Zero for Conduct* (1932) or
L'Atalante (1934); Louis Jouvet's performance in the 1933 *Dr. Knock*
would probably be patronizingly put down as a curiosity. Fortunately, most
of the best work from France plays regularly at revival houses and at colleges and doesn't depend on the daily reviewers to find its audience. Books
and magazine articles over three decades, a reference here and there, even
affectionate parental memories send new people each year to the Carné-
Prévert *Bizarre, Bizarre* (1937) or Pagnol's adaptation of Jean Giono's
Harvest (1937), to Renoir's *A Day in the Country* (1936) or *La Grande
Illusion* (1937), as well as to revivals of the French films of the forties and
fifties.

Other works by Renoir have come late and are taking their rightful

* First released in the United States in 1967.

place: the great 1939 *The Rules of the Game,* one of the key works in the history of movies, first seen here in a cut version and then restored in the sixties; and, a lesser but still important film, *The Crime of Mr. Lange* (1935), not subtitled for American audiences until the sixties. But with *Boudu,* it's different: it belongs to an earlier era, it gives a different kind of pleasure. The style and rhythm of *Boudu,* that whole way of looking at things, is gone, and so it may be a movie only for those who know and care about that way.

Boudu is a more leisurely film than we are used to now, not that it is long, or slow, but that the camera isn't in a rush, the action isn't overemphatic, shots linger on the screen for an extra split second — we have time to look at them, to take them in. Renoir is an unobtrusive, unselfconscious storyteller: he doesn't "make points," he doesn't rub our noses in "meaning." He seems to find his story as he tells it; sometimes the improvisation falters, the movie gets a little untidy. He is not a director to force things; he leaves a lot of open spaces. This isn't a failure of dramatic technique: it's an indication of that movie-making sixth sense that separates a director like Renoir from a buttoned-up-tight gentleman-hack like Peter Glenville or a genius-hustler like Sidney Lumet. Glenville suffocates a movie; Lumet keeps giving it charges to bring it to life. *Boudu* is a simple shaggy-man story told in an *open* way, and it is the openness to the beauty of landscape and weather and to the varieties of human folly which is Renoir's artistry. He lets a movie breathe.

Boudu is a tramp saved from suicide by a bookseller who takes him into his home and tries to do for him what decent, generous people *would* try to do — make him over in their own solid-bourgeois image, make him one of them. But *Boudu* is not a lovable tramp like Chaplin nor a Harry Langdon innocent nor a precursor of the artist-in-rebellion tramp like Alec Guinness's Gulley Jimson or Sean Connery's Samson Shillitoe. Boudu, bearded and long-haired like a premature Hell's Angel, is a dropout who just wants to be left alone. And this may help to explain why the movie wasn't imported earlier: he doesn't want romance or a job or a place in society (like the forlorn little hero of *À Nous La Liberté*), he isn't one of the deserving poor. There's no "redeeming" political message in *Boudu* and no fancy Shavian double-talk either.

Boudu is the underside of middle-class life, what's given up for respectability. We agree to be clean and orderly and responsible, but there is something satisfying about his *refusal*. There's a kind of inevitability — like someone acting out our dream — about the way he spills wine on the table, leaves the water running in the sink, wipes his shoes on the bedspread. There's some disorderly malice in him. He's like a bad pet that can't be trained: he makes messes. If Boudu's character were reformed, that would be defeat. The bookseller, despite his mistress-maid, is unmanned by the female household — and by being a householder. Boudu is, at least, his own dog.

Michel Simon, who plays Boudu, is better known for his masochistic roles, as, earlier, in Renoir's *La Chienne,* and, later, in Duvivier's *Panique* and *La Fin du jour.* But his Boudu, like his tattooed Père Jules of *L'Atalante,* which Agee described as "a premental old man . . . a twentieth-century Caliban," is a misfit loner. The loose walk, the eyes that don't communicate, the Margaret Rutherford jaw and the Charles Laughton sneaky self-satisfaction are not those of a man who rejects society: rejection is built into him, he merely acts it out. This, too, does not make the film easy for audiences: it is so much nicer to respond to a *Georgy Girl,* knowing that a pretty actress is putting us on. One of those four reviewers complained that Michel Simon "misses completely. . . . He is gross where he should be droll. He does wrong all the things that Fernandel later was to do right." That's rather like complaining that Olivier in *The Entertainer* is no Tony Bennett.

Renoir's camera reveals the actors as if they were there naturally or inadvertently — not arranged for a shot but found by the camera on the streets, in the shop, on the banks of the Seine. The camera doesn't overdramatize their presence, it just — rather reticently — picks them up, and occasionally lets them disappear from the frame, to be picked up again at a later point in their lives.

Despite the problems of sound recording in 1931, Renoir went out of the studio, and so *Boudu* provides not only a fresh encounter with the movie past but also a photographic record of an earlier France, which moved in a different rhythm, and because of the photographic equipment and style of the period, in a softly different light. The shop fronts look like Atget; the houses might have modeled for Bonnard. It is a nostalgic work, not in the deliberate, embarrassing way we have become inured to, but in spite of itself — through the accidents of distribution. And because Renoir is free of the public-courting sentimentality of most movie directors, our nostalgia is — well — clean.

The New Anne Bancroft,
Already Boxed In

Seven Women and The Slender Thread

MANY years ago, after the kind of Hollywood career that didn't go much further than a role in which her cute little bottom was featured as she was carried off by a gorilla, a young starlet named Anne Bancroft left the movies and made an auspicious, fresh start on the stage. Returning to Hollywood in glory, she won an Academy Award in 1962 for *The Miracle Worker* and then went to England, where she made *The Pumpkin Eater,* a remarkable study of modern sexual tensions (that too few people have seen). And now, in John Ford's *Seven Women,* she is back to being carried off by a gorilla. He's a gigantic Mongolian barbarian named Tunga Khan (played seriously, as far as we can tell, by that familiar strong-arm man, Mike Mazurki), and she is a "freethinking," cussing, drinking doctor who "gives herself" to him in order to save the lives of a group of missionary ladies. Which is a lot further than she went with the gorilla. But then, times have changed — but movies not as much as you might think, because she kills herself rather than face a fate worse than death, over and over again. This picture is more absurd than the deliberate spoof movies, because each cliché character and situation is played in apparent earnest; it's almost deadpan farce. Although it's not in the class of wildly extravagant kitsch like *The Fountainhead* or *Specter of the Rose* or *Duel in the Sun* or *The Barefoot Contessa,* it's on a level with *The Sandpiper.* It's rather like watching an old movie on TV and thinking, "No, no, they're not really going to do that next" — but they do, they do, and superior as you feel to it, you're so fascinated by the astounding, confident senselessness of it all that you can't take your eyes off it.

When you see Anne Bancroft in *The Slender Thread,* another of her recent films, you wonder if she really ever left Hollywood, because although she's playing an ordinary sort of woman, she has become expensive-looking, more Beverly Hills than Seattle, where the story is set. It's not that she's bad in the movie; it's just that she can't seem to help looking and acting like a big movie star — although she really isn't one quite yet. Not yet a queen, she already carries herself like the queen-mother.

The movie itself is distended essence of TV drama. Based on a *Life* magazine article about a crisis clinic that mans a telephone twenty-four hours a day, in an attempt to talk potential suicides out of the act, *The Slender Thread* is the telephone connection between Bancroft, who has taken a fatal dose of pills, and Sidney Poitier, as the student volunteer alone at the clinic. It's well acted and well directed (by Sydney Pollack). What's the matter with it is more basic than either acting or direction: it has no imaginative substance. It is merely an "idea" for a movie "worked out" by a TV writer (Stirling Silliphant) to be plausible.

What's the matter with it is what's the matter with most attempts at "intelligent" TV drama: we are told just enough about the characters to keep the action going; indeed, they are invented for that purpose and don't exist except to keep the action going. They never say or do anything that doesn't contribute to the "idea"; nothing spills over the edges. And oh how well we know them by now, these modern action stereotypes, these "real" television people on their plot strings of real-life stories.

The movie is stretched tight — which is supposed to keep us in suspense. But this clean, economical, well-organized production is fraudulent naturalism — details that are carefully arranged, so that we will accept them as normal, as true, though they are drawn not from observation but from the exigencies of plot need. We could do the job ourselves; it's simple mechanical engineering; it might even make a good party game: what is likely to make an ordinary person attempt suicide and call for help, and what kind of perfectly plausible obstacles might delay the help?

The motives, the obstacles are bound to be banal, unless you make them quirky (i.e., spoofing) or really draw upon some experience or imagination — getting away from "the ordinary," in which case it's no longer TV drama, it might even begin to be art.

We're supposed to relate to these people because they're just like us. But are we like them? I'm not, and I've never met anyone who was a type like these people when you got to know him. On TV they're all *types,* and maybe that's why we feel so blank and unrelated to anything after watching them. TV took it from radio and movies, of course, reduced it to its components, and perfected it in its own way — predictability plus switches, that's the formula; plays that drone on and on and never sting.

It's not drama; it's more like a jukebox. You put your money in, push the lever, and you know exactly what tune you'll hear — just what the sales representative stuck in and labeled for you. And of course there are lots of people who are content to put their dimes in and listen to the tunes that are popular that season and have no desire for music beyond what's in that box. There are also those people who stand all day pushing the levers on the one-armed bandits at Reno and Las Vegas — people to whom life and fate are reduced to this insane luck-machine. Their capacity for life seems to have been taken away; they can only diddle the machine, which they think has their fate inside it. And if they think so, it does.

TV drama may be the ultimate box. Is there a novel, a play, a movie that you remember that is so tight in eliminating nonessentials? You may conclude that it's the nonessentials, the loose and tangled and dangling threads, that you really care about. TV drama is all function, so clean and "ingenious" that it has no resonance, no reverberations. *The Slender Thread* never deals with the irony that the audience is constantly soaking in: that the man at the end of the telephone wire is a Negro. So much more graceful, so much *easier* to stay on a slender thread and not risk crossing wires.

At the end, when the woman's life has been saved and Telly Savalas, the decent, human doctor, asks Poitier if he'd like to meet her, he thinks for a moment and then says, "No." Gulp. I was happy to hear a voice behind me in the theatre: "They already met at the Academy Awards show."

The Living Library

Fahrenheit 451

THERE are some rather dumb — but in a way brilliant — gimmicks that have a strong, and it would almost seem a perennial, public appeal. Books or plays or movies based on them don't even have to be especially well done to be popular: readers and audiences respond to the gimmick. Sometimes this kind of trick idea is so primitive that it's particularly attractive to educated people — perhaps because they're puzzled by why they're drawn to it and so take it to be a much more complex idea than it is. *Frankenstein* is one of these fantastic, lucrative "ideas"; *The Pawnbroker* is almost one. A classic example of the use of one of them is Albert Lewin's 1945 movie adaptation of *The Picture of Dorian Gray*. Even the basic notion of Dorian Gray's remaining young and fresh and handsome while his portrait aged with the ravages of his evil soul wasn't sustained in the production — Hurd Hatfield's Dorian was never really young: he looked waxy and glacéed from the outset; and the other characters didn't age any more than he did. But audiences responded to the appeal of the idea, anyway, and are still responding to it on television re-runs and still arguing about how it should have been cast and carried out.

François Truffaut's *Fahrenheit 451* isn't a very good movie but the idea — which is rather dumb but in a way brilliant — has an almost irresistible appeal: people want to see it and then want to talk about how it should have been worked out. *Fahrenheit 451* is more interesting in the talking-over afterward than in the seeing. The movie is about a society in which books are forbidden, not censored or rewritten as in Orwell's vision of 1984, but simply forbidden, burned. Book lovers run off to the woods where each memorizes a book and they become a living library. It is in the difference between the movie's simple gimmick-idea and Orwell's approach to censorship as an integral part of totalitarianism that we can see some of the weakness of the idea. Stripped of the resonances of politics and predictions and all those other repressions and forms of regimentation which are associated with book burning, the idea is shallow: it operates in a void. The strength of the idea is that in removing book burning from any political context, in using it as an isolated fearful fancy, it turns into something both more primitive and superficially more sophisticated than a part of a familiar, and by now somewhat tiresome, political cautionary message.

Of course, a gimmicky approach to the emptiness of life without books cannot convey what books mean or what they're *for:* homage to literature and wisdom cannot be paid through a trick shortcut to profundity; the skimpy science-fiction script cannot create characters or observation that would make us understand imaginatively what book deprivation might be like. Among the books burned are Poe's *Tales of Mystery and Imagination* and *The Martian Chronicles* by Ray Bradbury, who also wrote the book of *Fahrenheit 451*. This decorative little conceit has the effect of making us more aware than ever of the coyness and emptiness and inadequacy of the central conceit. The idea that one of the book people at the end might be devoting his life to preserving a text by Ray Bradbury (or *No Orchids for Miss Blandish*, which we also see in flames) is enough to turn the movie into comedy. The next step is to imagine all the jerks we've known and what they might give their lives to preserving — *Anthony Adverse? Magnificent Obsession? The Robe? The Adventurers? Valley of the Dolls?* We have only to think about it to realize how absurd the idea is. Why should a society burn all books on the basis that books make people think and so disturb them and make them unhappy? Most books don't make people think, and print is not in itself a danger to totalitarianism. That is a crotchety little librarian's view of books. Print is as neutral as the television screen. And so we're back from the primitive appeal of the gimmick, to the Orwell vision of censorship and terror. And yet such is the power of the gimmick that I swear I heard people in the theatre murmur at the astuteness of that nonsensical explanation for book burning. You'd think they'd never read a book, they're so willing to treat books as magical objects. And that is, of course, how the movie treats them: the gimmick turns books — any books — into totems, and this is part of the gimmick's appeal to educated audiences, probably a stronger appeal than a more rational treatment of the dangers of censorship could make.

Book burning taps a kind of liberal hysteria and the audience supplies the fearful associations: Hitler, McCarthy (who was the inspiration for the book, which was published in 1953). A woman who taught at Berkeley dropped in on me once and saw a book burning in the fireplace. She pointed at it in terror. I explained that it was a crummy ghost-written life of a movie star and that it was an act of sanitation to burn it rather than sending it out into the world which was already clogged with too many copies of it.

But she said, "You shouldn't burn books" and began to cry. It's because of this kind of reaction, and because we don't think of book burning in a vacuum but of the historical horrors of taking away peoples' treasured possessions, of burning part of them, and of burning them, too, that the buggy little idea behind this movie is not easy to dismiss. *Frankenstein* preyed upon both our most primitive fears that man should not play God and our rather more sophisticated anxieties about scientists messing around with the order of things. *The Picture of Dorian Gray* brought back our childish fears that the bad secret things we did would show on our faces, as well as the more sophisticated fear, and perhaps envy, of all those beautiful people who could get away with murder, who could be ruthless and rotten and it would never show on their ingenuous faces. The banal suburban look of the future in *Fahrenheit 451* affects us at childish levels, too. The characters don't seem quite grown-up, and the notion of how to save books is peculiarly naïve — as in a fairy tale. The book people are a kid's idea of how to keep literature alive. They have no concept of carrying on a living literary tradition, of writing books, or of using books for knowledge or even against the state, but of turning themselves into books — as in a kids' game. Their notion of literature is a neighborhood library, and the book people at the end are coy and harmless eccentrics — bookworms.

For American art-house audiences who are both more liberal and more bookish than the larger public, book burning is a just-about-perfect gimmick. Yet even at the science-fiction horror-story level, this movie fails — partly, I think, because Truffaut is too much of an artist to exploit the vulgar possibilities in the material. He doesn't give us pace and suspense and pious sentiments followed by noisy climaxes; he is too tasteful to do what a hack director might have done. One can visualize the scene when the hero, Oskar Werner, reads his first book, *David Copperfield,* as it might have been done at Warners or MGM in the thirties, how his face would light up and change with the exaltation of the experience — the triumph of man's liberation from darkness. Well, ludicrous as it would have been, it might have been better than what Truffaut does with it — which is nothing. Truffaut is so cautious not to be obvious, the scene isn't dramatized at all, and so we're left to figure out for ourselves that Werner must have enjoyed the reading experience because he goes on with it. Soon we're left to figure out for ourselves why he has gotten so addicted to books that he's willing to kill for them. It would, no doubt, be obvious to have an adulterous romance between Werner and the girl who goads him to read, but Truffaut doesn't supply *any* relationship to help define their characters. And if he feels that too much characterization is wrong for the genre, couldn't he at least give them actions that would define their roles in the story? Yes, it would be too much of a movie cliché to have Julie Christie play the two roles of the wife and the book girl in sharply contrasting styles; but Truffaut makes nothing out of her being so much the same in both roles. It hardly helps us to see what books mean in human life if her range of expressiveness is as narrow for the book girl as for the bookless pill-head wife. The book girl's language is just as drab and she doesn't show any of the curiosity or imagination that might indicate that books had done something for her. Couldn't she have some quality that would help us understand why Werner reacts to her suggestion that he read a book? And shouldn't he have something that sets him apart, that makes him a candidate for heresy?

If the reply is that in this movie the books represent the life that is not in the people, then surely it is even more necessary to see that the book people have life. Shouldn't they speak differently from the others, shouldn't they take more pleasure in language? Couldn't they give themselves away by the words they use — the love of the richness of words? It's all very well for the director not to want to be obvious, but then he'd better be subtle. He can't just abdicate as if he thought it would be too vulgar to push things one way or another. Criticism, in this case, turns into rewriting the movie: we can generally see what was intended but we have to supply so much of the meaning and connections for ourselves that it's no wonder that when it's over we start talking about how we would have done it.

There are a few nice "touches": the loss of memory by bookless people so that they have no past and no history; their drugged narcissistic languor; and there is the rather witty bit about the chief book burner (Cyril Cusack) seeing the proof of the worthlessness of books in the fact that writers disagree. But these touches are made to pass for more than they should because there aren't enough of them. The movie is so listless we have what we should never have in a gimmicky thriller: time to notice inconsistencies. People know how to read; why are they taught? Why are the book people hiding libraries in town instead of smuggling them to the woods? (Do they have a secret lending library?) Why are we shown the hero revealing his guilt to his co-workers (in scenes like his inability to go up the fire pole) if it doesn't lead to any consequences? Why are we shown an antagonism between Werner and another fireman (Anton Diffring) which never develops into anything functional in the structure? Why is it so easy to escape to the woods? Couldn't Truffaut or anyone think up a better contrivance to bring the book girl back than the need to retrieve an incriminating list of names (of people who memorize books!)? The actions in this movie don't flow from the theme; O.K., we can accept that if, at least, they're ingenious. But they're not. Still, all the holes in the plot would just make it seem lacy and airy if the movie had rhythm, if it moved purposefully, if the moods surprised us or intrigued us. Why doesn't it?

True, this film is the first Truffaut has made in a studio, the first in color (which slows down and complicates shooting), and it was made in England, with English technicians, and in English (though Truffaut does not speak the language), which helps to explain why the timing and inflections are off in the dialogue and why the script sounds as if it were written by the bookless people. In other words, he has been totally uprooted and separated from his earlier co-workers. Business conditions made him a refugee, struggling against the same pressures of speed and efficiency and fixed shooting schedules that made the great refugee directors of Europe into modestly talented hacks in Hollywood in the thirties and forties, and so we cannot expect the spontaneity of *Shoot the Piano Player* and *Jules and Jim*. But not even a little bit of it? Truffaut *wanted* to make *Fahrenheit 451*: why then, even allowing for the hurdles of language and technology, isn't it more imaginatively thought out, felt, why are the ideas dull, the characters bland, the situations (like the hero breaking into the chief's office) flat and clumsy? Why is the whole production so unformed?

I would offer the guess that it's because Truffaut, in his adulation of Alfred Hitchcock, has betrayed his own talent — his gift for expressing the richness of life which could make him the natural heir of the greatest French director of them all, Jean Renoir. Instead, he is a bastard pretender to the commercial throne of Hitchcock — and his warmth and sensibility will destroy his chances of sitting on it. (Roman Polanski and dozens of others will get there before him.) Truffaut can't use Hitchcock's techniques because they were devised for something tightly controlled and limited and because they are based on coercing the audiences' responses (and, of course, making them enjoy it). Hitchcock is a master of a very small domain: even his amusing perversities are only two- or three-dimensional. Truffaut has it in him not to create small artificial worlds around gimmicky plots, but to open up the big world, and to be loose and generous and free and easy with it.

Southwestern

The Chase

IN a typical Western the sheriff-hero was trying to protect the good people of the town; in the socially conscious Western, *High Noon,* the town was used as a microcosm of the evils of capitalist society, and the sheriff was the lonely man of integrity. *The Chase* is a return to *High Noon,* which millions of people loved (I didn't). This time the sheriff is Marlon Brando (who is a great actor, though not in this movie) and the town isn't merely corrupt: it has an appetite for violence, it's a blood-lusting Texas town in the mythical United States of message movies. It's *evil.* Lillian Hellman wrote the screenplay (from Horton Foote's material), and the little foxes really took over. Our vines have no tender grapes left in this hellhole of wife swapping, nigger hating, and nigger-lover hating, where people are motivated by dirty sex or big money, and you can tell which as soon as they say their first lines. Why, even the kids are rotten: they *dance.* Satan's kids — weren't they born in the South? In this movie that's like original sin.

This is a hate-the-white-South movie. If you turned it around and showed Negroes doing what the white Southerners in the movie do, every Negro organization and civil rights group would have good cause to protest. The newest scapegoats are white Southerners; this time it's the liberals who are doing it, and they're using the oldest device — showing the white Southerners as sexually obsessed.

Many people all over the world blame Texas for the assassination of Kennedy — as if the murder had boiled up out of the unconscious of the people there. *The Chase* exploits and confirms this hysterical view, and goes so far as to provide a facsimile of Jack Ruby's shooting of Oswald, substituting a racist and, of course, Gentile white Southerner for Ruby, and a totally innocent hero (Robert Redford) for Oswald. It's as if Kennedy was killed because Texas is all heat and guns and violence — Sicily gone wild.

The director, Arthur Penn, tries to set things on fire with the old Elia

Kazan bazooka. He comes out with perhaps the most uncontrolled liberal sadomasochistic fantasy since *A Face in the Crowd.* This hysteria might not seem so preposterous if *The Chase* were a tawdry little movie trying to achieve big effects; but it's a big movie with what is advertised as "the Sam Spiegel imprimatur." Spiegel, who has become the new Sam Goldwyn (expensive, careful productions, famous writers, "distinguished" artists, etc.), has given it the largess of rich color and a big cast — which makes us even more conscious of the semi-psychotic material.

The attitudes of the moneymen behind movies show through the film's attack on moneymen. They try to make a big action picture that will "expose" the attitudes of white Southerners in lavish cross-section and at the same time they want to make sure the picture makes money, so they play up all that dirty rotten white Southern sex they're condemning. It's the gambit of which Cecil B. DeMille was a master. Condemn the decadence of the Romans who enjoy the spectacle of lions tearing Christians to pieces, and you can show the audience the same good time the Romans had. That way movies could provide the maximum of nudity, sex, and sadism and be as moral as Sunday in church. It's a standard movie device, used rather fulsomely recently in *The Cincinnati Kid,* which shows us how vicious Ann-Margret's eroticism is by emphasizing her excitement at a cock fight — which we are invited (in bloody close-ups) to enjoy just as she does. Sam Spiegel says *The Chase* is about "the consequences of affluence" — i.e., *La Dolce Vita* on the range. One of those consequences — if we are to believe the movie — is irrational, murderous intolerance. The silent comedies used to give us pie-throwing and ritualized destruction scenes; *The Chase* turns parties into throwing and destroying scenes but asks us to be revolted. I'm afraid we would have to be convinced first.

Instead of the attraction and moral disapproval we're supposed to feel, we're more likely to reject what we see as silly. There is a moment midway in the movie when the Lot-in-Sodom good sheriff Brando talks about the town to his good wife and says, "Some of those people out there are just nuts," and the audience cannot restrain its laughter. And when the wife inexplicably replies that maybe things would have been different if they'd had children, the audience laughs harder. I think there may be a general recognition in the theatre that the movie-makers lost track of what they were doing.

At the end, as at the end of *High Noon,* the sheriff and his wife leave the town. What makes the few good white Southerners different from the others? The only hint offered is that the sheriff used to be a farmer and wants to go back "to the land." That's hardly enough, since he and the other "good" people act as if they've come from another planet. (Perhaps they have: according to Reverend Lawrence W. Friedrich, S.J., Dean of the Graduate School at Marquette, "Space research is made all the more fascinating by the possibility that there are higher forms of life on other space bodies, perhaps some unaffected by original sin.")

I may have been unjust to Miss Hellman. The following interview between her and Irving Drutman was published in the New York *Times* on February 27, 1966:

I hear you did a year's work on The Chase, *but that you didn't see it until a few weeks ago.*

I wasn't allowed to see it until a few weeks ago.

What did you think of it?

That an old and foolish dream is ended, and there will be no such for me again.

What dream?

To write a picture the way you write anything else. Decision by democratic majority vote is a fine form of government, but it's a stinking way to create. So two other writers were called in, and that made four with Mr. Spiegel and Mr. Penn, and what was intended as a modest picture about some aimless people on an aimless Saturday night got hot and large, and all the younger ladies in it have three breasts, and ———. Well, it is far more painful to have your work mauled about and slicked up than to see it go in a wastebasket.

You feel that you lost a year's work?

I wouldn't care much about losing, that's the chance you take when you write anything ———. Ach. It's too old a Hollywood story for anybody to want to hear it again. Anyway, I've got a new theory, or maybe an old one dressed up. Want to hear?

Sure.

Movies always belonged to one man — the director — and early movie-makers like Griffith and Chaplin knew it. Then along came talking pictures. Words are something else again, and they frightened the boys who didn't know many, so they brought out good writers like Faulkner and Fitzgerald. But such people can't and don't take, or even understand, fiddling and mangling, and so they were lost or went away. Right then and there it should have been obvious that a new method had to be found. The Europeans began to find it right after the War — the director wrote the picture or he had a man, or six men, who worked so closely with him that it looked as if one person had made the picture.

Then you admire European movies?

Sometimes, certainly not always. Even the best of them, like Fellini's, often go wandering around, too loose and lush and aimless for my taste. They need more script as our pictures need less. Why not a new kind of script? A kind of outline of action, the sequences in order, the characters loosely defined, the end in view. Beyond that — and that, of course, is a great deal — you would write only the first few lines of each scene, leaving the rest to be improvised, going loose with what is there, or throwing it out if something better came along. The director would have something solid to rest on, but nothing so rigid that he would feel as cramped as he often does now. That's the kind of script I'd like to try someday. But never, never again these old, weary disappointments.

A Man for All Seasons

A Man for All Seasons is tasteful and moderately enjoyable; Robert Bolt's dialogue is crisp, lucid, and well spoken; the actors are generally efficient. Fred Zinnemann's direction is placed at the service of Bolt's material — in the manner of a good, modest stage director who does not attempt more than a faithful, respectful interpretation of the play. It's pleasant to see a movie made with integrity and sensibility: *A Man for All Seasons* wasn't that easy to do and it wasn't "safe" — though it appears to have turned out well for all concerned.

But that's really just about all I can say for it. As conceived by Bolt, Sir Thomas More isn't *A Man for All Seasons:* he isn't particularly relevant to this season, I doubt if he's relevant to any season. Bolt's presentation of More's martyrdom is so totally one-sided that we don't even get to understand *that* side — as we might if it were challenged and engaged in conflict. Though the principle for which he dies (his belief that the Pope represents divine law so that he is saving his soul in taking the Catholic position against Henry VIII's marriage to Anne Boleyn) seems doubtful at best, it is given as beyond question in this film that a man should follow the dictates of his conscience. (The Afrikaners willing to die for apartheid — and they find their justifications in divine law also — could probably make as good a case.) This More is simply *right* and he's smart and good and just about omniscient (he even knows his Judas); his great opponent, Henry VIII, is vain and childish, and everyone else is weak, stupid, cowardly, or corrupt. More (Paul Scofield) is the only man of honor in the movie, and he's got all the good lines.

Bolt's More is the kind of hero we used to read about in the biographies of great men written for twelve-year-olds: the one against the many. Perhaps people think *A Man for All Seasons* is so great because unlike the usual movie which is aimed at twelve-year-olds, this one is aimed at twelve-year-old intellectuals and idealists. And if they've grown into compromising and unprincipled people, they can hail *A Man for All Seasons* as a masterpiece: heroism so remote, so totally the property of a suprahuman figure, absolves them of human weakness. It becomes romantic.

There's more than a little of the school pageant in the rhythm of the movie: though it's all neater than our school drama coaches could make it, the figures group and say their assigned lines and move on. The camera, ever faithful to the author, does not open them up to us: they are set faces, fully — rigidly — formed from the start. For a too-brief sequence, Orson Welles's Wolsey overpowers the orderly progression of attitudes, but then we are left with Scofield — so refined, so controlled, so dignified, so obviously "subtle" — just the way a man of conscience in a school play would be expected to behave.

Fantastic Voyage

A miniaturized medical team going into the bloodstream of a scientist to destroy a blood clot on his brain, with sixty minutes for the journey and operation and getting out — the idea of *Fantastic Voyage* promised poetry, mystery, excitement, "with gun and camera up the alimentary canal." But Richard Fleischer and his crew have managed to make a standard, stereotyped adventure picture for the wholesome family "inside" the human body (a male body and the action doesn't go below the waist). No frontiers are crossed. You know you're not leaving the sod of Hollywood when you hear the messenger come for the hero, Stephen Boyd, with the words, "Sorry to get you up so early" and the hero (wiping away a lipstick smear) reply, "I thought I was on vacation. What's it all about?" Soon there's the usual little argument about whether to take the heroine, Raquel Welch, along: "A woman has no place on a mission like this," etc. And everybody who's ever seen an adventure movie or a science-fiction movie knows that of course they'll take her along because the picture needs a sex interest. And of course we know who the villainous saboteur is as soon as we hear one of the scientists spouting atheism, just as we know he's going to die horribly before the picture is over — because in family entertainment a man doesn't dirty-mouth God and live.

The ingenious idea of *Fantastic Voyage* sets off reverberations in our minds. What has been done with it is to kill the reverberations by reducing the idea to commonplaces — the un-characters inside the body with their moldy platitudes about man and the universe, and the medical and military men outside with their homey little ironies. "What a time to run out of sugar," says government-man Edmond O'Brien, like a "housewife" in a commercial.

The big sets are full of sweet little bubbles, shiny and clean. The interior of the body looks new and pretty and expensive, like a colored refrigerator. It's probably just because we're always conscious of the effects as effects and because they don't involve us imaginatively that people admire them. The beauties and terrors of fantasy are in our imaginative assent to its seeming reality. These effects are so obviously *made* that they are cozy examples of Hollywood's banal technology. Six-and-a-half-million dollars worth of special effects that you keep noticing must be good, and there are the reviewers' comments in the ads: "A lavishly produced marvel made possible through the technical wizardry of Hollywood!", "Should sweep the Oscar field for special effects!", etc. Yet the process shots are so clumsily mated with the figures that the actors look as if a child has cut them out with a blunt scissors (an effect that might be witty in a different context.)

The quote from Bosley Crowther that heads the ads is, in its way, perfect: "A bubbly, fantastic quality you won't find this side of Disneyland." Right, but if you weren't intending to go to Disneyland looking for "fantasy," you may not be so pleased to find it "this side."

Perhaps a film like *Fantastic Voyage* succeeds commercially just because it initially excites you and then puts your fantastic thoughts to rest by showing you that the mysteries of the human body are no more mysterious than a trip through Disneyland.

Darling

THE key sequence in *Darling* invites us to laugh at documentary footage of boobish "little" people in the street answering a television interviewer (played by Dirk Bogarde) who is asking "What is wrong with England?" Ironically, the film itself presents an answer just as silly and badly thought out as theirs and yet seems to congratulate itself for having made such a clever, sophisticated statement about modern society.

The darling of the title, played by Julie Christie, is a mod-ish, middle-class girl who drifts upward. She casually models, has a bit part in a movie, leaves a husband, deceives a lover, goes to new ones; after such tribulations as an abortion, an orgy, and a religious conversion, she winds up unhappily married to a prince. If some women in the audience will say, "There but for the grace of . . ." and the tender-minded will say, "She missed her chance for happiness when she left the one man who truly loved her," others will think, "It doesn't look half bad." We know what we're *supposed* to think: that this girl has no direction in life. We know the story has been developed out of English headlines. We can see that she's supposed to be as bored and as jealous of what she doesn't understand as Mildred in *Of Human Bondage:* there she is screaming, "I hate books," as she throws them off the shelves. We can see that she's supposed to be as empty and lonely and loveless as *The Goddess:* there she is in her palace not enjoying her finery one little bit. We can see that she's as starved for playful companionship as Jo in *A Taste of Honey:* there she is saying to a homosexual photographer, "We could do without sex. I don't really like it that much." She even spells it all out for us: "If I could just feel complete." But since she was empty and pushing at the beginning and is still empty at the end, all we can really feel is, "Well, if she's going to be unhappy, rich is better."

It used to be, when we went to a movie and the heroine sinned, she suffered, and we had to suffer along with her. And she suffered so much longer than she sinned that we paid a heavy price for that early bit of fun.

Darling employs the new post–*La Dolce Vita* formula: the heroine (who suggests an androgynous version of a male hustler) has no concept of sin, all she cares about is fun and now. And the author and director show us as good a time as they can while introducing little bits of social comment that are intended to "expose" how sick that good time *really* is.

The author Frederic Raphael and the director John Schlesinger are no more imaginatively gifted at vice than they are at virtue. This may be the making of the film, commercially speaking. Their vice has a prosaic Welfare State look to it: the horrors of jazz and transvestism and "shocking" pompous epigrams and eyes glinting with wicked pleasure at dim wit are democratically available to everybody. Schlesinger's vice is as homey as wife-swapping in the suburbs. Even the orgy can easily be staged on a modest budget in a small home or apartment.

But what is *Darling*'s point of view, what is it saying beyond the decorative jabs — as when the overstuffed rich people are served by little Negro boys in livery and powdered wigs while they listen to an appeal for funds to fight hunger? It is saying that the boobs on the street are taken in by this girl and believe that she's an ideal success story, while we in the audience are being taught better. We are prodded to see that this bitch is a child of our times. But is this movie with its loving, peeping, and deriding any different from, or more profound than, the "inside-story" magazines and columns which also show how dirty the lives of celebrities *really* are? And aren't they favorite reading matter for those people on the street who will also eat up this movie?

The film-makers, quick to make their satiric point, open the movie with a famine poster which is then replaced by the titles — a poster advertising *Darling*. Not *Darling*'s way of life, but their movie. Their satire is double-edged: *Darling* is as empty of meaning and mind as the empty life it's exposing.

Zorba the Greek and *The Pawnbroker*

IF we are formalists and reject a work because it isn't totally good, then we may close ourselves off from the few emotional experiences possible in recent films. It's easy to be aesthetically fastidious and put down *Zorba the Greek* or *The Pawnbroker* as clumsy or mechanical or pretentious (as they are) and to point out that despite their superficial modernism of language or technique, they are basically traditional.

Responding to Michael Cacoyannis's *Zorba the Greek* is like taking a job with bad pay but marvelous fringe benefits. The central Life Force conception, banal and forced as it is, yet yields up something to us, something we want to believe in, and so it helps us enjoy the good things in the movie. The script is unconvincing, and Cacoyannis's worst fault is choreographed grand sequences — set pieces — which the camera exposes as too neatly grouped, too obviously planned. The villagers' knifing of the young widow is almost enough to wreck any movie, and the sequence of the old ladies stripping the dying courtesan's hotel goes on past necessity, goes on so long we want to say, enough, enough. It's too thorough, too "classic."

Yet Anthony Quinn's glee in his role as Zorba is wonderfully satisfying — like the pleasure we might feel seeing a pretty girl who's usually dressed in cheap, ugly clothes in exquisite finery, and she's not just pretty, she's beautiful. It makes us feel good to look at her. Ironically, despite the phoniness of the Life Force he's *supposed* to embody, there *is* life force in Quinn's performance. And in the grandeur of Irene Pappas's beauty, and the acting of Lila Kedrova, as the coquettish old ruin who thinks she can cheat age and death if she's still attractive enough to get a man. Cacoyannis lingers too long over this great old tart, wanting a little too much of a good thing; but it's human, we want to hold on to her, too.

Sidney Lumet's *The Pawnbroker* could be dismissed as a Jewish *Christmas Carol* trying to be *King Lear;* most of its vignettes are trite, and the movie is obviously trying too hard for a powerful effect. Yet it achieves one. I think the movie wrenches us not because it reveals how most or some or even a few concentration-camp survivors are or might be, but because this is how we fantasize and fear that we could be — unable to feel again, deadened, past pain, past caring. We fear that we could become mummies, walking dead; that, subjected to the worst possible things that could happen to us, we would become like this man, who can't feel because pain has destroyed his capacity for more suffering. If this Scrooge should reform, the movie would collapse into mechanics; but his awakening is only to sharper pain and the helplessness of one who then can feel, but can feel nothing but pain, what the numbness protected him from.

In this movie, too, most of the intensity comes from the actors. The great old Juano Hernandez, as the man who wants to talk, gives the single most moving performance I saw in 1965, and Rod Steiger's power makes our questioning of much of the action seem like quibbling. *The Pawnbroker* is a terrible movie and yet I'm glad I saw it: it helps to remind us that there are qualities in bad movies that have been lost in good ones, just as there is something in James Michener's novels (even though I can't get through them) that has been lost in our literature.

ⁱⁱⁱⁱⁱⁱ

The Glamour of Failure

La Guerre est finie

AN aging actress, finishing up her fifth marriage, and in her third decade of analysis, used to entertain friends by explaining her affairs. She'd go on something like this: "There's all that talk about the eternal triangle, but we run around in the eternal circle. When I was fifteen, there was a kid I liked. Once he chased me all around the living room and then upstairs. I was running around the bedroom for I don't know how long when he stopped and said, 'You wanted to stay. The doors were wide open all the time. You could have run out instead of running around the room.' That's it, after a while with compulsions, you lose the facts involved; you just get lost in the movement. Nothing leads up to anything. Running from one trap to another, leaving somebody desperately, running to somebody else, and feeling trapped the minute you get in."

She didn't believe in love, but she sure loved to go through the motions. She would explain her latest involvement with, "Every sex relationship I've ever had has been degrading. I could stop having anything to do with men, but I guess I'd rather be degraded." And after she told everybody exactly how impossible her latest affair had become, she would still go on with it. She'd say, "I'll probably never have this experience again. I might as well get all the sensations out of it. What I've had I don't have to miss." Her baby face was going hard, her upper arms were flabby, but she made herself seem more gallant and more appealingly romantic than those who still hoped for something. She made so much capital out of failure she almost passed for a success.

At its best, *La Guerre est finie* is an attempted elegy on the theme of exile, on living on old ideals, on living in the past, on not relating to the life that is actually being lived. But the variant of existentialism that is used in presenting the hero is embarrassingly close to the old actress's whorey

Freudianism. Though in her version of her life she was the heroine because so obviously willing to go on being victimized, we listeners didn't necessarily view her that way. In *La Guerre est finie,* however, we are asked to believe in the hero's humanity because although he no longer believes in the effectiveness of his "anti-Fascist" activity, he goes through the motions just the same.

Diego — Yves Montand — is a "professional" (euphemism for "paid") revolutionary in Spain, a courier in the Communist underground, a man for whom the conspiratorial life has become a matter of habit and reflexes. The movie opens as he crosses from Spain into France to warn another agent that a trap has been set for him if he goes into Spain, and it ends as Diego goes back and we learn that the trap is set for him. Diego goes on, without conviction, carrying out plans and policies he knows are futile because that's what he does, or, as we used to be told in those pre-existential pukka-sahib pictures when C. Aubrey Smith or Sir Guy Standing sent the regiment out to defend a hopeless position, "He does what he has to do." But movies have changed — a little — and the director, Alain Resnais, is careful to play down the heroism; Montand is like a weary commuter who's been through it all so many times he can see what's coming. And so do we, in anticipatory flash forwards — jump cuts into an imagined future, one of those peculiarly naïve, long-abandoned devices that are frequently hailed as technical innovations. These flashes (some of them may be projections of the past into the future) are obviously supposed to be fast as the speed of thought (though does anybody think this way, with fully detailed visual apprehensions cutting into the present?). As there isn't time to figure out what they relate to, we are forced to admire them for themselves or ignore them. The technique doesn't work, but we get the idea behind it that for Diego past and future are one.

It's easy to satirize force of habit — as W. C. Fields demonstrated when he blew the head off an ice-cream soda — but Resnais, although he allows most of the other revolutionaries to appear ridiculous, protects Diego very tenderly. He's not presented as a fool or a tool but as a noble, almost-extinct animal — the exile who cannot forget, who cannot make a new life. And the liberal audience, which sees so few screen heroes it can call its own, may be so touched by a film on a contemporary political subject or a contemporary experience of any kind that some may be willing to overlook the nature and quality of the contact, like Dwight Macdonald when he hailed *To Die in Madrid* as a masterpiece. It's a simple mistake in the arts to assume that anything that moves us must be a masterpiece, that we wouldn't be affected if it weren't great (it's the same mistake made by those who call *Gone with the Wind* or *The Sound of Music* or *The Pawnbroker* great).

Although those most sympathetic to the theme have a way of concluding that the technique is masterly, *La Guerre est finie* is smooth and rather banal in its technique despite the little hiccups of earlier Resnais "style" — some pretentious "ritualistic" narration (that recalls *Marienbad*) and those obtrusive jump-cuts (out of *Muriel*). They are tossed in almost as a Hollywood director imitating Resnais would toss them in — to prove that he can do it too; they become mildly irritating devices of conventional movie storytelling.

It is on whether we can accept Resnais's (and presumably scenarist Jorge Semprun's) attitude toward Diego that our own attitudes toward the movie will almost certainly be based. Diego the incorruptible failure, committed to irrelevance, is the very model of an aging liberal's idea of a good man. Can we go along with his glamorized melancholy (and the assumption that his political activity was once useful though now out of touch), or do we see it as a Frenchman's Hollywoodization of a lummox of a party hack? One might speculate that for some the futility of Diego's commitment has the beauty of making them feel there was no way they could have done anything anyway: Diego can only go slogging along on those same stupid errands, accomplishing nothing. The audience can transpose the elegy to the grateful hymn, "There but for some instinct of self-preservation. . . ."

In the most interesting sequence, Diego encounters a group of the young new left, who propose bombs to scare off the tourists who are supporting the Spanish economy, but he does not connect with them. He goes back to try to plot a general strike. (As that old actress used to say, "I thought it was so bad that I could only learn from experience that I refused to learn from it.") What a relief to the sentimental audience that their hero rejects such wild suggestions and goes back to passing out illegal pamphlets; they may look for one as a souvenir of their trip to Spain this summer.

In movies today, perhaps the clearest indication of how we are meant to feel about a character is the quality of his sex life. Diego has such high quality sex that when he goes to bed we hear a heavenly choir. Resnais provides him with a little sex kitten (Genevieve Bujold) as well as a handsome, mature mistress (Ingrid Thulin). Of course he doesn't make the overtures to the kitten: she propositions him and, being a gentleman, he doesn't turn her down. After all, he's human — which is the movie's explanation of all he does and doesn't do (and, as in Hollywood pictures, being human means giving in). In the bed sequence with the girl, the disconnected limbs of her body are treated abstractly for an amusing suggestiveness: toes, hands, thighs parting — it's so chic and economically done, it's very funny (and probably a conscious parody of the abstract treatment of body parts in *The Married Woman*). The contrasting sequence when Diego visits his mistress is chic, too, but is, unfortunately, not intended as parody but as the way it should be — satisfying, deep. Now the woman's torso is featured — her trunk — and she is no mere casual diversion, she is the true wife, the woman who waits, the woman who is too good to be anything but too good. It's a long way from the thirties and tunes like "I kissed a Communist, is my face red?" Now a woman gets a halo when she goes to bed with a Communist. Sex in this movie (and not only in this movie) is so uplifting and so solemnly sanctified, it seems to have taken the place of going to church. That soprano vocalizing reminds one of Colette's description of the courtesan who trilled when she was pretending to be thrilled.

Resnais and Semprun have hit upon perhaps the only way a radical can be acceptable as a screen hero: when he's too numb and apathetic to argue. And Yves Montand has the stoic manner of a man whose emotional and intellectual limits were set early — so that he's loyal to his old mistakes. We know, from past experience at the movies, that he would be about the same if he were playing a tired businessman or a State Department man carrying on a war he doesn't believe in, but he's good to watch anyway. He has that face that looks as if it's been lived in — not an actor's face — and he's got a bit of a pot that hasn't been hoisted into an actor's chest. Watching him in *La Guerre est finie* is like being with those people who are more convincing when you're with them than when you think about them afterward.

La Guerre est finie is a moderately good movie, but what I'm trying to get at here is how it works on the preconceptions of an audience, how a moderately good movie can be taken (by liberals in this case) to be an important work of art if it rubs them the right way.

Fifteen years ago Yves Montand appeared in a movie that *was* an existential melodrama, and the contrast between the toughness of Clouzot's *The Wages of Fear* (which was an art-house success) and the gentleness of *La Guerre est finie* (which is also an art-house success) suggests a change — a softening — in the audience. As *The Wages of Fear* has not played in this country for almost a decade, I'll attempt to refresh memories. It was made in France, though it re-creates a South American town with nearby American oil installations. The opening sequence shows us the town and its inhabitants — an insect heap, a final human melting pot of primitivism, corruption, and decadence, and without any civilizing elements. The only ambition of the Europeans trapped in it is to get enough money to escape. An oil well three hundred miles away has caught fire, and the fire might be put out by exploding it out with nitroglycerine. The oil company offers four men two thousand dollars each to drive two trucks loaded with explosives over primitive roads. The four men are Mario, a Corsican (Yves Montand); Jo, a Frenchman (Charles Vanel); Luigi, an Italian (Folco Lulli); and Bimba, a German (Peter Van Eyck). The body of the film deals with the men's responses to the crucial test of driving the trucks.

Jo has gone to extreme measures to get the chance to drive (possibly he has even murdered for the chance) and once in the truck he tries to run away. Mario drives the truck over Jo because he thinks that is the only way to get the truck through an oil-filled crater — and the truck stalls anyway; he has destroyed Jo for nothing. Bimba's extraordinary courage is rewarded: Luigi takes off his cap to him. A little while later they are both blown to bits.

Courage, caution are, finally, irrelevant to fate; they are human gestures — necessary but absurd. The truck with Bimba and Luigi explodes; it could just as easily have been the truck with Mario and Jo — and though theirs doesn't explode, they die anyway.

It is a senseless kind of human situation: the men are not even as flies to wanton boys; there is not even the control of careless malevolence. No one's to blame; destruction is impersonal. In this violent thriller-parable, human (that is to say, decent, civilized) gestures — whether based on decision or impulse — are all that is left to man; they appear to be desperate, absurd holdovers from some archaic human period when character had something to do with fate, or from the human delusion that it does.

Well, Diego has his gestures, too, but they are not all that is left to man: he's lost the facts involved. And so we may wonder why Resnais makes him a sad, classic hero — as if a man who went on doing something dumb long enough acquired nobility. *La Guerre est finie* is soaked in romantic defeatism, in a mushy poetry of hopelessness, in existentialism used decoratively to make a hero of a man who just got lost in the movement. *La Guerre est finie* is damp from the Marseilles fog of the French films of the thirties — which is what, in the fifties, we admired Clouzot for cleaning away.

꧁꧂꧁꧂꧁꧂

10:30 P.M. Summer

DID you have daring ideas for sophisticated sexual dramas when you were in high school, and then, realizing how ludicrously lurid they were, laugh at yourself whenever you thought of them? Well, not everybody discarded those moldy-gaudy fantasies, as the Tony Richardson-Jean Genet collaboration on *Mademoiselle* demonstrated. And now there's another of these movies to diddle by, *10:30 P.M. Summer* directed by Jules Dassin out of Marguerite Duras — too preposterously purple to be successfully blue. This fantasy of the international set is loaded with absurdly gorgeous photography, crowd scenes out of Goya, and pregnant close-ups (which have supplanted the old pregnant silences). The ads show three intertwined bodies — Melina Mercouri, Peter Finch, Romy Schneider — and the picture is about the agonized eroticism of a traveling *ménage à trois*. The pivot is Melina Mercouri who is like some great ravenous sex-obsessed witch; she has the wingspread to carry you off, though all she does is croak in her drag-queen baritone about the pain of living.

Sample dialogue — Romy to Melina: "Maria, what would you do if you came face to face with a murderer?" Melina: "I would take heem in my arms."

This is a long way from Janet Gaynor, though we may be hard put to say which is worse — the virgin that good boys were afraid to touch for fear she might break, or this grandiose apparition — too-much-woman — who would gurgle with passion while eating up little men, and now little women, too.

Movies always seem to be both behind and ahead of the culture. Though the sexual revolution has scarcely found its way onto the screen, and movies rarely deal with the simplest kinds of heterosexual life in our time, they're already treating bisexuality — like the kids who are on pot and discussing the merits of LSD before they've had their first beer. The extra-woman-in-the-house (which is said to be the latest alteration in the domestic arrangements of a number of analysts in Southern California) is turning up in other, unexpected places. I think this element was at least a partial source of the discomfort so many people felt about *Le Bonheur*. In addition to the obviously disturbing aspect of the film — the lack of personal differentiation in one woman taking the place of the other — there was, underneath, a breakdown also of sexual differentiation: the husband must have wanted the two women to love each other, also. He wanted them all to be one happy family. And *that,* given the simple bourgeois characters of *Le Bonheur,* is unsettling, while *10:30 P.M. Summer* with its world-weary trio is to howl at.

Ulysses

JOYCE wrote *Ulysses* in the form of a movie and that's probably why so many people, including Joyce himself, thought it should be made into one. In the modern novels which are influenced by movies the novelists describe what the characters say and do and where they are and what they see but rarely what they think. (And when they do think, it's not likely to be about abstract or large concepts, but very specifically — almost, one might say, photogenically.) But how does one photograph intellectual pride? Pride can be photographed (Autant-Lara did it in the Michèle Morgan–Françoise Rosay section of *The Seven Deadly Sins*), but *intellectual* pride? Zinnemann did it in the sequence of *The Nun's Story* when the nun was told to fail her examinations, but that was a simpler kind and there were actions planned to dramatize it. Joyce gives us the drama within Stephen's consciousness. The movie *Ulysses* can provide the meeting between Stephen and his sister when she is buying the penny French primer, but what made us *care* about that scene in the novel — the agenbite of inwit — is missing.

The actor Maurice Roeves looks a bit like Stephen-Joyce, but we can't see the guilt and emotion and mind that made him an artist. Leopold Bloom (Milo O'Shea), who is easier to represent, takes over — the Everyman whose thoughts are of food and sex and daily affairs. But how does one photograph *thoughts* about food or desire? Watching Bloom fry a kidney is a reminder of the passage beginning

Mr. Leopold Bloom ate with relish the inner organs of beasts and fowls. He liked thick giblet soup, nutty gizzards, a stuffed roast heart, liver slices fried with crustcrumbs, fried hencod's roes. Most of all he liked grilled mutton kidneys which gave to his palate a fine tang of faintly scented urine.

For those who don't know the passage it is only a dear, funny little man frying a kidney. Or, much worse, we see Bloom watching Gerty McDowell, and without her fantasies we have nothing.

The movie is an act of homage in the form of readings from the book plus illustrated slides, and though it has no life of its own, it provides some interesting facsimiles of Joyce's characters (Buck Mulligan, particularly), and some of the readings are very good. The movie clarifies the physical actions of the book — the comings and goings in town and nighttown, providing a surface map of the novel. A man of intelligence and taste, Joseph Strick could probably be an excellent movie producer. As a director, his ambitions are coordinate with his taste rather than his talent. He has taken few liberties with the material except the basic liberty of attemping it: conceptually this movie is so respectful, so pedestrian, so ordinary it might have been made by O'Shea's gentle cuckold Bloom. But, Everyman, why should we go with thee? We've already been there with Raimu and Pagnol and all those others who tried to convince us that those who lived close to the soil were warm, witty, and wise.

In one sense, perhaps the best thing about the movie is its total inadequacy: it shouldn't result in any damage to our feelings about the book because the images in the movie aren't strong enough to supplant our own. The visual imagery is uneven but mostly flat and weak, and the editing rhythm is both static and jerky: visually the movie never comes near to achieving an acceptable rhythmic equivalent for Joyce's prose. On the soundtrack are the lines we want to hear and it's good to be reminded of them, but they don't have the weight they had in the novel. They are merely quotations from a classic, well selected, intelligently read.

There is a widespread assumption that a film version of *Ulysses* must be an important film. But a movie director doesn't become great by association. Joseph Strick has gone from one brothel world to another — from *The Balcony* to *Ulysses* — and he has succeeded only in becoming culturally respectable. *The Balcony,* visually even flatter than *Ulysses,* had some sex drive in it. His *Ulysses,* though it's explicit in images and words, *is* respectable — which doesn't mean that this is an occasion for rejoicing about how-far-we-have-come. Although as lovers of the book we should be indebted to Judge Woolsey for his famous decision of 1933 which permitted us to obtain it lawfully, I never believed his concluding statement that "nowhere does it tend to be an aphrodisiac." He cleared it *legally* of exciting "sexually impure and lustful thoughts," and so we are grateful to him for all the gloriously impure, lustful thoughts we've had while reading it. But the movie is so lacking in sensuality that it's no wonder it has escaped prosecution. There's nothing in it to get excited about.

※※※※※

Persona

THERE is a brief passage in Ingmar Bergman's *Persona* — Bibi Andersson tells about a day and night of sex — that is so much more erotic than all of *Ulysses* that it demonstrates what *can* be done on the screen with told material. We do not need to see images of the beach and the boys and the return to the fiancé that she describes, because the excitement is in how she tells it. Bergman has the capacity to create images that set off reverberations: in the early part of *Summer Interlude* an old woman appears for just a moment on a road — walking — and this image, like the croquet game in *Smiles of a Summer Night,* seems to be suspended in time. In moments like these, Bergman is a great artist. In *Persona* Bibi Andersson's almost fierce reverie has that kind of beauty. As she goes on talking, with memories of summer and nakedness and pleasure in her words and the emptiness of her present in her face, we begin to hold our breath in fear that Bergman can't sustain this almost intolerably difficult sequence. But he does, and it builds and builds and is completed. It's one of the rare, truly erotic sequences on film.

Bergman's movies have almost always had some kind of show within the show: a ballet, a circus, a magic show, a bit of animation, many pieces of plays and even whole plays. In *Persona,* as in the very early *Prison,* Bergman involves us in the making of a movie. He gives us a movie within a movie, but he seems hardly to have made the *enclosing* movie, and then he throws away the inner movie. (I thought I even *felt* it go — at the repeated passage, when the director seems to be trying an alternate way of shooting a sequence.) It's a pity because the inner movie had begun to involve us in marvelous possibilities: an actress (Liv Ullmann) who has abandoned the power of speech is put in the care of a nurse (Bibi Andersson); and the nurse, like an analysand who becomes furious at the silence of the analyst, begins to vent her own emotional disturbances. In the dramatic material the women don't change identity; it is merely their roles that change as the nurse becomes hysterical and uncontrollable. But the two look very much alike, and Bergman plays with this resemblance photographically by suggestive combinations and superimpositions.

Most movies give so little that it seems almost barbarous to object to Bergman's not giving us more in *Persona,* but it is just because of the expressiveness and fascination of what we are given that the movie is so frustrating. Though it's possible to offer interpretations, I don't think that treating *Persona* as the pieces of a puzzle and trying to put them together will do much more than demonstrate ingenuity at guesswork. It's easy to say that the little boy reaching up to the screen is probably Bergman as a child; and he may also represent the nurse's aborted baby and/or the actress's rejected son. But for this kind of speculation (and one would have to go through almost every image in the movie this way) to have any purpose, there must be a structure of meanings in the work by which an interpretation can be validated; I don't think there is one in *Persona.* If there is, it is so buried that it doesn't function in the work. We respond to the image of the little boy — not because he's Bergman or an abortion but simply in terms of the quality and intensity of the image — but we don't know why it's in this film.

It may be that an open puzzle movie like this one, which affects some people very profoundly, permits them to project into it so much of themselves that what they think the movie is about has very little to do with what happens on the screen. This kind of projection — which we used to think of as the precritical responsiveness of the mass audience — is now common in the educated audience. People can be heard saying that they "didn't worry about whether it was good or bad," they "just let it happen to them." And if the educated audience is now coming around to the larger audience's way of seeing movies, I would suggest that they are also being sold in the same way as the larger audience, that advertising and the appearance of critical consensus it gives to certain movies are what lead people to "let" certain prestigious movies "happen to them," just as the larger audience lets an oversized musical spoof like *Thoroughly Modern Millie* happen to them. The idea is that "art" should be experienced, not criticized. There seems to be little sense that critical faculties are involved in experience, and that if they are not involved, advertising determines what is accepted as art.

Laurence Olivier as Othello

Othello with Laurence Olivier is a filmed record of the theatrical production; it would be our loss if we waited for posterity to discover it. Olivier's Negro Othello — deep voice with a trace of foreign music in it; happy, thick, self-satisfied laugh; rolling buttocks; grand and barbaric and, yes, a little lewd — almost makes this great, impossible play work. It has always made more than sense; now it almost makes sense, too — not only dramatic poetry, but a comprehensible play. Frank Finlay's pale, parched little Iago is not a plotting maniac who's lucky for theatrical convenience, but a man consumed with sexual jealousy and irrational hatred. And because Iago is consumed by sexual jealousy, he infects Othello with the same disease. Maggie Smith's Desdemona is strong and quiet and willful enough to have wanted Othello and gone after him. And Othello, who thought himself almost accepted by these civilized whites, is destroyed by primitive, irrational forces in them that he has no knowledge of. His "civilization" is based on theirs and goes because he believed in theirs.

Olivier is the most physical Othello imaginable. As a lord, this Othello is a little vulgar — too ingratiating, a boaster, an arrogant man. Reduced to barbarism, he shows us a maimed African prince inside the warrior-hero. Iago's irrationality has stripped him bare to a different kind of beauty. We are sorry to see it, and we are not sorry, either. To our eyes, the African prince is more beautiful in his isolation than the fancy courtier in his reflected white glory.

Part of the pleasure of the performance is, of course, the sheer feat of Olivier's transforming himself into a Negro; yet it is not wasted effort, not mere exhibitionism or actor's vanity, for what Negro actor at this stage in the world's history could dare bring to the role the effrontery that Olivier does, and which Negro actor could give it this reading? I saw Paul Robeson and he was not black as Olivier is; Finlay can hate Olivier in a way José Ferrer did not dare — indeed did not have the provocation — to hate

Robeson. Possibly Negro actors need to sharpen themselves on white roles before they can *play* a Negro. It is not enough to *be:* for great drama, it is the awareness that is everything.

Every time we single out the feature that makes Olivier a marvel — his lion eyes or the voice and the way it seizes on a phrase — he alters it or casts it off in some new role, and is greater than ever. It is no special asset, it is the devilish audacity and courage of this man. Olivier, who, for Othello, changed his walk, changed his talk, is a man close to sixty who, in an ordinary suit in an ordinary role, looks an ordinary man, and can look even smaller in a role like Archie Rice in *The Entertainer*. What is extraordinary is inside, and what is even more extraordinary is his determination to give it outer form. He has never leveled off; he goes on soaring.

Olivier once said of his interpretation of Henry V: "When you are young, you are too bashful to play a hero; you debunk it. It isn't until you're older that you can understand the pictorial beauty of heroism." And perhaps there is a tendency for people to debunk the kind of heroism necessary to develop your art in a society that offers so many rewards and honors to those who give up and sell out early at the highest market price. One might suspect that in a democratic society the public is on better terms with the mighty after they have fallen. Our mass media are full of the once mighty: they are called "celebrities." Olivier's presence on the screen is the pictorial beauty of heroism. Perhaps that is why we may leave the photographed version of *Othello* with a sense of exaltation and the wonder of sheer admiration.

This *Othello* is history already; it's something to remember. And *Othello* isn't even much of a "movie." Just a reasonably faithful (one assumes) record of a stage interpretation. After thirty-five years in movies and masterpiece upon masterpiece acclaimed in the theatre — every new season seems to bring the tidings that Olivier has exceeded himself as Oedipus, as Lear, in Chekhov — he still could not raise the money to do a real movie version of his Othello. And of his Macbeth, acclaimed as the greatest since — Macbeth, we have not even a record.

Olivier's greatness is in his acting; as a movie director, he is merely excellent and intelligent. Yet his Shakespearean performances deserve — at the minimum — the kind of movie he or other talented directors might do, what he brought to *Henry V, Hamlet, Richard III*. It is a scandal, an indictment of Anglo-American civilization and values, that eight million dollars can go into a spy spoof, twelve into a comic chase, twenty-seven into a spectacle, and for Olivier in *Othello,* we and history must content ourselves with a quickie recording process. And yet the joke is on the spoofs, chases and spectacles. *Othello* lives.

Yes, it's lovely that foundations give all that money to regional theatres, to training ballet students, to raising the pay of symphony orchestras, to encouraging the young and promising and possibly gifted, and that our government is talking about encouraging "standards of excellence" — that eerie schoolteacher's terminology that suggests magical measuring sticks. But do artists have to *aspire* to "excellence" to get help? Where is the help when they have overachieved their promise? Where is the help when Orson Welles botched his great movie version of *Othello* for want of cash, when Olivier can only record a stage production on film? What, then, is the purpose of all the encouragement of "creativity"?

The movies, the one art that people don't have to be encouraged, prodded, or "stimulated" to enjoy, which they go to without the path being greased by education and foundations, are still at the mercy of the economics of the mass market, which have broken the heart of almost every artist who has tried to work in the movies.

The Sound of . . .

The Sound of Music and The Singing Nun

The Singing Nun will make you realize how good Fred Zinnemann's *The Nun's Story* was. Although the theme, the conflict and even the story line are similar, *The Singing Nun* reduces them to smiles, twinkles, banalities and falseness. It is almost a parody of *The Nun's Story* and, of course, without the courage of the conclusion of that earlier thoughtful, subtle film. Though *The Singing Nun* draws its ideas from *The Nun's Story,* its inspiration is obviously that movie phenomenon the trade press now refers to (very respectfully) as *The Sound of Money.* And perhaps to get at what goes on in a movie like *The Singing Nun,* we need to look at that phenomenon, which is so often called "wholesome" but which is probably going to be the single most repressive influence on artistic freedom in movies for the next few years.

The success of a movie like *The Sound of Music* makes it even more difficult for anyone to try to do anything worth doing, anything relevant to the modern world, anything inventive or expressive. The banks, the studios, the producers will want to give the public what it seems to crave. The more money these "wholesome" movies make, the less wholesome will the state of American movies be. "The opium of the audience," Luis Buñuel, the Spanish director, once said, "is conformity." And nothing is more degrading and ultimately destructive to artists than supplying the narcotic.

What is it that makes millions of people buy and like *The Sound of Music* — a tribute to "freshness" that is so mechanically engineered, so shrewdly calculated that the background music rises, the already soft focus blurs and melts, and, upon the instant, you can hear all those noses blowing in the theatre? Of course, it's well done for what it is: that is to say, those who made it are experts at manipulating responses. They're the Pavlovs of movie-making: they turn us into dogs that salivate on signal. When the cruel father sees the light and says, "You've brought music back into the house," who can resist the pull at the emotions? It's that same tug at the heartstrings we feel when Lassie comes home or when the blind heroine sees for the first time; it is a simple variant of that surge of warmth we feel when a child is reunited with his parents. It's basic, and there are probably few of us who don't respond. But it is the easiest and perhaps the most primitive kind of emotion that we are made to feel. The worst despots in history, the most cynical purveyors of mass culture respond at *this* level and may feel pleased at how tenderhearted they *really* are because they do. This kind of response has as little to do with generosity of feeling as being stirred when you hear a band has to do with patriotism.

I think it is not going too far to say that when an expensive product of modern technology like *The Sound of Music* uses this sort of "universal" appeal, it is because nothing could be safer, nothing could be surer. Whom could it offend? Only those of us who, *despite the fact that we may respond,* loathe being manipulated in this way and are aware of how self-indulgent and cheap and ready-made are the responses we are made to feel. And we may become even more aware of the way we have been *used* and turned into emotional and aesthetic imbeciles when we hear ourselves humming those sickly, goody-goody songs. The audience for a movie of this kind becomes the lowest common denominator of feeling: a sponge. The heroine leaves the nuns at the fence as she enters the cathedral to be married. Squeezed again, and the moisture comes out of thousands — millions — of eyes and noses.

And the phenomenon at the center of the monetary phenomenon? Julie Andrews, with the clean, scrubbed look and the unyieldingly high spirits; the good sport who makes the best of everything; the girl who's so unquestionably good that she carries this one dimension like a shield. The perfect, perky schoolgirl, the adorable tomboy, the gawky colt. Sexless, inhumanly happy, the sparkling maid, a mind as clean and well brushed as her teeth. What is she? Merely the ideal heroine for the best of all possible worlds. And that's what *The Sound of Music* pretends we live in.

Audiences are transported into a world of operetta cheerfulness and calendar art. You begin to feel as if you've never got out of school. Up there on the screen, they're all in their places with bright, shining faces. Wasn't there perhaps one little Von Trapp who didn't want to sing his head off, or who screamed that he wouldn't act out little glockenspiel routines for Papa's party guests, or who got nervous and threw up if he had to get on a stage? No, nothing mars this celebration of togetherness. Not only does this family sing together, they play ball together. This is the world teachers used to pretend (and maybe still pretend?) was the real world. It's the world in which the governess conquers all. It's the big lie, the sugarcoated lie that people seem to want to eat. They even seem to think they should feed it to their kids, that it's healthy, wonderful "family entertainment."

And this is the sort of attitude that makes a critic feel that maybe it's all hopeless. Why not just send the director, Robert Wise, a wire: "You win, I give up," or, rather, "We both lose, we all lose."

Yet there was a spider on the valentine: the sinister, unpleasant, archly decadent performance Christopher Plummer gives as the baron, he of the thin, twisted smile — my candidate for the man least likely to be accepted as a hero. Even the monstrously ingenious technicians who made this movie couldn't put together a convincing mate for Super-Goody Two-Shoes. The dauntless heroine surmounts this obstacle: in the romantic scenes, she makes love to herself. And why not? We never believed for a moment that love or marriage would affect her or change her. She was already perfection.

Debbie Reynolds, as the character based on Soeur Sourire in *The Singing Nun,* is less than perfection. Her eyes are not so clear and bright, indeed they're rather anxious and, yes, almost bleary; and her singing isn't pure and pretty, it's sort of tacky and ordinary. So is the whole production. Henry Koster doesn't succeed even in making it very convincingly "wholesome." The religion is a familiar kind of Hollywood Christianity. The nuns are even more smiley and giggly — like a mush-headed schoolteacher's dream of ideally happy schoolchildren; Ricardo Montalban is a simperingly simple priest; and though Agnes Moorehead plays a nun like a witch, she is more than balanced by Greer Garson as the Mother Prioress. With her false eyelashes and her richly condescending manner, Greer Garson can turn any line of dialogue into incomparable cant. It's a gift, of a kind.

The people in *The Singing Nun* behave like the animals in a Disney movie: they are so cute and so full of little tricks. There are chintzy little pedagogical songs that are supposed to be full of *joy,* and there is Debbie's excruciating humility. "I have a lot to learn," she tells us; but we didn't need to be told. She gives up her singing career — which was giving her too much attention and adoration — in order to find her simple faith again. And so, at the end, we see her working as a nurse in Africa, posed like a madonna holding a Negro baby, surrounded by attentive, adoring Africans. . . . But then, of course, this movie is the kind of spiritual exercise in which the nuns say a little prayer for Ed Sullivan every day.

Why am I so angry about these movies? Because the shoddy falseness of *The Singing Nun* and the luxuriant falseness of *The Sound of Music* are part of the sentimental American tone that makes honest work almost impossible. It is not only that people who accept this kind of movie tend to resent work which says that this is not the best of all possible worlds, but that people who are gifted give up the effort to say anything. They attune themselves to *The Sound of Money.*

Movies for Young Children

Born Free and Around the World
Under the Sea

I HAVE a friend who says, "Business is business, and anything you do in it is fair as long as you don't cheat children." But there's such a good profit in cheating children that businessmen can easily deceive themselves about what they're doing. They can even publicize themselves into honors and awards for it.

But parents shouldn't fall into the trap. Walt Disney's *The Ugly Dachshund* isn't a movie: it's a pacifier. After the interminable first half hour, I walked out. Yes, the children in the audience were laughing; but it sounded like the forced, sickly, attention-getting "childish laughter" of kids who are influenced, indeed corrupted, by their parents' insipid notions of what they should enjoy. A movie like this is supposed to be a treat for them, and so they'd better enjoy it.

It's easy to say that it's not intended for adults (meaning it isn't fit for them) but that kids will love it. But I can't think of a single *good* "children's" picture that intelligent adults can't enjoy, and I see no reason why we should not respect our children at least as much as we respect ourselves.

Before Disney began to dominate this market, it used to be assumed that good adventure movies could be enjoyed by adults and children; it was only after adventure movies and domestic comedies were reduced to formulas and silliness that this split developed between what *you* could enjoy and what you had to take your children to.

There's so much written about what slaves to advertising and group patterns teen-agers are; but parents often appear to be the worst slaves of all — letting advertisers convince them that children's movies must be innocuous and that their children will be deprived if they don't take them to every Disney picture. And even parents who are fed up with these pictures may be heard asking helplessly, "But what else is there to take our kids to?"

If you're interested in some alternatives, here are a few suggestions. These are some movies that can be shown at schools, clubs or Saturday afternoon theatre matinées: Albert Lamorisse's *White Mane* (which is infinitely more magical and beautiful than his better-known *The Red Balloon*); Arne Sucksdorff's superbly photographed nature study *The Great Adventure;* Robert Flaherty's early classic *Nanook of the North;* the Disney documentary *The African Lion,* which isn't hoked up too much; Karel Zeman's comic-fantasy *The Deadly Invention* (released in the United States as *The Fabulous World of Jules Verne*).

And, of course, there are all those marvelous adventure films. Why not have the pleasure of reliving some of the adventure movies of your youth and sharing your own sense of excitement with the younger generation — just as you do when you read them books you remember from your childhood?

At some time or other, haven't you tried to tell your children about the great moment in *The Adventures of Robin Hood* when Errol Flynn strode into the castle with a deer on his shoulders, or about the way Alan Hale, as Little John, roared with laughter? Perhaps you tried to describe the way Sam Jaffe in *Gunga Din* blew that beautiful bugle call? Maybe you tried to tell them about Cochise and the lovely Indian girl in *Broken Arrow,* or you tried to describe the beauty of the acrobatics in the buccaneer comedy *The Crimson Pirate?* Perhaps you've even taught them the little jingle Leslie Howard recited as the Scarlet Pimpernel?

The old movies will be as new to your children as *The Ugly Dachshund* or other movies of this ilk. And even if they've seen pieces of them on television, the children may be all the more pleased with the familiarity — just as they want to hear a story told over again. The older movies will probably be more new to the children than current ones, because by the time the movie companies have finished their saturation advertising, the kids know just about every detail of a new movie, anyway.

You may rediscover the pleasures of movies like *National Velvet, The African Queen* or *Ivanhoe* as your children and your friends' children discover them. And it's possible, too, that this kind of movie — with its excitements and plot anticipations — may help children develop the story sense, that sense of narrative structure which is becoming almost vestigial in the television era, yet is so necessary for the enjoyment of the traditional English novel, and which may even be necessary for a sense of history.

Born Free has the same basic story material as some of the fair to very good old child-loves-animal, child-loses-animal movies like *My Friend Flicka, Lassie Come Home, The Yearling,* and *Goodbye, My Lady.* You may recall that, for example, *My Friend Flicka* was about a dreamy boy (Roddy McDowall) and his strange colt, Flicka, and his West Point-type father, who understood neither boy nor horse. *Born Free* has a rather angular Englishwoman with a strange penchant for female lions, and although her coy, big, puppy-dog husband understands her (which may put him one up on the audience), they are faced with the necessity of putting their Elsa in a zoo or setting her free.

When it comes to animal movies, I'm as big a fool as anybody, and I stupidly hoped for a lot. The letdown was almost immediate: unfortunately for *Born Free,* the art of the film was not born yesterday. As a piece of movie-making, *Born Free* can't compare with the good films in this genre: the animal trainers must have worked very hard indeed, but weren't there any trained cameramen around? It's bad enough that instead of the anticipated animal lore, we get a lion that is just a big sweet puttytat; but there aren't even the visual delights of seeing animals beautifully photographed. Did the company really go to Kenya to shoot this movie? It looks as if it were made in the local park — with the two happy smiling Negroes stuck in for "authenticity."

After we have seen the grandeur of a movie like *Lords of the Forest* (released in the United States as *Masters of the Congo Jungle*), a vast and visually elegant record of the interrelations of men, animals and birds in Africa, with young Watusi girls performing a ritual dance in imitation of the courtship of the crowned cranes, how can we take pleasure in this drab affair that looks like a home movie?

The subject matter of *Born Free* touches the anxieties of all of us who keep animals: what would happen to our pets if we were forced to give them up or if they were lost? We develop these anxieties as part of our responsibility to the other kinds of living creatures we have somehow, perhaps even without thinking about it, made dependent on us and on our way of life. And the possible solutions are all ghastly — painful both for the animals and for the people. I wish that *Born Free,* like so many of the Disney movies, did not degrade our anxieties by treating us as if we were the sort of people who stick pink bows on animals and exclaim, "How cute!"

Is it obligatory for animal movies to jerk tears about a child or, even worse, to be a tear-jerking account of a trembling, stiff-upper-lipped, emotionally frustrated woman's obsession — as if there were no real problem?

And is it necessary to assume that we as audience have so little curiosity about animal life that we can care about an animal only in relation to its owner's emotional problems? *Born Free* begs the fundamental questions about men's responsibility to their pets and animals in general, by providing the basis for thinking that the heroine wouldn't be so involved with animals if she just had some children of her own. And in that way, the audience is let off the hook: they can feel she is concerned about animals because there is something the matter with her. They can feel sorry for her.

Movies are a great medium for showing us other ways of life, human as well as animal. Yet the market-oriented movie producers are so convinced that audiences want only the same old melodramatized versions of existence that not only are stories set in foreign countries distorted to make other people over in our image, but even animal behavior is sentimentalized to reassure us in our ignorance. They show us animal behavior which the trainers know does not mean what the movie audience will take it to mean, in order to deceive us. Movies like these assume that we in the audience are so idiotically narcissistic that we will not be interested in animals unless they are shown as funny, four-legged human children.

If a movie has a reason for being made — besides the hope of revenue — we can forgive the kind of amateurishness and ineptitude that blight *Born Free*. For example, *Serengeti Shall Not Die* was a straightforward picture, made by Dr. Bernhard Grzimek, director of the Frankfurt zoo, and his twenty-four-year-old son, Michael, to publicize the imminent danger of destruction of the last great wild animal herds left in the world. Dr. Grzimek went on to complete the film after his son, who appears in much of the footage, was killed when a vulture struck the small plane he was flying. The profits were contributed to the Serengeti National Park, in Tanganyika — which is the largest wild animal preserve in the world. The Grzimeks established that the Serengeti herds, usually estimated at a million animals, numbered fewer than four hundred thousand. And by capturing and marking zebra, wildebeest and other game, they were able to trace the migrations of the herds and to estimate that if the new boundaries proposed by the government were set up, the herds, already decimated by poachers and hunters, would have to leave the preserve at certain times of the year or starve. And if they left the preserve, they would be exposed to organized slaughter.

The message of the picture is simple and clear: African wild game — wonders and treasures of the earth — will soon be as extinct as the great herds of North America unless those who care do something to save them. The guilt for the destruction in Africa is revealed as both the black man's and the white man's. Within the Serengeti Park, the Masai tribesmen use wire snares and kill with poisoned arrows. But the white hunters have set a glorious example: in one sequence, we see a vast storehouse full of what look like tree stumps. They are elephants' feet being made into souvenir wastebaskets for civilized white people.

Serengeti Shall Not Die is not a highly organized or expensive film, but what it lacks in cinematographic skills, it more than compensates for in moral beauty. And the solid information it provides, to children and adults, and its undisguised message of indignation and its cry for help are an appeal to our intelligence. It demonstrates that there are good, brave causes left.

Around the World Under the Sea pretends to be about a good, brave cause. And the ten-year-old boy who accompanied me knew all about it: the mission of the submarine *Hydronaut* was to plant a network of seismic warning devices on the ocean floor, so that countries could be alerted about the direction of impending earthquakes and tidal waves. He was as disappointed as I when the movie slighted the scientific material for more conventional interpersonal byplay and a treasure hunt. It didn't live up to its title, either.

Does sea life differ greatly in different parts of the world? We never find out, because most of the time we're looking at a group of TV stars (Brian Kelly of "Flipper," David McCallum of "The Man from U.N.C.L.E.," Lloyd Bridges of "Sea Hunt," Marshall Thompson of "Daktari") going through the motions that their fans presumably enjoy seeing them go through. In olden movie times, the one woman on an expedition was the brilliant scientist's daughter or the bride seeking her lost groom. Now she's Shirley Eaton of *Goldfinger,* the shady-lady as scientist, with several of the men from her past right on that little *Hydronaut*. She wears diving gear with an uplift so sharply pointed she could probably spear two fish at a time; but her weapon turns out to be a hypodermic, which she keeps inserting lovingly into the muscular arms of her co-stars.

Around the World Under the Sea is competently made and intermittently entertaining; but it assumes we go to the movies for just a bigger-screen, brighter-colored version of what is available on television series shows. It provides a little melodrama, a little science fiction, a good monster (a giant moray eel), and some of the same kind of eerily magical underwater comic-strip action as *Thunderball*. But except for the rare shots, like the beautiful one of water so full of fish it's like a sea of grass, there is almost nothing of that great camera subject: the iridescent universe of undersea life.

Movie excursions undersea have too often been so mystic and didactic that we aren't allowed a look at anything without being told that each gelatinous blob reveals God's purpose; but there have been some good documentaries, like *Hunters of the Deep,* in which the camera follows the antique creatures of the sea — lolling sea elephants, gloomy mantas, giant groupers — and the soundtrack feeds our curiosity with unpretentious information. And the Cousteau films, even though they're strong on mystery and self-congratulation and weak on what and where, are so visually opulent that we can feast our eyes and imagination, if not our minds.

SOME SUGGESTED MOVIES FOR CHILDREN,
AVAILABLE IN 16 MM.

(Rental rates are from the catalogues current in 1966.)

The Adventures of Robin Hood. Errol Flynn, Olivia de Havilland, Basil Rathbone; color; 102 minutes. Brandon $27.50; Twyman $30.00; Films Inc. $35.00.

The African Lion. Disney True-Life Adventure; color; 72 minutes. AFC $24.50; Films Inc. $24.50; Twyman $24.50.

Anchors Aweigh. Gene Kelly, Frank Sinatra; color; 140 minutes. Films Inc. $42.50; Brandon $45.00.

The Bank Dick. W. C. Fields; 73 minutes. UWF $35.00.

Beau Geste. Gary Cooper, Ray Milland, Robert Preston; 114 minutes. UWF $35.00.

Broken Arrow. James Stewart, Jeff Chandler, Debra Paget; color; 93 minutes. Films Inc. $35.00.

Captain Blood. Errol Flynn, Olivia de Havilland, Basil Rathbone; 98 minutes. Twyman $20.00; Brandon $17.50; Films Inc. $22.50.

The Charge of the Light Brigade. Errol Flynn, Olivia de Havilland; 115 minutes. Brandon $17.50; Contemporary $17.50; Films Inc. $22.50; Twyman $20.00.

A Day at the Races. Marx Brothers; 109 minutes. Films Inc. $30.00; Brandon $32.50.

The Day the Earth Stood Still. Michael Rennie, Patricia Neal; 92 minutes. Films Inc. $25.00.

Days of Thrills and Laughter. Robert Youngson silent comedy compilation; 93 minutes. Films Inc. $32.50; Brandon $32.50.

Duck Soup. Marx Brothers; 72 minutes. UWF $35.00.

The Fabulous World of Jules Verne (*The Deadly Invention*). Embassy 16 mm. Division.

The General. Keaton; silent; 80 minutes. MG $25.00.

The Golden Age of Comedy. Robert Youngson silent comedy compilation; 85 minutes. AFC $20.00; Contemporary $20.00; Twyman $20.00; Brandon $20.00.

Go West. Marx Brothers; 80 minutes. Brandon $32.50.

The Great Adventure. Arne Sucksdorff documentary; 75 minutes. Contemporary $15.00. Also available free from many public library systems.

Gunga Din. Cary Grant, Douglas Fairbanks, Jr., Victor McLaglen; 107 minutes. Films Inc. $22.50.

Horse Feathers. Marx Brothers; 69 minutes. UWF $35.00.

Hunters of the Deep. Documentary; color; 64 minutes. Twyman $30.00.

The Incredible Shrinking Man. Grant Williams; 92 minutes. UWF $20.00. Not for the very little ones.

It's a Wonderful Life. James Stewart, Donna Reed; 130 minutes. Twyman $25.00.

Ivanhoe. Robert Taylor, Elizabeth Taylor, Joan Fontaine; color; 106 minutes. Films Inc. $35.00.

Journey to the Center of the Earth. Pat Boone, James Mason, Arlene Dahl; color; 132 minutes. Films Inc. $35.00.

Jumbo. Doris Day, Jimmy Durante, Martha Raye; color; 121 minutes. Films Inc. $35.00.

Jungle Book. Sabu; color; 115 minutes. Twyman $37.50.

King Kong. Bruce Cabot, Fay Wray; 111 minutes. Films Inc. $25.00; Brandon $32.50.

King Solomon's Mines. Deborah Kerr, Stewart Granger; color; 102 minutes. Films Inc. $35.00. Early part frightening to very young children.

Kon Tiki. Documentary; 80 minutes. Contemporary $32.50. More for boys than girls.

Lassie Come Home. Roddy McDowall, Elizabeth Taylor, Donald Crisp; color; 90 minutes. Films Inc. $35.00.

The Little Fugitive. Richie Andrusco; 75 minutes. Twyman $20.00.

The Lives of a Bengal Lancer. Gary Cooper, Franchot Tone; 111 minutes. UWF $22.50.

Man of Aran. Flaherty documentary; 70 minutes. Contemporary $25.00.
Man with a Million. Based on a Mark Twain story; Gregory Peck; color; 90 minutes. Twyman $30.00; AFC $25.00.
March of the Wooden Soldiers (Babes in Toyland). Laurel and Hardy; 78 minutes. Contemporary $25.00; AFC $15.00; Twyman $22.50. Note: Twyman print deletes horror scenes from end of film.
Meet Me in St. Louis. Judy Garland, Margaret O'Brien, Mary Astor; color; 113 minutes. Films Inc. $35.00; Brandon $45.00.
Monkey Business. Marx Brothers; 81 minutes. UWF $35.00.
Mr. Hulot's Holiday. Jacques Tati; English version; 90 minutes. Continental $60.00.
My Friend Flicka. Roddy McDowall, Preston Foster, Rita Johnson; color; 90 minutes. Films Inc. $35.00.
Nanook of the North. Flaherty documentary; silent with music and narration added in 1939; 55 minutes. Contemporary $25.00. Also available from many public library systems.
National Velvet. Elizabeth Taylor, Mickey Rooney; color; 123 minutes. Films Inc. $35.00.
Never Give a Sucker an Even Break. W. C. Fields; 63 minutes. UWF $35.00.
A Night at the Opera. Marx Brothers; 93 minutes. Contemporary $27.50; Films Inc. $30.00; Brandon $32.50.
Roman Holiday. Audrey Hepburn, Gregory Peck, Eddie Albert; 118 minutes. Films Inc. $25.00; Brandon $45.00.
The Sea Hawk. Errol Flynn, Brenda Marshall, Claude Rains; 120 minutes. Films Inc. $22.50; Twyman $20.00; Brandon $17.50.
Serengeti Shall Not Die. Documentary. Allied Artists 16 mm Division, 165 W. 46 St., New York, N. Y.
The Silent World. Cousteau documentary; color; 86 minutes. Brandon $27.50; Contemporary $27.50; Twyman $30.00; AFC $25.00.
Singin' in the Rain. Gene Kelly, Donald O'Connor, Debbie Reynolds: color; 103 minutes. Films Inc. $35.00; Brandon $50.00.
The Thief of Bagdad. Sabu, Conrad Veidt and Rex Ingram; color; 106 minutes. Twyman $37.50.
Thirty Years of Fun. Robert Youngson silent comedy compilation; 85 minutes. Films Inc. $32.50; Brandon $32.50.
The Time Machine. Rod Taylor, Yvette Mimieux; color; 103 minutes. Films Inc. $30.00.
A Tree Grows in Brooklyn. Dorothy McGuire, Peggy Ann Garner, Joan Blondell; 128 minutes. Films Inc. $22.50; Twyman $35.00.
When Comedy Was King. Robert Youngson comedy compilation; 81 minutes. Contemporary $20.00; Films Inc. $32.50; Twyman $35.00; Brandon $32.50.
White Mane. Lamorisse film; 39 minutes. Contemporary $22.50. Also available from many public library systems.
World Without Sun. Cousteau documentary; color; 91 minutes. Twyman $52.50. Also available from Brandon, Contemporary and AFC.
The Yearling. Gregory Peck, Jane Wyman, Claude Jarman, Jr.; color; 135 minutes. Films Inc. $35.00.

If you send for the distributors' catalogues, you may turn up all sorts of movies you remember with pleasure — for example, musicals like *Where's Charley?* with Ray Bolger, or *Calamity Jane* with Howard Keel and Doris Day, or *Annie Get Your Gun* with Betty Hutton; or Westerns like *The Plainsman* with Gary Cooper and Jean Arthur, or *Destry Rides Again* with Marlene Dietrich and James Stewart; or comedies like *Million Dollar Legs* with Jack Oakie and W. C. Fields (not to be confused with a later film of the same title featuring Betty Grable), or *Mr. Deeds Goes to Town* with Gary Cooper and Jean Arthur.

Several of the principal distributors' codes and addresses:

AFC: Audio Film Center, 10 Fiske Place, Mt. Vernon, New York 10550; 2138 East 75th Street, Chicago, Illinois 60649; and 406 Clement Street, San Francisco, California 94118.

Brandon: Brandon Films, Inc., 221 West 57th Street, New York, New York 10019; 20 East Huron Street, Chicago, Illinois 60611; and 381 Bush Street, San Francisco, California 94104.

Contemporary: Contemporary Films, Inc., 267 West 25th Street, New York, New York 10001; 614 Davis Street, Evanston, Illinois 60201; and 1211 Polk Street, San Francisco, California 94109.

Continental: Continental 16, Inc., 241 East 34th Street, New York, New York 10016; 614 Davis Street, Evanston, Illinois 60201; and 1211 Polk Street, San Francisco, California 94109.

MG: Em Gee Film Library, 3246 Veteran Avenue, Los Angeles, California 90034.

Films Inc.: Films, Incorporated, 38 West 32nd Street, New York, New York 10001; 161 Massachusetts Avenue, Boston, Massachusetts 02115; 277 Pharr Road N.E., Atlanta, Georgia 30305; 4420 Oakton Street, Skokie, Illinois 60076; 1414 Dragon Street, Dallas, Texas 75207; 5625 Hollywood Boulevard, Hollywood, California 90028; and 2129 N.E. Broadway, Portland, Oregon 97232.

Twyman: Twyman Films, Inc., 329 Salem Avenue, Dayton, Ohio 45401.

UWF: United World Films, Inc., 221 Park Avenue South, New York, New York 10003; 287 Techwood Drive, N.W., Atlanta, Georgia 30313; 542 South Dearborn Street, Chicago, Illinois 60605; 6434 Maple Avenue, Dallas, Texas 75235; 1025 North Highland Avenue, Los Angeles, California 90038; and 5023 N.E. Sandy Boulevard, Portland, Oregon 97213.

IV

Careers

Marlon Brando:
An American Hero

THE history of the motion-picture industry might be summed up as the development from the serials with the blade in the sawmill moving closer and closer to the heroine's neck, to modern movies with the laser beam zeroing in on James Bond's crotch. At this level, the history of movies is a triumph of technology. I'm not putting down this kind of movie: I don't know anybody who doesn't enjoy it more or less at some time or other. But I wouldn't be much interested if that were the only kind of movie, any more than I'd be interested if all movies were like *Last Year at Marienbad* or *The Red Desert* or *Juliet of the Spirits*. What of the other kinds?

While American enthusiasm for movies has never been so high, and even while teachers prepare to recognize film-making as an art, American movies have never been so contemptible. In other parts of the world there has been a new golden age: great talents have fought their way through in Japan, India, Sweden, Italy, France; even in England there has been something that passes for a renaissance. But not here: American enthusiasm is fed largely by foreign films, memories, and innocence. The tragic or, depending on your point of view, pitiful history of American movies in the last fifteen years may be suggested by a look at the career of Marlon Brando.

It used to be said that great clowns, like Chaplin, always wanted to play Hamlet, but what happens in this country is that our Hamlets, like John Barrymore, turn into buffoons, shamelessly, pathetically mocking their public reputations. Bette Davis has made herself lovable by turning herself into a caricature of a harpy — just what, in one of her last good roles, as Margo Channing in *All About Eve,* she feared she was becoming. The women who were the biggest stars of the forties are either retired, semi-retired, or, like Davis, Crawford, and de Havilland, have become the mad queens of Grand Guignol in the sixties, grotesques and comics, sometimes inadvertently.

Marlon Brando's career indicates the new speed of these processes. Brando, our most powerful young screen actor, the only one who suggested tragic force, the major protagonist of contemporary American themes in the fifties, is already a self-parodying comedian.

I mean by protagonist the hero who really strikes a nerve — not a Cary Grant who delights with his finesse, nor mushy heartwarmers like Gary Cooper and James Stewart with their blubbering sincerity (sometimes it seemed that the taller the man, the smaller he pretended to be; that was his notion of being "ordinary" and "universal" and "real"), but men whose intensity on the screen stirs an intense reaction in the audience. Not Gregory Peck or Tyrone Power or Robert Taylor with their conventional routine heroics, but James Cagney or Edward G. Robinson in the gangster films, John Garfield in the Depression movies, Kirk Douglas as a postwar heel. These men are not necessarily better actors, but through the accidents of casting and circumstances or because of what they themselves embodied or projected, they *meant* something important to us. A brilliant actor like Jason Robards, Jr., may never become a protagonist of this kind unless he gets a role in which he embodies something new and relevant to the audience.

Protagonists are always loners, almost by definition. The big one to survive the war was the Bogart figure — the man with a code (moral, aesthetic, chivalrous) in a corrupt society. He had, so to speak, inside knowledge of the nature of the enemy. He was a sophisticated, urban version of the Westerner who, classically, knew both sides of the law and was tough enough to go his own way and yet, romantically, still do right.

Brando represented a reaction against the postwar mania for security. As a protagonist, the Brando of the early fifties had no code, only his instincts. He was a development from the gangster leader and the outlaw. He was antisocial because he knew society was crap; he was a hero to youth because he was strong enough not to take the crap. (In England it was thought that *The Wild One* would incite adolescents to violence.)

There was a sense of excitement, of danger in his presence, but perhaps his special appeal was in a kind of simple conceit, the conceit of tough kids. There was humor in it — swagger and arrogance that were vain and childish, and somehow seemed very American. He was explosively dangerous without being "serious" in the sense of having ideas. There was no theory, no cant in his leadership. He didn't care about social position or a job or respectability, and because he didn't care he was a big man; for what is less attractive, what makes a man smaller, than his worrying about his status? Brando represented a contemporary version of the free American.

Because he had no code, except an aesthetic one — a commitment to a *style* of life — he was easily betrayed by those he trusted. There he was, the new primitive, a Byronic Dead End Kid, with his quality of vulnerability.

His acting was so physical — so exploratory, tentative, wary — that we could sense with him, feel him pull back at the slightest hint of rebuff. We in the audience felt protective: we knew how lonely he must be in his assertiveness. Who even in hell wants to be an outsider? And he was no intellectual who could rationalize it, learn somehow to accept it, to live with it. He could only feel it, act it out, be "The Wild One" — and God knows how many kids felt, "That's the story of my life."

Brando played variations on rebel themes: from the lowbrow, disturbingly inarticulate brute, Stanley Kowalski, with his suggestions of violence waiting behind the slurred speech, the sullen face, to his Orpheus standing before the judge in the opening scene of *The Fugitive Kind,* unearthly, mythic, the rebel as artist, showing classic possibilities he was never to realize (or has not yet realized).

He was our angry young man — the delinquent, the tough, the rebel — who stood at the center of our common experience. When, as Terry Malloy in *On the Waterfront,* he said to his brother, "Oh Charlie, oh Charlie . . . you don't understand. I could have had class. I could have been a contender. I could have been somebody, instead of a bum — which is what I am," he spoke for all our failed hopes. It was the great American lament, of Broadway, of Hollywood, as well as of the docks.

I am describing the Brando who became a star, not the man necessarily, but the boy-man he projected, and also the publicity and the come-on. The publicity had a built-in ambivalence. Though the fan magazines might describe him alluringly as dreamy, moody, thin-skinned, easily hurt, gentle, intense, unpredictable, hating discipline, a defender of the underdog, other journalists and influential columnists were not so sympathetic toward what this suggested.

It is one of the uglier traditions of movie business that frequently when a star gets big enough to want big money and artistic selection or control of his productions, the studios launch large-scale campaigns designed to cut him down to an easier-to-deal-with size or to supplant him with younger, cheaper talent. Thus, early in movie history the great Lillian Gish was derided as unpopular in the buildup of the young Garbo (by the *same* studio), and in newspapers all over the country Marilyn Monroe, just a few weeks before her death, was discovered to have no box-office draw. The gossip columnists serve as the shock troops with all those little items about how so-and-so is getting a big head, how he isn't taking the advice of the studio executives who know best, and so forth.

In the case of Brando, the most powerful ladies were especially virulent because they were obviously part of what he was rebelling against; in flouting their importance, he might undermine their position with other new stars who might try to get by without kowtowing to the blackmailing old vultures waiting to pounce in the name of God, Motherhood, and Americanism. What was unusual in Brando's case were the others who joined in the attack.

In 1957, Truman Capote, having spent an evening with Brando and then a year writing up that evening (omitting his own side of the conversation and interjecting interpretations), published "The Duke in His Own Domain" in the *New Yorker*. The unwary Brando was made to look public ass number one. And yet the odd thing about this interview was that Capote, in his supersophistication, kept using the most commonplace, middlebrow evidence and arguments against him — for example, that Brando in his egotism was not impressed by Joshua Logan as a movie director. (The matter for astonishment was that Capote *was* — or was willing to use anything to make his literary exercise more effective.) Despite Capote's style and venomous skill, it is he in this interview, not Brando, who equates money and success with real importance and accomplishment. His arrows fit snugly into the holes they have made only if you accept the usual middlebrow standards of marksmanship.

It was now open season on Brando: Hollis Alpert lumbered onto the pages of *Cosmopolitan* to attack him for not returning to the stage to become a great actor — as if the theatre were the citadel of art. *What* theatre? Was Brando really wrong in feeling that movies are more relevant to our lives than the dead theatre which so many journalists seem to regard as the custodian of integrity and creativity? David Susskind was shocked that a mere actor like Brando should seek to make money, might even dare to consider his own judgment and management preferable to that of millionaire producers. Dwight Macdonald chided Brando for not being content to be a craftsman: "Mr. Brando has always aspired to something Deeper and More Significant, he has always fancied himself as like an intellectual" — surely a crime he shares with Mr. Macdonald.

If he had not been so presumptuous as to try to think for himself in Hollywood and if he hadn't had a sense of *irony,* he could have pretended — and convinced a lot of people — that he was still a contender. But what crown could he aspire to? Should he be a "king" like Gable, going from one meaningless picture to another, performing the rituals of manly toughness, embracing the studio stable, to be revered, finally, because he was the company actor who never gave anybody any trouble? Columnists don't attack that kind of king on his papier-mâché throne; critics don't prod him to return to the stage; the public doesn't turn against him.

Almost without exception, American actors who don't accept trashy assignments make nothing, not even superior trash. Brando accepts the trash, but unlike the monochromatic, "always dependable" Gable, he has too much energy or inventiveness or contempt just to go through the motions. And when he appears on the screen, there is a special quality of recognition in the audience: we know he's too big for the role.

Perhaps, as some in picture business say, Brando "screws up" his pictures by rewriting the scripts; certainly he hasn't been very astute in the directors and writers he has worked with. What he needed was not more docility, but more strength, the confidence to work with young talent, to try difficult roles. But he's no longer a contender, no longer a protagonist who challenges anything serious. Brando has become a comic.

The change was overwhelmingly apparent in the 1963 *Mutiny on the Bounty,* which, rather surprisingly, began with a miniature class conflict between Brando, as the aristocratic Fletcher Christian, and Trevor Howard, as the lowborn Captain Bligh, who cannot endure Christian's contempt for him. Brando played the fop with such relish that audiences shared in the joke; it was like a Dead End Kid playing Congreve. The inarticulate grunting Method actor is showing off, and it's a classic and favorite American joke: the worm turns, Destry gets his guns, American honor is redeemed. He can talk as fancy as any of them, even fancier. (In the action sequences he's uninteresting, not handsome or athletic enough to be a stock romantic adventure hero. He seems more eccentric than heroic, with his bizarre stance, his head held up pugnaciously, his face unlined in a peculiar bloated, waxen way. He's like a short, flabby tenor wandering around the stage and not singing: you wonder what he's doing there.)

In *The Ugly American* (1963) once again he is very funny as he sets the character — a pipe-smoking businessman-ambassador who parries a Senate subcommittee with high-toned clipped speech and epigrammatic sophistication. When he plays an articulate role, it is already rather a stunt, and in this one he is talking about personal dignity and standards of proper behavior. His restraint becomes a source of amusement because he is the chief exponent of the uncouth, the *charged.* Even his bull neck, so out of character, adds to the joke. His comedy is volatile. It has the unpredictable element that has always been part of his excitement: at any moment we may be surprised, amazed. When he submerges himself in the role, the movie dies on the screen.

Brando is never so American as when his English or foreign accent is thickest. It's a joke like a child's impersonation of a foreigner, overplaying the difference, and he offers us complicity in his accomplishments at pretending to be gentlemen or foreigners. What is funny about these roles is that they seem foreign to the Brando the audience feels it knows. When he does rough, coarse American serviceman comedy, as in *Bedtime Story,* he is horribly nothing (except for one farcical sequence when he impersonates a mad Hapsburg). Worse than nothing, because when his vulnerability is gone, his animal grace goes too, and he is left without even the routine handsomeness of his inferiors.

He had already implicated us in his amusement at his roles earlier in his career, in 1954 with his Napoleon in *Désirée,* in 1957 with his hilarious

Southern gentleman-officer in *Sayonara,* but these could still be thought of as commercial interludes, the bad luck of the draw. Now he doesn't draw anything else. Is it just bad luck, or is it that he and so many of our greatest talents must play out their "creative" lives with a stacked deck?

It is easy these days to "explain" the absence of roles worth playing by referring to the inroads of television and the end of the studio system. Of course, there's some truth in all this. But Brando's career illustrates something much more basic: the destruction of meaning in movies; and this is not a new phenomenon, nor is it specially linked to television or other new factors. The organic truth of American movie history is that the new theme or the new star that gives vitality to the medium is widely imitated and quickly exhausted before the theme or talent can develop. Everything good can be turned into a trick.

What's left of the rebel incarnate is what we see of Brando in the 1965 *Morituri:* his principal charm is his apparent delight in his own cleverness. Like many another great actor who has become fortune's fool, he plays the great ham. He seems as pleased with the lines as if he'd just thought them up. He gives the best ones a carefully timed double-take so that we, too, can savor his cleverness and the delight of his German accent. And what else is there to do with the role? If his presence did not give it the extra dimension of comedy, it would be merely commonplace.

In *Morituri* all we need is one look at the cynical aesthete Brando in his escapist paradise, telling us that he's "out of it," that war never solves anything, and we know that he's going to become the greatest warrior of them all. It can be argued that this hurdle of apathy or principle or convictions to be overcome gives a character conflict and makes his ultimate action more significant. Theoretically, this would seem to explain the plot mechanism, but as it works, no matter how absurd the terms in which the initial idealism or cynicism or social rejection is presented (as in such classic movie examples of character reformation as *Casablanca, To Have and Have Not, Stalag 17*), it is the final, socially acceptable "good" behavior which seems fantasy, fairy tale, unbelievable melodrama — in brief, fake. And the initial attitudes to be overcome often seem to have a lot of strength; indeed, they are likely to be what drew us to the character in the first place, what made him pass for a protagonist.

In *Morituri,* as in movies in general, there is rarely a *difference* shown, except to bring it back to the "norm." The high-minded, like the Quakers in *High Noon* or *Friendly Persuasion,* are there only to violate their convictions. They must be brought down low to common impulses, just as the low cynical materialists must be raised high to what are supposed to be our shared ideals. This democratic leveling of movies is like a massive tranquilizer. The more irregular the hero, the more offbeat, the more necessary it is for him to turn square in the finale.

Brando's *career* is a larger demonstration of the same principle at work in mass culture; but instead of becoming normal, he (like Norman Mailer) became an eccentric, which in this country means a clown, possibly the only way left to preserve some kind of difference.

When you're larger than life you can't just be brought down to normalcy. It's easier to get acceptance by caricaturing your previous attitudes and aspirations, by doing what the hostile audience already has been doing to you. Why should Bette Davis let impersonators on television make a fool of her when she can do it herself and reap the rewards of renewed audience acceptance?

Perhaps Brando has been driven to this self-parody so soon because of his imaginative strength and because of that magnetism that makes him so compelling an expression of American conflicts. His greatness is in a range that is too disturbing to be encompassed by regular movies. As with Bette Davis, as with John Barrymore, even when he mocks himself, the self he mocks is more prodigious than anybody else around. It's as if the hidden reserves of power have been turned to irony. Earlier, when his roles were absurd, there was a dash of irony; now it's taken over: the nonconformist with no roles to play plays *with* his roles. Brando is still the most exciting American actor on the screen. The roles may not be classic, but the actor's dilemma is.

Emerson outlined the American artist's way of life a century ago — "Thou must pass for a fool and a churl for a long season." We used to think that the season meant only youth, before the artist could prove his talent, make his place, achieve something. Now it is clear that for screen artists, and perhaps not only for screen artists, youth is, relatively speaking, the short season; the long one is the degradation *after* success.

[March 1966]

ଵଵଵଵଵ

Orson Welles: There Ain't No Way

Falstaff

WHAT makes movies a great popular art form is that certain artists can, at moments in their lives, reach out and unify the audience — educated and uneducated — in a shared response. The tragedy in the history of movies is that those who have this capacity are usually prevented from doing so. The mass audience gets its big empty movies full of meaningless action; the art-house audience gets its studies of small action and large inaction loaded with meaning.

Almost everyone who cares about movies knows that Orson Welles is such an artist. Even audiences who don't know that Welles is a great *director* sense his largeness of talent from his presence as an actor. Audiences are alert to him, as they often were to John Barrymore, and later to Charles Laughton, as they sometimes are to Bette Davis, as they almost always are to Brando — actors too big for their roles, who play the clown, and not always in comedy but in roles that for an artist of intelligence can only be comedy. Like Brando, Welles is always being attacked for not having ful-filled his prodigious promise; but who has ever beaten the mass culture fly-by-night system of economics for long? What else could Welles do with his roles in *Black Magic* or *Prince of Foxes* or *The Black Rose* or *Trent's Last Case* but play them as comedy? Could one take such work seriously? The mediocre directors and the cynical hacks got money when he couldn't. His ironic playing is all that one remembers from those movies anyway; like Brando, he has the greatness to make effrontery a communicated, shared experience — which lesser artists had better not attempt. It takes large *latent* talent to tell the audience that you know that what you're doing isn't worth doing and still do it better than anyone else in the movie.

Waiting for a train in Grand Central station recently, I was standing next to a group of Negroes. To everything that they talked about, one of them — a young girl — said, "There ain't no way"; and it fit perfectly each time.

Orson Welles's *Falstaff* came and went so fast there was hardly time to tell people about it, but it should be back (it should be around forever) and it should be seen. It's blighted by economics and it will never reach the audience Welles might have and should have reached, because there just ain't no way. So many people — and with such complacent satisfaction, almost, one would say, delight — talk of how Welles has disappointed them, as if he had willfully thrown away his talent through that "lack of discipline" which is always brought in to explain failure. There is a widespread notion that a man who accomplishes a great deal is thus a "genius" who should be able to cut through all obstacles; and if he can't (and who can?), what he does is too far beneath what he should have done to be worth consideration. On the contrary, I think that the more gifted and imaginative a director, the greater the obstacles. It is the less imaginative director who has always flourished in the business world of movies — the "adaptable," reliable fellow who is more concerned to get the movie done than to do it his way, who, indeed, after a while has no way of his own, who is as anonymous as the director of *Prince of Foxes*. And the more determined a man is to do it his way or a new way, the more likelihood that this man (quickly labeled a "troublemaker" or "a difficult person" or "self-destructive" or "a man who makes problems for himself" — standard Hollywoodese for an artist and, of course, always true at some level, and the greater the artist, the more true it's likely to become) won't get the support he needs to complete the work his way. In the atmosphere of anxiety surrounding him, the producers may decide to "save" the project by removing him or adding to or subtracting from his work, or finally dumping the film without publicity or press screenings, consigning it to the lower half of double bills.

All these things have happened to Welles (*Citizen Kane* was not big enough at the box office and it caused trouble; he was not allowed to finish his next picture, *The Magnificent Ambersons*). Treatment of this sort, which usually marks the end of great movie careers, was for Welles the beginning. Most of these things have happened to men as pacific as Jean Renoir, whom few could accuse of being "undisciplined." (Renoir turned to writing a novel, his first, in 1966, when he could not raise money to make a movie, though the budget he required was less than half that allotted to movies made to be premiered on television.) And they are still happening to men in Hollywood like Sam Peckinpah. Such men are always blamed for the eventual failure of whatever remains of their work, while men who try for less have the successes (and are forgiven their routine failures because they didn't attempt anything the producers didn't understand). Joseph L. Mankiewicz's *Julius*

Caesar was considered a success and Orson Welles's *Othello* a failure. The daring of doing Shakespeare at all was enough for Mankiewicz and his producer, John Houseman, who was to be ritualistically referred to as "the distinguished producer John Houseman" because of this film — not from his early theatre work with Orson Welles — much as George Schaefer is referred to as "the distinguished director" because of his specialty of embalming old war horses for television. Mankiewicz's luck held good on *Julius Caesar*: it's perfectly suited to the small screen, where it recently appeared, while Welles's *Othello* — with its disastrous, imperfectly synchronized soundtrack — isn't even intelligible. How could it be? A movie shot over a period of four years with Welles dashing off periodically to act in movies like *The Black Rose* to earn the money to continue; and then, his cast scattered, trying to make a soundtrack, reading half the roles himself (not only Roderigo, but if my ear is to be trusted, parts of Iago, too), selecting long shots and shots with the actors' backs to the camera to conceal the sound problem. This, of course, looked like "affectation." And his splendid, flawed production — visually and emotionally a near-masterpiece — was a "failure." Earlier, working on a Republic Pictures budget (for Republic Pictures), Welles had shot his barbaric *Macbeth* — marred most by his own performance — in twenty-three days because "no one would give me any money for a further day's shooting."

In the early fifties, Welles as an actor was in top flamboyant form. Nobody seemed to enjoy the sheer physical delight of acting as much as he in roles like his Lord Mountdrago in *Three Cases of Murder*. Still very young, he played like a great ham of the old school — which was marvelous to watch in his Father Mapple in *Moby Dick* and in *The Roots of Heaven*. This lesser talent that he could live on was a corollary to his great talent. It was a demonstration of his love of (and prowess in) traditional theatre — like the way Vittorio De Sica (also an actor from adolescence) could go from being the romantic singing star of Italian musical comedy to make *Shoeshine* and then back again (he, too, to raise money for his own films) to playing in an ornate style, Gina's lawyer or Sophia's papa, a whole Barzini gallery of glory-ridden, mustachioed Italians. But Welles was beginning to turn into America's favorite grotesque. Like Barrymore and Laughton and Brando, he seemed to be developing an obsession with false noses, false faces. He had once, at least, played a role in his own face, Harry Lime in *The Third Man,* a role he had written for himself; by the sixties he was encased in makeup and his own fat —like a huge operatic version of W. C. Fields. Audiences laughed when he appeared on the screen. He didn't need to choose the role of Falstaff: it chose him.

When Welles went to Europe, he lost his single greatest asset as a movie director: his sound. (He had already lost the company that *talked* together, the Mercury players he had brought to Hollywood — Joseph Cotten, Agnes Moorehead, Everett Sloane, et al. — who were now working separately.) Welles had first skyrocketed to public attention on radio, and what he had brought to movies that was distinctively new was the radio sound — with an innovative use of overlapping dialogue — which was used for trick shock purposes, almost playfully, in *Citizen Kane*. But by the time of *The Magnificent Ambersons* he was using this technique for something deeper (the family bickering was startling in its almost surreal accuracy; the sound was of arguments overheard from childhood, with so many overtones they were almost mythic). Welles himself had a voice that seemed to carry its own echo chamber; somehow, in becoming the whiz kid of vocal effects, in simulating so many deep, impersonal voices, he had emptied his own voice of emotion, and when he spoke his credit at the end of *The Ambersons,* audiences laughed at the hollow voice (and perhaps at the comic justice of the *spoken* credit). Ironically, sound — the area of his greatest mastery — became his worst problem as he began to work with actors who didn't speak English and actors who did but weren't around when he needed them (for the post-synchronization which is standard practice in Europe, because the actors don't speak the same language, and is becoming standard here, too, because it saves shooting time). Welles compensated by developing greater visual virtuosity.

Yeats said "Rhetoric is heard, poetry overheard," and though I don't agree, I think I see what he means, and I think this assumption is involved in much of the rejection of a talent like Welles's. His work is often referred to as flashy and spectacular as if this also meant cheap and counterfeit. Welles is unabashedly theatrical in a period when much of the educated audience thinks theatrical flair vulgar, artistry intellectually respectable only when subtle, hidden. Welles has the approach of a *popular* artist: he glories in both verbal and visual rhetoric. He uses film *theatrically* — not stagily, but with theatrical bravado. He makes a show of the mechanics of film. He doesn't, if I may be forgiven the pun, hide his tracks. Movies gave him the world for a stage, and his is not the art that conceals art, but the showman's delight in the flourishes with which he pulls the rabbit from the hat. (This is why he was the wrong director for *The Trial,* where the poetry needed to be overheard.) I think that many people who enjoy those flourishes, who really love them — as I do — are so fearfully educated that they feel they must put them down. It's as if people said he's a mountebank, an actor showing off. But there's life in that kind of display: it's part of an earlier theatrical tradition that Welles carries over into film, it's what the theatre has lost, and it's what brought people to the movies.

Welles might have done for American talkies what D. W. Griffith did for the silent film. But when he lost his sound and his original, verbal wit, he seemed to lose his brashness, his youth, and some of his vitality. And he lost his American-ness; in Europe he had to learn a different, more exclusively visual language of film. An *enfant terrible* defeated ages fast. At fifty-one, Welles seems already the grand old master of film, because, of course, everybody knows that he'll never get in the position to do what he might have done. Governments and foundations will prattle on about excellence and American film companies will rush to sign up Englishmen and Europeans who have had a hit, hoping to snare that magic moneymaking gift. And tired transplanted Europeans will go on making big, lousy American movies, getting financed because they once had a hit and maybe the magic will come back. And Welles — the one great creative force in American films in our time, the man who might have redeemed our movies from the general contempt in which they are (and for the most part, rightly) held — is, ironically, an expatriate director whose work thus reaches only the art-house audience. And he has been so crippled by the problems of working as he does, he's lucky to reach that. The distributors of *Falstaff* tested it out of town before risking Bosley Crowther's displeasure in New York.

You may want to walk out during the first twenty minutes of *Falstaff*. Although the words on the soundtrack are intelligible, the sound doesn't match the images. We hear the voices as if the speakers were close, but on the screen the figures may be a half mile away or turned from us at some angle that doesn't jibe with the voice. In the middle of a sentence an actor may walk away from us while the voice goes on. Often, for a second, we can't be sure who is supposed to be talking. And the cutting is maddening, designed as it is for camouflage — to keep us from seeing faces closely or from registering that mouths which should be open and moving are closed. Long shots and Shakespearean dialogue are a crazy mix. It's especially jarring because the casting is superb and the performance beautiful. It's not hard to take Shakespeare adapted and transformed by other cultures — like Kurosawa's *Throne of Blood,* a *Macbeth* almost as much related to Welles's as to Shakespeare's — but the words of Shakespeare slightly out of synch! This is as intolerable as those old prints of *Henry V* that the miserly distributors circulate — chewed up by generations of projection machines, crucial syllables lost in the splices. The editing rhythm of *Falstaff* is at war with the rhythm and comprehension of the language. Welles, avoiding the naturalistic use of the outdoors in which Shakespeare's dialogue sounds more stagey than on stage, has photographically stylized the Spanish locations, creating a theatrically darkened, slightly unrealistic world of angles and low beams and silhouettes. When this photographic style is shattered by the cuts necessary to conceal the dialogue problems, the camera angles seem unnecessarily exaggerated and pretentious. But then despite everything — the angles, the doubles in long shots, the editing that distracts us when we need to concentrate on the dialogue — the movie begins to be great. The readings in *Falstaff* are great even if they don't always go with the images, which are often great, too.

Welles has brought together the pieces of Falstaff that Shakespeare had strewn over the two parts of *Henry IV* and *The Merry Wives of Windsor*, with cuttings from *Henry V* and *Richard II*, and fastened them into place with narration from Holinshed's Chronicles (read by Ralph Richardson). Those of us who resisted our schoolteachers' best efforts to make us appreciate the comic genius of Shakespeare's fools and buffoons will not be surprised that Welles wasn't able to make Falstaff very funny: he's a great conception of a character, but the charades and practical jokes seem meant to be funnier than they are. This movie does, however, provide the best Shakespearean comic moment I can recall: garrulous Falstaff sitting with Shallow (Alan Webb) and Silence (Walter Chiari), rolling his eyes in irritation and impatience at Silence's stammer. But Welles's Falstaff isn't essentially comic; W. C. Fields's Micawber wasn't either: these actors, so funny when they're playing with their own personae in roles too small for them, are not so funny when they're trying to measure up. The carousing and roistering in the tavern doesn't seem like such great fun either, though Welles and the cast work very hard to convince us it is. Oddly, we never really see the friendship of Prince Hal — played extraordinarily well by Keith Baxter — and Falstaff; the lighter side in *Henry IV, Part I* is lost — probably well lost, though we must take it for granted in the film. What we see are the premonitions of the end: Hal taking part in games that have gone stale for him, preparing himself for his final rejection of his adopted father Falstaff in order to turn into a worthy successor of his father the king. And we see what this does to Falstaff, the braggart with the heart of a child who expects to be forgiven everything, even what he knows to be unforgivable — his taking the credit away from Hal for the combat with Hotspur (Norman Rodway). Falstaff lacks judgment, which kings must have.

John Gielgud's Henry IV is the perfect contrast to Welles; Gielgud has never been so monkishly perfect in a movie. Welles could only get him for two weeks of the shooting and the makeshift of some of his scenes is obvious, but his performance gives the film the austerity it needs for the conflict in Hal to be dramatized. Gielgud's king is so refined — a skeleton too dignified for any flesh to cling to it, inhabited by a voice so modulated it is an exquisite spiritual whine. Merrie England? Falstaff at least provides a carcass to mourn over.

Welles as an actor had always been betrayed by his voice. It was too much and it was inexpressive; there was no warmth in it, no sense of a life lived. It was just an instrument that he played, and it seemed to be the key to something shallow and unfelt even in his best performances, and most fraudulent when he tried to make it tender. I remember that once, in *King*

Lear on television, he hit a phrase and I thought his voice was emotionally right; it had beauty — and what a change it made in his acting! In *Falstaff* Welles seems to have grown into his voice; he's not too young for it anymore, and he's certainly big enough. And his emotions don't seem fake anymore; he's grown into them, too. He has the eyes for the role. Though his Falstaff is short on comedy, it's very rich, very full.

He has directed a sequence, the battle of Shrewsbury, which is unlike anything he has ever done, indeed unlike any battle ever done on the screen before. It ranks with the best of Griffith, John Ford, Eisenstein, Kurosawa — that is, with the best ever done. How can one sequence in this movie be so good? It has no dialogue and so he isn't handicapped: for the only time in the movie he can edit, not to cover gaps and defects but as an artist. The compositions suggest Uccello and the chilling ironic music is a death knell for all men in battle. The soldiers, plastered by the mud they fall in, are already monuments. It's the most brutally somber battle ever filmed. It does justice to Hotspur's great "O, Harry, thou hast robbed me of my youth."

Welles has filled the cast with box-office stars. Margaret Rutherford, Jeanne Moreau, Marina Vlady are all in it (though the girl I like best was little Beatrice Welles as the pageboy). And Falstaff is the most popular crowd-pleasing character in the work of the most enduringly popular writer who ever lived. Yet, because of technical defects due to poverty, Welles's finest Shakespearean production to date — another near-masterpiece, and this time so very close — cannot reach a large public. There ain't no way.

[June 1967]

‹¿‹¿‹¿‹

The Intentions of
Stanley Kramer

Ship of Fools

AT college there was a salesman named Conrad who used to hang around
the coffeehouses, joining in the conversations on art and politics, submitting
vulgar commonplaces as if they were brilliant insights. One afternoon he
arrived a little confused but on the whole elated. He had been taking some
psychological and vocational tests and had just been told the result: he was
a phenomenon, according to the testing center, because of the enormous
discrepancy between his abilities and his professional and artistic aspirations. Poor Conrad! If the tests had covered the classification of movie
producer, he might have found his vocation. He is not alone.

Stanley Kramer's reputation as a great director is largely based on a
series of errors: he is widely assumed to be the director of *Champion* and
Home of the Brave (both by Mark Robson), *High Noon, The Men,* and
The Member of the Wedding (all by Fred Zinnemann), *Death of a Salesman* and *The Wild One* (both by Laslo Benedek), as well as *Cyrano de
Bergerac* (Michael Gordon), *The Happy Time* (Richard Fleischer), *My
Six Convicts* (Hugo Fregonese), *The 5000 Fingers of Dr. T.* (Roy Row-
land), *The Caine Mutiny* (Edward Dmytryk), etc. This misconception is
understandable, as Kramer is one of those producers who refers to "When I
was *making*" this or that picture, and the names of the actual directors are
rarely mentioned. The standard procedure for producers is to publicize
their names if the movie is a hit and the directors' names if it is a flop (which
it often is because of the producer's interference). Kramer is unusual in
publicizing himself no matter *what* the film.
Some of his productions, like *The Men* and *The Member of the Wedding,*

were very good; others, like *The Wild One,* though not so good, had a kind of contemporary excitement. Most were "small" movies with young players, and they were often cleverly and economically directed. They were melodramas with — to use legalese — redeeming social importance; and if their messages were often irritatingly self-righteous, the situations and settings were, nevertheless, excitingly modern, relevant. There was talent in his productions, though there was no more reason to think it was *his* talent than to confuse a magazine editor with his writers. The producer, like an editor, needs only the talent to buy talent — then all too frequently he attempts to shape it in his own image. The shaping in Stanley Kramer productions was harsh, shallow, opportunistic.

Kramer spoke of each new production as "his dream," and in his own words, he became a director so that he could "protect his dream." His dreams have silver linings. The pictures he has directed himself are not skillful; they are not small and inexpensive; the casts are more than likely to be all-star; and despite his reputation as a "courageous" director and a serious thinker, the subject matter when it isn't already pulp is turned into pulp.

In 1955, having directed one film — the appalling, highly successful *Not as a Stranger* — he wrote in *Theatre Arts:*

You have to realize that there are two schools of thought on the Hollywood film. One school — and it's by far the larger — looks on it as an industry. The other, smaller school considers it an art.

I've tried not to straddle this issue. I believe the film is an art form. I think this is the only form in which it can survive. Those who say it's not an art form are creating unnecessary limitations. They are allowing themselves to become sitting ducks for alert competition.

Or, in other words, "art" means being ahead of the industry. And he explained how he got ahead:

Actually, I'm not particular where the material comes from. The idea is to buy for impact — total impact — and not because something is well-phrased or because it's a successful play. A story becomes important if it represents a blow for or against something — if it has great impact.

"Total impact" requires "massive retaliation" — or at the very least, a "confrontation."

Not as a Stranger was adapted from a big (948-page) best seller about idealism and corruption in the medical profession. The film lacked what used to be called sensibility, and formally it lacked rhythm and development. It jerked along from crisis to crisis: epidemics, adultery, and plenty of surgery, including an exposed pulsing heart and an autopsy. The hero and villainess fornicated to the accompaniment of a stallion and mare rearing and screaming. Lawdy, it was gaudy. And it observed an inglorious convention of ancient tear-jerkers: the hero's proud, egotistic, adulterous character was finally improved when he blundered in an operation and killed a friend (Ah, how many best friends have been killed off to make the heroes better men!).

Kramer didn't stint on "production values." The cast (Robert Mitchum, Frank Sinatra, Olivia de Havilland, Gloria Grahame, Broderick Crawford, Charles Bickford, Lee Marvin, et al.) included four Academy Award winners. There were two more, the Anhalts, on the screenplay, the great Franz Planer as cinematographer, and George Antheil, famed in Hollywood for his ability to supply what the director failed to, as musical director — or doctor. It may also be worth noting that this first effort ran for two hours and fifteen minutes — longer, that is, than Kramer had ever permitted a director working for him to go. This might just possibly be construed as self-indulgence. (I was almost removed from the theatre because I laughed at what others did not take to be funny: the hero's long-suffering wife calls his office during the big epidemic and is informed by the nurse that "the doctor is out giving his last shot to the widow Lang" — as the camera moves to Mitchum and Grahame in the stable.)

His next film, the 1957 *The Pride and the Passion,* based on C. S. Forester's *The Gun,* was a vast, expensive epic-spectacle about Napoleon's campaign in Spain — which, on advice, I managed to avoid. It featured a large cannon, Cary Grant, Frank Sinatra, and Sophia Loren. As to its scale, according to the *New Yorker:*

Mr. Kramer and his associates must have spent on this film the equivalent of the national debt of the Spanish dictatorship, under whose mercenary eye the picture was made, and employed as many extras as Mr. DeMille used when he was turning back the waters of the Red Sea in *The Ten Commandments.* As a matter of fact, Mr. Kramer may be a few thousand extras up on Mr. DeMille . . .

It was after the failure of *The Pride and the Passion* that Kramer (his character improved?) returned to the kind of material with which he had been identified as a producer.

The Defiant Ones is probably Kramer's best picture: the subject matter is relatively simple, though "powerful"; the action is exciting; the acting is good. But the singleness of purpose behind it all is a little offensive. The theme is irrational hatred between two escaping convicts, a white man (Tony Curtis) and a Negro (Sidney Poitier); chained together, pursued by a bloodthirsty posse, they learn brotherhood. Q.E.D. If, instead of creating a false premise of incredible, primitive hatred between two very good men, Kramer showed some Negroes less attractive than Sidney Poitier, with less virtuous problems, some of the congratulations he got for daring would be deserved. The joker in *The Defiant Ones* was that although white liberals were pleased at the demonstration of solidarity, Negroes in theatres could be heard jeering at Poitier for sacrificing himself for his white "brother." Moviegoers with good memories amused themselves by pointing out that *The Defiant Ones* was *The Thirty-Nine Steps* in drag, and by noting that the episode about the farm woman was badly lifted from *La Grande Illusion* — with the convenient substitution of Negro for Jew (a familiar device in Kramer productions).

His next film, in 1959, shows the almost complete Kramer syndrome. *On the Beach,* according to its initial publicity, was designed to act "as a deterrent to further nuclear armament." And the treatment it got in the press was not incommensurate with the importance of the objective. Here, as a sample, are some quotes from Arthur Knight in the *Saturday Review:*

. . . he trains his cameras on what is surely the most important question on earth — survival in the atomic age. And he gives an answer.

. . . Kramer has arranged for the simultaneous release of *On the Beach* in eighteen world capitals in mid-December. He still hopes to include Moscow and Warsaw. It can only do good.

This same awareness of his theme's importance also influenced Kramer's budgeting and casting. Although his reputation stems from relatively inexpensive pictures featuring relatively unknown players, he gambled the works on this one — a budget of well over $4,000,000 and such costly stars as Gregory Peck, Ava Gardner, Fred Astaire, and Anthony Perkins. But where most producers of an expensive picture would have used these names as insurance, casting them in safe, scintillating roles, Kramer has sought to create additional excitement by casting against type. Ava Gardner, for the first time in her career, is downright unglamorous as a woman who has lived too hard and drunk too much. And Astaire, as the scientist, neither sings a note nor dances a step.

Remarkably, Kramer who had earlier, as a producer, been much praised for using the inexpensive actors he could afford, now got credit for using stars like everybody else in Hollywood. He even got credit for the oldest gambit in the game — casting an aging star as "a woman who has lived too hard and drunk too much." Knight concluded with:

. . . a film that aims at something big, and emerges as something tremendous. . . . Faced with an alternative so graphically drawn, the world can only strive harder for peace, supporting and implementing all those agencies and organizations that are working today to avert the holocaust of *On the Beach.* The date of that holocaust by the way, is 1964. We don't have too much time, brother.

It may be noted that this picture set the strange pattern of Kramer — the bold one — getting an even better press than his pictures. Influential critics — eager to get credit for saving the world? — wrote prose worthy of his publicity department. From Bosley Crowther of the New York *Times:*

Deeply moving . . . The great merit of this picture, aside from its entertainment qualities, is the fact that it carries a passionate conviction that man is worth saving, after all. . . . The basic theme of this drama and its major concern is life, the wondrous thing that man's own vast knowledge and ultimate folly seem about to destroy. And everything done by the characters, every thought they utter and move they make, indicates their fervor, tenacity and courage in the face of doom. . . . In putting this fanciful but arresting story of Mr. Shute's on the screen, Mr. Kramer and his assistants have most forcibly emphasized this point: life is a beautiful treasure and man should do all he can to save it from annihilation, while there is still time. To this end, he has accomplished some vivid and trenchant images that subtly fill the mind of the viewer with a strong appreciation of his theme.

Esquire, in the person of George P. Elliott, sounded the same stirring note: "To make this movie indeed took courage; people resent having their consciences stirred." And Linus Pauling was quoted as saying, "It may be that some years from now we can look back and say that *On the Beach* is the movie that saved the world."

Six years have passed: does anyone remember *On the Beach* as anything more than a lousy movie? Yet, curiously, the notion hovers in the air that Kramer is some sort of savior, that we are somehow in his debt. And Kramer, who turned it all on himself, seems to share in this delusion. In 1963, he spoke of *On the Beach* in these terms: "I was satisfied that it was made, but not satisfied with the film itself." Does he, then, think that he accomplished the good he set out to do — a good separable from the quality of the film? The bigger the head, the more easily turned.

When you carry the creative man's burden as Kramer does, after a film like *On the Beach* it must be difficult to find big enough subjects, subjects a thinker can sink his teeth into. He looked around and found God waiting in the wings. *Inherit the Wind,* of 1960, a fictionalized account of the Scopes trial, continued the formula of using "controversial" subjects in noncontroversial ways. The courageous Kramer even treated us to the spectacle of Fredric March as William Jennings Bryan and Spencer Tracy as Clarence Darrow joining forces to expose the "cynic" — Gene Kelly as H. L. Mencken. We might suspect that Kelly-Mencken was standing in for those of us critics who had been derisive about Kramer's messianic movies as we heard the warning to Mencken, "Where will your loneliness lead you? No one will come to your funeral." It is the voice of purest Hollywood, a threat worthy of Louis B. Mayer himself — whose funeral, according to legend, was mobbed by those who wanted to make sure the sonovabitch was really dead.

If Tracy-Darrow in all his virtue (carrying a Bible under one arm, Darwin under the other) had looked startlingly like an aged Stanley Kramer, Kramer indulged the narcissism to the full in his next picture, *Judgment at*

Nuremberg — which Gavin Lambert, one of the cynics, has described as "an All-Star Concentration Camp Drama, with Special Guest Victim Appearances." In addition to Tracy as the simple, humane superjudge, a Yankee version of Tolstoy's clean old peasant, the cast included Burt Lancaster, Richard Widmark, Maximilian Schell, and Marlene Dietrich, with Judy Garland and Montgomery Clift as the guests. He had been showered with publicity and plaudits for the "daring" "offbeat" casting of Fred Astaire as a nuclear physicist; who knows what glory might come of this multiple offbeat casting?

The real star was Abby Mann. At long last, Stanley Kramer had found the screenwriter for him: Abby Mann compounded his faults, carried him beyond movies, beyond merely saving the world, into Ethics. The Kramer syndrome was complete.

Abby Mann had a new cops and robbers formula with a depth charge. The world was divided between Nazis and Jews, and the twist was how you told one from another, because some Gentiles, though they might look like Nazis, risked their lives for Jews and so were as good as Jews, while some Jews might not be proud of being Jews, might even consider themselves Germans (— or Americans?), which made them dupes for the Nazis.

Brutally sure how everyone *should* have acted, Kramer and Mann were not slowed down by indecision, doubts, ambiguities. We weak mortals might not be so sure how the world worked, so they explained it to us. Abby Mann distended his small talent for ironic humor, bending twigs and demonstrating how Nazis grow. Kramer's direction became a matter of throwing strong, bright lights on Mann's labeling. They were quick to examine other people's guilts, quicker to judge — the greatest fingerpointing team since Cohn and Schine.

Critics could see the signposts all right and knew if they didn't like the film, they were as bad as Nazis. The reviews were urgent. This is how a San Francisco paper put it:

> . . . if you have the slightest concern about the future course of civilization, I would suggest that you see *Judgment at Nuremberg*. It is an object lesson in how a compromise with evil, no matter how slight it might seem at first, inevitably leads to disaster.

Under the moral coercion of Kramer and Mann, reviewers didn't say "This is a good movie, go see it." They said, in the words of one influential paper: "Few films are important. *Judgment at Nuremberg* is." The critics were impacted. The *Illustrated London News* told its readers that "To evade this film is a weakness in courage." (Surely this would not be said of a work of art — even if it were as "difficult" as a Greek tragedy?) The critic went on: "This picture is a voice like a clarion call for peace, fair dealing, mercy, and absolute justice." An absolutely intelligent critic. He was responding, no doubt, to Kramer and Mann's demonstration that justice should not be tempered with mercy — a principle that might well be used against them. Only a few critics pointed out that the largeness of the issues contrasted sharply with the feeble intellectual and imaginative approach to them and that the large issues were dramatized in ludicrous terms. Abby Mann, with excruciating humility, accepted his Academy Award not only for himself but for all intellectuals.

When Kramer decided to make his first comedy, it had to be the funniest picture ever made — "as overpowering an assault of the risibilities as possible." He said he wanted to make "a comedy to end all comedies." If he can't achieve greatness any other way, he'll be one of the world's great destroyers. *It's a Mad, Mad, Mad, Mad World* lasts over three and a quarter hours and cost over nine and a half million dollars, and in the words of J. B. Priestley, "There is in it not a glimmer of affection for anybody or anything."

After a vacation from each other — Kramer on his vast *Mad World,* Mann berating the Nazis some more in *The Condemned of Altona* — they had their second honeymoon on *Ship of Fools.* No longer innocent, they went through the motions. Not of an act of love but of a ritual of judgment, condemnation, and false illumination.

The cynics said Kramer and Mann counted on people going to see the movie to find out how the book they never finished came out. But Kramer and Mann know the terrible truth that for the kind of movies they make — the big expensive kind — they need the people who never open a "literary" book. They are men of a certain consistency — bewildering though that consistency may be to the rest of us. Abby Mann put it all in place: "It is the most important book of the decade because it deals with momentous things." The movie, we could then assume, would be important the same way, the Kramer way.

The book reviewers had already described what seemed to be a Kramer and Mann movie. *Time* said that the novel "tells in parable form of the slothful, harmless and irresponsible people who made possible the rise of fascism." Mary Lasswell, in a fairy typical newspaper review, wrote, "I hurt all over, which is probably the normal reaction to such a lengthy and detailed account of man's inhumanity to man. After fifty pages, one is already prepared for the atrocities of World War II, a mere enlargement of the hates and aggressions of the microcosm aboard the S.S. *Vera.*" They bought a best-selling title, and a book that could be pushed to mean what they wanted it to mean. Miss Porter, "a charming, old Southern belle," as Abby Mann characterized her, could hardly be expected to ram the old point home. They began by moving the date up from 1931 to 1933.

These two men, joined together by their holy hindsight as they condemn Germany — and the world — for putting expediency above justice and humanity, perform the equivalent crime in the arts. They want to make movies that mean something, but in order to ensure reaching the biggest audience possible, they calculate each portion of that meaning, balancing the controversial areas against the drawing power of the big stars, the name property, etc. They point out to others that there is no compromising with justice; but they ignore what V. S. Pritchett has called "the law ruling the arts" — that they must be pursued to excess. They think they can be businessmen *and* artists. This "balanced" view is destroying movies just as surely as the balancing of risks and profits against justice morally degrades those who accept the compromise. They violate what is perhaps the only possible basic moral code: to refuse compromise for ourselves, and to have sympathy and understanding for those who *do* compromise. Kramer and Mann reverse this code.

In a not too reassuring opening note, Katherine Anne Porter had explained her title as "this simple almost universal image of the ship of this world on its voyage to eternity . . . I am a passenger on that ship." Whatever the ship might mean in the course of the book — and at times it did seem to be intended as a microcosm of the pre-Nazi world — there was no doubt that the author *was* a passenger on that ship. Kramer and Mann are not mere passengers on the movie ship: they are masters of their fate, captains of their soul. They *know,* apparently, what would have stopped Hitler.

At the opening of the movie, the dwarf Glocken comes on just like the disfigured outsider played by Lewis Stone in *Grand Hotel* to tell us: "This is a ship of fools. I'm a fool. You'll meet more fools as we go along . . . all kinds . . . and it may be, if you look closely enough, you will find yourself on board." And at the end, he informs us of what we have seen: "I told you they were fools, didn't I? Fools, pimps, whores, cowards, potential murderers. Is there any hope for such people? I'll tell you. I have a feeling that lives don't have to be wasted this way. They can have meaning. That there is some beauty in people." This speech is completed by the Abby Mann speciality, the show business twist — "But you'd be crazy to take my word for it. Who am I? I'm just a fellow who's three feet six and wants to be six feet three." And then, in Abby Mann's own words in the script, the dwarf "walks on. As he does, his figure reminds us of life itself, misshapen, fragile, a little shabby even, but it does give off a tawdry beauty. *Fade out.*"

Original sin meets Mr. Fixit.

Although writers have learned to avoid the pathetic fallacy, they are often congratulated on their depth when they do something that may be just as fallacious: showing the faults in human character as the explanation of a war, a political event, an economic catastrophe. The novel *Ship of Fools,* for all its complexity and despite some brilliantly realized scenes of sexual torment and intermittent moments of beauty and power, is a rather naïve allegory. How, the author implicitly asks, did the ship of this world sail into the barbarism of the death camps? And her answer, as she herself has said is, "the collusion between good and evil . . . most of the evil in this world occurs because good people allow it. . . . There is always something in good people that sympathizes with the evil people. Good people help them without even knowing it. . . . We cannot attain perfection. We can only try for it. And of course we always fail."

Which doesn't explain the death camps anymore than it explains the New York World's Fair. Universal evil can lead to *anything*. But this sort of statement about the responsibility people must share for evil *passes for* an explanation in the arts, and in recent years these platitudes and redundancies have appeared so often in fiction, in the theatre, in movies and television, and their authors have been so frequently commended for their courage in *speaking out* that this inane, lofty it-tolls-for-thee-ism is taking a toll of our good sense.

What is rather shocking in the novel is that the bell doesn't quite toll for the German characters or the Spaniards, adult or child. Miss Porter has a fine eye with a fearfully large mote in it, and surely it is this mote which has attracted Kramer and Mann, who discard the eye and look out of the mote — her attitude toward Germans.

In their view the fools are those who do not see that Nazism is coming: such wisdom is easily acquired in 1965. Their charming Jew, the waltzing Lowenthal, is a humorous, compassionate man whose failing is that he considers himself a German: this will lead to his downfall.

Lowenthal is supposed to show his weakness, his blindness, when he says to Glocken, "Do you think this boat is a cross-section of the German people? No, you don't know the average German the way I know him."

GLOCKEN: Gott in Himmel, Lowenthal! You're blind, you're absolutely blind! You don't see what's going on in front of your face!
LOWENTHAL: What do you mean? (*Looks at Glocken a moment, then laughs derisively*) You mean about the Jews? You don't understand us. The German Jew is something special. We're Germans first, and Jews second. We've done so much for Germany, Germany has done so much for us, what are we supposed to do — pack up our bags and leave because of a few troublemakers? . . . Listen. There are six million of us. What are they going to do? Kill all of us? (*Laughs*)

Really, it's more than nit-picking to point out that the German Jews numbered closer to a half million than six million,* and that the silly Lowenthal is, in a sense, more astute than Abby Mann. For Germany, before 1939, did allow German Jews — who were, after all, *German* Jews — some

* This was later changed to "there are almost a million of us." After release the movie was also trimmed by several minutes: Kramer observed audiences in a number of theatres and cut out what he thought they didn't respond to.

chance to escape; they were not slaughtered like the Polish and Russian Jews.

In Katherine Anne Porter's novel, the uncharming Lowenthal is first a Jew ("Me, I'm a jew, and if sometimes I think that's hard luck, why I just try to imagine being a Goy"), and in her view, his hatred of Gentiles makes him more or less even with the anti-Semitic Christians. Abby Mann has altered his character to make him more amiable and attractive, and then suggests that this very amiability is the weakness that will lead to his death. Does Abby Mann know what would save him anymore than *we* do? "I wanted," he says, "to show the basis of the tragedy of the German Jew, to find his human frailty." It's a strange place to look for the reasons for Hitler's policies — in the hearts of Jews. He's so busy with his fast-buck ironies about assimilation ("When the holocaust was at their heads, the most tragic people were those Jews who were heroes in World War I and considered themselves completely German." — Why?) he doesn't seem to have taken the trouble to find out what actually happened to the German Jews before telling us how it could have been prevented.

If this ship is supposed to be a cross-section of the German people — and obviously this is what Mann intends — then he has failed (as indeed Katherine Anne Porter did also) to make the characters representative of the major elements in that society; and even more significantly, he has failed (as she did also) to demonstrate how the flaws in character and outlook even in a representative group might have led to the specific consequence of Nazism. Hitlerism was not produced because people don't love each other enough and it is arrant nonsense to give us dinner-party snubs as the beginnings of the gas chambers. I can easily imagine avoiding Kramer and Mann at a party; but I would not incinerate them. (I wish I could be sure they would treat me the same way.)

Probably the only way to enjoy the book is to read it as a trip, not an allegory, and to enjoy the points of interest along the way — just as we might get involved in a story about life in a small town in California in the forties even if the author, by showing the racial prejudices against Japanese farmers, intended to provide a microcosm of the rotten society that would drop the bomb over Hiroshima. But when Kramer and Mann get to work on the "commercial" side of the picture — the romance and sex — they manage to destroy and distort even the good things in the novel. The best relationship in the book, the sexual entanglement of the two young artists, Jenny who is trying to be free, and puritanical David who wants to own her, has been altered so that it now (1) appeases the large audience's suspicious hostilities toward talented women; (2) flatters the masculine vanity of Kramer and Mann; (3) gets the jump on the movie of *Who's Afraid of Virginia Woolf?* by introducing a simulated-Albee sex hatred.

David, now rewritten to represent, as Abby Mann has said, Abby Mann, and played by George Segal who looks like a *young* Stanley Kramer, has become a proletarian artist of great animal vitality who is being kept by adoring, rich-bitch Jenny. Asked about David, the movie Jenny says, "David? He's a real artist, a wonderful one. He's a bit swept-up with social consciousness right now, but he'll get over that." David knows the truth, of course: "You hate my work, don't you Jenny?" And *we* are tipped off that she hates his painting not only because of its revolutionary content but also because she can't really paint — she's only a *commercial* artist. It's as much a vulgarization of the original as if Katherine Anne Porter hated Abby Mann's writing because she's just a hack jealous of his genius. And Jenny later admits it — "David, you say I hate your paintings. I do . . . Maybe it's because I'm not very good at it myself. Maybe because it means so much to you, more than anything, more than even me." David answers, "You're so full of competition. You're so full of God knows what kind of sickness." Once more a male director and a male scenarist have turned a woman's writing upside down and have come up with male fantasies. Jenny, the only chance of a protagonist, becomes Elizabeth Ashley snapping her eyes and projecting like a house afire as the untalented, neurotic, competitive woman.

They turn the exquisite Vivien Leigh, who would seem perfectly cast as Mrs. Treadwell, into an inexplicable, jerky little Pinocchio. Everything is staccato, loud, crude. It would almost seem that Kramer thought quiet observations, revelation, subtlety, beneath him. More likely he's incapable of it. The deepest feelings, the most complex involvements may seem unimportant to those who mistake every breath they take for a blast of emotion.

But audiences will "buy" the doomed lovers right out of *One Way Passage:* Oskar Werner's Dr. Schumann compassionately giving injections and adoring love to his La Condesa, Simone — sexy-sad, never-met-the-right-man-until-too-late — Signoret.

DOCTOR: You're so strange, sometimes you're so bitter. Then you're like a child, soft and warm.
LA CONDESA: I'm just a woman.

Elinor Glyn used to be good at this sort of thing — a kind of ur-kitsch. Oskar Werner, smiling mistily throughout a sickly, romantic performance, is undoubtedly the hit of the film. His Dr. Schumann is a good man who loves sweetly yet falters, oh so humanly, in his devotion; he dies smack bang on the deck. In his forties, Oskar Werner has turned into a startling synthesis of William F. Buckley, Jr., and Wernher Von Braun. And Kramer and Mann, trying to be six foot three, have made him the new romantic hero.

"In art," Sir Kenneth Clark has said, "you cannot achieve accuracy without emotion." And the only emotion you can achieve without accuracy is embarrassment. In Kramer's work the artist's accuracy is missing. That is why he is so often congratulated for his *intentions*. Intentions, despite what schoolteachers say, are what we shouldn't have to think about in the arts and don't think about except when they're not achieved. Kramer asks for congratulations on the size and importance of his unrealized aspirations. In politics a·candidate may hope to be judged on what he intends to do, but in art we judge what is done. Stanley Kramer runs for office in the arts.

[September 1965]

V

The Movie Past

‎
‎
‎‎

Movies on Television

A FEW years ago, a jet on which I was returning to California after a trip to New York was instructed to delay landing for a half hour. The plane circled above the San Francisco area, and spread out under me were the farm where I was born, the little town where my grandparents were buried, the city where I had gone to school, the cemetery where my parents were, the homes of my brothers and sisters, Berkeley, where I had gone to college, and the house where at that moment, while I hovered high above, my little daughter and my dogs were awaiting my return. It was as though my whole life were suspended in time — as though no matter where you'd gone, what you'd done, the past were all still there, present, if you just got up high enough to attain the proper perspective.

Sometimes I get a comparable sensation when I turn from the news programs or the discussion shows on television to the old movies. So much of what formed our tastes and shaped our experiences, and so much of the garbage of our youth that we never thought we'd see again — preserved and exposed to eyes and minds that might well want not to believe that this was an important part of our past. Now these movies are there for new generations, to whom they cannot possibly have the same impact or meaning, because they are all jumbled together, out of historical sequence. Even what may deserve an honorable position in movie history is somehow dishonored by being so available, so meaninglessly present. Everything is in hopeless disorder, and that is the way new generations experience our movie past. In the other arts, something like natural selection takes place: only the best or the most significant or influential or successful works compete for our attention. Moreover, those from the past are likely to be touched up to accord with the taste of the present. In popular music, old tunes are newly orchestrated. A small repertory of plays is continually reinterpreted for contemporary meanings — the great ones for new relevance, the not so great rewritten, tackily "brought up to date," or deliberately treated as period pieces.

By contrast, movies, through the accidents of commerce, are sold in blocks or packages to television, the worst with the mediocre and the best, the successes with the failures, the forgotten with the half forgotten, the ones so dreary you don't know whether you ever saw them or just others like them with some so famous you can't be sure whether you actually saw them or only imagined what they were like. A lot of this stuff never really made it with any audience; it played in small towns or it was used to soak up the time just the way TV in bars does.

There are so many things that we, having lived through them, or passed over them, never want to think about again. But in movies nothing is cleaned away, sorted out, purposefully discarded. (The destruction of negatives in studio fires or deliberately, to save space, was as indiscriminate as the preservation and resale.) There's a kind of hopelessness about it: what does not deserve to last lasts, and so it all begins to seem one big pile of junk, and some people say, "Movies never really were any good — except maybe the Bogarts." If the same thing had happened in literature or music or painting — if we were constantly surrounded by the piled-up inventory of the past — it's conceivable that modern man's notions of culture and civilization would be very different. Movies, most of them produced as fodder to satisfy the appetite for pleasure and relaxation, turned out to have magical properties — indeed, to *be* magical properties. This fodder can be fed to people over and over again. Yet, not altogether strangely, as the years wear on it doesn't please their palates, though many will go on swallowing it, just because nothing tastier is easily accessible. Watching old movies is like spending an evening with those people next door. They bore us, and we wouldn't go out of our way to see them; we drop in on them because they're so close. If it took some effort to see old movies, we might try to find out which were the good ones, and if people saw only the good ones maybe they would still respect old movies. As it is, people sit and watch movies that audiences walked out on thirty years ago. Like Lot's wife, we are tempted to take another look, attracted not by evil but by something that seems much more shameful — our own innocence. We don't try to reread the girls' and boys' "series" books of our adolescence — the very look of them is dismaying. The textbooks we studied in grammar school are probably more "dated" than the movies we saw then, but we never look at the old schoolbooks, whereas we keep seeing on TV the movies that represent the same stage in our lives and played much the same part in them — as things we learned from and, in spite of, went beyond.

Not all old movies look bad now, of course; the good ones are still good — surprisingly good, often, if you consider how much of the detail is lost on television. Not only the size but the shape of the image is changed, and, indeed, almost all the specifically visual elements are so distorted as to be all but completely destroyed. On television, a cattle drive or a cavalry charge or a chase — the climax of so many a big movie — loses the dimensions of space and distance that made it exciting, that sometimes made it great. And since the structural elements — the rhythm, the buildup, the suspense — are also partly destroyed by deletions and commercial breaks and the interruptions incidental to home viewing, it's amazing that the bare bones of performance, dialogue, story, good directing, and (especially important for close-range viewing) good editing can still make an old movie more entertaining than almost anything new on television. (That's why old movies are taking over television — or, more accurately, vice versa.) The verbal slapstick of the newspaper-life comedies — *Blessed Event, Roxie Hart, His Girl Friday* — may no longer be fresh (partly because it has been so widely imitated), but it's still funny. Movies with good, fast, energetic talk seem better than ever on television — still not great but, on television, better than what *is* great. (And as we listen to the tabloid journalists insulting the corrupt politicians, we respond once again to the happy effrontery of that period when the targets of popular satire were still small enough for us to laugh at without choking.) The wit of dialogue comedies like Preston Sturges's *Unfaithfully Yours* isn't much diminished, nor does a tight melodrama like *Double Indemnity* lose a great deal. Movies like Joseph L. Mankiewicz's *A Letter to Three Wives* and *All About Eve* look practically the same on television as in theatres, because they have almost no visual dimensions to lose. In them the camera serves primarily to show us the person who is going to speak the next presumably bright line — a scheme that on television, as in theatres, is acceptable only when the line *is* bright. Horror and fantasy films like Karl Freund's *The Mummy* or Robert Florey's *The Murders in the Rue Morgue* — even with the loss, through miniaturization, of imaginative special effects — are surprisingly effective, perhaps because they are so primitive in their appeal that the qualities of the imagery matter less than the basic suggestions. Fear counts for more than finesse, and viewing horror films is far more frightening at home than in the shared comfort of an audience that breaks the tension with derision.

Other kinds of movies lose much of what made them worth looking at — the films of von Sternberg, for example, designed in light and shadow, or the subleties of Max Ophuls, or the lyricism of Satyajit Ray. In the box the work of these men is not as lively or as satisfying as the plain good movies of lesser directors. Reduced to the dead grays of a cheap television print, Orson Welles's *The Magnificent Ambersons* — an uneven work that is nevertheless a triumphant conquest of the movie medium — is as lifelessly dull as a newspaper Wirephoto of a great painting. But when people say of a "big" movie like *High Noon* that it has dated or that it doesn't hold up, what they are really saying is that their judgment was faulty or has changed. They may have overresponded to its publicity and reputation or to its attempt to deal with a social problem or an idea, and may have ignored the banalities surrounding that attempt; now that the idea doesn't seem so daring, they notice the rest. Perhaps it was a traditional drama that was new to them and that they thought was new to the world; everyone's "golden age of movies" is the period of his first moviegoing and just before — what he just missed or wasn't allowed to see. (The Bogart films came out just before today's college kids started going.)

Sometimes we suspect, and sometimes rightly, that our memory has improved a picture — that imaginatively we made it what we knew it could have been or should have been — and, fearing this, we may prefer memory to new contact. We'll remember it better if we don't see it again — we'll remember what it meant to us. The nostalgia we may have poured over a performer or over our recollections of a movie has a way of congealing when we try to renew the contact. But sometimes the experience of reseeing is wonderful — a confirmation of the general feeling that was all that remained with us from childhood. And we enjoy the fresh proof of the rightness of our responses that reseeing the film gives us. We re-experience what we once felt, and memories flood back. Then movies seem magical — all those *madeleines* waiting to be dipped in tea. What looks bad in old movies is the culture of which they were part and which they expressed — a tone of American life that we have forgotten. When we see First World War posters, we are far enough away from their patriotic primitivism to be amused at the emotions and sentiments to which they appealed. We can feel charmed but superior. It's not so easy to cut ourselves off from old movies and the old selves who responded to them, because they're not an isolated part of the past held up for derision and amusement and wonder. Although they belong to the same world as stories in *Liberty,* old radio shows, old phonograph records, an America still divided between hayseeds and city slickers, and although they may seem archaic, their pastness isn't so very past. It includes the last decade, last year, yesterday.

Though in advertising movies for TV the recentness is the lure, for many of us what constitutes the attraction is the datedness, and the earlier movies are more compelling than the ones of the fifties or the early sixties. Also, of course, the movies of the thirties and forties look better technically, because, ironically, the competition with television that made movies of the fifties and sixties enlarge their scope and their subject matter has resulted in their looking like a mess in the box — the sides of the image lopped off, the crowds and vistas a boring blur, the color altered, the epic themes incongruous and absurd on the little home screen. In a movie like *The Robe,* the large-scale production values that were depended on to attract TV viewers away from their sets become a negative factor. But even if the quality of the image were improved, these movies are too much like the ones we can see in theatres to be interesting at home. At home, we like to look at those stiff, carefully groomed actors of the thirties, with their clipped, Anglophile stage speech and their regular, clean-cut features — walking profiles, like the figures on Etruscan vases and almost as remote. And there is the faithless wife — how will she decide between her lover and her husband, when they seem as alike as two wax grooms on a wedding cake? For us, all three are doomed not by sin and disgrace but by history. Audiences of the period may have enjoyed these movies for their action, their story, their thrills, their wit, and all this high living. But through our window on the past we see the actors acting out other dramas as well. The Middle European immigrants had children who didn't speak the king's English and, after the Second World War, didn't even respect it so much. A flick of the dial and we are in the fifties amid the slouchers, with their thick lips, shapeless noses, and shaggy haircuts, waiting to say their lines until they think them out, then mumbling something that is barely speech. How long, O Warren Beatty, must we wait before we turn back to beautiful stick figures like Phillips Holmes?

We can take a shortcut through the hell of many lives, turning the dial from the social protest of the thirties to the films of the same writers and directors in the fifties — full of justifications for blabbing, which they shifted onto characters in oddly unrelated situations. We can see in the films of the forties the displaced artists of Europe — the anti-Nazi exiles like Conrad Veidt, the refugees like Peter Lorre, Fritz Kortner, and Alexander Granach. And what are they playing? Nazis, of course, because they have accents, and so for Americans — for the whole world — they become images of Nazi brutes. Or we can look at the patriotic sentiments of the Second World War years and those actresses, in their orgies of ersatz nobility, giving their lives — or, at the very least, their bodies — to save their country. It was sickening at the time; it's perversely amusing now — part of the spectacle of our common culture.

Probably in a few years some kid watching *The Sandpiper* on television will say what I recently heard a kid say about *Mrs. Miniver:* "And to think they really believed it in those days." Of course, we didn't. We didn't accept nearly as much in old movies as we may now fear we did. Many of us went to see big-name pictures just as we went to *The Night of the Iguana,* without believing a minute of it. The James Bond pictures are not to be "believed," but they tell us a lot about the conventions that audiences now accept, just as the confessional films of the thirties dealing with sin and illegitimacy and motherhood tell us about the sickly-sentimental tone of American entertainment in the midst of the Depression. Movies indicate what the producers thought people would pay to see — which was not always the same as what they *would* pay to see. Even what they enjoyed seeing does not tell us directly what they believed but only indirectly hints at the tone and style of a culture. There is no reason to assume that people twenty or thirty years ago were stupider than they are now. (Consider how *we* may be judged by people twenty years from now looking at today's movies.) Though it may not seem obvious to us now, part of the original appeal of old movies — which we certainly understood and responded to as children — was that, despite their sentimental tone, they helped to form the liberalized modern consciousness. This trash — and most of it was, and is, trash — probably taught us more about the world, and even about values, than our "education" did. Movies broke down barriers of all kinds, opened up the world, helped to make us aware. And they were almost always on the side of the mistreated, the socially despised. Almost all drama is. And, because movies were a mass medium, they had to be on the side of the poor.

Nor does it necessarily go without saying that the glimpses of something really good even in mediocre movies — the quickening of excitement at a great performance, the discovery of beauty in a gesture or a phrase or an image — made us understand the meaning of art as our teachers in appreciation courses never could. And — what is more difficult for those who are not movie lovers to grasp — even after this sense of the greater and the higher is developed, we still do not want to live only on the heights. We still want that pleasure of discovering things for ourselves; we need the sustenance of the ordinary, the commonplace, the almost-good as part of the anticipatory atmosphere. And though it all helps us to respond to the moments of greatness, it is not only for this that we want it. The educated person who became interested in cinema as an art form through Bergman or Fellini or Resnais is an alien to me (and my mind goes blank with hostility and indifference when he begins to talk). There isn't much for the art-cinema person on television; to look at a great movie, or even a poor movie carefully designed in terms of textures and contrasts, on television is, in general, maddening, because those movies lose too much. (Educational television, though, persists in this misguided effort to bring the television viewer movie classics.) There are few such movies anyway. But there are all the not-great movies, which we probably wouldn't bother going to see in museums or in theatre revivals — they're just not that important. Seeing them on television is a different kind of experience, with different values — partly because the movie past hasn't been filtered to conform to anyone's convenient favorite notions of film art. We make our own, admittedly small, discoveries or rediscoveries. There's Dan Dailey doing his advertising-wise number in *It's Always Fair Weather,* or Gene Kelly and Fred Astaire singing and dancing "The Babbitt and the Bromide" in *Ziegfeld Follies.* And it's like putting on a record of Ray Charles singing "Georgia on My Mind" or Frank Sinatra singing "Bim Bam Baby" or Elisabeth Schwarzkopf singing operetta, and feeling again the elation we felt the first time. Why should we deny these pleasures because there are other, more complex kinds of pleasure possible? It's true that these pleasures don't deepen, and that they don't change *us,* but maybe that is part of what makes them seem our own — we realize that we have some emotions and responses that *don't* change as we get older.

People who see a movie for the first time on television don't remember it the same way that people do who saw it in a theatre. Even without the specific visual loss that results from the transfer to another medium, it's doubtful whether a movie could have as intense an impact as it had in its own time. Probably by definition, works that are not truly great cannot be as compelling out of their time. Sinclair Lewis's and Hemingway's novels were becoming archaic while their authors lived. Can *On the Waterfront* have the impact now that it had in 1954? Not quite. And revivals in movie theatres don't have the same kind of charge, either. There's something a little stale in the air, there's a different kind of audience. At a revival, we must allow for the period, or care because of the period. Television viewers seeing old movies for the first time can have very little sense of how and why new stars moved us when they appeared, of the excitement of new themes, of what these movies meant to us. They don't even know which were important in their time, which were "hits."

But they can discover *something* in old movies, and there are few discoveries to be made on dramatic shows produced for television. In comedies, the nervous tic of canned laughter neutralizes everything; the laughter is as false for the funny as for the unfunny and prevents us from responding to either. In general, performances in old movies don't suffer horribly on television except from cuts, and what kindles something like the early flash fire is the power of personality that comes through in those roles that made a star. Today's high school and college students seeing *East of Eden* and *Rebel Without a Cause* for the first time are almost as caught up in James Dean as the first generation of adolescent viewers was, experiencing that tender, romantic, marvelously masochistic identification with the boy who does everything wrong because he cares so much. And because Dean died young and hard, he is not just another actor who outlived his myth and became ordinary in stale roles — he is the symbol of misunderstood youth. He is inside the skin of moviegoing and television-watching youth — even educated youth — in a way that Keats and Shelley or John Cornford and Julian Bell are not. Youth can respond — though not so strongly — to many of our old heroes and heroines: to Gary Cooper, say, as the elegant, lean, amusingly silent romantic loner of his early Western and aviation films. (And they can more easily ignore the actor who sacrificed that character for blubbering righteous bathos.) Bogart found his myth late, and Dean fulfilled the romantic myth of self-destructiveness, so they look good on television. More often, television, by showing us actors before and after their key starring roles, is a myth-killer. But it keeps acting ability alive.

There is a kind of young television watcher seeing old movies for the first time who is surprisingly sensitive to their values and responds almost with the intensity of a moviegoer. But he's different from the moviegoer. For one thing, he's housebound, inactive, solitary. Unlike a moviegoer, he seems to have no need to discuss what he sees. The kind of television watcher I mean (and the ones I've met are all boys) seems to have extreme empathy with the material in the box (new TV shows as well as old movies, though rarely news), but he may not know how to enter into a conversation, or even how to come into a room or go out of it. He fell in love with his baby-sitter, so he remains a baby. He's unusually polite and intelligent, but in a mechanical way — just going through the motions, without interest. He gives the impression that he wants to withdraw from this human interference and get back to his real life — the box. He is like a prisoner who has everything he wants in prison and is content to stay there. Yet, oddly, he and his fellows seem to be tuned in to each other; just as it sometimes seems that even a teen-ager locked in a closet would pick up the new dance steps at the same moment as other teen-agers, these television watchers react to the same things at the same time. If they can find more intensity in this box than in their own living, then this box can provide *constantly* what we got at the movies only a few times a week. Why should they move away from it, or talk, or go out of the house, when they will only experience that as a loss? Of course, we can see why they should, and their inability to make connections outside is frighteningly suggestive of ways in which we, too, are cut off. It's a matter of degree. If we stay up half the night to watch old movies and can't face the next day, it's partly, at least, because of the fascination of our own movie past; *they* live in a past they never had, like people who become obsessed by places they have only imaginative connections with — Brazil, Venezuela, Arabia Deserta. Either way, there is always something a little shameful about living in the past; we feel guilty, stupid — as if the pleasure we get needed some justification that we can't provide.

For some moviegoers, movies probably contribute to that self-defeating romanticizing of expectations which makes life a series of disappointments. They watch the same movies over and over on television, as if they were constantly returning to the scene of the crime — the life they were so busy dreaming about that they never lived it. They are paralyzed by longing, while those less romantic can leap the hurdle. I heard a story the other day about a man who ever since his school days had been worshipfully "in love with" a famous movie star, talking about her, fantasizing about her, following her career, with its ups and downs and its stormy romances and marriages to producers and agents and wealthy sportsmen and rich businessmen. Though he became successful himself, it never occurred to him that he could enter her terrain — she was so glamorously above him. Last week, he got a letter from an old classmate, to whom, years before, he had confided his adoration of the star; the classmate — an unattractive guy who had never done anything with his life and had a crummy job in a crummy business — had just married her.

Movies are a combination of art and mass medium, but television is so single in its purpose — selling — that it operates without that painful, poignant mixture of aspiration and effort and compromise. We almost never think of calling a television show "beautiful," or even of complaining about the absence of beauty, because we take it for granted that television operates without beauty. When we see on television photographic records of the past, like the pictures of Scott's Antarctic expedition or those series on the First World War, they seem almost too strong for the box, too pure for it. The past has a terror and a fascination and a beauty beyond almost anything else. We are looking at the dead, and they move and grin and wave at us; it's an almost unbearable experience. When our wonder and our grief are interrupted or followed by a commercial, we want to destroy the ugly box. Old movies don't tear us apart like that. They do something else, which we can take more of and take more easily: they give us a sense of the passage of life. Here is Elizabeth Taylor as a plump matron and here, an hour later, as an exquisite child. That charmingly petulant little gigolo with the skinny face and the mustache that seems the most substantial part of him — can he have developed into the great Laurence Olivier? Here is Orson Welles as a young man, playing a handsome old man, and here is Orson Welles as he has really aged. Here are Bette Davis and Charles Boyer traversing the course of their lives from ingenue and juvenile, through major roles, into character parts — back and forth, endlessly, embodying the good and bad characters of many styles, many periods. We see the old character actors put out to pasture in television serials, playing gossipy neighbors or grumpy grandpas, and then we see them in their youth or middle age, in the roles that made them famous — and it's startling to find how good they were, how vital, after we've encountered them caricaturing themselves, feeding off their old roles. They have almost nothing left of that young actor we responded to — and still find ourselves responding to — except the distinctive voice and a few crotchets. There are those of us who, when we watch old movies, sit there murmuring the names as the actors appear (Florence Bates, Henry Daniell, Ernest Thesiger, Constance Collier, Edna May Oliver, Douglas Fowley), or we recognize them but can't remember their names, yet know how well we once knew them, experiencing the failure of memory as a loss of our own past until we can supply it (Maude Eburne or Porter Hall) — with great relief. After a few seconds, I can always remember them, though I cannot remember the names of my childhood companions or of the prizefighter I once dated, or even of the boy who took me to the senior prom. We are eager to hear again that line we know is coming. We hate to miss anything. Our memories are jarred by cuts. We want to see the movie to the end.

The graveyard of *Our Town* affords such a tiny perspective compared to this. Old movies on television are a gigantic, panoramic novel that we can tune in to and out of. People watch avidly for a few weeks or months or years and then give up; others tune in when they're away from home in lonely hotel rooms, or regularly, at home, a few nights a week or every night. The rest of the family may ignore the passing show, may often interrupt, because individual lines of dialogue or details of plot hardly seem to matter as they did originally. A movie on television is no longer just a drama in itself; it is part of a huge ongoing parade. To a new generation, what does it matter if a few gestures and a nuance are lost, when they know they can't watch the parade on all the channels at all hours anyway? It's like traffic on the street. The television generation knows there is no end; it all just goes on. When television watchers are surveyed and asked what kind of programming they want or how they feel television can be improved, some of them not only have no answers but can't understand the questions. What they get on their sets is television — that's it.

Notes on 280 Movies

From *Adam's Rib* to *Zazie*

Over the past fifteen years I've written about four thousand notes on movies in one form or another — ads for theatres and colleges, notes for students, broadcasts and magazine articles — and I've made a selection from them here. Such a selection may indicate something usually left out of the histories of movies — may get at some of the experiences that were possible at the movies, some of what we went to movies for and what we reacted to when we got there. I hope that no one will confuse my purpose by attempting to see significance in what I've left out. There are enormous gaps — not just of movies and directors and periods of film I've written about elsewhere, or hope to write about more intensively in the future, but also movies I just never got around to writing about. Mostly I was writing about movies years after I'd seen them (for revivals at theatres and colleges), so what I said about them was what had stayed with me.

Perhaps there is something to be gained from an individual's ranging over old moviegoing experiences this way. I think the sense of feeling qualified to praise and complain in the same breath is part of our feeling that movies belong to us. Going to the movies was more satisfying than what the schools had taught us was art. We responded totally — which often meant contemptuously, wanting more, wanting movies to be better. Moviegoing meant experiencing possibilities so seldom realized that we lived in a state of constant frustration, perpetual eagerness. Maybe this comes through in the notes. We may be reaching the end of the era in which individual movies meant something to people. In the new era, movies may just mean a barrage of images. But these movies I've written about are all going into the stew of the future; they can still be seen in theatres, at film societies, or on television, and perhaps the notes will be useful.

◉ ◉ ◉

Adam's Rib. This "uncinematic" but well-played and often witty comedy derives its humor from modern variations on the battle of the sexes. Katharine Hepburn, thin, nervous, and high-strung, keeps pecking away at Spencer Tracy, who is solid, imperturbable, and maddeningly sane. She attacks, he blocks; their skirmishes are desperately, ludicrously civilized. They are married lawyers on opposing sides in a court battle; the case involves equal rights for women, i.e., does Judy Holliday have the right to shoot her husband, Tom Ewell, in order to protect her home against Jean Hagen? The stars are well matched (though Tracy frequently indulges in coy mugging); the script by Ruth Gordon and Garson Kanin is lively and ingenious (though it stoops to easy laughs now and then). The phenomenal supporting cast includes David Wayne (who almost walks away with the movie), Polly Moran, and Hope Emerson (as a circus strong woman). Holliday and Ewell, both later starred, are best when taken in small doses, as in this picture. Directed by George Cukor. 1949.

◉　◉　◉

The Adventures of Robin Hood. In 1938 Warner Brothers produced one of the most popular of all adventure pictures. Errol Flynn was the image of Robin Hood, almost improbably pretty Olivia de Havilland was Maid Marian, Alan Hale was Little John, Eugene Pallette was Friar Tuck, Ian Hunter was Richard the Lion-Hearted, Basil Rathbone and Claude Rains were wicked, and Herbert Mundin was cute. The story was clear, the color ravishing, the direction (by Michael Curtiz and William Keighley) simple, the acting simple and crude. And it was wonderful! Mean men get themselves killed off; good men triumph. Vice is intriguing; virtue is charming. Who could ask for anything more? Well, of course, we do, we must . . . yet action is good, our senses demand it. Three Academy Awards, including Best Original Score (Erich Wolfgang Korngold).

◉　◉　◉

The Adventures of Robinson Crusoe. Luis Buñuel's version of the Defoe novel is free of that deadly solicitude that usually kills off classics. *Sight and Sound* selected this as the Best Picture of 1954 — "a picture destined to give pleasure in twenty years" — and one critic described it as "a classic of a classic." The film is a simple, unsentimental account of Defoe's basic themes: a man alone face to face with nature; then a man terribly alone, unable to face lack of love and friendship; and finally, after the lacerations of desire, a man ludicrously alone. The great, controversial Spanish director used Dan O'Herlihy, a fine actor with a beautiful voice, and photographed him in the jungle of Manzanillo near Acapulco. In the delirium sequence, Buñuel is the same untamed director who made film history, and when O'Herlihy as Crusoe shouts to the hills in order to hear the companionable echo, when he rushes to the sea in desperate longing for a ship, loneliness is brought, in sudden shocks, to the pitch of awe and terror. Crusoe's eventual meeting with Friday (James Fernandez) changes the tone to irony. Color.

⊙ ⊙ ⊙

The African Queen. In 1951 an inspired piece of casting brought Humphrey Bogart and Katharine Hepburn together in *The African Queen*. This is a comedy, a love story, and a tale of adventure, and it is one of the most charming and entertaining movies ever made. The director, John Huston, has written that the comedy was not present either in the novel by C. S. Forester or in the original screenplay by James Agee, John Collier, and himself, but that it grew out of the relationship of Hepburn and Bogart, who were just naturally funny when they worked together. Hepburn has revealed that the comedy didn't just grow, it was planted — that the picture wasn't going well until Huston came up with the inspiration that her Rosie should be played as Mrs. Roosevelt. After that, Bogart and Hepburn played together with an ease and humor that makes their love affair — the mating of a forbidding, ironclad spinster and a tough, gin-soaked riverboat captain — seem not only inevitable, but perfect. The story, set in central Africa in 1914, is so convincingly acted that you may feel a bit jarred at the end; after the lovers have brought the boat, the "African Queen," over dangerous rapids to torpedo a German battleship, Huston seems to stop taking the movie seriously, and the conclusion presages his later careless madness in *Beat the Devil*. With Robert Morley as Hepburn's missionary brother. Bogart won the Academy Award as Best Actor of 1951. Color. (Peter Viertel, who worked on the dialogue while the company was on location in Africa, wrote the novel *White Hunter, Black Heart* about his experiences with Huston.)

⊙ ⊙ ⊙

Alice Adams. Apart from her comedies, Katharine Hepburn has been best in *Little Women*, in *Alice Adams,* and, later in her career, in *Long Day's Journey into Night*. As Alice Adams, her beautiful angularity and her faintly absurd Bryn Mawr accent are perfect for Booth Tarkington's desperately pretentious small-town social climber. The scene in which Alice, dressed in simple, exquisite taste, attends a party full of plushy, overdressed "society" belles is a pointed commentary on American taste and social standards. Hepburn's pantomiming in some of the scenes is as fine as the best American acting I've ever seen — she makes Alice one of the few authentic American movie heroines. But there's no question that for some people the movie has its nerve-wracking side — the revolting, nagging, massive-bosomed mother; the painfully funny, calamitous dinner scene. This 1935 movie helped to make the reputation of its young director

George Stevens; his sense of detail and milieu is in marked contrast to his later inflated style. With that nightmare of a ghastly family: Fred Stone as the infantile father; Ann Shoemaker as the pushing mother; Frank Albertson as the vulgar brother; and, as the classic slovenly servant, Hattie McDaniel. There are also the "society" people: the fleshy young Evelyn Venable, Hedda Hopper, and, regrettably, as the hero, the young Fred MacMurray, who looks utterly incapable of appreciating Alice. The happy ending is a bad enough falsification of the material; as acted by MacMurray, it's hopeless (Alice's disbelieving "Gee whiz!" is matched by the audience's disbelief).

◉ ◉ ◉

All About Eve. This is ersatz art of a very high grade, and one of the most enjoyable movies ever made. Eve, a young actress (Anne Baxter), intrigues to take the place of an aging star (Bette Davis) on stage and in bed, and the battle is fought with tooth, claw, and a battery of epigrams. The dialogue and atmosphere are so peculiarly remote from life that they have sometimes been mistaken for art. The synthetic has qualities of its own — glib, over-explicit, self-important, the You're-sneaky-and-corrupt-but-so-am-I-We-belong-to-each-other-darling style of writing. Author-director Joseph L. Mankiewicz's bad taste, exhibited with verve, is more fun than careful, mousy, dehydrated good taste. His nonsense about "theatre" is saved by one performance that is the real thing: Bette Davis is at her most brilliant. Her actress — vain, scared, a woman who goes too far in her reactions and emotions — makes the whole thing come alive (though it's hard to believe Anne Baxter could ever be a threat to Bette Davis). With George Sanders, Celeste Holm, Gary Merrill, Thelma Ritter, Gregory Ratoff, Hugh Marlowe, and Marilyn Monroe. Academy Awards for 1950: Best Picture, Director, Screenplay, Supporting Actor (Sanders), etc.

◉ ◉ ◉

All Quiet on the Western Front. Made in Hollywood in 1930, this is a remarkable, angry, and important film — not because it is a work of film art, but because it is part of human history by now. Over one hundred million people have seen this film and — perhaps — responded to its pacifist message. One could be cynical about the results, but the film itself does not invite cynical reactions, and the fact that it has frequently been banned in countries preparing for war suggests that it is a touchstone that makes even militarists uncomfortable.

Remarque's novel was already famous when Lewis Milestone directed this attack on the senseless human waste of war. We follow a handful of young German volunteers in World War I from school to battlefield, and we see the disintegration of their romantic ideas of war, gallantry, and fatherland in the squalor of the trenches. Except for Louis Wolheim, who is capable of creating a character with a minimum of material, the actors (Lew Ayres, Slim Summerville, Russell Gleason, Billy Bakewell, John Wray, Raymond Griffith, Ben Alexander, et al.) are often awkward, uncertain, and overemphatic, but this does not seem to matter very much. This is a film in which sincerity and intention matter more than style, and though one may wince at the lines Maxwell Anderson wrote (every time he opens his heart, he sticks his poetic foot in it), one knows what he means.

The year 1930 was, of course, a good year for pacifism — which always flourishes between wars. (Milestone didn't make pacifist films during World War II — nor did anybody else working in Hollywood.) It might be noted also that a later pacifist film, Kubrick's *Paths of Glory,* is conveniently set in World War I, rather than in the more complicated moral and political environment of Nazism and World War II. And wasn't it perhaps easier to make *All Quiet on the Western Front* just because its heroes were Germans? War always seems like a tragic waste when told from the point of view of the losers. It would be an altogether different matter to present the death of, say, R.A.F. pilots in World War II as tragic waste.

George Cukor worked on the production with Milestone; Arthur Edeson did the photography; George Abbott, Del Andrews, and Milestone also worked on the script. (Fred Zinnemann, who had just arrived in Hollywood after studying film in Paris and Berlin, is a bit player, doing double duty as a German soldier and a French ambulance driver.) Academy Awards for 1930: Best Picture, Best Director.

◉ ◉ ◉

Amici per la Pelle. (Shown in various countries as *Friends for Life;* released in the United States as *The Woman in the Painting.*) Franco Rossi's 1955 film is an intuitive study of the emotional involvement of two boys — glittering little fawns who suggest an earlier stage in the lives of the schoolboys of *Les Enfants Terribles.* Films that deal with the pains of love in the undifferentiated period of early adolescence are usually crude and coy; this one is almost too tender, too "sensitive" to the beauty of youthful agony. But it respects the dreams and the humor of its subjects. Dark, incredibly beautiful Geronimo Meynier is the assured Mario; blond Andrea Scire (the more gifted actor of the two) is Franco. This movie is conceived on a small scale and it never attracted much of an audience here except among homosexuals — although it doesn't have any overt homosexual content.

◉ ◉ ◉

Arsenic and Old Lace. This isn't much of a movie but it's a demonstration of what was considered black comedy in the forties — and *Arsenic and Old Lace* was just different enough in its time to be enormously popular (as it also had been on the stage). Wholesome black comedy we might call it now. Multiple murder has never been so deliberately amoral and innocent as in this American quasi-classic farce. Cary Grant tries to convince his sweetly lethal little aunts (Josephine Hull and Jean Adair) that it isn't nice to put arsenic in the elderberry wine, but they just don't understand why he gets so upset. You may not either: the director, Frank Capra, has Grant performing in such a frenzied, dithering manner that throughout much of the action he seems crazier than anybody else. The villains, Peter Lorre as himself and Raymond Massey impersonating Boris Karloff, are also murderers, and extremely uncouth in their methods. With James Gleason, Edward Everett Horton, Priscilla Lane, Jack Carson, and thirteen corpses. From Joseph Kesselring's play. 1944. (For about fifteen years afterward, any film society or school movie series could count on *Arsenic and Old Lace* to make money. But nobody paid much attention to a funnier, less labored movie in the same genre, the 1945 *Murder, He Says.*)

◉　◉　◉

Baby Doll. The Legion of Decency: "It dwells almost without variation or relief upon carnal suggestiveness." *Life:* "The most fiercely controversial film of the decade." *Time:* "Just possibly the dirtiest American-made motion picture that has ever been legally exhibited . . . Priapean detail that might well have embarrassed Boccaccio."

No, *Baby Doll* may not be all that, but it is a droll and engrossing carnal comedy. Tennessee Williams's teen-age heroine (Carroll Baker) lives on the edge of reality in infantile erotic dreams (reality is Mississippi white trash — Southern decadence at the gin level). Her middle-aged husband (Karl Malden) has agreed not to consummate the marriage until she is twenty; meanwhile her husband's enemy, a sharp Sicilian (Eli Wallach) lays expert hands on her (his performance is also expert). Elia Kazan directed. 1956.

◉　◉　◉

The Bad and the Beautiful. The same year as the great Hollywood Dunciad *Singin' in the Rain,* there was a rather hysterical piece of Hollywoodian self-analysis — *The Bad and the Beautiful.* The former was a satire, the latter a satire in spite of itself — which recalls the fabled little old lady who said in the middle of *Quo Vadis?,* "Look, there's a sweet little lion who hasn't got a Christian." *The Bad and the Beautiful,* a loaded, glossy melodrama about a "bad" megalomaniac Hollywood producer, Kirk Douglas, and a "beautiful" alcoholic star, Lana Turner, is a piquant example of what it purports to expose — luxurious exhibitionism. The course of what is described as a "rat race" to success is the softest turf ever. The structure is reminiscent of *Citizen Kane,* and there is the "Rosebud" of Mr. Douglas's ill-defined Oedipal confusion, but there are good scenes and, for those who enjoy gossip, incidents derived from a number of famous careers. With Dick Powell as the author, Gloria Grahame as his Southern wife, Walter Pidgeon as a studio head, Barry Sullivan as a director, Gilbert Roland as "Gaucho" the actor, Elaine Stewart as the starlet, Leo G. Carroll, etc. Vincente Minnelli directed. 1952. Five Academy Awards, including Best Supporting Actress (Miss Grahame), Screenplay (Charles Schnee), Cinematography (Robert Surtees).

⊙   ⊙   ⊙

Bad Day at Black Rock. The title suggests a banal Western, but this 1954 film was the first to bring up the wartime outrages against Japanese-Americans (treated also in 1960 in Phil Karlson's *Hell to Eternity*). The story is set in the mythical Southwestern town of Black Rock where the inhabitants are bound together by the guilty secret of their mistreatment of a Japanese farmer; on this bad day a one-armed stranger (Spencer Tracy) arrives and begins to ask questions. Though *Bad Day at Black Rock* is crudely melodramatic, it is a very superior example of motion picture craftsmanship. John Sturges is an excellent director — each movement and line is exact and economical; the cinematographer, William C. Mellor, uses composition and color intelligently. With Robert Ryan, Dean Jagger, Walter Brennan, Anne Francis, John Ericson, Lee Marvin, Ernest Borgnine. CinemaScope, color.

⊙   ⊙   ⊙

The Baker's Wife (*La Femme du Boulanger*). When Marcel Pagnol's film opened in this country, the New York *Times* wrote, "It also happens to be one of the very greatest pictures ever made: pagan, poetic, and incomparably witty. If the cinema could only live up to its standards, we should all very soon be spoiled." Far from living up to its standards, the French soon produced a rash of imitations — and everybody got sick of "earthy," "peasant" comedies, each claiming to be another *Baker's Wife*. Pagnol adapted this classic of cuckoldry from Jean Giono's *Jean Le Bleu*. The village baker cannot work because he laments his wife's departure with a stupid, sexy shepherd; the villagers, who want their bread, organize to bring her back. Raimu's baker is an acting classic — a true tragicomic hero; and you may find the movie a perfect comedy (as did Orson Welles, who cited it as proof that "a story and an actor — both superb" could result in "a perfect movie" even if the direction and editing were not "cinematic"). With Charpin, and the openmouthed Ginette Leclerc as the wife. 1938.

⊙   ⊙   ⊙

The Band Wagon. If you love musicals, you may be forced to conclude that the *idea* of musicals is better than musicals themselves. Try to think of the good ones, ones you could actually invite civilized people to look at, and there aren't many. There are *Singin' in the Rain, It's Always Fair Weather,* the Rogers-Astaire series, *The Wizard of Oz, Gold Diggers of 1933,* the lovely, neglected Rodgers and Hart *Hallelujah, I'm a Bum, Where's Charley?, Annie Get Your Gun, Calamity Jane.* And then you begin to get to pieces of *An American in Paris, Cabin in the Sky, On the Avenue, Be Yourself,* and *Up in Arms,* to Hermes Pan's choreography in *Kiss Me Kate* and Jack Cole's in *The "I Don't Care" Girl,* and to Danny Kaye singing "Ballin' the Jack" and doing his Spanish dance in *On the Riviera,* and to parts of *Jumbo* — especially the Busby Berkeley parts — etc. There are dozens of musicals that have one or two good numbers, but that's all they've got; and to get that much you may have to writhe in sympathy while poor Gene Kelly, rose clenched between his teeth, ogles Kathryn Grayson as she shrills a high C.

There were few as good as *The Band Wagon* with Fred Astaire and Jack Buchanan — and Jack Buchanan's dancing and rosy-ripe readings of the satirical theatre cant provided by Comden and Green take precedence even over Astaire. Except for three minutes of "classical" ballet by Cyd Charisse, which the charitable will overlook, the film is a series of urbane delights, culminating in the dance sequence parodying the Mickey Spillane genre of bloody boudoir fiction. And when the bespangled Miss Charisse wraps her phenomenal legs around Astaire, she can be forgiven everything — even the fact that she reads her lines as if she learned them phonetically. Nanette Fabray and Oscar Levant (who are both good) play at being Comden and Green; Vincente Minnelli directed; Michael Kidd did the choreography; the songs are by Howard Dietz and Arthur Schwartz. 1954, color.

⊙ ⊙ ⊙

The Barefoot Contessa. Insiders' exposés usually tell little that isn't known, but they are great for exposing the intellectual pretensions of the insider. And those pretensions are sometimes very appealing to movie fans . . .

In the forties Ben Hecht impressed some people with a whoppingly ludicrous movie called *Specter of the Rose* (sample dialogue: "My heart is dancing a minuet in the ashcan"). Joseph L. Mankiewicz had apparently been concealing *his* load of florid deep thoughts, and in 1954 he unburdened himself, telling All about Hollywood — where the men aren't men and the women are magnificent, frustrated animals. Flamenco dancer Ava Gardner is discovered in the slums of Madrid by a millionaire movie producer (Warren Stevens), a gutless, sycophantic press agent (Edmond O'Brien), and an alcoholic, broken-down director (Humphrey Bogart). She becomes a glamorous star but only feels at home with her feet in the dirt (symbolized by a guitar player, a chauffeur, and a gypsy dancer — one played by Riccardo Rioli). The movie, absurdly garrulous about telling the dirty truth, is so ornate and so acidulous that a lot of people took it very seriously. *Contessa* is a trash masterpiece: a Cinderella story in which the prince turns out to be impotent. It's hard to believe Mankiewicz ever spent an hour in Hollywood; the alternative supposition is that he spent too many hours there. With Rossano Brazzi as the castrated Italian count, Marius Goring as a rich South American playboy, Valentina Cortesa, Elizabeth Sellars, etc. Academy Award for Best Supporting Actor (O'Brien). Color.

◉   ◉   ◉

Bay of the Angels (*La Baie des Anges*). What would this film be like without Jeanne Moreau? Even if the dialogue and direction were the same, the meanings would be subtly different. *Bay of the Angels* is almost an emanation of Moreau, is inconceivable without her. Written and directed by Jacques Demy in 1964, the film is rather like a French attempt to purify, to get to the essence of a Warners movie of the thirties. Demy not only gets to it, he gets beyond it. His virtuoso sense of film rhythm makes the flimsy, capricious story about a gambling lady a lyrical study in compulsion and luck, a passionate comedy. The concept of gambling as almost total spontaneity and irresponsibility — as giving in to chance (as if that were the most complete acceptance of life) — is oddly suggestive, and we begin, in this film, to feel its pull and appeal, to feel that gambling is a bum's existentialism. And Jeanne Moreau, in a very Bette Davis sort of way, dramatizes herself superbly. (There are times when she's as white and unreal as Constance Bennett in her satins and you think how marvelous she'd be singing "The Boulevard of Broken Dreams.") This is a magical, whirling little film, a triumph of style — even though it runs down to nothing in the last — too quick, too ambiguous — shot. With Claude Mann. Photographed, in dazzling sunlight, by Raoul Coutard. The music by Michel Legrand is integral to the film — in a way music has rarely been used since René Clair's first talkies.

◉   ◉   ◉

Beat the Devil. "The formula of *Beat the Devil*," its director John Huston once remarked, "is that everyone is slightly absurd." The story was unknown to the cast, but presumably known to Huston and his writer, Truman Capote; however, Capote later remarked that he had "a suspicion that John wasn't too clear about it." Commercially speaking, the movie courted — and achieved — disaster. According to most accounts, Capote wrote the script as they went along (reading it aloud to the cast each morning,

Robert Morley says), and Huston didn't show any signs of anxiety. This improvisation was not necessarily an actor's delight, and Humphrey Bogart, who looks rather bewildered through much of it, as if he hadn't been let in on the joke, said, "Only the phonies think it's funny. It's a mess." *Beat the Devil* is a mess, but it's probably the funniest mess — the screwball classic — of all time. It kidded itself, yet it succeeded in some original (and perhaps dangerously marginal) way by finding a style of its own.

Bogart and his wife, Gina Lollobrigida, are on a ship bound for British East Africa; their traveling companions are a gang of uranium swindlers — Robert Morley, Peter Lorre, Marco Tulli, and Ivor Barnard. A creative liar, Jennifer Jones, turns up, surprisingly in a blonde wig (the other surprise is that she's the funniest performer in the picture); she's married to a bogus British lord, Edward Underdown. Then there's a shipwreck — but need we go on? This 1954 picture is something special: the straight-faced parody of the international thriller that killed off the whole genre. (It also ended the Huston-Bogart working relationship: Bogart had had his own money in *Beat the Devil*.)

⊚ ⊚ ⊚

Beauty and the Beast (*La Belle et la Bête*). Jean Cocteau wrote and directed his first full-length movie in 1946; he created a fairy-tale atmosphere of sensuous elegance. As a child escapes from the everyday family life to the magic of a storybook, so, in the film, Beauty's farm with its Vermeer simplicity fades in intensity as we are caught up in the Gustave Doré extravagance of the Beast's enchanted landscape. In Christian Bérard's makeup, Jean Marais is a beautiful Beast; Beauty's self-sacrifice to him holds no more horror than a satisfying romantic fantasy should have. The transformation of the Beast into Prince Charming is ambiguous — what we have gained cannot take the place of what we have lost. (When shown the film, Greta Garbo is reported to have said at the end, "Give me back my beast.") Josette Day is, quite properly, Beauty. With Marcel André as the father, Michel Auclair as the brother, Mila Parely as the sister. Music by Georges Auric.

⊚ ⊚ ⊚

Il Bell'Antonio. This minor, but very fine, film was badly mistreated by the American press. The New York *Times* led off the attack with, "Much ado about something that any average intelligent couple in this day would straighten out with a good marriage counselor or perhaps a psychiatrist." The Yankee notion that a good psychiatrist can cure anything dies hard; if this therapeutic concept of life and criticism were widely applied, Hamlet and Macbeth and Oedipus and all the rest of the great characters of drama also needed nothing more than a little straightening out.

Bell'Antonio isn't a great character, but he's a desolate, and finally painful, figure — the young man who has accepted the myths of his mother, his father, and his church and cannot reconcile them. He believes in purity, but he also acts out his father's belief that sexual prowess is the measure of the man. Antonio (Marcello Mastroianni in a delicate, muted performance that may be his best) is a Sicilian Don Juan whose life is destroyed by the conflict between sacred and profane love. A great ladies' man with women he doesn't respect or care about — loose women or women of a lower social class — he is impotent with the pure, highborn girl that he loves and marries. Mauro Bolognini directed this gentle but satirical study of virility and social position in a Catholic culture, with Pierre Brasseur as the strutting rooster of a father, Rina Morelli as the mother, Claudia Cardinale as the pure bride, and Tomas Milian as the cousin.

In Pier Paolo Pasolini's adaptation of Vitaliano Brancati's novel, the man who is incapable of making love when he is in love represents the whole pattern of social and religious decadence. Antonio is expected to profess a belief in purity without believing in it — but Antonio really believes in purity and love. He is the victim of the system.

The reactions of the American critics — almost all male — to this film may tell us something about American concepts of virility. The critics found the hero's problem rather ludicrous or "droll"; some complained that the problem was too special to be of general interest — as if Americans were so virile they couldn't possibly be interested in an impotent character. Sometimes when you get to know these men, you wonder who they think they're kidding. (A friend who worked for a mail-order publishing house that put out one of those manuals on how to cure impotence told me that his firm received thousands of orders, and every man who wrote in said he was ordering it for a cousin or a friend. No one ordered it for anyone so close to himself as a brother.) Problems of virility are not localized in Sicily, nor problems of sacred and profane love either. The sexual boasts of salesmen and merchants and junior executives betray a split life: they rarely talk about what they do with their wives. One gathers that it's not worth bragging about. "My wife is a *lady*," they often say. And sometimes they add, "That's what's the matter with her." But it doesn't take too much imagination to catch on that the inhibition is just as much theirs.

It is the special quality of sympathy, and even of tragedy, in *Il Bell'Antonio* that the proud, handsome hero is never for an instant comic, that what is so often treated, from the outside, as a subject for comedy is here treated from the inside. Impotence may seem funny if you're that insensitive, but it's not at all funny seen from the point of view of the humiliated and despised impotent male. All his life, Antonio will long to possess the ideal, and the very intensity of his longing for idealized love will defeat him. And perhaps there is no cure. 1960.

⊙ ⊙ ⊙

Big Deal on Madonna Street (*I Soliti Ignoti,* literally, the police term —
the usual unknown, or unidentified, persons). Mario Monicelli's gentle,
casually underplayed little comedy, made in 1958, has no ugliness, no brutality, no villains, and no heroes, just a bunch of good-natured, hopeful but
incompetent crooks. Even their goal — a safe with some jewelry — is
modest. The most prominent members of the cast are Vittorio Gassman,
Marcello Mastroianni (as a simpleton), Renato Salvatori, and Claudia
Cardinale. Totò is featured as a sort of guest star. It isn't a particularly
interesting role, but Totò, who died in 1967, was beyond such considerations: a world unto himself. Totò, a stylized image of age, sadness, and
decadence, is usually called a clown, but he is a clown the way champagne
is a wine. He was, perhaps not incidentally, the living embodiment of the
old sentimental plot clichés about the aristocrat or disillusioned lover or
man guilty of a crime of passion who disguises himself as a clown. Off stage
and screen he was Antonio, Prince De Curtis, and his titles included Prince
of Byzantium, Cilicia, Macedonia, Thessaly, and Ponte; Duke of Cyprus
and Epirus; Count of Drivasto and Durazzo, Noble Knight of the Holy
Roman Empire. No wonder he looked at us with those tired eyes that had
seen everything.

⊙ ⊙ ⊙

The Big Knife. This film — in the same genre as *The Bad and the Beautiful* — is thoroughly immoderate. Everything in it is garish and overdone:
it's paced too fast and pitched too high, immorality is attacked with almost
obscene relish, the knife turns into a buzz saw. But with all these faults of
taste, perhaps because of them, who can take his eyes off the screen? Rod
Steiger gives a classic performance as the Hollywood magnate; Jack Palance is surprisingly effective as the overwrought John Garfield-type star.
With Wendell Corey, Shelley Winters, Everett Sloane, Jean Hagen, Ilka
Chase, and Ida Lupino and Wesley Addy as sanctimonious characters who,
I'm afraid, are the author's mouthpieces. James Poe adapted Clifford
Odets's play. Robert Aldrich directed. 1955.

⊙ ⊙ ⊙

The Big Sleep. Humphrey Bogart is Raymond Chandler's private eye in
this incredibly complicated thriller. You may not be able to figure out the
plot, even after the dénouement (Chandler reported that while the film was
in production, William Faulkner and the other screen writers had to appeal
to him for guidance, and apparently Chandler couldn't exactly figure it out,
either), but it's the dialogue and the entertaining qualities of each sequence,
not the plot, that make this movie. *The Big Sleep* is a shoddy, though amus-

ing detective-genre piece. It takes place in the big city of displaced persons — the night city where sensation is all. The action is tense and fast, and the film catches the lurid Chandler atmosphere. The characters are a collection of sophisticated monsters — blackmailers, pornographers, apathetic society girls (Lauren Bacall and Martha Vickers are a baffling pair of spoiled sisters; the latter sucks her thumb), drug addicts, nymphomaniacs (a brunette Dorothy Malone seduces the hero in what must surely be record time), murderers. All of them talk in innuendoes as if that were a new stylization of the American language, but how reassuring it is to know what the second layer of meaning refers to. Howard Hawks directed — and so well that you may even enjoy the fact that, as he says, "Neither the author, the writer, nor myself knew who had killed whom." 1946.

⊚　⊚　⊚

The Blood of a Poet (*Le Sang d'un Poete*). Jean Cocteau: "I can give you an interpretation which is my own. I can tell you: the poet's solitude is so great, he so lives what he creates, that the mouth of one of his creations lives in his hand like a wound, and that he loves this mouth, that he loves himself, in short, that he wakes up in the morning with this mouth against him like a pick-up, that he tries to get rid of it, and that he gets rid of it on a dead statue — and that this statue begins to live — and that it takes its revenge, and that it sets him off upon awful adventures. I can tell you that the snowball fight is the poet's childhood, and that when he plays the game of cards with his Glory, with his Destiny, he cheats by taking from his childhood that which he should draw from within himself." The four sequences of *The Blood of a Poet* are illogical and timeless: they happen in the instant that a chimney topples. (More than the chimney toppled — thousands of cans of film fell into disrepute.) The first time you see Jean Cocteau's 1930 film, you're likely to find it silly, auto-erotic, static, absurd, and you may feel cheated after having heard so much about it. But though it may seem without any depth, you're not likely to forget it — it has a suggestiveness unlike any other film. Cocteau dedicated "this ribbon of allegories" to the "painters of blazons and enigmas." Almost twenty years later, in *Orpheus,* he orchestrated the themes of the dreams and ecstasies of the poet and his obsession with the unknown. Music by Georges Auric. Photographed by Georges Périnal.

⊚　⊚　⊚

The Blue Angel (*Der Blaue Engel*). Josef von Sternberg's almost legendary film is popularly known as the movie that launched the career of Marlene Dietrich; among film historians it is acclaimed as a work of screen art, among psychologists as the classic study of sadomasochism. Heinrich Mann's novel *Professor Unrath* deals with a man who descends to complete degradation after his first sexual experience. Emil Jannings plays the inhibited, tyrannical high-school professor who is prudishly indignant about his students visiting Lola Lola (Dietrich), the singer at the Blue Angel; he goes to put a stop to this, and himself succumbs to her callous, impassive sexuality. Dietrich's Lola Lola is a rather coarse, plump young beauty — who suggests sex without romance, love, or sentiment. *The Blue Angel* is a movie you can look at and admire sequence by sequence because it's brilliantly made, and yet you may feel (with me) that you don't really *like* it that much. I prefer the lovely romantic nonsense of *Morocco* to all this heavy breathing.

This 1930 work, which revived the German cinema, was meant to star Emil Jannings, who was part of the international tradition of the silent screen. He was popular enough in this country to win the first Academy Award in 1927–28 for two American movies, *The Way of All Flesh,* and *The Last Command* (directed by von Sternberg). The director of *The Blue Angel* had been working in Hollywood for more than fifteen years before he went to Germany, at Jannings's request, to direct this crucial film — the first sound film for both Jannings and von Sternberg. They set in motion the Dietrich myth that was eventually to surpass their fame.

◉　◉　◉

Born Yesterday. Judy Holliday took the Academy Award as Best Actress of 1950 for this classic portrait of the dumb blonde — brassy, vacuous Billie Dawn. Broderick Crawford plays her keeper, a junkman lately become "a dealer in scrap metal" in the world of cartels. Afraid that Billie will disgrace him in Washington, he hires a newspaperman, William Holden, to make Billie more "couth." Unfortunately, both for the junkman and the picture, the journalist reforms Billie, and as she gains in virtue she diminishes in interest. But you'll remember the early, acquisitive Billie with her truculent voice and glassy eyes, and her gin-rummy game. Directed by George Cukor, from the play by Garson Kanin.

◉　◉　◉

Breaking the Sound Barrier. The screen heroes who had been winning the war by killing Japanese or Germans gave way to the quiet, worried-eyed heroes of our time in David Lean's 1952 British epic of the air. The most worried of them all is Ralph Richardson — the courageous, civilized modern man — sober-faced, businesslike, keeping his inner tensions under exquisite control (though we are always tipped off that he is suffering more than other men who crudely vent their emotions). Terence Rattigan, who wrote the film, didn't exactly break any new ground in the air: he provides Ann Todd with that inevitable role of the prescient wife (the "please don't go up to break the sound barrier tonight, dear" type), and Nigel Patrick,

John Justin, and the others say and do just what you might expect were they carrying the White Man's Burden in remote Outposts of Empire. If you're tolerant, you'll just relax through all this low-keyed English valor and enjoy the soaring photography and the amazing supersonic sound effects. (In his review of the film, Henry Hart of *Films in Review* contributed this rich, deep thought: "When, in the cockpit of a plane, Ann Todd and Nigel Patrick kiss by rubbing the ends of their oxygen masks together, even the idlest mind is alerted to the poignant fact that the solaces of the human past will have different manifestations in the exigencies of the human future.")

⊙ ⊙ ⊙

Bringing Up Baby. Katharine Hepburn had been a magnificent Jo in *Little Women,* and as the thirties prototype of an ultramodern career girl (*Christopher Strong, Break of Hearts,* etc.), she was just about the whole Mary McCarthy *Group.* But by the late thirties, despite her exquisite performances, such films as *The Little Minister* and *Quality Street* (which were not bad) had made her box-office poison. The public didn't want tremulous anguish in crinoline: James M. Barrie had had his day, quaintness was out. *Bringing Up Baby,* Hepburn's first comedy, made in 1938, rescued her.

Lunatic comedy of the thirties generally started with an heiress; this one starts with an heiress (Hepburn) who has a dog, George, and a leopard, Baby. Cary Grant is a paleontologist who has just acquired the bone he needs to complete his dinosaur skeleton. George steals the bone, Grant and Baby chase each other around, the dinosaur collapses — but Grant winds up with Hepburn, and no paleontologist ever got hold of a more beautiful set of bones. Howard Hawks keeps all this trifling nonsense in such artful balance that it never impinges on the real world; it may be the American movies' closest equivalent to Restoration Comedy. Though *Bringing Up Baby* hasn't the prestige or reputation of Hepburn's later comedy success, *The Philadelphia Story,* it's her best comedy. The cast includes Charles Ruggles as an explorer, Barry Fitzgerald as a drunk, May Robson as the dowager, Walter Catlett as the sheriff, and Fritz Field as the frenzied psychoanalyst. (George is played by Asta of *The Thin Man* series.) The screenplay is by Dudley Nichols and Hager Wilde from Wilde's story.

⊙ ⊙ ⊙

Broken Arrow. I've never heard of anybody — man or child — who didn't enjoy this movie. Not that it's film art. But it's full of legend and romance and action. The setting is Arizona in those confused days after the Civil War when renegades from both armies are causing trouble among the Indians. James Stewart plays the ex-Union officer who befriends the Apache, Cochise (Jeff Chandler), and marries an Apache princess (Debra

Paget). Delmer Daves directed this adaptation by Michael Blankfort of the novel *Blood Brother* by Elliott Arnold, and though it never won any Academy Awards or brotherhood awards, it has probably done more to soften racial hostilities than most movies designed to instruct, indict, and inspire. (That Indian princess was no squaw.) Indians vs. settlers have been a movie staple from the beginning, but this 1950 production manages to be acceptably modern without violating the conventions of the genre. Color.

⊙ ⊙ ⊙

The Bullfighter and the Lady. A dark horse in the same field and in the same year (1951) as Robert Rossen's *The Brave Bulls,* this less pretentious and much less expensive film has a more authentic, seamy aspect. Though marred by synthetic plot ingredients, it is a better film than its heavily glamorized and publicized rival. Robert Stack plays the American who wants to be a bullfighter; Gilbert Roland, in the best performance of his amazingly long career, is the aging matador. With Katy Jurado and Joy Page. Produced and directed by Budd Boetticher.

⊙ ⊙ ⊙

The Cabinet of Dr. Caligari. The audience, confined in the madman's universe, sees what he sees: distorted perspectives, eerie painted lights and shadows, an angular, warped world of fears and menace. The sets are used expressionistically to convey the madman's thoughts, to intensify the characters' emotions, and to emphasize the meanings of the action. This film is so entrenched in the "masterpiece" classification that a few cautionary remarks should be added, lest your initial reaction be disappointment: you may be delighted that the flats express something, because most of the actors don't; you may find that the décor, which is highly experimental in terms of space and distance but is derivative from the stage use of expressionism, is a monotonous zigzag (too many hooks and no fish, if you know what I mean). The decorative use of an insane landscape — startling though it is — is not popular and is rarely imitated. *Caligari,* the most complete essay in the décor of delirium, is one of the most famous films of all time, and it was considered a radical advance in film technique, yet it stands almost alone — and you'll know why.

But it does have a style, crazy though it is, and style is the most difficult achievement in the movie medium. And it has Werner Krauss as the nightmare image of the psychoanalyst — the mountebank Caligari — and in his cabinet, the somnambulist Cesare — the extraordinary young Conrad Veidt. (For the really dedicated, there is an elaborate exposition of the film and its supposed subversive political implications in Siegfried Kracauer's *From Caligari to Hitler,* though Kracauer may be the mountebank of film exegesis.) Directed by Robert Wiene; scenario by Carl Mayer and Hans Janowitz. 1919.

⊚ ⊚ ⊚

Camille. Like parents crowing over baby's first steps, MGM announced "Garbo talks!" (in *Anna Christie*) and "Garbo laughs!" (in *Ninotchka*), but they missed out when they should have crowed: "Garbo acts!" That was in *Camille* in 1936. Garbo's Camille is too intelligent for her frivolous life, too generous for her circumstances; she is a divinity trying to succeed as a whore. It's a sublime, ironic performance. The slow, solemn production is luxuriant in its vulgarity; it achieves that glamor which MGM traditionally mistook for style. As Armand, Robert Taylor is inept, but not completely unforgivable: in 1936 he had, at least, a romantic profile. As M. Duval, Lionel Barrymore *is* unforgivable. The one actor who rises to the occasion is Henry Daniell, who makes a brilliant Baron de Varville. With Lenore Ulric as Olympe, Laura Hope Crews as Prudence, Elizabeth Allan, Jessie Ralph. In spite of MGM, Garbo's artistry triumphs, and the tear-jerker *Camille* is transformed into the "classic" the studio claimed it to be. Directed by George Cukor.

⊚ ⊚ ⊚

The Captain's Paradise. Alec Guinness leads a double life, and acts out one of the most common fantasies of Western man: as the captain of a ferry steamer, he alternates nights between a cozy middle-class cottage with homebody wife Celia Johnson on the Gibraltar end, and a torrid, opulent apartment with passionately exuberant wife Yvonne De Carlo on the Morocco end. "Two women," he says, "each with half of the things a man wants," and, happily split between two lives and two wives, he doesn't realize that he is satisfying only half of each wife's desires. This comedy never quite finds its style, but the two wives are better than any man (or the film) deserves. With Charles Goldner, Miles Malleson, Bill Fraser. Directed by Anthony Kimmins, written by Alec Coppel and Nicholas Phipps. 1953.

⊚ ⊚ ⊚

Un Carnet de Bal. In 1932 Julien Duvivier established his mastery of the sound film with *Poil de Carotte* (*Redhead*) starring Harry Baur, the great character actor whose position in France in the thirties was similar to that of Emil Jannings in Germany in the twenties. The film had lyric intensity and psychological complexity — the qualities which were to become the characteristic style of the French sound film. The subject of *Poil de Carotte* is the desperate estrangement of a young boy (Robert Lynen), and this is communicated by images, rhythm, and editing rather than by didactic dialogue (in an American film a doctor or analyst would explain that the mother felt unloved and so she rejected the child, etc.). The influence of this film may still be seen in passages of Tony Richardson's *The Loneliness of the Long Distance Runner*.

But Duvivier became famous for a different kind of film-making: in 1937 he made *Pépé Le Moko* starring Jean Gabin — the greatest French romantic-gangster movie until *Breathless*. Few Americans saw *Pépé Le Moko,* as it was held back until an American version, *Algiers,* starring Charles Boyer and "introducing" Hedy Lamarr, could be released. *Algiers* was a peculiar backhanded tribute to Duvivier — reproducing many of his sequences shot by shot, with actors selected and costumed to look like his, and yet with a totally different "glamorized" spirit. But that same year, 1937, Duvivier had one of the great commercial successes here in the emerging foreign film theatres with the most famous (and widely imitated in Hollywood and Europe) of all episodic star-studded films, *Un Carnet de Bal*.

A wealthy, nostalgic widow (Marie Bell) goes in search of what might have been; she sets out to find the men listed on the dance program of her first ball, and manages to locate the most famous French actors of the day — Harry Baur, who has become a monk; Pierre-Richard Willm, an Alpine guide; Raimu, a town mayor; Louis Jouvet, a crook; Pierre Blanchar, a shady doctor; Fernandel, a hairdresser. The performances form an astonishing catalogue of acting styles. Even Françoise Rosay turns up. People who saw this movie in their youth still talk about its big scene — the revelation of the discrepancy between what the widow remembered as her first great ball and the poor little provincial dance it actually was. But they tend to have the same kind of nostalgia toward *Un Carnet de Bal* — which despite its stars and its Grand Prix at Venice is a little tawdry, too. It doesn't compare, artistically, with *Poil de Carotte,* nor as a work of romantic entertainment with *Pépé Le Moko*. But it's redolent of the thirties, and it could serve as a text on the varieties of French acting.

◉   ◉   ◉

Carnival in Flanders (*La Kermesse Héroïque*). One of the rare, perfect works of the screen, this comedy masterpiece suggests a fusion of Breughel and Boccaccio. It is a morning in 1616; a Spanish regiment comes to a town in occupied Flanders. The cowardly burghers collapse, and their charming ladies meet the challenge: with the dawn the Spaniards depart, poorer in worldly goods, richer in experience. Jacques Feyder directed, from a script by Charles Spaak. Nothing is attempted which is not achieved. The drawback to this kind of classical perfection is a trace of dullness — expectations are too neatly fulfilled; movies with rough edges and bad spots are sometimes more exciting. This is a classic movie comedy which isn't really very funny — not so much because the thirties' "sophisticated" treatment of sexual collaboration is undermined by our awareness of what happened in the forties but because it's just too archly classic. With Françoise Rosay, Louis Jouvet, Jean Murat, Alerme, Micheline Cheirel. Designed by Lazare Meerson; photographed by Harry Stradling. Grand Prix du Cinema Française, First Prize at Venice, New York Film Critics' Award, etc. 1935.

⊙ ⊙ ⊙

Casablanca. Ingrid Bergman became a popular favorite when Humphrey Bogart, as Rick, the most famous saloonkeeper in screen history, treated her like a whore in *Casablanca* — a movie that demonstrates how entertaining a bad movie can be. Although their romance was certified by a collection of Academy Awards, they didn't press their luck and never appeared together again. In the role of the cynic redeemed by love, Bogart became the great adventurer-lover of the screen during the war years. There isn't an actor in American films today with anything like his assurance, his magnetism, or his style. In *Casablanca* he established the figure of the rebellious hero — the lone wolf who hates and defies officialdom (and in the movies he fulfilled a universal fantasy: he got away with it). Questioned about his purposes and motives, he informs the police: "I came to Casablanca for the waters." "But there are no waters in Casablanca." "I was misinformed." The international cast includes Paul Henreid, Conrad Veidt, Sydney Greenstreet, Claude Rains, Peter Lorre, Marcel Dalio, Helmut Dantine, S. Z. Sakall, Joy Page, Leonid Kinsky, Madeleine LeBeau, John Qualen, and, memorably, Dooley Wilson singing "As Time Goes By." One's tender sentiments will probably still be stirred, but in the cool night air afterward one may wonder a bit that this received the Academy Award as Best Picture of 1943, and that awards were given to Michael Curtiz as Best Director, to Julius and Philip Epstein and Howard Koch for the Best Screenplay, and the Thalberg Award to producer Hal Wallis.

⊙ ⊙ ⊙

Casque d'Or. Simone Signoret had her finest role (until *Room at the Top*) as the gigolette with the glorious helmet of golden hair in Jacques Becker's sultry, poetic account of the Paris underworld of 1900. Her performance — a triumph of sensuality and physical assurance — took the British Film Academy Award for 1952. Becker introduces a world of cutthroats, apaches, and gun molls, and then subtly evokes an atmosphere that gives meaning and passion — and an overdose of doom — to their rivalries and intrigues. The love scenes between Signoret and Serge Reggiani are unusually simple and tender; perhaps because of this, the grim conclusion is almost insupportably painful. The movie is very well done, and yet I don't really like it. There's something fundamentally trashy and touristy about its look at lowlife — "Look, *they* have feelings, too." With Claude Dauphin as the gang leader; Raymond Bussières, Gaston Modot. Becker and Jacques Companeez did the script.

◎ ◎ ◎

A Cat and Two Women (*Neko to Shozo to Futari no Onna*). Shiro Toyoda made this film in 1956, and it was widely regarded as the best Japanese film of that year. *A Cat and Two Women* is a wry psychological comedy about a man who prefers his cat to his two wives. The tart flavor of the film derives from the familial nastiness: one can't like any of them, one can't even really like the cat. Some of the most famous Japanese players are the leads: the first wife is the fabulous Isuzu Yamada (she has been in over three hundred movies since 1929, has been married six times, and still plays romantic roles . . .); Kyoko Kagawa, usually a demure heroine, plays the unsympathetic second wife; Hisaya Morishige is the indolent, cat-loving husband; the character actress, Cheiko Naniwa, plays his mother. The manner in which these four scheme for affection and power, using the cat as a decoy, is a perverse object lesson in Japanese manners and mores. The story (by Junichiro Tanizaki) is set among shopkeepers at a small seaside town near Osaka, in the Kansai district. Shiro Toyoda is a more traditional Japanese director than Kurosawa or Ichikawa, and the narrative (rather than dramatic) construction of the film makes it a bit trying for American moviegoers; but if one makes the effort of adjustment, this film yields many subtle pleasures. Japanese films are notorious for badly selected, derivative music (even *Rashomon* was marred by a score that sounded like Ravel's *Bolero*); this is one of the rare examples of an interesting Japanese film score.

◎ ◎ ◎

The Cat People. Among the films produced as B thrillers, there are occasional ingenious works; one of the most famous of these is Val Lewton's ironic horror film, produced in 1942 — the first of a series of eleven Lewton productions. The psychoanalyst (Tom Conway) calmly explains to his patient (Simone Simon) that her idea that she is turning into a member of the cat family is a fantasy; she silences him with fang and talon. Such charming ironies in the American horror genre, dedicated for many years to gorillas, haunted houses, and disembodied arms, were the contribution of Lewton. For a brief period he revolutionized scare movies with suggestion, imaginative sound effects and camera angles, leaving everything to the fear-filled imagination. But it's only in the context of almost totally incompetent trash that Lewton's minor kind of ingenuity can loom large. It doesn't take much to make a revolution in Hollywood. Lewton's horror pictures aren't good, they're just better than the other cheap horror pictures Hollywood had been grinding out. With Kent Smith. Directed by Jacques Tourneur. Edited by Mark Robson.

◉ ◉ ◉

The Children Are Watching Us (*I Bambini Ci Guardano*). In 1942 Vittorio De Sica found his author, Cesare Zavattini, and his theme — the destruction of innocence. As in his later works, the enemy is human injustice — not intentional injustice, but what people are driven to do to each other. This is one of those rare movies that are too finely felt, too painful, and too intransigent ever to reach a large audience. Like De Sica's *Umberto D.,* it is a picture of loneliness, but at the other end of the life-span. Umberto has so little time left; Prico, the four-year-old, has his whole ruined life ahead. His mother, sensually drawn to her lover, hasn't the strength to cling to the child; his ego-shattered father kills himself. Prico is left, agonized and inarticulate, walking the corridors of a boarding school. Except for *Forbidden Games* there has probably never been such a view of the antagonism and desolation that separates adult and child life.

◉ ◉ ◉

Children of Paradise (*Les Enfants du Paradis*). This lushly romantic creation by director Marcel Carné and writer Jacques Prévert seems to burst the bounds of the medium. At first it may seem a romance set in the Paris of Balzac; it is likely to turn into an aesthetic problem on the relations of art and life; it even turns into a comparison of dramatic modes — for it includes at least five kinds of theatrical performances. And, encompassing these, it is a film poem on the nature and varieties of love — sacred and profane, selfless and possessive. Made during the Occupation, when some of its makers were being hunted by the Gestapo, this extraordinarily sumptuous production was filmed in garages and Maquis hideaways where starving extras made away with some of the banquets before they could be photographed. With Jean-Louis Barrault (he sucks in his cheeks a bit much for my tastes) as the mime Deburau — the Pierrot; Arletty as Garance; Pierre Brasseur as the Shakespearean actor Lemaître — the Harlequin; Louis Salou as the count; Marcel Herrand as the philosophic murderer; Pierre Renoir as the ragpicker-informer; and Maria Casarès has the unrewarding role of the theatre manager's daughter, who produces an abominable offspring. 1945.

◉ ◉ ◉

Citizen Kane. In 1941 the most controversial one-man show in film history was staged by twenty-five-year-old writer-director-star Orson Welles when he dramatized the life of William Randolph Hearst, who had quite a reputation for his own one-man show, i.e., the Spanish-American War.

Kane, the figure Welles creates, is the American as imperialist — a Faust who sells out to the devil in himself. Welles's striking study of unscrupulous egotism was nevertheless withdrawn for over a decade and reissued only after Hearst's death. *Citizen Kane* was the only American movie of the sound period to be among the top selections at Brussels in 1958, and the 1962 international poll of critics voted it first among the greatest films of all time; I wonder if the judges appreciated what Americans enjoy in the film — the exuberant, sophomoric, devil-may-care effrontery of it all. Welles not only teases the film medium with a let's-try-everything-once-over-lightly, he teases his subject matter once over heavily. It's exhilarating to see the mechanics of movie-making (usually more concealed) exploited for theatrical effect. (Welles's devices were like visual counterparts of the booming voice, the echoes, the hollow sounds, and his other old radio techniques.) *Citizen Kane* is more fun than any great movie I can think of, and it's also a rare example of a movie that seems better today than when it first came out: in 1941 many of us were disappointed by the shallowness of the film's political treatment, but now even that shallowness seems evocative of the period. With Joseph Cotten, Dorothy Comingore, Agnes Moorehead, George Coulouris, Everett Sloane, etc. Academy Award for Best Original Screenplay of 1941 (Welles and Herman J. Mankiewicz). Photography by Gregg Toland; edited by Robert Wise and Mark Robson.

◉ ◉ ◉

City of Gold. This twenty-three-minute film from Canada, a reconstruction of the Yukon gold rush from period photographs, shows the men who left all ties behind in the quest for gold and glory; the film provides more sense of what gold fever is, and of what these people were actually like and what they were after, than all the dozens of Hollywood epics on the theme. One marvelous photograph shows the climb through Chilkoot Pass — the climb re-created by Chaplin in *The Gold Rush.* And there are photographs of the girls who actually entertained the men of the Yukon: fat, plain, lewd, they don't look much like the dance-hall girls in Hollywood Westerns. But the young men have a beauty Hollywood has never been able to reproduce. Written and narrated by Pierre Berton. Directed by Colin Low and Wolf Koenig. 1957.

◉ ◉ ◉

Cluny Brown. A girl with a passion for plumbing is terribly repugnant to stuffy people who don't want to admit that they have drains. This wonderfully suggestive idea is the basis of Margery Sharp's mischievous satire on English propriety, filmed by Ernst Lubitsch in 1946. Lubitsch cast Jennifer Jones as Cluny (it's her only performance, except for *Beat the Devil,* that I'd look at twice) and Charles Boyer as the debonair scrounger — two happy iconoclasts who violate social conventions. He surrounded them with a prime collection of English class and mass types — the wheezy Richard Haydn, Una O'Connor as his mother, Reginald Owen, Margaret Bannerman, Peter Lawford, Helen Walker, Ernest Cossart, Sara Allgood, Florence Bates, Reginald Gardiner, C. Aubrey Smith, etc. It's a good-natured comedy.

◉ ◉ ◉

The Cobweb. By 1955 nobody was surprised that the new variant of *Grand Hotel* was an expensive, exclusive loony bin. Plots and subplots tangle and untangle as the staff and patients rush through their intrigues and affairs. Lillian Gish, even with a small part, comes closest to being the star (no, I'm not being sentimental, and my nostalgia is under firm control). Charles Boyer is the weary director of the asylum: when things start to go to hell, he flees, bottle in hand, to a motel. Richard Widmark, tense and fairly unconvincing as the "dynamic" new psychoanalyst, shuttles between his petulant wife (Gloria Grahame), who makes trouble for everybody, and an idealized occupational therapist (Lauren Bacall), who is having an affair with him. John Kerr and Susan Strasberg are young, sick, and in love. The prize comic maniac is Oscar Levant — shown, at one point, under a restraining sheet, in a continuous warm bath, gulping sedatives and singing "Mother." Vincente Minnelli directed, and to his credit, most of the confusion is calculated. With Fay Wray (in wonderful shape, considering the way King Kong used to squeeze her), Paul Stewart, etc. Based on a novel by William Gibson. This picture, not much better than *Private Worlds* of 1935 and much less fresh, has a special cachet because so many famous people have been at Austin Riggs Center at Stockbridge, which is obviously the "inspiration." Color.

◉ ◉ ◉

A Cold Wind in August. When people who work in the movie industry get together, they often talk about the little offbeat pictures — the ones that encourage them to think that maybe *something* can be done now and then. One of the movies that almost inevitably comes up for discussion is the 1961 *A Cold Wind in August.*

This low-budget, extremely "commercial" movie is a shrewdly conceived and well-acted piece of what might be called tawdry but frank eroticism. It's about an aging stripper who amuses herself by seducing a seventeen-year-old boy and discovers a sexual gratification that she has never known. He finds out she's a stripper, is disgusted and leaves her (to play around at his own age level), and she's left in despair. That's all there is to it — or that's all there might be except for the intensity Lola Albright brings to the stripper's role. Unquestionably the movie was made as an exploitation film, as an American ersatz version of Radiguet's *Devil in the Flesh* and Colette's

The Game of Love, but it does not pretend to be set on a high plane, and it is saved by the honesty and clarity of its low intentions.

The stripper's attitudes toward men and sex are convincing; but in order to point up the boy's unawareness and basic indifference to the meaning the affair has for her, the boy is made too simple. He's not much more than a concept of callow, heedless youth, and although the actor who bears the name Scott Marlowe (he doesn't look like a Scott Marlowe) plays the part well, the role is out of high-class soap opera. Still, Marlowe is a good man with his Method, and he manages to convey an emotional nature without indulging in the hysteria which so many young actors seem to confuse with feeling. His good Italian papa (Joe De Santis) seemed far more attractive to at least one older woman until the writer and director loaded him down with a piece of business that would have sunk even John Barrymore (except he would have had the wit to play it for laughs). Papa delivers quiet words of wisdom and decency — good counsel — to his son and then sits back philosophically to read his well-thumbed leatherbound volume. It was hard to concentrate on the next scene: what *could* that book be? We never found out.

Apart from the performances and Alexander Singer's direction, the movie's chief strength — Burton Wohl's economical, well-organized script — is also its weakness. It's as if "low-budget" production had been interpreted to mean a script without nonessentials. But if you set out to be a flesh merchant, you should offer more than a skeleton of material; we want more — even if it's a little extra. What's there is good in a cheap, sleazy way, but there isn't enough. *A Cold Wind in August* has a low-budget conception: it's too tight to do justice to a "loose woman."

◉ ◉ ◉

Compulsion. Here we have the case of two Raskolnikovs, brilliant students but miserably sloppy murderers. This 1959 movie has a stylish, jazz-age format, but the script can't make up its little bit of mind — is it an exploitation of thrills and decadence, a piece of crime research, or an attack on capital punishment? The three principals — Dean Stockwell, Bradford Dillman, and Orson Welles — were jointly given the Best Actor Award at Cannes; I thought Stockwell as Judd Steiner (i.e., Nathan Leopold) gave the only remarkable performance. I love to see Welles, but as a spokesman for humanity and humility, he's a terrible humbug, and it's a vapid, mealy-mouthed oration he's called upon to deliver (Clarence Darrow's two-day summation is reduced to twelve minutes of spongy sentiment). There are interesting possibilities in the material; it's too bad they're not developed. With Diane Varsi, Richard Anderson, E. G. Marshall, and Martin Milner as the student-reporter (if the murderers had really been aesthetes, he would have been the victim). Richard Fleischer directed. CinemaScope.

⊚ ⊚ ⊚

The Confessions of Felix Krull. Thomas Mann's last novel (a debonair expansion of his early short story) is a lively account of a cherubic young confidence man, an amoral charmer who uses his natural endowments in a variety of liaisons. One might think it would be difficult to find an actor handsome enough and ambiguous enough to impersonate the fortunate Felix, but fox-eyed Horst Bucholz plays the role as if born to it. Kurt Hoffmann shot the film in Germany, Paris, and Lisbon in 1957, and — like the book — it bounces along from affair to affair. Among Felix's admirers are Liselotte Pulver as Zaza, Ingrid Andree as Zouzou, Susi Nicoletti as Madame Houpfle (who tears off Felix's clothes, forces him to steal from her, and then cries, "Oh, how delightfully you debase me!"), Walter Rilla as Lord Killmarnoch (who wants to adopt Felix and offers him a ring as a token of his affection), etc. The screenplay was written by Robert Thoeren in cooperation with Erika Mann (she can be seen in the film in the bit part of an English governess). The fun isn't sustained but the first part of the picture is pretty good.

⊚ ⊚ ⊚

Confidential Agent. A tired, aging Spanish Loyalist (tired, aging Charles Boyer, and still better than almost any actor in the business) starts out by trying to prevent a Fascist business deal in England, and is variously chased, beaten, and framed by some of the most unsavory characters who ever intrigued. The cast includes Peter Lorre, Katina Paxinou, Victor Françen, George Coulouris, Wanda Hendrix, John Warburton, Miles Mander, George Zucco, etc. It also includes Lauren Bacall, but this young lady, so elegantly feline in *To Have and Have Not,* which preceded, and *The Big Sleep,* which followed, is at her wooden worst. What should have been a good thriller wasn't. Despite the cast and the possibilities in the material (out of Graham Greene) the movie is pedestrian, and Herman Shumlin, the "distinguished" stage producer who directed, showed little evidence that he'd learned anything about the medium since his earlier melodrama, *Watch on the Rhine. Confidential Agent* marked the end of his movie career. Those unfamiliar with the melodrama of the forties may be shocked at the brutalities that were indulged in under cover of the anti-Fascist theme. 1945.

⊚ ⊚ ⊚

Counsellor-at-Law. John Barrymore seems an unlikely choice for the ghetto-born lawyer of Elmer Rice's play, but this is one of the few screen roles that reveal his measure as an actor; his fabulous "presence" is apparent in every scene; so are his restraint, his humor, and his zest. The material

is a success-story-with-heartbreak, a typical American well-made play —
energetic, naïve, melodramatic, and rather touchingly goodhearted. The
1933 production has by now the patina of a period piece, and what a good
movie period it was, full of gold-diggers, social climbers, dedicated radicals,
etc. William Wyler directed, and despite his later reputation for such "pol-
ished" works as *The Little Foxes, The Best Years of Our Lives, Roman
Holiday, The Desperate Hours,* etc., I prefer this earlier Wyler, fresh from
more than fifty two-reel Westerns, willing to tell his story simply. With
Bebe Daniels, Melvyn Douglas, Doris Kenyon, Mayo Methot, Thelma
Todd, Onslow Stevens, Isabel Jewell, and, as the horrid stepson, Richard
Quine.

◉ ◉ ◉

Crime and Punishment (*Crime et Châtiment*). Marcel Aymé's adaptation has clarity and power; the director, Pierre Chenal, uses the controversial but interesting technique of conveying the characters' disassociation
from their environment by a slight distortion in the settings. As Raskolnikov, Pierre Blanchar is older, more eccentric than one expects: he emphasizes the tortured isolation, the near madness, of the character. It is in
Harry Baur's performance as Inspector Porfiry that the film achieves its
stature; Graham Greene long ago described the performance as "the finest
in the cinema this year, with his tortoise movements, his streak of cruelty,
his terrible good humor" — it is one of the great performances of any year.
1935.

◉ ◉ ◉

The Crimson Pirate. The Hecht-Lancaster travesty of the buccaneer film
combines comedy with the physical exuberance of the early Douglas Fairbanks pictures. Burt Lancaster and his old circus partner Nick Cravat tum-
ble and jump with exhilarating grace. They charge the film with physical
sensations, and, if you wanted to dance after seeing the Rogers-Astaire
musicals, you'll want to get in condition after experiencing the acrobatics
here. Robert Siodmak's direction is lively; Roland Kibbee's script is bright
and improvisatory (much of the film's wit derives from a series of casual
anachronisms). With James Hayter as a wildly improbable inventor who
looks like Benjamin Franklin; Eva Bartok, Torin Thatcher, Margot Grahame. 1952, color.

◉ ◉ ◉

Il Cristo Proibito (*Strange Deception*). Curzio Malaparte's only film is a
visually exciting but emotionally upsetting allegory of justice, guilt, and ex-
piation. Malaparte, author of *Kaputt* and *The Skin,* stopped at many stations — Fascist, Communist, pro-American — and here, in this rather

ghastly, even ludicrous semi-Christian lament for man's inability to solve his moral problems, he finds his strongest image in the masked, robed procession for the Game of the Cross. The hero, Raf Vallone, returns to his Italian village after the war and tries to hunt down the man who caused his brother's death. The villagers, sick of blood and vengeance, refuse to tell him anything; to stop the terrible hunt, his best friend (Alain Cuny) falsely confesses that he was the betrayer. The movie was condemned by the Catholic Church, attacked by the Communists, and ignored by the public. Perhaps there is a kind of writer's cinema that despite talent and originality, despite "art," is too self-serious and is doomed at the box office: *Il Cristo Proibito* is very similar to Pasolini's *Accatone*. They are boring, fascinating, maddening movies. 1951.

⊙ ⊙ ⊙

Crossfire. Psychological depths are sounded, though not deeply: the murder victim is a Jew, the murderer an anti-Semite. (The depths in the original novel by Richard Brooks were a little different: the victim was a homosexual.) This tense thriller, well acted and directed, was turned out in 1947 by producer Adrian Scott, director Edward Dmytryk, and writer John Paxton. Robert Ryan brings his considerable talent for portraying obsessive, isolated individuals to the role of the sly, anti-Semitic ex-sergeant. With Robert Mitchum, Gloria Grahame, Robert Young, Sam Levene. There are condescending little messages on the evils of race prejudice that make one squirm; this is the patina of forties melodrama.

⊙ ⊙ ⊙

Dancing Mothers. Clara Bow, Alice Joyce, and Conway Tearle are the stars in this flapper period piece — a scandalous success of 1926. The clothes of the twenties are worn triumphantly by the alarmingly active Miss Bow and the languidly patrician Miss Joyce. The sentiments are frightfully noble, though the serviceable theme was later used for less noble (and less amusing) effects in movies such as *Mildred Pierce*. Glittering sheaths enclose Elsie Lawson, Dorothy Cummings, and Leila Hyams, while Norman Trevor is an impeccable figure in white tie and tails. Herbert Brenon directed, from a play by Edgar Selwyn and Edmund Goulding.

⊙ ⊙ ⊙

Day Dreams. Silent slapstick comedy rarely encompassed visual elegance, but in England in 1928 an oddly assembled company — the director Ivor Montagu (known to film scholars as the translator of Pudovkin), the author H. G. Wells, and the heroine Elsa Lanchester, assisted by pudgy young Charles Laughton as the mock villain, and absurdly lean Harold Warrender as the mock hero — produced this little (twenty-three-minute) triumph of cinematic editing and art nouveau décor, within the slapstick form. Wells's story — a servant girl fantasizes herself in the throes of aristocratic passions, as a great actress, as a leader of fashion, etc. — has more sly wit than the later, more labored variations on the same theme. *Day Dreams* is the sort of inventive, playful use of the medium that makes you want to go right out with your friends and make a movie.

◉ ◉ ◉

A Day in the Country (*Partie de Campagne*). An innocent young girl comes of age in Jean Renoir's short (thirty-seven-minute) film based on de Maupassant. This lyric tragedy ranks with Renoir's greatest (*La Grande Illusion, La Règle du Jeu*). Visually, it recaptures the impressionist period; in tone, it accomplishes a transformation from light nostalgic comedy to despair. In the late 1800s a merchant (Gabriello) takes his family for an outing on the banks of the Marne; there, his wife (Jeanne Marken) and his daughter (Sylvia Bataille) are seduced — the one delightedly, the other tremblingly, like a captured bird. Renoir plays the innkeeper. Music by Kosma. 1937.

◉ ◉ ◉

Day of Wrath. It has been said that Carl Dreyer's art begins to unfold just at the point where most other directors give up. Witchcraft and martyrdom are his themes — but his witches do not ride broomsticks; they ride the erotic fears of their persecutors. In *Day of Wrath,* as in his earlier *The Passion of Joan of Arc,* he carries the heroine to the limits of human feeling, to the extremes of isolation, fear, and torment. In 1623 the young second wife of an austere pastor desires his death because of her love for his son; when the pastor falls dead, she is tried as a witch. As the girl is trapped, and as all possibility of hope is stripped away, one's identification with her fear becomes unbearable; then Dreyer dissolves our terror as we see that the individual is now laid bare, purified beyond even fear. It is a world that suggests a dreadful fusion of Hawthorne and Kafka: the young wife *becomes* what she and the others believe a witch to be. This psychological masterpiece is the expression of a single personality, built up from Dreyer's script, choice of camera angles, editing, and his control of every nuance of performance; it is one of the most complexly moving films ever made. Completed in 1943, but not shown outside Denmark until after the war. With Lisbeth Movin as the wife and Anna Svierkier as the old woman burned at the stake.

◉ ◉ ◉

Dead of Night. Michael Redgrave turns a horror episode into a memorable work of art in this civilized omnibus movie about the "supernatural."

The five ghost stories in this 1945 English production accumulate in intensity, until the trap closes in the surrealist climax — the encompassing ghost story. Perhaps because the people are matter of fact and contemporary and the settings are of the reasonably sophisticated forties, the horror seems more shocking than if the characters and settings were Gothic or Transylvanian.

When the film was first shown in this country, two of the stories were omitted — and though these were the weakest stories, the omission made the climax partly unintelligible. The complete version begins with Mervyn Johns's arrival at the house and proceeds through five episodes: Antony Baird and Miles Malleson in "room for one more"; Sally Ann Howes in the murdered child sequence (good material poorly done); Googie Withers and Ralph Michael in the story of the mirror that reflects the crime of an earlier century; Basil Radford and Naunton Wayne in the golfers' story told by Roland Culver (which is pretty awful); Michael Redgrave in his electrifying portrait of the schizophrenic ventriloquist, with Hartley Power as his rival and Frederick Valk as the psychoanalyst; then the nightmarish summation. John Baines and Angus MacPhail did the screenplay, using stories by H. G. Wells, E. F. Benson, and themselves; the master author of English film comedy, T. E. B. Clarke, did the additional dialogue. Directed by Robert Hamer (the mirror story), Basil Dearden, Charles Crichton, and Alberto Cavalcanti (the ventriloquist sequence). Score by Georges Auric.

⊚ ⊚ ⊚

The Deadly Invention (*Vynalez Zkazy;* released in the United States with narration and dialogue in English as *The Fabulous World of Jules Verne*). In 1895 the French magician Georges Méliès was among those invited when the Lumières gave their first exhibition of motion pictures; by 1896 he was making movies that explored the possibilities of using trick photography to create a world of irrational, comic fantasy. Among his most popular creations was his 1902 version of Jules Verne's *A Trip to the Moon* (which was used at the beginning of Michael Todd's production of *Around the World in Eighty Days*). For a half century, the magical side of film-making was almost totally neglected; even animation became routinized. In 1958, a great new movie magician, the Czech Karel Zeman, also turning to Jules Verne for inspiration, made a brilliantly stylized science fantasy.

Like Méliès, Zeman employs almost every conceivable trick, combining live action, animation, and puppet films. For many scenes, several film strips are printed on one film strip. The variety of tricks and superimpositions seems infinite, and the spectator can't help wondering how the designers, the animators, miniature-makers, and photographers have worked their magic. Just when we have one effect figured out, another image comes on that baffles us. For example, we see a drawing of half a dozen sailors in a boat on stormy seas; the sailors in their little striped outfits are foreshortened by what appears to be the hand of a primitive artist. Then the waves move, the boat rises on the water, and when it lands, the little sailors — who are live actors — walk off, still foreshortened. There are underwater scenes in which the fishes swimming about are as rigidly patterned as in a child's drawing (yet scientists say they are also perfectly accurate drawings). There are more stripes, more patterns on the clothing, the décor, and on the image itself than a sane person can easily imagine, and the painted sets are a triumph of sophisticated primitivism.

The purpose of the trickery is to create the atmosphere of the Jules Verne books which is associated in readers' minds with the steel engravings by Bennet and Riou. Zeman designed the film to look like this world-that-never-was come to life, and he retains the antique, make-believe quality by the witty use of faint horizontal lines over some of the images. Like Méliès, Zeman has wit and taste. He sustains the Victorian tone that is so necessary to the spirit of Jules Verne, and the delight in the magic of science which makes Verne seem so oddly archaic, perhaps just because his prophecies are being fulfilled.

Based on *Facing the Flag* and other works by Jules Verne. Grand Prize, International Film Festival, Brussels, 1958.

⊙   ⊙   ⊙

Destry Rides Again. "Marlene Dietrich! . . . When you wear feathers, and furs, and plumes, you wear them as the birds and animals wear them, as though they belonged to your body." — Jean Cocteau. "She possesses the rarest of civilized virtues, irony." — Kenneth Tynan.

These two gifts were combined in her classic comedy role as Frenchy, the quixotic harlot of a frontier saloon. George Marshall directed this satiric revitalization of the Tom Mix Western, based on a Max Brand novel. By taking her spangles and feathers into the Old West and dropping her sultry voice to a howling baritone, Dietrich revitalized her own career. James Stewart is Destry; in 1939 he was a younger and much more appealing hero. With a large group of people who all contribute to the flavor, some in good-sized parts — Mischa Auer, Brian Donlevy, Charles Winninger, Una Merkel, Samuel Hinds, and, in lesser parts — Jack Carson, Allen Jenkins, Irene Hervey, Warren Hymer, Billy Gilbert.

⊙   ⊙   ⊙

The Detective. Father Brown, the detective priest of G. K. Chesterton's stories, is perhaps too facile a role for Alec Guinness, and he shows a hitherto unsuspected tendency toward endearing, owlish coyness. But the film is an amusing series of chases, well directed by Robert Hamer (*Kind Hearts* *and Coronets*), and well acted by Joan Greenwood, Peter Finch, Cecil Parker as the bishop, and beautifully desiccated Ernest Thesiger as the librarian. 1954.

⊚ ⊚ ⊚

Devil in the Flesh (*Le Diable au Corps*). Raymond Radiguet, a prodigy and now a legend, wrote the novel when he was seventeen; at twenty he was dead. But his account of the clandestine love affair between an adolescent schoolboy and the discontented wife of a soldier hounded the woman who was his model all her tragic life (she insisted that the precocious Radiguet had invented the sexual aspects of their relationship). Working during the Second World War, Claude Autant-Lara re-created this story of the First World War with nostalgic tenderness. His sensitive dramatization treats the affair with such delicacy that many critics consider the love scenes to be among the most beautiful ever photographed. *Devil in the Flesh* is perhaps the kind of wartime love story that people hoped to see when they went to *A Farewell to Arms:* it has the beauty and despair of lovers attempting to save something for themselves in a period of hopeless confusion. It isn't really as good a movie as people want to believe it is, but the young Gérard Philipe was so extraordinary a camera subject that despite the dozens of roles which followed, he is best known for his incarnation of the passionate, egocentric schoolboy. Micheline Presle is the woman. Grand Prix, Brussels, 1947; International Critics Prize, etc.

⊚ ⊚ ⊚

The Devil Strikes at Night (*Nachts, Wenn der Teufel Kam*). Robert Siodmak's Hollywood films, such as *The Spiral Staircase, The Suspect, Phantom Lady, The Killers,* and *The Crimson Pirate,* are much better known than he is — perhaps because his films are often mistakenly attributed to other directors or to highly publicized producers. In the twenties in Berlin he directed *People on Sunday* (with a crew that included Billy Wilder and Fred Zinnemann); in France he directed films with Harry Baur and Maurice Chevalier; and after many years in Hollywood he returned to Germany in 1958 where he directed this thriller based on the Bruno Luedke case.

Luedke was a half-witted mass murderer who killed about eighty women — a fantastic criminal record that was so inopportune for the Nazi government that Hitler himself decided to suppress the case. The Nazis had been publicizing the trial of a French murderer to demonstrate the degeneracy of France, and the idiot-maniac Luedke was not a foreigner nor a Jew nor a hereditary misfit. He was a "pure Aryan" — and thus an embarrassment to the Nazis who were trying to promote the Aryans as a "superior

258 · THE MOVIE PAST

race." Then, too, in the midst of the Nazi genocide, Luedke's individual initiative in mass murder might, if publicized, have seemed almost a parody of Hitler, who apparently was not flattered by imitation.

The film is more interesting in the ideas and ironies it suggests than in itself. As a thriller it doesn't achieve a satisfactory unity or style, but it does something few thrillers do — it sends one out arguing about the characters and the possible courses of action; it's a movie that nags at the mind. Perhaps German "thrillers" dealing with war themes are necessarily ambiguous: the simple virtuous hero in this (as in *The Third Man*) is maddeningly inadequate to deal with the complexities of corruption. With Mario Adorf as Bruno; Hannes Messemer as the SS officer Rossdorf; Claus Holm as the "good" police officer; Werner Peters as the Nazi fall guy Willi Keun.

◉ ◉ ◉

The Devil's General (*Des Teufels General*). The devil takes his reckoning of a gallant Luftwaffe general (based on the famous ace Ernst Udet, who was so popular he used to make guest appearances in movies — as in *The White Hell of Pitz Palu*). The general works for Hitler because he loves his air force; he is a man of conscience who becomes aware of what he is doing, and "can't eat as much as I want to vomit." Though the film is a melodrama of conscience, it derives much of its impact from the sexual assurance of Curt Jurgens in the leading role: Jurgens creates a mature but dashing figure that is one of the most satisfying romantic images of masculinity that has ever adorned the screen. (When I was running theatres, I was used to schoolgirls phoning for pictures of stars, but only after showings of *The Devil's General* were there such requests from ladies with M.D.s and Ph.D.s.) His performance took a first prize at Venice. Helmut Kautner's direction is not imaginative, but for a solid story, well-told, about characters and obstacles, it doesn't need to be: it has the necessary pulse and excitement. From Carl Zuckmayer's play — which was the biggest stage success of postwar Germany. With Marianne Koch, Victor de Kowa. 1955.

◉ ◉ ◉

Diabolique (*Les Diaboliques*). "I only sought to amuse myself and the little child who sleeps in all our hearts — the child who hides her head under the bedcovers and begs, 'Daddy, Daddy, frighten me.' " — Henri-Georges Clouzot. Perhaps the dear little thing didn't know what a coldblooded daddy she had. The setting is a provincial school for boys; the headmaster's wife (Vera Clouzot) and mistress (Simone Signoret) conspire to murder him. It sounds simple but there are overtones and undertones of strange, tainted pleasures and punishments; the characters seem fearfully knowing (and what, in this context, can they know but the extremes of perversion?). Clouzot corners the Grand Guignol market — some may feel he gluts it.

Preposterously sensational as all this is, there is no doubt that thinking about it makes one feel queasy and sordid and scared. With Paul Meurisse as the malignant murder candidate, and Charles Vanel, Noel Roquevert, Michel Serrault. 1955.

◉ ◉ ◉

Dial M for Murder. Those who like drawing-room murder and cold, literate, gentlemanly skulduggery will find this ingenious and almost entertaining. Ray Milland is the suitably suave husband who hires unsavory, penny-dreadful Anthony Dawson to kill his rich, unfaithful wife, Grace Kelly; he then calmly goes out for the evening with her lover, Robert Cummings. The unexpected happens: the wife dispatches her would-be assassin with scissors; the determined husband goes to work to make the murder look premeditated. All this is related with Alfred Hitchcock's ghoulish chic but everyone in it seems to be walking around with tired blood. Amusingly, John Williams, as the inspector who unravels the case, is so wryly, archly dexterous, that he makes everybody else's underplaying look positively boisterous. (A mystery more dark than any propounded in the film: why does Hitchcock persist in using actors as unattractively untalented as Robert Cummings?) Based on Frederick Knott's play. 1954, color.

◉ ◉ ◉

Diary of a Country Priest (*Journal d'un Curé de Campagne*). Robert Bresson's adaptation of the Georges Bernanos novel is one of the small body of film masterpieces which are hopelessly doomed to commercial failure. It is a pure and intense account of the anguish of a young priest whose faith is neither understood nor accepted by his village. An austere director of astonishing integrity, Bresson offers no sops to the public — no humorous or romantic asides; he pulls you down into the depths of the priest's suffering and refuses to give you a glad hand up. What he does offer is one of the most profound emotional experiences in the history of film; no other director, with the possible exception of Dreyer with *The Passion of Joan of Arc,* has come so close to communicating a religious experience. With Claude Laydu as prisoner of the holy agony. Photography by L. H. Burel; music by Jean-Jacques Grünenwald. Grand Prix du Cinema Français; Venice special award. 1950.

◉ ◉ ◉

Don Quixote. In 1934 an international group of artists collaborated on a rather overwhelming project. The great Russian basso Feodor Chaliapin, under the direction of the great German G. W. Pabst, filmed Cervantes' masterpiece in three versions, with different supporting casts. The English version features the English comedian George Robey as Sancho Panza. The film is not completely satisfying — Jacques Ibert's music is undistinguished, and despite beautiful photography and a stunning piece of cinematography in the windmill sequence, the treatment seems rather cold. But if the film fails as *Don Quixote,* it succeeds in transmitting to new generations the grandeur of Chaliapin — one of the rare great singers who was also a great actor. He isn't just a singer photographed: the voice is part of the actor's equipment. This is one of those privileged experiences the movie medium affords us: to be in the presence of a great performer who is already a legend.

◉ ◉ ◉

Dreaming Lips. That extraordinary chameleon Elisabeth Bergner, who could be alternately a drab little mouse or an astonishingly sophisticated sensual animal, had a triumph in this 1937 English production. As the wife of one artist (Romney Brent) and the mistress of another (Raymond Massey), she moves like a starved cat, *talks* on tiptoe, and ever so cleverly breaks your heart. Henri Bernstein, the greatest boudoir dramatist of them all, wrote the play (*Melo*). Carl Mayer adapted it, and Paul Czinner directed. This film is one of the best examples of a genre that has all but disappeared: the bittersweet conflict of desire versus responsibility — pure romance.

◉ ◉ ◉

Earth. The masterwork of Dovzhenko is a passionate lyric on collectivization and the continuity of man, death, and nature. The theme is perhaps most startlingly expressed in the sequence about the man who has just celebrated the arrival of — don't scream — a tractor. He starts to dance — for sheer love of life — on his way home, and as he dances in the middle of the moonlit road, he is suddenly struck by a bullet. 1930, silent.

◉ ◉ ◉

Ecstasy (*Extase*). In the early sixties there was the scandalous *The Lovers,* with Jeanne Moreau as a deep-watery Madame Bovary; in 1933 it was *Ecstasy,* with Hedy Lamarr, directed by Gustav Machaty in Czechoslovakia, which was always being "banned" and released and withdrawn and reissued and all the rest of the sex/art exploitation routine. What's in these movies? Well, in *Ecstasy,* along with some explicit sequences there is symbolic erotic imagery — romantic, poetic, and despite a kind of innocent absurdity about it, sensuous and exciting. In "Reflections on Extasy," Henry Miller wrote, "This is a Laurencian theme, and Machaty is the one man in the movie world capable of giving adequate expression to Lawrence's ideas." There were always people around to say, "But you must see the original, complete version!" Yes, but how many original versions were there, and where were they to be seen? (One distributor I know swears he has handled prints with two different men playing the engineer.) And have people really seen what they say was in the "original" film or have they just fantasized their own particular sexual predilections onto the screen? Recently, I was held spellbound as a writer described what had gone on in the *Ecstasy* he'd seen; later I remembered that, as an undergraduate, I'd gone to the picture with him. In recent versions, someone has decided to prolong the ecstasy by printing climactic sequences over and over again. Still, whichever *Ecstasy* one sees, it's a sweeter, more tender movie than *The Lovers,* which is the planned poetry of sex.

⊙   ⊙   ⊙

Edge of the City (*A Man Is Ten Feet Tall*). Sidney Poitier is startlingly good as the intelligent Negro who is destroyed by his friendship with a weak, unstable white man (John Cassavetes). Martin Ritt, directing his first movie, sustains the tension with great skill but cannot resist clinching the case with gratuitous violence; the author, Robert Alan Aurthur, works with such precision that he reduces the quest for human values to a quick fix. But it's a powerful movie. With Jack Warden and Ruby Dee. The music is by Leonard Rosenman; when he completed the score, he must have cut another notch on his gun — as a composer he's out to slaughter the audience. 1957.

⊙   ⊙   ⊙

El (literally, *He,* but in this country it has sometimes been called *This Strange Passion*). In Mexico in 1952 the great Spanish director Luis Buñuel made this mocking study of irrational love and jealousy — a film with suggestions of Freud and the Marquis de Sade which, as one critic put it, is "an Othello with the hero as his own Iago." Francisco, a wealthy Catholic (Arturo de Cordova) marries Gloria (Delia Garces) and the symptoms begin on their honeymoon: imagining that her former fiancé is in the next room spying on them, he thrusts a knitting needle through the keyhole. As the symptoms mount in an absurd but frightening crescendo, Buñuel makes his own thrusts at the church. By the time Francisco takes needle and thread to his wife, one is still not convinced that the movie isn't ludicrous; but when we see Francisco's last crooked little steps in the monastery, Buñuel's daring is fully apparent. Except for the brilliantly edited anti-clerical sequences, however, one must be prepared to enjoy the daring despite the careless, cheaply-made look of the film. His joke is a black one: by carrying the Spanish male's obsession with female chastity to paranoia, he exposes the insanity that's inherent in it.

⊙   ⊙   ⊙

The Emperor Jones. Eugene O'Neill's play is a study of disintegration conceived in a semi-expressionistic style, and it was filmed in that style by Dudley Murphy in 1933, with painted sets, exaggerated décor, artificial jungle, etc. The effects are sometimes powerful, sometimes absurd, but they seem appropriate to the material. O'Neill's violent emotions are accurately rendered by Paul Robeson and Dudley Digges. It's as if a time machine transported one to the "daring" theatre of the twenties.

◉ ◉ ◉

Les Enfants Terribles (American title, *The Strange Ones*). The director, Jean-Pierre Melville, expands Cocteau's novel about the shared disorder and confused narcissism of a brother and sister into a baroque tragi-comedy in which the characters move, as compulsively as in a dream, toward self-destruction. With Nicole Stéphane, brilliant as the dominating Elizabeth; Edouard Dermithe as Paul; Renée Cosima as Dargelos and Agatha; Jacques Bernard as Gerard. This film, almost voluptuous in its evocation of temperament and atmosphere, was shot, on a shoestring, in "real" settings (the director's flat, the lobby of the Petit Journal, the stage of the Théâtre Pigalle — and when Melville was ill, Cocteau directed the summer beach scene in Montmorency, under snow). Dismissed as "arty" and "embalmed" by many critics, this film is "embalmed" in the memory of those of us who think it one of the most exciting films of our time. Cocteau provides cryptic, emblematic narration. The music (Bach-Vivaldi) is one of the few effective film usages of great music. (Melville appeared in *Breathless* as the celebrity being interviewed.) 1951.

◉ ◉ ◉

The Eternal Husband. There were glimpses of Dostoyevsky's brilliance and complexity in Harry Baur's performance as Porfiry in the French *Crime and Punishment,* in Peter Lorre's Raskolnikov in the American production, in Edwige Feuillère's role in *The Idiot.* But none of the films has ever communicated Dostoyevsky in more than flashes. *The Eternal Husband,* perhaps because it copes with a smaller work, is more sustained, although it is too thin and lacks texture. Dostoyevsky's short novel was filmed in France in 1946 and circulated under the eccentric title *L'Homme au Chapeau Rond.* It is the last film of Raimu, for decades the tragicomic spirit of French films. His performance, a startling climax to his career, may be something of a shock: the humane master cuckold of the screen (*The Baker's Wife*) is gone, and in his place is a tight, bitter, cold cuckold. Raimu is Trusotsky, ridiculous on the surface, but spiritually dead, the man who hates the child he knows is not his own, who hates the lover (Aimé Clariond) of his dead wife. It's a masterful performance. Directed by Pierre Billon.

⊚ ⊚ ⊚

The Exiles. American Indians were granted citizenship in 1924, given civil rights in 1934; now some have left the reservations. Dispersed, they are strangers — exiles — within the big American cities. In each city it is the same: many of the Indians live "communally" — sponging off each other, drinking, brawling, working for a few days, committing petty thefts. And in each city there is a gathering place — a hill, a park, a beach, where, late at night, the Indians gather to sing tribal songs, beat the drums and dance. *The Exiles* follows a group in Los Angeles through a day and a night of eating, drinking, and fighting, and to Hill X — where, high above the lights of the city, they sing and dance until dawn.

This account of people lost in our midst was made over a period of several years by a dedicated group of young USC film school graduates, headed by Kent Mackenzie; their convictions about movie-making were strong enough to impress some two dozen people into financing the film. The film is what used to be called an eye-opener. It justifies their faith, though it may not have repaid their investment. 1961.

⊚ ⊚ ⊚

Expresso Bongo. It opens with the camera roving around the teen-age haunts and entertainment palaces of London, and one might be led to expect a continuation of the new "frankness" of *Room at the Top* and *Look Back in Anger*. Instead, this film treats contemporary fads with humor, commenting on them in stylized musical numbers (a record manufacturer describes his product in a song called "Nausea"). It's a satire which accepts its targets with good-natured incredulity.

Expresso Bongo is more brash than the other films written by Wolf Mankowitz (*The Bespoke Overcoat, A Kid for Two Farthings*), but one would have to be very prissy to be offended. Although the American reviewers made it sound like another *Sweet Smell of Success,* all they have in common is the stylized theatrical idiom with its Yiddish flavor, which, however, Mankowitz uses affectionately. In *A Kid for Two Farthings* he performed the remarkable feat of turning a narcissistic weightlifter into a fairy-tale character; here he lifts a segment of the modern world to the level of fantasy. Laurence Harvey (in this role he has that amusing theatrical habit of adapting his speech to the accents of the characters he talks to) is the glib Soho agent who owns 50 percent of a young, bewildered rock 'n' roll singer; Cliff Richard seems as childlike and withdrawn, and yet as opportunistic, as a number of successful American pop singers. He's perfectly cast as he informs the juveniles that he is a "deeply religious boy" and sings a song about mom and home called "The Shrine on the Second Floor." With Sylvia Syms, Yolande Donlon, Wilfred Lawson. Val Guest directed. 1959.

⊙ ⊙ ⊙

An Eye for an Eye (*Oeil pour Oeil*). For the first half this movie is peculiarly compelling — the sequences in which Curt Jurgens, as a successful, sophisticated European doctor, is stranded in a remote, corrupt Arab settlement where he can communicate with no one, are worthy of the best Paul Bowles stories and have the same fascination and horror. Unfortunately, André Cayatte (he is the damnedest director!) always destroys his own best effects, and he winds up with his two principal characters in an apparently endless desert — which is what the movie also turns into. The plot is one of those terrible, trick ideas that sometimes make wonderful movies; in this case, the idea doesn't come off, but the atmosphere is so good that the movie is worth seeing anyway. Christian Matras' photography (of southern Spain) had me convinced that we were really in strange Levantine byways, within walking distance of Damascus. With Folco Lulli, Lea Padovani, Pascale Audret. 1957, color.

⊙ ⊙ ⊙

Fanfan the Tulip (*Fanfan la Tulipe*). This is a sort of Louis XV Western. Fanfan (Gérard Philipe) is a handsome peasant lout with good physical equipment and no excess weight of mind or morals; his agility in bed and battlefield provides a light burlesque on the arts of love and war (although the humor, unfortunately, is sometimes of the type that can best be described as "irrepressible" or "roguish"). Gina Lollobrigida is his most decorative playmate; other ladies bursting their bodices include Genevieve Page as La Pompadour and Sylvie Pelayo as Henriette de France. With Marcel Herrand as the king, and Noel Roquevert. Christian-Jacque directed: as usual, he seems to mistake archness for style. 1953.

⊙ ⊙ ⊙

Film Without a Name (*Film Ohne Titel*). This is one of the more original and charming comedies of the postwar period; ironically, it is a satirical improvisation on the theme that there are *no* movie themes in the German shambles. The star is Hildegarde Neff, the hungry-voiced, alluringly sad-eyed actress who is more or less the female equivalent of Curt Jurgens. Miss Neff is joined by Willy Fritsch and Hans Sohnker as they act out a group of romantic episodes, including a succulent little parody of *The Blue Angel* and a divertissement on the actor's pox — vanity. Made in the British Zone in 1947, this film is a rare bird — wit and nonchalance are scarcely what one expects from a German film. Helmut Kautner, Ellen Fechner, and Rudolf Jugert did the script; Jugert directed.

⊙ ⊙ ⊙

The Final Test. Robert Morley doesn't enter until the scene has been so thoroughly prepared that he can trundle off with the rest of the picture. He looks, as one critic remarked, like a "debauched panda," and he plays a famous aesthete and man of letters. Terence Rattigan did the surprisingly affectionate script for this 1953 English comedy, directed by Anthony Asquith. Jack Warner is the aging cricket batsman who is going to the wicket for the last time; Ray Jackson is his poet son, who couldn't care less. For American audiences, the movie provides a visiting American senator, who cannot understand what cricket is all about, and a superbly contemptuous Englishman who explains the game to him. Rattigan has cleverly underlined the meaning of the game by having it apply to the movie itself — and by extension, to English humor and character. With Valentine Dyall in the pseudo-Greek play. There's something detestably, comfortably smug about films like this, yet they're so cleverly done that we enjoy them in spite of ourselves.

◉ ◉ ◉

The Five-Day Lover (*L'Amant de Cinq Jours*). In the arms of her lover, the dreamy, role-playing little nymphomaniac (Jean Seberg) looks out over the rooftops of Paris (a scene that inevitably recalls René Clair) and rhapsodizes, "all those cells for love." There is no bitterness at the end of an affair — "Love's a lie, a bubble," she says, "when it touches earth, it's over." Philippe De Broca's lyric boudoir comedy stays aloft in its own sphere, and his technique calls up similar pleasures and the same sweet melancholy. His originality is in his use of incongruities; he choreographs the follies of love. The astonishingly gifted Jean-Pierre Cassel is the lover; François Périer is the scholarly husband; and Micheline Presle — like a younger Tallulah Bankhead — is the couturière-mistress who pays the bills. These four are joined in a network of romance and deceit; the threads move and snap, and suddenly we see the people from different angles, here a feeling exposed, there a dream dissolved. The dialogue is graceful and often inexplicably touching: Périer, the bustling little cuckold, puts the children to bed and explains their mother's absence, "You're wondering why Mummy's late. It's because she wears high heels and they're difficult to walk on." With a lovely score by Georges Delerue. 1961.

◉ ◉ ◉

Folly To Be Wise. This 1952 English comedy is in the nature of an anecdote — it's an unusual one because it seems to get funnier the longer it's spun out. Alastair Sim is the chaplain assigned as entertainment officer to an army camp. He decides to stage a quiz show, and innocently gathers together a panel of experts that includes some rather sophisticated types. Martita Hunt, Miles Malleson, and Edward Chapman are reasonably safe, but Roland Culver, Elizabeth Allan, and Colin Gordon are, unfortunately, husband, wife, and lover. Once the question is asked, "Is marriage a good idea?" everything begins to fall apart. Directed by Frank Launder.

⊙ ⊙ ⊙

Forbidden Planet. The best of the science-fiction interstellar productions of the fifties lifts its plot and atmosphere from Shakespeare: the magical island of *The Tempest* becomes the planet Altair-4, where the sky is green and the sand is pink and there are two moons. More serviceable than one might suspect, *The Tempest* in the forties had been set in a ghost town at the edge of a desert in *Yellow Sky,* and with a humor frequently indulged in under cover of the Western genre, Miranda became Anne Baxter's Mike. In *Forbidden Planet* the magician Prospero becomes the mad scientist Morbius (Walter Pidgeon); Prospero's daughter Miranda, who knows no man except her father, is Altaira (Anne Francis); and (though this is less clear) the sprite Ariel becomes Robby, the friendly robot. It's a pity the film-makers didn't lift some of Shakespeare's dialogue: it's hard to believe you're in the heavens when the diction of the hero (Leslie Nielsen) and his spaceshipmates flattens you down to Kansas. But, in keeping with Shakespeare's fantasy, in which Prospero's will is supreme and the island seems to be the caves, plains and towers of his mind, Caliban has become a marvelously flamboyant monster out of Freud. Pure id, the monster is certainly "not honor'd with a human shape." The fiery visual style employed for this monster id is peculiarly odd in the science fiction setting — though it *almost* works. Fred Wilcox directed. 1956, CinemaScope, color.

⊙ ⊙ ⊙

The Forty-First. Visually, this Soviet film is extraordinary — magnificent scenes in the Asian desert, storms at sea in exquisite silvery blues; for the poetic use of color, it was at the time (1956) one of the few films that could be discussed alongside *Gate of Hell*. The content is a "tragic" love story set in the civil war period. The tragedy — indeed, the whole point of the film — is supposed to be that the Red Army girl, who has killed forty men, falls in love with a White officer, but learns that class conflicts are stronger than love — and he becomes her forty-first. This is not likely to be what you'll make of the film: it is immensely entertaining, and runs along rather like a good Hollywood action movie of the old John Ford type, and the decadent Cossack is so much more attractive than the good Red Army men that you may begin to wonder if sex appeal is a right-wing deviation. His suggestion that he and the girl get the hell out of Russia seems remarkably sensible, and when the rather monolithic heroine shoots him down, you're very likely to take the politically frivolous view that she's simpleminded — where would she find another man like that? This was the first film directed by Grigori Chukhrai, fresh out of the State Institute of Cinematography.

◉   ◉   ◉

Four Bags Full (*La Traversée de Paris*). When Marcel Aymé's long short story was published in *Partisan Review,* it was called simply *Crossing Paris;* the movie version is known in England as *Pig across Paris;* in the United States it is called *Four Bags Full,* and is unknown under any title. Claude Autant-Lara's explosively witty comedy took the French award as Best Film of 1957. The period is the German occupation: a petty, anxious blackmarketeer (Bourvil) hires a helper (Jean Gabin) for a night's work — transporting a slaughtered pig across Paris to a butcher in Montmartre. The helper, a famous painter who has taken on the job for the mischief of it, has an uproarious night, teasing his dull companion, outwitting both the French police and the German soldiers. Bourvil was selected Best Actor at Venice for his performance, but the star of the film is Gabin, lusty and powerful as the man who loves life so much he can play with it. When in the midst of sordid little perils, the artist devises quick-witted solutions, and then howls with delight, "This pig's making a genius of me!" the contrast between him and the terrified, sweating petit bourgeois at his side makes it apparent that Autant-Lara has tossed off a little fable.

◉   ◉   ◉

Gaslight. Ingrid Bergman is the cherubic bride who is terrorized by the grisly, dirty tricks of husband Charles Boyer. She runs the gamut from antimacassar to antimacassar and it's good scary fun all the way (with a prize at the end — the Academy Award as Best Actress of 1944). This pseudo-Victorian thriller is rather more enjoyable than one might expect. Bergman is, intermittently, genuinely moving (and though one may suspect that she is feeling, rather than acting, her hysteria in the musicale sequence is a good demonstration of how hard it sometimes is to tell the difference); Boyer is expert, and the cast includes Joseph Cotten, Dame May Whitty, and Angela Lansbury (only in her teens but you couldn't guess it). Patrick Hamilton's play has been toned up with smooth dialogue from John Van Druten, Walter Reisch, and John Balderston; and the full-dress production is directed by George Cukor. When you watch a picture like this one you're so aware of how expensively careful it is, you can't help being a little impressed and more than a little depressed. (In this case, the expense included suppressing the 1941 English version by Thorold Dickinson.)

◉   ◉   ◉

Gate of Hell (*Jigokumon*). Famed for its use of color, this exquisitely stylized tragedy of passion tells the subtle story of a warrior's desire for a married noblewoman and her way of defeating him. I've listened to many interpretations of the heroine's action; most of them devolve on Oriental points of honor that I'm not qualified to credit or discredit. As we look at the movie, we don't worry too much about the story anyway: it's as if the director, Kinugasa, had read those loathsome critics who compare every Japanese movie to a Japanese print, and decided to give them more than they could handle — delicately choreographed battles, the flow and texture of garments, and everywhere grace of movement and composition. The setting is twelfth-century Kyoto, where the abstract patterns of interiors and architecture suggest that modern décor may catch up to medieval Japan in a few decades. With Machiko Kyo as the Lady Kesa, and Kazuo Hasegawa as the demonic warrior Moritoh. Grand Prix, Cannes; Special Academy Award, 1954.

⊙ ⊙ ⊙

Il Generale Della Rovere. Great leaders have often turned into confidence men working on a gigantic scale; *Il Generale Della Rovere* gives us a reverse image: a petty swindler who becomes a leader among men. There are some remarkable ironies involved in this production: it is the most widely honored movie made in many years by Roberto Rossellini, and it provides perhaps the greatest role in his career for Vittorio De Sica who, as an actor, commands one of the top salaries in the world (he gets as much as three thousand dollars a day for presenting his courtly magnificence to the camera) and who reaches a new acting peak in this role which — in all likelihood — he performed gratis to help Rossellini's comeback. *Il Generale,* which took the grand prizes at both the Venice and San Francisco festivals, is a memorable movie; but it stays in the mind not because of Rossellini's direction but because of De Sica's performance.

Il Generale Della Rovere is set in Genoa in 1943. De Sica is a small-time scrounger with the classic con man's grand manner; the Germans induce him to impersonate a Resistance general whom they have inadvertently shot, and send him to a political prison where he is supposed to ferret out information for them. But the petty, self-loathing crook, experiencing for the first time the respect and admiration — even the awe — of other men, becomes as great as the man he impersonates. The mask has molded the man, and the Nazis must destroy their own creation.

The role does not appear to have been written with any great depth, but it is performed as if it were. Some facts about De Şica's career may help to explain how he developed the insights for this extraordinarily intuitive transformation in character. De Sica first appeared in films in 1913, at the age of twelve, as the boy Clemenceau in the Italian film *Clemenceau;* during World War I he toured hospitals for the wounded with an amateur group of Neapolitan singers. Later, in an attempt at a respectable, settled career, he took a degree in accountancy at the University of Rome. But after his army service, he went on the stage, and in the twenties became popular as a musical comedy star; by 1928 he was appearing in films. If you have ever seen any of his dozens of film musicals, you have probably been dazzled by his charming voice and light, romantic comedy style. By 1939, disgusted with the inadequacies of the directors he worked with, he decided to try his own hand at directing; his first efforts were highly successful light comedies, but his first really important film (and first collaboration with the scenarist Cesare Zavattini), *The Children Are Watching Us,* was a financial failure.

During the German occupation, De Sica was, indeed, involved in a confidence game. He saved himself from making movies for the Nazis by arranging to make a religious movie about the sick who journeyed to the sanctuary at Loreto in search of miracles. He managed to keep this project going for two years — at times with as many as three thousand people taking refuge with him in the Basilica of St. Paul's, where he had built a replica of Loreto. As soon as the Allies took over, he completed the film in a week. The Church, indignant at the way his thousands had carried on within the holy precincts, was not mollified by the movie — *The Gates of Heaven* — in which, as De Sica put it, "The miracle which had been invoked did not take place, but the resignation which the sick people learned seemed to me to be the real miracle." *The Gates of Heaven* was suppressed.

After the war he made his first great work, *Shoeshine* (which, through an error, also helped to make Rossellini's reputation — for when Rossellini's big success, *Open City,* came to the United States, *Life* and much of the American press ascribed *Shoeshine* to him), and followed it with *The Bicycle Thief, Miracle in Milan,* and *Umberto D.* De Sica is a man who has been known to drop ten thousand dollars at the gambling tables night after night; he has also made movies which international juries rate among the best of all time — and paid for them himself. Perhaps it is this fantastic background and character which we respond to as we watch his evolution from worm to Il Generale.

Il Generale Della Rovere was made on a slender budget and it was shot and edited in six weeks (in Hollywood that's a schedule for a "quickie"). Oddly enough, its principal fault is that it is too long: the screenwriters don't seem to have discovered their best material until it was too late to pull the story together. At its best — and most original — it is a shockingly funny black comedy: the con man, battered and bleeding from torture, weeps sentimentally over a photograph of the real Generale's children — a scene as excruciatingly comic as the almost surrealist torture scenes in *Bend Sinister,* Nabokov's novel about the Nazis.

In a sense, Rossellini's comeback picture is also a throwback. The compositions, the groupings of actors, the ideas and the milieu are like a reprise of *Open City;* but the rawness and immediacy are gone. The faces are actorish and often not very interesting; the sets are obviously sets. Italian neorealism is somehow so associated with the war and postwar period from which it emerged that many people have applauded *Il Generale Della Rovere* as a return to the creative fount. But this 1959 restaging of Partisan activities in World War II is no more neorealist than a restaging of the War of the Roses. With Hannes Messemer, Sandra Milo, Giovanna Ralli, Anne Vernon.

⊚ ⊚ ⊚

Genevieve. Genevieve is a venerable motor vehicle, a 1904 Darracq; this English film is on its way to becoming a venerable little vehicle in its own right. John Gregson and Dinah Sheridan race the Darracq against Kenneth More and Kay Kendall in a 1904 Spyker. That the two men should be testing their masculine prowess in these antiques gives the comedy a double edge of human absurdity. Kenneth More is wonderfully smug and infuriating as the advertising man; Kay Kendall is quite irresistible as the trumpet-playing model. Written by William Rose, directed by Henry Cornelius, score by Larry Adler. 1953, color.

⊚ ⊚ ⊚

The Ghost Goes West. Americans loved this barb thrust at them by René Clair — perhaps because the satire isn't on a much higher plane than what it satirizes. However, the movie is fortunate in its star: Robert Donat brings elegance and melancholy and his memorable voice to the dual role of Donald Glourie and his phantom ancestor, Murdoch Glourie. Murdoch is the unhappy ghost whose abode, Glourie Castle, is purchased by a rich American (Eugene Pallette), dismantled, shipped across the ocean, and reconstructed in Sunnymede, Florida, with modern plumbing. René Clair provides some rhythmic editing, but the script by Robert Sherwood is painfully frolicsome. With Elsa Lanchester, Jean Parker. 1936.

⊚ ⊚ ⊚

A Girl in Black. The heroine is the classic beauty, Ellie Lambetti, whose thoughtful, passionate Mediterranean face is one of the glories of Greek films. In *A Girl in Black* she plays the shy daughter of an impoverished, once-genteel family, a family that has become the victim of the meanness, pettiness, and harsh sexual standards of the villagers. She is caught in the shame of her widowed mother's sordid sexual activity, trapped in an island village where everyone knows everyone else and where throngs of children call out the news of her mother's latest fornication.

The young writer-director, Michael Cacoyannis, made *A Girl in Black* on the island of Hydra on a budget of approximately sixty thousand dollars, with a single camera in the hands of Walter Lassally. It is a strongly individual work — the camera moves fluidly over the dark expressive faces and the narrow streets; the Greek sunlight hits the white houses and the whole island seems exposed (one feels there would be no place to hide on Hydra). Cacoyannis's script is much smoother than in his earlier *Stella,* but he still has some construction problems: there is no adequate preparation for the startling last sequence, which may give you the uncomfortable feeling that a group of children are drowned in order to strengthen the hero's character.

But the film has a simplicity and a vibrancy that make it stand out from even the best of foreign films. We experience the emotions and temperament and style of a new film artist who is trying to find his own way and whose limitations and defects are his own (and interesting because they are his own), rather than the results of the commercialized conditions of most modern film-making.

Dimitri Horn is intelligent and sensitive in the difficult role of the weak Athenian writer; Georges Foundas is the handsome but loutish and smallminded fisherman. The other principals include Notis Pergialis as the writer's friend, Eleni Zafiriou as the widow, and Anestis Vlachos as the son. 1956.

◉ ◉ ◉

A Girl in the Mist (Kiri no Naka no Shojo). The most charming Japanese film to reach the West, Hideo Suzuki's forty-four-minute pastoral comedy has a simplicity and freshness that have gone out of American films (and you won't find them in other Japanese films, either). It's an idyll about a college student who has returned to her small-town home for the summer vacation and is visited by her Tokyo boyfriend. She, her younger sister, and the boy are three of the most beautiful people ever seen on the screen. At times, their youth and radiance are so alive and so unlike the usual people in movies that we forget this is a film: we seem to be watching country neighbors, eavesdropping as the mother and father argue, the grandmother drinks, the adolescent sister worries about propriety, etc. Though the westernization of Japanese life is apparent, the provincial family (representing the values shattered in the sun-tribe films like *Affair in Kamakura*) is presented with grace and humor, and it appears that intellectual college students have the same gaucherie and pretentiousness the world over. 1955.

◉ ◉ ◉

The Goddess. Paddy Chayefsky's 1958 attack on the American dream of success hews to the main line and won't let us escape the central neurosis — an unloved child who grows up incapable of loving and becomes a big, empty wreck of a movie star. *The Goddess* is a fascinating, conscientious, bad movie, the most ambitious and the most interesting of the Paddy Chayefsky films, though, as usual, Chayefsky's famous ear for dialogue is in full cauliflower —

RITA: How kind you look.

TOWER: I was just thinking you're so unchanged. I wish I were meeting you now for the first time.

RITA: Hold me, John. I never loved anybody but you.

TOWER: You never loved me either, Emmy. You needed me, but you never loved me. You never knew what love was. Whoever taught it to you? Life is unbearable if you don't love something, Emmy. Don't I know that as well as you? . . .

THE SECRETARY: Leave her alone.

RITA: I'm no good! I'm no good!

TOWER (*to the Secretary*): Would you rather she clutches at life for half hours in cheap hotel rooms?

RITA: I had my mother in labor for seventeen hours and I've been nothing but pain to everybody since!

— and so forth.

Probably because the characters are not so embarrassingly "little" as in the other Chayefsky films, *The Goddess* manages to hold interest despite its clinical and transparent motivations. The heroine's "quality of availability" has enriched the American idiom with a new and amusing euphemism, even though as a heroine she lacks the power and the qualities to be convincing as a Marilyn Monroe-type "star" and a representative of the bitch goddess Success. Chayefsky is so concerned with her weakness — pitiful, and self-centered on a hopelessly unformed self — that he fails to distinguish her from many other girls with problems.

In the thirties (and again in the fifties) we had the legend of *A Star is Born;* in *The Goddess,* as Dilys Powell put it, "A Star is Made." In both cases the legend is basically and sentimentally false: *The Goddess* is the oversimplified, psychiatric and sociological new public image of the star as a stupid neurotic whom we should feel sorry for, just as *A Star is Born* was the fan magazine's version of the old-fashioned idiocies of gallant heartbreak and the-show-must-go-on.

John Cromwell directed the highpowered cast of *The Goddess* — the intense Kim Stanley in the lead (her compelling over-non-acting makes the poor writing even more painful); Betty Lou Holland as the mother; Patty Duke as the child ("Kitty, I got promoted today"); Steven Hill as the first husband (an impossible role, as he's called upon to deliver the author's prophetic insights, i.e., the lines that should have been cut); Lloyd Bridges (in a good performance) as the prizefighter husband; and Elizabeth Wilson as the final gorgon. The score is by Virgil Thomson. (Collectors of fascinating errata may note that Chayefsky has the heroine say she was in *Stage Door,* "by Moss Hart and George S. Kaufman." Her error or his?)

◉ ◉ ◉

Gold Diggers of 1933. This movie sums up what is now meant by the phrase "pure thirties." It's a funny, good-natured backstage musical, and a Depression period piece as well. It was directed by the not conspicuously talented Mervyn LeRoy (the year after *I Am a Fugitive from a Chain Gang*), and it is memorable chiefly because the choreographer, Busby Berkeley, created a mad geometry of patterned chorines. It features the unforgettably absurd "In the shadows let me come and sing to you" sequence, with countless electrically wired young ladies playing violins and then merging to form one big screaming violin — brilliantly illuminated. (Collectors of only-in-Hollywood memorabilia may recall that there was an earthquake while this sequence was being staged, and several of the wired lovelies were short-circuited.) The innocent vulgarity of the big numbers is charming and uproarious, and aesthetically preferable to the pretentious ballet finales of fifties musicals like *An American in Paris.* Even those of us who were children at the time did not mistake *Gold Diggers* for art — and certainly no one took it for "life." The cast is a Who's Who of Warners types: Joan Blondell, Dick Powell, Warren William, Aline MacMahon, Ginger Rogers (singing "We're in the Money" in pig Latin!), Ned Sparks, Guy Kibbee, and Ruby Keeler (the most leaden-footed of all tap dancers). Busby Berkeley appears in a bit part as the backstage call-boy (can this really be the correct term?) shouting such directions as, "On stage for the Forgotten Man number!" The Negro singer was Etta Moten. The songs are by Harry Warren and Al Dubin.

◉ ◉ ◉

The Gold Rush. He enters, "pursued by a bear," the man who for generations of filmgoers has been the embodiment of "the little fellow" — humanity. In this extraordinarily sweet and graceful comedy, Chaplin is the weak and helpless perfect gentleman in the world of bears and brutes; yet his gallantry wins him the gold and the girl, too. This 1925 film was selected by the international jury at Brussels as second (to *Potemkin*) of the greatest films of all time. With Mack Swain as Big Jim, and Georgia Hale.

◉ ◉ ◉

The Golden Age of Comedy. These sequences from Mack Sennett and Hal Roach two-reelers made between 1923 and 1928 show off the talents of Ben Turpin, Harry Langdon, Will Rogers, the Keystone Cops, the Sennett Bathing Beauties, etc., and best of all, they exhibit Stan Laurel and

Oliver Hardy in several classics of demolition-style silent comedy. Their custard pie sequence is perhaps the high point of the collection — a demonstration that throwing a pie can be both art and science. In *The Cosmological Eye* Henry Miller called it "the ultimate in burlesque" and "the greatest comic film ever made — because it brought pie-throwing to apotheosis." Their paint-brush routine is a beauty, and there is also the methodical, fatalistic car-wrecking ritual. Jean Harlow makes a stunning appearance in black teddies, but Carole Lombard is, unfortunately, not at her best. Robert Youngson compiled these clips (the original directors include Frank Capra, Leo McCarey, and George Stevens) in 1957; he added a tireless narrator who lards the unpretentious artistry with a layer of sentiment about how "beloved" these players were, and what "tragic" fates they met, and worse, explanations of gags that are perfectly clear to the eye. But the irritations are minor when you are looking at the best collection of sight gags ever brought together.

Photographs of Fred Karno's *A Night in an English Music Hall* company, which arrived in the United States in 1913, show a beaming Charles Chaplin and, in the back row, a shy figure that looks startlingly like Alec Guinness. Upon scrutiny, it turns out to be Stan Laurel. Laurel had had twenty years of theatre experience and was working as a director when he was teamed with Oliver Hardy, an American, who had also been in the theatre for twenty years, and who was himself doing some direction. Their partnership, at first accidental, became inevitable — Laurel, the fragile, timid Cockney, and Hardy, the graceful elephantine Southerner, were complementary. Laurel was to be forever the innocent cause of misfortunes that fell on the exasperated Hardy. From the first days of their partnership, they produced destruction scenes like the ones in *The Golden Age of Comedy;* later they worked these rituals into features like *Way Out West.*

They did their best work when the nominal director of their films was left on the sidelines and Laurel directed; he worked on the editing as well. They created their "business" and timing on the set and shot each film in continuity; it was a matter of continuous improvisation. When studio methods changed, they were not allowed to use their own techniques: a script was insisted on; then, for economy, sequences had to be shot out of continuity, and soon the nominal directors became the real directors. Films were ground out in rapid succession: Laurel and Hardy made more than two hundred shorts and features over a period of twenty years, and as the quality went down, their reputations sank even lower than the quality. But while many comedians do end tragically, when these two gentlemen were finished in Hollywood, they packed up, went abroad, and made tour after tour of the English music halls — playing to delighted audiences. (Their features are, perhaps, a little too relaxed in tempo — I can't sit through them, but their routines — as in this compilation — are impeccable.)

⊙ ⊙ ⊙

Goodbye, Mr. Chips. James Hilton's gentle tribute to his schoolmaster father became an American best seller when that old sentimentalist, Alexander Woollcott, touted it on the radio. MGM bought the novel and sent Sam Wood to England to film it. Robert Donat's portrait of the frightened young Junior Master, rigid and forbidding in his twenties, who is humanized by marriage and mellowed by sixty years of contact with youth, brought him the Academy Award as Best Actor of 1939. Greer Garson, in her screen debut, played his warm and gracious wife. And a rather overripe little boy named Terry Kilburn played the ubiquitous Little Colley. The movie is not so good as the critics once thought it, but it is an ingratiating, bittersweet record of a good life — the kind of thing that may clog your nose even if you can keep your head clear when nuns are looking at a bride.

⊙ ⊙ ⊙

Grand Hotel. From her first line, "I have never been so tired in my life," Greta Garbo sets the movie in vibration with her extraordinary presence. She is a *première danseuse* whose career is fading, a weary, disillusioned woman briefly reconciled to life by a passion for a shady nobleman — John Barrymore. Garbo was only twenty-six when she played this role (Barrymore was fifty), but the fatigue, the despair seem genuine. Intellectually you have every reason to reject *Grand Hotel* as an elaborate chunk of artifice and hocus-pocus: there are no redeeming qualities in Vicki Baum's excruciating concepts of character and fate, and anyone who comes to see this movie expecting an intelligent script or even "good acting" should have his head examined. But if you want to see what screen glamour used to be and what, originally, "stars" were, this is perhaps the best example of all time. *Grand Hotel* survives because of the same factors that made it a huge hit in 1932 (it even won the Academy Award as Best Picture) — the force of the personalities involved in the omnibus story. There is a sexy minx named Joan Crawford, who bears only a slight resemblance to the later zombie of that name; there are Wallace Beery, Lionel Barrymore, Lewis Stone, and in minor parts, Jean Hersholt, Raffaela Ottiano, Ferdinand Gottschalk, etc. Striding through it all there is the living legend of the screen, Garbo, in her chinchilla polo coat, with her anguished "I want to be alone," with her clothes that seem to get in her way, and with a ridiculous little bobby pin that keeps her hair firmly in place during her big love scenes with Barrymore. Directed by Edmund Goulding.

⊙ ⊙ ⊙

The Grapes of Wrath. To Americans over forty, it may be inconceivable that there could be a younger generation that doesn't know the subject matter of John Steinbeck's most famous novel; in the Depression years it was compared with *Uncle Tom's Cabin* and *Les Miserables* and widely, though with a shocking want of judgment, regarded as the greatest novel written by an American. The Joads are sharecroppers who leave their eroded, dust-bowl farm in Oklahoma and come to the promised land of California, where they become the lowest of the low — migratory farm laborers. *The Grapes of Wrath* is full of the "they can't keep us down, we're the people" sort of thing, and one's outrage at the terrible social injustices the film reveals is blurred by its gross sentimentality. This famous film, high on almost all lists of the great films of all time, seems all wrong — phony when we want it to be "true" — and yet, because of its raw material, it is moving in spite of the acting, the direction, and the pseudo-Biblical pore-people talk. John Ford directed the production which, in externals, is as authentic as a documentary; the cast includes Henry Fonda as Tom, John Carradine as Casey, Charley Grapewin as Grampa, John Qualen as Muley, Eddie Quillan as Connie, Doris Bowden as Rosasharn, Russell Simpson as Pa, Zeffie Tilbury as Granma, Darryl Hickman as Winfield, and Ward Bond, Grant Mitchell, Joe Sawyer, Frank Faylen. Screenplay by Nunnally Johnson; photography by Gregg Toland. Academy Awards of 1940: Best Director, Best Supporting Actress — Jane Darwell as Ma Joad (I thought she was impossibly fraudulent, but she was good as the lewd old bitch in *The Ox-Bow Incident*).

⊚ ⊚ ⊚

The Great Adventure. Arne Sucksdorff's documentary — one of the handful of great nature films — is a sensuous mixture of beauty and cruelty. Refusing, as he says, "to rape reality," Sucksdorff waits until he gets the shot he wants — extraordinary shots of lynx and otter, fox and woodgrouse, framed in dazzling compositions. Swedish, 1955.

⊚ ⊚ ⊚

Great Expectations. The arrival of *Look Back in Anger* makes Dickens's world seem farther away than ever — and perhaps because of that, one may feel more nostalgia for that period in English letters when heroes had nice manners, a story had sweep and flourish, and all the stray subplots were gathered up and "rhymed." In this handsome 1946 production, David Lean, with the help of Ronald Neame on the adaptation, managed to evoke the special Dickens atmosphere, though the rather creamy look (like an expensive gift edition of a classic) is not particularly appropriate to Dickens's style. With Anthony Wager and then John Mills as Pip; Jean Simmons and then Valerie Hobson as Estella (though it's inconceivable that one could grow into the other); Alec Guinness as Herbert Pocket; Finlay Currie as Magwich; Martita Hunt as Miss Havisham; Bernard Miles as Joe Gargery;

Freda Jackson as Mrs. Gargery; Ivor Barnard as Wemmick; Torin Thatcher as Bentley Drummel; and Francis L. Sullivan as that most alarming upholder of the law, Jaggers. Three Academy Awards, including Best Cinematography (Guy Green).

⊚ ⊚ ⊚

The Great Man. "The great man," a popular and influential radio-television personality, has died; it is the task of a commentator (José Ferrer) to prepare a memorial broadcast. If it is successful, he may become the great man's replacement. Though the outcome of the research is predictable, the further step in the plot is so efficiently cynical that the venality we have explored appears to be merely a childish prelude to a new venality. The film's inside-story style is set by the kind of nasty literacy that never quite works, but it does carry one along and the movie is almost over before one realizes what a slick, fast sell it is (resembling nothing so much as what it is attacking). Ed Wynn brought off his long scene, a six-minute monologue, in a single take, and it is said that when he finished, the technicians applauded and the director (Ferrer) wept. With Keenan Wynn, Julie London, Dean Jagger, Russ Morgan, Joanne Gilbert. From the novel by Al Morgan. 1957.

The next year Ferrer was again director and star for the comedy about organization men, *The High Cost of Loving,* which had a good sense of the inadequacies and anxieties that you laugh at out of the wrong side of your face. Neither of these films was a hit, though both had the bite of contemporary material, and *Loving* (which had a very funny opening sequence) was one of the few even passable comedies of 1958.

⊚ ⊚ ⊚

The Green Man. Alastair Sim is so limpid of eye, so arch in speech, and so gentle, unctuous, and tragic of demeanor, that he suggests the modern epitome of agonized courtesy: the undertaker. In this macabre farce, he is cast just one jump away: as an aesthetic assassin. It is unlikely that anybody in the history of the cinema has ever matched his peculiar feat of flipping expressions from benign innocence to bloodcurdling menace in one devastating instant. He dispatches an assortment of expendable types: headmasters, businessmen, dictators, etc., but gets snarled up while trying to liquidate a distasteful cabinet minister. *The Green Man* isn't genteel: it has the virtues of English comedy combined with the more energetic style of satirical American comedy of the thirties. This movie makes you laugh out loud. With George Cole, Terry-Thomas, Jill Adams, Dora Bryan, Raymond Huntley, and a string trio of ladies right out of a George Price cartoon. Frank Launder and Sidney Gilliat wrote and produced; Robert Day directed. 1956.

⊚ ⊚ ⊚

Gunga Din. This is one of the most enjoyable nonsense-adventure movies of all time — full of hokum and heroism and high spirits. George Stevens directed; Ben Hecht and Charles MacArthur wrote the story, "inspired" by the Rudyard Kipling poem, and William Faulkner worked on it, too. The stars are a rousing trio: Cary Grant at his athletic, satirical best; the dashing, gentlemanly Douglas Fairbanks, Jr.; and the eternal vulgarian, Victor McLaglen. Who has forgotten Eduardo Ciannelli in one of the classics of absurd makeup as some sort of mad high priest, or Sam Jaffe as Gunga Din, the essence, the soul of loyalty? Who remembers Joan Fontaine as the pallid and proper heroine? 1939.

⊚ ⊚ ⊚

The Happiest Days of Your Life. If you are the helpless victim of English comedy, you have probably had the dismaying experience of trying to share this taste with someone who has been stonily impervious while you were breaking up. The disease simply isn't communicable — either you get it or you don't, and a plot synopsis of a movie like this one would be no inducement and would probably result in the charge of supreme silliness. But for those who need no inducement: through a bureaucratic error, a boys' school is billeted with a girls' school; there is spinster-grandmother-sergeant Margaret Rutherford as headmistress of St. Swithin's, feuding with soulful-eyed Alastair Sim as headmaster of Nutbourne; there is gangly, gurgling Joyce Grenfell, the undermistress, with her copy of *The New Statesman;* and there are troops of boys and girls with oaths, sports, mottoes, Grecian dances, and all the hideous paraphernalia of pubescent youth. Frank Launder directed, from John Dighton's play. Ronald Searle provides the drawings for the titles. 1950.

⊚ ⊚ ⊚

Harlow. There is not a single line in the Joseph E. Levine production *Harlow,* starring Carroll Baker, that sounds as if the speaker felt it or thought it, or could possibly have said it. The falseness is total: from "Oh, Mama, all they want is my body" to "She died of life. She gave it to everyone else and there wasn't enough left for her." Even the title is false; what we see should be called *Landau.* It's about this wonderful agent, Landau (Red Buttons), who wanted to bring this beautiful talent to the world — a story which seems to parallel Levine's faith in Carroll Baker. She's about as talented as Harlow but in different ways. When Landau says to her, "You have the body of a woman and the emotions of a child," we can see it's just the reverse. The script is loaded with such choice epigrams as: "A bedroom with only one person in it is the loneliest place in the world." Not lonelier, I hope, than theatres playing *Harlow*. With Raf Vallone, Angela Lansbury, Peter Lawford. Directed by Gordon Douglas. 1965.

⊚ ⊚ ⊚

Harper. *Harper* sounded promising — Paul Newman in an attempt to recapture the Bogart private-eye world of *The Big Sleep,* with its spoiled people and overripe Southern California civilization. But it's a despicably incompetent attempt. This kind of movie requires wit (which the scenarist, William Goldman, fails to provide) and thoroughly professional directorial skill. Jack Smight is a bungler from start to finish. Nothing needs justification less than entertainment; but when something planned only to entertain fails, it has no justification. A private-eye movie without sophistication and style is ignominious.

I don't know a woman or a girl-child who doesn't ordinarily enjoy looking at Paul Newman; but he performs coarsely in this — it's his worst performance since his first (*The Silver Chalice*). In mitigation of his offensiveness: what can an actor do with a role that calls for him to be half-drowned and beaten to a bloody pulp — all of which merely serves him as an aphrodisiac? He could at least stop mugging; it would be better if he just walked through (and probably better for him if he walked out). Shelley Winters gives the picture artificial respiration for a few minutes, but it soon relapses. Lauren Bacall appears in an in-joke: not in her old role in *The Big Sleep* but as the rich old paralytic in the wheelchair. Funny like a crutch. A lot of famous and some talented people like Julie Harris and Arthur Hill are in this picture, which is even badly photographed. This opinion of *Harper* was not shared by the public: it was a big hit. 1966, color.

⊚ ⊚ ⊚

Harvest (*Regain*). In the thirties, a handful of superb French films — adult, atmospheric, and tender — created a new American movie audience, and the art house came into existence. *La Grande Illusion, The Baker's Wife, Regain, Le Jour se Lève* reawakened an interest in motion pictures among people who had grown up on Hollywood's standard product and had grown beyond it. *Regain* (1937), adapted from the 1930 novel by the great Provençal primitivist, Jean Giono, is perhaps as refreshing now as when it jolted its first American audiences by the extraordinary purity of its love story, set in an abandoned village. (Typically, the New York censors at first refused to pass it.) Marcel Pagnol made the film in Provence with a superlative cast — the young Fernandel (in what I still think his finest role) as the itinerant tinker who sells his slavey-mistress, Orane Demazis (the Fanny of the Pagnol trilogy), to the magnificent, wild hunter, Gabriel Gabrio. With Marguerite Moreno, Delmont, Le Vigan. Music by Arthur Honegger.

⊙ ⊙ ⊙

Having a Wild Weekend (*Catch Us If You Can* in England). Hardly anyone I know seems to have gone to see John Boorman's *Having a Wild Weekend,* a little English movie featuring the Dave Clark Five and Barbara Ferris, which came into this country in 1965, quietly failed, and disappeared. With few exceptions, the reviewers treated it as a poor imitation of a Beatles picture; but although it began like that, it turned into something else. *Having a Wild Weekend* is partly a reaction against the pop world. It isn't sure of itself, its tone is uneven, its style is faltering and somewhat confused; but it's trying to get at something. Like many of us, it tries to be a success and question the meaning of success — and inevitably fails on both counts.

It begins as just another pop-music happening; but then, as if the inanity of the project overwhelmed the participants, the hero and heroine try to escape their advertising milieu. They don't want to be turned into products, they don't want to be sold. They begin to look at various escape routes from modern commercialism: drugs, antique collecting, yearning for an island. They see middle-aged failures when they're picked up by a dreadful yet sympathetic couple (Robin Bailey and Yootha Joyce), who suggest the Almans, the horribly bickering pair of *Wild Strawberries* (she with her hysteria, he with his Catholicism). The movie seems to discover tentatively, with regret and bewilderment, that the cures are illusory, are only more symptoms. It's as if pop art had discovered Chekhov — the Three Sisters finally set off for Moscow and along the way discover that there isn't any Moscow.

The young refugees from urban corruption look for pastoral innocence and solitude and find that the corruption has infected the countryside. It is total. And the island the girl had dreamed of turns out — at low tide — to be attached to the mainland. They were drawn together by the quest; when they are defeated, they split. This movie has an aftertaste. It's bittersweet — which is an old-fashioned word with connotations of sadness, of nostalgia, and perhaps of something one might call "true." It is one of those films that linger in the memory — a forlorn little Cinderella that the public never took to the big box-office ball.

⊙ ⊙ ⊙

High Noon. It could be, as some film enthusiasts tell us, a poem of force comparable to the *Iliad*. On the other hand, it might be a portentous account of what the reviewers called "a moment of crisis" for a little cow town. Gary Cooper is the marshal who fights alone for law and order when the town is paralyzed by fear. Much has been made of the film's structure: it runs from 10:40 A.M. to high noon (coinciding with the running time of the film); of the stark settings and the long shadows; of the screen writer Carl Foreman's build-up of suspense and his psychological insights. I'm inclined to think his insights are primer sociology passing for dramatic motive, that the town's cowardice is Q.E.D., and that the Western form is being used for a sneak civics lesson. Given this hokum for what it is, it's good, and Fred Zinnemann's direction is excellent. With Grace Kelly, Katy Jurado, Thomas Mitchell, Lloyd Bridges, Otto Kruger, etc. 1952 Academy Awards went to Gary Cooper (Best Actor!), the film editors, and Dimitri Tiomkin (Best Movie Score!!).

⊚   ⊚   ⊚

His Girl Friday. In 1928 Ben Hecht and Charles MacArthur wrote *The Front Page,* the greatest newspaper comedy of them all; in 1940 Howard Hawks directed this adaptation of the play by Charles Lederer, starring Cary Grant as the domineering editor and Rosalind Russell as the unscrupulous crime reporter with printer's ink in her veins. (The difference between Miss Russell here and in a later vehicle like *Auntie Mame* is the difference between a comedienne and an institution.) Overlapping dialogue carries the movie along at breakneck speed; word gags take the place of the sight gags of silent comedy, as this vanished race of brittle, cynical, childish people rush around on corrupt errands. And what a pleasure to know that they will not have misunderstood sex problems and that we can laugh at off-color jokes instead of killing sex with kindness and good taste. The reporters — a fine crew — are Ernest Truex, Cliff Edwards, Porter Hall, Roscoe Karns, Frank Jenks, Regis Toomey; with Gene Lockhart as the sheriff, Billy Gilbert as the messenger, John Qualen, Helen Mack, and with Ralph Bellamy as chief stooge — a respectable businessman — and Alma Kruger as his mother.

This peculiarly American genre of verbal slapstick was admired throughout the world for its vitality and freshness, and envied because of its freedom from certain kinds of political censorship. (If you didn't — and still rarely do — see corrupt politicians, a venal press, shocking prison conditions, and crooked cops in European films, it's not because Europe doesn't have them.) The target in all these impudent, irreverent comedies was always America itself; perhaps no other country could so freely criticize and satirize itself. Ironically, this freedom was lost not because of governmental pressure but because of box-office pressure — the fear of giving offense. Even those marvelous character actors with their idiosyncrasies of accent and appearance, their *idées fixes,* are gone — one is not supposed to make fun of people.

⊚ ⊚ ⊚

Hobson's Choice. Charles Laughton is superbly vulgar in this whack at
the backside of Victorianism. He makes a great vaudeville turn out of the
role of an egocentric scoundrel, the prosperous bootmaker who doesn't
want to part with his three marriageable daughters because they are too
useful as unpaid labor. As the oldest daughter, the spinster in spite of herself, Brenda De Banzie is so "right" that when she marries her father's best
workman and puts belching, drunken old Dad out of business, one feels the
good old-fashioned impulse to applaud. John Mills is the fortunate young
man whom she overpowers. David Lean directed — with more life than
usual — this 1954 English comedy based on the Harold Brighouse play,
with photography by Jack Hildyard.

⊚ ⊚ ⊚

Home before Dark. Jean Simmons gives a reserved, beautifully modulated performance that is so much better than the material that at times her
exquisite reading of the rather mediocre lines seems a more tragic waste
than her character's wrecked life. The script starts with a good idea. A professor (Dan O'Herlihy) commits his young wife to a state mental hospital;
she returns home after a year, exhausted from eight rounds of shock treatment, her hair gray, but feeling cured — reasonable and happy, rid of her
former delusions. Then as she slowly discovers that the delusions the doc-
tors were shocking out of her were actually the truth, she loses her bearings
and begins to go mad. Unfortunately, the script makes the heroine too sympathetic, and it has an edge of fashionable, self-congratulatory virtue — the
"one must be more understanding toward discharged mental patients" attitude, and Mervyn LeRoy directs in a glossy, uninspired style that drags the
material out at least half an hour too long. 1958.

⊚ ⊚ ⊚

The Horse's Mouth. Joyce Cary's painter-hero, Gulley Jimson, is a fabulous creation: the modern artist as a scruffy, dirty little bum. His antics
were partly based on the marvelous, gargantuan self-destructive behavior of
Cary's friend Dylan Thomas, and his approach as a painter was derived
from the tradition of William Blake. Alec Guinness's portrait of Gulley isn't
all that one might hope (it lacks passion and innocence and the real fire of
insolence) and the movie isn't all it should be, but with that said and out of
the way, let's admit how marvelously enjoyable it is. With Ernest Thesiger
as Hickson, Renee Houston as wily old Sarah, Kay Walsh (less successful)
as Coker, the conscience-ridden barmaid, and Michael Gough (wretched)
as the sculptor. Ronald Neame directed Guinness's adaptation; paintings by
John Bratby. 1959, color.

◎ ◎ ◎

I Am a Fugitive from a Chain Gang. In 1932 a grim document about so-cial injustice awakened the country to what was going on in some of the Southern states. Those involved in making the movie hoped it might help to ameliorate the condition of convicts. Its phenomenal success did ameliorate financial conditions at Warner Brothers and was a factor in making it the "socially conscious" studio. *Fugitive* is still one of the best of the social protest films — naïve, heavy, artless, but a straightforward, un-adorned social horror story. There are moments that haunted a generation (the hero, Paul Muni, trying to pawn his Congressional Medal of Honor), and there is one of the great closing scenes in the history of film: the hero is asked, "What do you do? How do you live?" and he answers, "I steal . . ." With Glenda Farrell, Edward Ellis, Helen Vinson, David Lan-dau. Directed by Mervyn LeRoy.

◎ ◎ ◎

Inside Daisy Clover. Natalie Wood plays the teen-age singing movie star (fill in Judy Garland, Deanna Durbin, etc.) of *Inside Daisy Clover,* Robert Mulligan's version of the Gavin Lambert novel. Natalie Wood's way of being teen-age is to act like Tom Sawyer; her way of being a movie star we already know. She's brassy and mechanical, with wind-up emotions.

The movie is short on characters, detail, activity, dialogue, even music: it's as if it's so determined to be stylish and sophisticated that rather than risk vulgarity or banality, it eliminates almost everything. The result is far from stylish: it's empty, but long on sinister, funereal pauses and a few ghoulish people, like the head of the studio, Christopher Plummer (whose performance mightn't be so deadly if it were just speeded up).

The people who make Daisy a star seem to have some terrible secret that we're never let in on; the movie is full of lurking evil that seems to be unrelated to anything. It's an inside-Hollywood movie with a Gothic atmos-phere — all portent, no content. *A Star is Born* was full of heartbreak, but this is practically "A Star Dies": *horror* and heartbreak. And oddly enough, just as the star's "fading" husband, James Mason, walked off with *A Star Is Born,* the no-good husband, Robert Redford, in one of the most cryptic roles ever written, gives the only fresh performance in *Inside Daisy Clover.* With Ruth Gordon, Katharine Bard, Roddy McDowall. 1966, color.

◎ ◎ ◎

Intruder in the Dust. Lucas Beauchamp, the "stubborn and insufferable" hero of *Intruder in the Dust,* is very much like another modern example of pride, isolation, and intransigence — De Sica's great Umberto D. Both men, in their insistence on their rights and dignity, alienate themselves from the community that does not want to be reminded of their existence. Umberto is old, Lucas is a black man who enrages the white people of Mississippi by his refusal to play "nigger" for them.

If this movie had been produced in Europe, it would probably be widely acclaimed among American students of the film as a subtle, sensitive, neorealist work. It was, in fact, made under the same kind of conditions: it was filmed in William Faulkner's home town, Oxford, Mississippi, with the inhabitants playing the bit parts and the crowd scenes. The authenticity of the backgrounds does not, of course, necessarily confer any truth on the foreground action; but *Intruder in the Dust* is faithful to its subject. "All in all I think it is a good movie," Faulkner said at the première in 1949. When you consider how novelists generally react to screen adaptations of their work, this may be considered a cry of hosanna. It *is* a good movie, but it came at the end of a cycle of melodramas about Negroes (*Home of the Brave, Lost Boundaries,* etc.), and few people seemed to realize that *Intruder in the Dust* was a work of integrity and depth. The advertising campaign didn't help to differentiate it from any other movie: "It's Sensational . . . the Picture You'll Never Forget . . . From the Moment You See the Gaunt Figure of a Mysterious Man . . . Silhouetted Against the Hot Sky . . . To the Last Flurry of Bullets . . . When a Bloody Manhunt . . . Flushes the Killer . . . The Picture That Dares to Tell the Truth . . . Tearing Asunder the Veils of Hate and Persecution," etc.

Instead of the good Negro (Sidney Poitier is his prophet), *Intruder in the Dust* presents the maddening Negro: in both novel and film, inflexible Lucas is conceived — and beautifully — as a focus of white ambivalence. He refuses to accept condescension or patronage, he insists on his right to be no better than a white man, and what is truly intolerable — he acts as if he *were* white. The other central character, Chick, the white boy who has made the wretched, stupid mistake of treating Lucas as a Negro by offering him money as payment for hospitality is so humiliated by Lucas's stony refusal that he writhes in impotent fury at himself and at Lucas. He isn't the only one who is upset about Lucas: "He was to learn every white man in that whole section of the country had been thinking about him for years, 'We got to make him be a nigger first. He's got to admit he's a nigger. Then maybe we will accept him as he seems to intend to be accepted.'" When Lucas is arrested for killing a white man, the townspeople get their chance to turn him into a "nigger"; they couldn't teach him, but they can lynch him. But Chick, still suffering from the debt he has been unable to discharge, finds his opportunity to pay Lucas back — by saving him from death. This melodrama serves as a framework for an ironic study of the dignity of man. Chick is trying to get back his pride, trying to restore the balance of his relationship with Lucas; Lucas, even at the risk of burning alive, never risks his pride.

Had *Intruder in the Dust* been directed by a young unknown, it might have been called a masterpiece. But it was directed by Clarence Brown, a man whose sensibility and taste have been less publicized than his ability to handle stars. Some of his most famous and successful films have been artistically atrocious; others have been surprisingly good. If you think back on the big MGM films, chances are that he directed much of what you remember. Here are some of the titles: *The Last of the Mohicans* (1920), *The Eagle* (Valentino, 1925), *The Goose Woman* (1925), *Flesh and the Devil* (Garbo and Gilbert, 1927), *A Woman of Affairs* (Garbo, 1928), *Anna Christie* (Garbo, 1930), *Inspiration* (Garbo, 1931), *A Free Soul* (Gable and Shearer, 1931), *Possessed* (Crawford, 1931), *Emma* (Marie Dressler, 1932), *Letty Lynton* (Crawford, 1932), *Night Flight* (1933), *Anna Karenina* (Garbo, 1935), *Ah, Wilderness!* (1935), *Wife Versus Secretary* (Gable and Loy, 1936), *Conquest* (Garbo and Boyer, 1937), *Idiot's Delight* (1939), *The Rains Came* (1939), *Edison the Man* (1940), *The Human Comedy* (1943), *The White Cliffs of Dover* (1944), *National Velvet* (1944), *The Yearling* (1946), *Song of Love* (Hepburn, 1947), *Intruder in the Dust* (1949).

Intruder in the Dust bears little resemblance in directorial style to the bulk of Brown's glamorous, star-ridden productions. But surely it is the years of range and experience which have given him a control of the medium so calm, sure, and — apparently — easy that he can make a complex story seem simple and straightforward, without any of that straining for effect or vulgar overemphasis which is Hollywood's usual approach to a "classic" (for example, the way Richard Brooks overloaded *Elmer Gantry* with gigantic sets, enormous crowds, fires, riots, and human stampedes). As Karel Reisz pointed out in his analysis of *Intruder in the Dust,* Brown's "deliberate, unspectacular direction" often extends and sharpens the impact of the novel by capturing in a single image the effects that Faulkner had to catalogue one by one; but, of course, the movie simplifies the internal conflicts, the long passages of minute analysis of motives and reactions. As Reisz says, "This, perhaps, is inevitable. But it means that the novelist's most sensitive instrument of perception has been lost." It is evidence of Brown's craftsmanship that he achieved in a single take the sequence which most impressed European critics: the gathering of the crowd in the town square — expectant, waiting for the lynching.

The performances Brown gets are astonishing — although no doubt his years of pulling emotions out of the great ladies of the screen constituted monumental training. Many will recall that in his *National Velvet,* the child Elizabeth Taylor gave what is still the finest performance of her career, and that in *The Yearling* (his last location production before *Intruder in the Dust*), he not only got marvelous results from the two boy actors, but a surprisingly effective performance from Jane Wyman. Juano Hernandez's interpretation of Lucas deserved its two European awards; Claude Jarman, Jr., who had already demonstrated his fine responsiveness to Brown in *The Yearling,* plays Chick. Two American character actors perform with great skill and even beauty: Porter Hall as the murdered man's father and Elizabeth Patterson as the little old lady who believes in doing what's right. Only at the very end is a false note struck in a few lines of explicit comment delivered by David Brian as Chick's uncle — "It will be all right, as long as some of us are willing to fight — even one of us" and the ultimate cliché, "Lucas wasn't in trouble; *we* were in trouble." It's the movie that gets in trouble. Fortunately, the character of Lucas is so dominating that what we have witnessed cannot be reduced to such commonplaces: we know that Lucas has won, that the sheepish, guilty townspeople will now have to accept him on his own terms, that, as Faulkner put it, Lucas is "now tyrant over the whole county's white conscience." The screenplay is by Ben Maddow; photography by Robert Surtees.

⊙ ⊙ ⊙

Invasion of the Body Snatchers. This unpretentious science-fiction movie may be crudely written and inexpensive, and it employs few of the resources of the cinema (to put it mildly), but it has an idea that confirms everyone's suspicions: people are being turned into vegetables and who can tell the difference? It is, of course, a parable of modern society; the hero and heroine (Kevin McCarthy and Dana Wynter), who try to cling to their animality and individuality, seem inexplicably backward to the rest of the town. The supporting cast includes Carolyn Jones and Sam Peckinpah. Directed by Don Siegel. 1956.

⊙ ⊙ ⊙

The Island. This work has been widely acclaimed as a masterpiece, largely I suspect because it is so ponderously, pretentiously simple. A lot of serious-minded people will think it must be art because it sure as hell isn't entertainment. It's the kind of movie that aims at universality by stripping away all the particularities — which are considered to be the nonessentials of civilization and personality. The result is something so barren that those who praise it seem to be asserting proof of virtue, of moral superiority over those of us who are bored by false purity.

This Japanese film by Kaneto Shindo is about a family living on an island without fresh water: their life is a succession of trips to the mainland for water, which they then carry by shoulder yoke up steep paths, to pour over their crops. The film is made without dialogue, and this silence of the characters has been widely commended as the perfect use of silence — the demonstration that the family gives all its energy to the effort to stay alive and has no need for idle talk. We are supposed to regard their preverbal existence, their silent struggle with elemental forces as more basic, more "true to nature" and hence greater — more beautiful — than our talky and hence superficial lives. (If this island family — so sure of their relationships to each other and to the earth and water and plants that they have nothing to say — ever figure out how to get a pipeline in from the mainland, they'll be liberated from that primal struggle with the elements and soon they'll be on their path to conversation and what — in Kaneto Shindo's view — is, I suppose, sophistication, corruption, and decadence.)

The Island, striving for poetry, gives us endless repetition of simple tasks — plenty of time to observe that the carrying of those buckets has been choreographed as a stark ballet of human existence (and to notice that the actors' shoulders sag as much when the buckets are supposed to be empty). Though we are spared the kind of uplifting folk conversation that film-makers with this approach usually provide — the lean, true words of real people — the images are saturated with a musical score of prodigious monotony. *The Island* was made on a small budget and I suppose something should be said about its pictorial qualities. They have been highly praised. They're pictorial, all right.

This film was co-winner of the Grand Prize at the Moscow Film Festival in 1961. A cynic might suggest that it may have had a special appeal for the Russians — as one of the few foreign films that could be absolutely counted on to make life outside the Soviet Union look more grim than life inside.

⊙   ⊙   ⊙

The Italian Straw Hat (*Un Chapeau de Paille d'Italie*). Bergson used the Eugène Labiche and Marc Michel play to illustrate his theory of the comic. René Clair took the basic situations of the play as the starting point for his own inventiveness and made what has become a model of visual wit. *The Italian Straw Hat* is very simply one of the funniest films ever made and one of the most elegant as well. A silent satire on the pretensions of the middle classes, it is so expertly timed and choreographed that farce becomes ballet. With Albert Préjean as the bridegroom. Designed by Lazare Meerson. The picture was a commercial failure. 1927.

⊙   ⊙   ⊙

It's Always Fair Weather. The title is a misnomer. Written by the same team that did *On the Town* (Betty Comden and Adolph Green) and directed by the same team (Gene Kelly and Stanley Donen), this is like a delayed hangover from the earlier film. The three buddies are now Kelly, Dan Dailey, and Michael Kidd; at war's end they swear eternal friendship and promise to meet in ten years. They have their reunion and find that they haven't a thing to say to each other; their boredom turns to mutual disgust, and then to self-disgust and a longing for the hopes they have abandoned.

Unlike *On the Town,* this musical isn't ever-so-cheerful; it manages to compromise with its own cynicism, but the peculiar mixture of social criticism, cynicism, and song and dance in *It's Always Fair Weather* is perhaps too tart — even a little sour — for popular success. As the sickened advertising man, Dan Dailey has the best number in the film — a bitter, drunken solo at a business party in which he mercilessly ridicules "advertising-wise" jargon. (To a great extent this is Dailey's movie, and at times his little moustache gives him a Chaplin look that's rather intriguing.) Dolores Gray's role is too broadly written, but her smooth, glib style is refreshingly brassy and she has one wonderful big number, "Thanks a lot but no thanks"; Cyd Charisse is benumbed until she unhinges those legs. 1955, color, CinemaScope.

⊚ ⊚ ⊚

It's Love I'm After. This thoroughly incredible light farce begins with a burlesque of the tomb scene from *Romeo and Juliet* and proceeds like a somewhat deranged *Taming of the Shrew.* Leslie Howard is a matinée idol, Bette Davis his leading lady, and they play their shallow, vanity-ridden actors as if they relished every slapstick minute (when you consider how much suffering they had to go through in most of their roles, it's no wonder). They are surrounded by that set of millionaires (George Barbier), valets and butlers (Eric Blore, E. E. Clive), and heiresses (Olivia de Havilland) that were at one time as much of a convention in American comedy as the fops of Restoration theatre. The pace is sluggish and Archie Mayo's direction (from Casey Robinson's screenplay) is — to put it kindly — uninspired, but the movie is a rather pleasant bad movie. With Bonita Granville, Patric Knowles, Spring Byington. 1937.

⊚ ⊚ ⊚

Ivan the Terrible. Eisenstein's two-part film is obviously a magnificent work and it imposes its style on the viewer; yet it's so lacking in human dimensions that we may stare at it in a kind of outrage. True, every frame in it looks great — it's a brilliant collection of stills — but as a movie, it's static, grandiose, and frequently ludicrous, with elaborately angled, overcomposed photography, and overwrought, eyeball-rolling performers slipping in and out of the walls, dragging their shadows behind them. Though no doubt the extraordinarily sophisticated Eisenstein intended all this to be a nonrealistic stylization, it's still a heavy dose of décor for all except true addicts. Millions of rubles worth of sets, beards, and brocades went into it. The city of Kazan was built full scale in Central Asia with lumber imported from Siberia.

In Part I, released in 1945, Ivan is crowned, and then because of the opposition of the boyars (or nobles) he is forced to abdicate. (Their dastardly deeds include the murder of his wife.) At the end, he is restored to power with the help of "the people." Part II, which Eisenstein called *The Boyars' Plot,* was his last film. Made in 1945–46, censured by the Central Committee and suppressed, it was not released until five years after Stalin's death (the director, still in disgrace, had died in 1948). In Part II the boyars strike again. Under the leadership of Ivan's ratty old aunt Efrosinia, who hopes to put her (crazy? queer?) son on the throne, they plot to assassinate Ivan. But he outwits them and destroys their power in a big, bloody purge.

Does this read like the libretto for a rather dreary night at the opera? The movie isn't dreary, but it *is* operatic — and opera without singers is a peculiar genre. Something momentous seems about to be imparted to us in each great frozen composition — it's almost as if the aria were about to begin (in one of the most satisfying moments in Part I there *is* a song). The style is so overpowering — like a gigantic expressionist mural — that we expect some content that would measure up to it. But in this exhausting extravaganza of evil tyranny, the figures are like giant spiders and rodents: as in science fiction, some horrible mutation seems to have taken place. The conflict in Ivan is between the good man dedicated to the welfare of his people and the power-mad despot (and, given when it was made, it's easy to read in parallels). Oddly, the makeup that Nikolai Cherkasov uses as Ivan seems to be based on Conrad Veidt's makeup in Paul Leni's 1924 film *Waxworks,* in which Ivan was used simply as a horror figure (the décor and camera work also recall *Waxworks*). And as James Agee pointed out, Eisenstein gave Cherkasov "a chin and cranium which becomes ever more pointed, like John Barrymore as Mr. Hyde." Perhaps *Ivan the Terrible* is closer to the horror genre than has been recognized. It's as mysterious to the American eye and mind as Kabuki, to which it is often compared. Voted sixth among the greatest films of all time by the British Film Institute's 1961 international poll of critics. Music by Prokofiev. Photographed by Edward Tisse, assisted by Andrei Moskvin on Part II. (Part II has one sequence in color.)

⊚ ⊚ ⊚

Jezebel. Bette Davis is impulsive, complex Julie, the Southern belle who destroys her chances for happiness by perversely flouting conventions. William Wyler produced and directed this sumptuous, moss-hung evocation of pre-Civil War New Orleans, with its great balls where tradition decreed that unmarried ladies dress in white — and where Julie's red dress wrecks her life. It's hard to know which is Davis's "big scene" in the movie — the painful, flamboyant error of her appearance in red, or the breathtaking moment of her apology in white. She took the Academy Award of 1938 for this role, and rarely has it been awarded so justly. The screenplay has some remarkable passages, possibly contributed by John Huston, who was one of the writers. This kind of material was already dated by 1938, of course, but was brought out of mothballs and refurbished because of the popularity of *Gone with the Wind* — which it beat to the screen. Without the zing Davis gave it, it would have looked very mossy indeed. With Henry Fonda, George Brent, Margaret Lindsay, and Fay Bainter, who received the Academy Award for Best Supporting Actress, and Richard Cromwell, John Litel, Donald Crisp, Spring Byington, Irving Pichel.

◉   ◉   ◉

Jour de Fête (*The Big Day*). As director, Jacques Tati has a spare, quick, improvisatory touch. As comedian, buoyancy and impersonal eccentricity in the face of disaster are his special style. In his 1950 film, photographed in Saint Severs, with villagers playing many of the parts, Tati is the postman who attends the village fair and sees a documentary on the advanced, mechanized American postal system. He is overcome with enthusiasm for speed, and though he has no helicopter, he has his bicycle. He takes off, and causes the unpredictable to happen.

◉   ◉   ◉

Kameradschaft. Based on an actual incident in which German miners crossed the border to go to the assistance of French miners trapped by an explosion, G. W. Pabst's 1931 study of disaster and rescue is a powerful and imaginative re-creation of a high moment in human comradeship. The socialist-pacifist implications which Pabst sees in the episode had tremendous international impact in the days when people were more idealistic. In the early thirties it was still possible for large audiences to believe in the symbolic revolutionary meaning of smashing through artificial frontiers for the sake of natural brotherhood. This movie belongs to a genre that has disappeared. Technically a brilliant achievement, *Kameradschaft* is famous among film craftsmen for the experimental use of sound, and for magnificent creative editing. The subterranean scenes have a nightmarish authenticity. The cast of French and German players includes Alexander Granach and Elizabeth Wendt.

◉   ◉   ◉

A Kid for Two Farthings. Wolf Mankowitz takes the language of the East End of London and uses it as a poetic idiom. His characters are also transformed by his imaginative gift into creatures of fantasy and fable. *A Kid for Two Farthings,* directed by Carol Reed in 1955, has some of the same verbal magic of *The Bespoke Overcoat* and *Expresso Bongo,* and many of the characters could step in and out of any of these films. A boy looks for the unicorn that can work miracles and finds a sick goat with one horn. Reed is a fine director, and the film achieves enough small miracles to lift it to an unfamiliar realm, but he can't quite solve the problem of *how* to tell the Mankowitz story. The success of this type of fantasy depends on the contrast between the child's world and the adult's: in *The Rocking Horse Winner,* for example, the director stays outside the child's world and we view what goes on inside with terror and apprehension; in *White Mane,* Albert Lamorisse helped us to enter and experience the child's domain. Here we are caught in a fairy-tale set somewhere between. The East End is made so fascinating that reality and fantasy are inextricable; and though a child may well apprehend them this way, the fabulous reality confuses the point for us. With Jonathan Ashmore, David Kossoff, Celia Johnson, Brenda De Banzie, Sidney James, Alfie Bass, Vera Day, Diana Dors, Joe Robinson, and Primo Carnera as the ogre. Color.

◉ ◉ ◉

The Killers. Ernest Hemingway's short story about the man who does not try to escape his killers is acted out tensely and accurately, and, for once, the material added to it is not just padding, but is shrewdly conceived (by Anthony Veiller and John Huston, although Huston's name does not appear in the script credits) to show why the man didn't care enough about life to run away. Under the expert direction of Robert Siodmak, Burt Lancaster gives his first and probably best screen performance, and Siodmak has also done wonders for Ava Gardner. With Edmond O'Brien, Albert Dekker, Sam Levene, Donald MacBride, Vince Barnett, Jeff Corey. 1946.

◉ ◉ ◉

The Killing. It's a mercy to Stanley Kubrick to forget his juvenilia — *Fear and Desire* and *Killer's Kiss.* If he were a novelist instead of a film director, he would be able to destroy them. He was young enough (twenty-seven) when he made *The Killing,* which is the real beginning of his career. *The Killing* is an expert suspense film, with fast, incisive cutting, a nervous, edgy style, and furtive little touches of characterization. The film is no more than a good tense thriller, but it has movement, and dialogue that doesn't sound as if it were written by the IBM machine that's been processing most recent film speech. It includes many familiar second-string actors, but they go through enough unfamiliar movements to keep you in an agreeable state of anxious expectation. Sterling Hayden is excellent as the lead; with Elisha Cook, Jr. and fierce, tight (over-rated) Marie Windsor as his mismate; the generally under-rated good little actress Coleen Gray, Jay C. Flippen, Timothy Carey as the sharpshooter, Ted De Corsia, Joe Sawyer, and Kola Kwarian as the chess-playing wrestler. Photographed by Lucien Ballard. 1956.

⊚ ⊚ ⊚

Kind Hearts and Coronets. This tart black comedy on the craving for social position and the art of murder has a brittle wit that came as a bit of a shock: such amoral lines were not generally spoken in forties movies. We were surfeited with movies that try to move us and push us around; *Kind Hearts* is heartless, and that is the secret of its elegance. Ninth in line to inherit a dukedom, the insouciant young hero (Dennis Price) systematically eliminates the intervening eight — a snob, a general, a photographer, an admiral, a suffragette, a clergyman, a banker, and the Duke — all, by a casting stroke of genius, played by Alec Guinness. Secure in the knowledge that Guinness will return in another form, the audience suffers no regret as each abominable D'Ascoyne is coolly dispatched. And as the murderer takes us further into his confidence with each foul deed, we positively look forward to his next success. With purring little Joan Greenwood as the minx-nemesis Sybilla, Valerie Hobson as the high-minded Edith, Miles Malleson as the poetasting executioner. Based upon the 1907 novel *Israel Rank* by Roy Horniman, adapted by Robert Hamer and John Dighton, Hamer directed. 1949.

⊚ ⊚ ⊚

Knock on Wood. This film has been fairly universally certified as a howl, but I found myself moaning. I'm not the Danny Kaye enthusiast I used to be. His talents are violently evident, but they're sunk in the mud of "family entertainment." The tiresome, naïve young man occasionally breaks out into frenzied satire, but more frequently he just pushes his way through some clumsy routines (if he uses that Irish impersonation again, even the infants may crawl out for a cigarette). In this one, he's a ventriloquist who can't control his dummy (the plot resemblance to the brilliant Redgrave episode in *Dead of Night* may not be wholly coincidental) and Mai Zetterling is his analyst. Norman Panama and Melvin Frank wrote and directed. Michael Kidd did the choreography. 1954, color.

⊚ ⊚ ⊚

The Koumiko Mystery. This hour-long documentary about a modern Japanese girl, her attitudes and her life, was made by a Frenchman, Chris Marker, who shot it in Tokyo during the Olympics. The mystery is simply the mystery of human individuality, a *true* mystery. Marker's approach is personal, lyrical. Earlier, Marker made the short *La Jetée,* which is the greatest science-fiction movie I've ever seen. His Tokyo has something of science fiction, too: it looks as if it were built the day after tomorrow. It seems almost inconceivable that it was ever intended to endure. And as Koumiko, with her archaic Oriental beauty, walks through this transient, commercial World's Fair kind of civilization and talks about what she likes and what she doesn't and how she feels — seeing herself as an outsider, as so many young Americans do — the movie begins to express something new, a new modern mood, perhaps, of acceptance of estrangement. 1966, color.

⊚ ⊚ ⊚

The Ladykillers. This sinister black comedy of murder accelerates until it becomes a hilarious fantasy of murder; the more grotesque, the funnier it becomes. When it's over, you realize that even the actors have been having a boisterous good time getting themselves knocked off. Alec Guinness, almost crucified by great, hideous teeth — so enormous they give him master criminal status — is the leader of the horrendous gang. Katie Johnson is the cheerful old lady who upsets their fiendish plans simply by living in a world of her own. As her victims are, in some ways, even less real than she (she, at least, is as real as a good fairy), the disasters that befall them are extravagantly absurd. With Cecil Parker, Herbert Lom, Peter Sellers (remember? he was Harry, the awkward Teddy Boy), Danny Green, Jack Warner, and Frankie Howard as the barrow boy. Written by William Rose, directed by Alexander Mackendrick. 1956, color.

⊚ ⊚ ⊚

The Lady Vanishes. This 1938 murder mystery about a fussy, jolly old lady who boards a train and disappears on it is directed with such skill and velocity that it has come to represent the quintessence of screen suspense. It provides some of the finest examples of Hitchcock touches — the little shocks and perversities of editing and detail that give his early movies a satanic kind of humor. The hero is played by a tall, callow young man making his film debut — Michael Redgrave; the heroine is Margaret Lockwood, and the lady is Dame May Whitty. With Paul Lukas, Cecil Parker, Margaretta Scott, Catherine Lacey, Googie Withers, and the team of Naunton Wayne and Basil Radford creating that often-to-be-repeated parody of the "jolly-good-show" type of Britisher. Screenplay by Sidney Gilliat, Frank Launder, Alma Reville.

⊚ ⊚ ⊚

Last Holiday. The 1950 production of J. B. Priestley's ironic comedy stars Alec Guinness as the ordinary little fellow who is told that he has only six weeks to live, and liberated from anxieties about the future, finds in that time all the opportunities for wealth, fame, and happiness that he had never found before. It's just about a perfect little picture. The dexterity, the impeccable "rightness" of Priestley's screenplay is almost infuriating: within his middle-class, socialist-mystic limits he is an unerring master. With Kay

Walsh, Wilfred Hyde-White, Beatrice Campbell, Gregoire Aslan, David McCallum as the blind violinist, Sidney James, and that great asset of English comedy, Ernest Thesiger. Henry Cass directed.

◎ ◎ ◎

The Last Ten Days (*Der Letzte Akt*). G. W. Pabst, who directed this 1955 account of the last ten days in Hitler's headquarters, employs a restrained style which makes the collapse of discipline and the final disintegration seem like an enveloping nightmare. Remarque's script, based on Musmanno's *Ten Days to Die,* perhaps errs in systematically constructing little episodes to illuminate chaos; the atmosphere is so compelling that these vignettes seem trite and unnecessary. Albin Skoda's Hitler is an intelligent approach to a terribly difficult role; Oskar Werner's heroic role is a flamboyant invention and he gives it a fine flourish. Surrounding Hitler there are Lotte Tobisch as Eva Braun, Willi Krause as Goebbels, and, of course, the generals of all kinds and attitudes: General Krebs, for example, who asks if God exists, and General Burgdorf who replies, "If he did, we wouldn't." Whatever your judgment of the picture's value as historical interpretation (did Hitler flood the subways?), it is an experience to spend two hours in that claustrophobic bunker with Pabst and his actors.

◎ ◎ ◎

Laughter in Paradise. Audiences love this 1951 English comedy, and for good reason. Michael Pertwee's script is amusingly contrived: an old prankster dies, leaving a will that outlines the tasks his relatives must complete before receiving their inheritance — such tasks as robbery, marriage, etc. Alastair Sim has a classic comic sequence (trying to get arrested) and a classic fiancée (Joyce Grenfell, a WAAF whom he describes as "an officer and gentleman"). Mario Zampi's direction is not all it should be, but the cast is so good it hardly matters: George Cole, Ernest Thesiger, A. E. Matthews, Beatrice Campbell, Guy Middleton, Fay Compton, Hugh Griffith, John Laurie, Anthony Steel, and "introducing" Audrey Hepburn.

Pertwee's good script ideas often come across despite the ways they are carried out. His *Your Past is Showing* (English title, *The Naked Truth*) of 1958 was about a blackmailing publisher (Dennis Price in one of his best roles since *Kind Hearts and Coronets*) of a *Confidential*-type magazine. His victims included Peter Sellers as a peculiarly nasty television celebrity, and Sellers captured the horror and hypocrisy of the role with great finesse (particularly in the sequence with the old man from the Gorbals); Terry-Thomas as a racketeering peer; Shirley Eaton as a model; and the formidable Peggy Mount (a female Charles Laughton crossed with a young Margaret Rutherford) as a novelist. Again Mario Zampi directed, and although no one could describe his style as subtle, he allows for good bits by Miles

Malleson and Joan Sims as the novelist's daughter. This is one of the few moderately good English comedies that hasn't been played to death.

Another of the good Pertwee ideas was for the 1959 *Too Many Crooks:* a gang of crooks (George Cole, Sidney James, and company) kidnap the wife (Brenda De Banzie) of a tycoon (Terry-Thomas) and discover they are holding a cold potato. The tycoon, who is having an affair with his secretary, is delighted to be rid of his wife and has no intention of ransoming her. Furious, the wife becomes the mastermind of the gang. Zampi, directing rather laboriously, confuses frenzy and disorder with action, and shouted dialogue with wit. But compared to the way Elliot Silverstein handled the same idea in *The Happening* in 1967, Zampi — in retrospect — seems a master.

⊚ ⊚ ⊚

The Lavender Hill Mob. As the prim, innocuous little bank clerk with a hidden spark of nonconformity, Alec Guinness carries out the universal dream of larcenous glory: robbing a mint. A man who steals three million in gold bullion may be permitted to coin a word: Guinness describes his gleaming-eyed, bowler-hatted little man as the "fubsy" type. (Would it be stretching the point to suggest that, in the modern Western world, this sneaky, paper-weighted civil servant is the new image of Everyman?) T. E. B. Clarke's script, Charles Crichton's direction, and Auric's music contribute to what is probably the most perfect fubsy comedy of all time. Stanley Holloway is the genteel, artistic accomplice; Alfie Bass and Sidney James the professional assistants, and one of the beneficiaries of Guinness's wrongdoing is a bit player, Audrey Hepburn. Academy Award for Best Story and Screenplay. 1951.

⊚ ⊚ ⊚

The Letter. *The Letter,* Bette Davis's forty-third movie, marked her tenth year in films; it is one of her few good vehicles. Somerset Maugham's melodrama (generally believed to be based on an actual incident) had been a Broadway success for Katherine Cornell and was filmed in 1929 with Jeanne Eagels (those blessed with movie-loving parents may still retain images of her strangely corrupt beauty, and of the frenzied scene when she told off her husband). The central figure is the wife of a rubber plantation owner — a woman of such unimpeachable respectability that she can empty a gun into her lover and get by with it (in the courts, at least, because in Singapore the white ruling class must stick together). Davis gives what is very likely the best study of female sexual hypocrisy in film history. Cold and proper, she yet manages to suggest the fury and frustration of a murderess. She is helped by a good script (by Howard Koch) and by two excellent performances — James Stephenson as her lawyer and Herbert

Marshall as her husband (it is one of his few commendable acting jobs in a career of staggering mediocrity). The cast also includes two formidable women — Frieda Inescourt (who has always struck me as ineffably absurd) as the lawyer's wife, and Gale Sondergaard (whose performance used to be taken seriously) as the Eurasian. With Bruce Lester, Cecil Kellaway, and Doris Lloyd. The music is pure, adulterated Max Steiner. It demeans William Wyler's clear, excellent direction. 1940.

⊙   ⊙   ⊙

Letter from an Unknown Woman. Max Ophuls made this film in Hollywood in 1948, but its evocation of late nineteenth-century Vienna is as romantically stylized and as beautifully textured as his European work. His theme (it was almost always his theme) is the difference in approaches to love. A pianist, Louis Jourdan, seduces an impressionable adolescent, Joan Fontaine, and promptly forgets her; years later he meets her again, and, thinking her a fresh conquest, seduces her again. But in the intervening years she has borne him a child and remained hopelessly in love with him. This ironic love story, based on Stefan Zweig's *Brief Einer Unbekannten,* is told from the woman's point of view (one suspects the Production Code had something to do with the attitudes taken toward the man), and there are moments when one wants to clobber the poor wronged, suffering creature. But the director's artistry raises the film above the heroine's point of view. With Mady Christians. Script by Howard Koch.

The following year Ophuls made an "American" American movie, *Caught,* about a millionaire (Robert Ryan — in what was possibly a portrait of Howard Hughes) who, to spite his analyst, marries a young innocent (Barbara Bel Geddes). James Mason appeared as a doctor, Curt Bois as a slimy pimp, a worm who turned. This little-publicized movie was a financial failure, but I think it is the most interesting and emotionally complex of Ophuls's American pictures.

⊙   ⊙   ⊙

Les Liaisons Dangereuses. Valmont and Juliette, the eighteenth-century characters in the Laclos novel, were former lovers who, writing to each other about their strategies, targets, and conquests, turn love into something as studied and planned and calculated as war. They take the love out of love. Modernizing the story, Roger Vadim ties things up rather neatly by having Valmont (in a rather tired, too-sweet performance by Gérard Philipe — his last) and Juliette (Jeanne Moreau at her ravaged best) married; for who plots more than married people? Boredom with "love" leads to games of love. In Laclos the pleasure seems to be in carrying out the plan, achieving the victory — a triumph of austere, rational conquest; in Vadim's version a sensuous aura surrounds and permeates the objects.

The first scene of Marianne (Annette Stroyberg Vadim) in the snow, her mouth open in laughter for a romantic eternity, isn't on a much higher level than the *Playboy* bunnies of the month; Vadim also uses jazz and Negroes and sex all mixed together in a cheap and sensational way that, I assume, is exotic for the French. But, using these elements, he attempts to give them a rhythm and feeling that are, at least, unusually high-class commercialism. Vadim's erotic cleverness is so transparent and shoddy that it verges on the comic; yet the snowflower lyric innocence about Marianne gives pathos and a suggestion of spirituality to Valmont's feeling for her.

It is Juliette's independence when Valmont wants to halt their activities that gives the film its character. She is not, then, pursuing this life of conquest *merely* to hold her husband: she has developed a passion that, once he has softened and reneged, can only destroy them both. When Valmont and Juliette declare their war on each other, the film becomes less corrupt, more interesting. Though it is he who wants to give up the game, it is she who breaks the rules of the game by using his letters against him. They were both talented at long, drawn-out military maneuvers, but when it comes to the passions of war, they finish each other off as viciously and destructively as if they had never heard of finesse.

Seeing the film, I had a sense of confusion when I saw the vaccination mark on Moreau's arm and I was distracted until, a few seconds later, I recalled that in the novel Juliette was, at the end, disfigured by smallpox. Vadim serves her up flaming and the result is the same. I think it's a much better movie than the American reviews indicated. With Jeanne Valerie, Jean-Louis Trintignant, Simone Renant. Background music by Thelonious Monk; party music played by the Jazz Messengers with Kenny Clarke. 1959.

⊙   ⊙   ⊙

The List of Adrian Messenger. The detective story film has become rare; this one revives many of the pleasures of the genre — especially the opportunities it provides for all sorts of odd, specialized information and odd characters. In this case there are phonetic clues, some fancy murder methods, a fox hunt, war-hero detectives; and even the disguised guest stars are rather like those maddening, suspicious characters in detective novels who seem to be introduced for the sole purpose of throwing dust in our eyes. The stardust is slightly irritating: you find yourself trying to clear up the incidental mystery and losing track of the action. But it's not so bad as some of the reviewers indicated. Burt Lancaster is amusing as a woman (though his drag sequence here doesn't compare with his prancing maiden in *The Crimson Pirate*). And there is a joker in the disguised pack: Robert Mitchum, who defies makeup — when he peels off the layers, the wonder is that he could be wearing so much to so little purpose. John Huston directed, from Anthony Veiller's screenplay, based on Philip MacDonald's novel. The cast includes George C. Scott, Kirk Douglas, Clive Brook, Gladys Cooper, Dalio, Jacques Roux, John Merivale, Herbert Marshall, Noel Purcell, and a couple of Hustons; and there are also guests bits by Tony Curtis and Frank Sinatra. 1963.

⊙ ⊙ ⊙

Long Day's Journey into Night. After such an experience, I don't see how one can niggle over whether it's "cinema" or *merely* "filmed theatre." Whatever it is, it's great. (And I am prepared to defend it as a movie.) I'm not sure, however, that *Journey* is, in the fullest sense, exportable. This portrait of the artist as an Irish-American has the worst American failings: it's obvious, sprawling yet crabbed. It's the naked, trite, naggingly self-expressive art of a new, almost pathetically self-conscious country. But if you respond at all, I think you go all the way to exaltation. Perhaps just because of all its hideous familiarity, its grinding, ludicrous wrestling with expressiveness, *Journey* is, at last, an American family classic: the usual embarrassments have been transcended and the family theme is raised to mythic heights.

Katharine Hepburn has surpassed herself — the most beautiful comedienne of the thirties and forties has become our greatest tragedienne; seeing her transitions in *Journey,* the way she can look eighteen or eighty at will, experiencing the magic in the art of acting, one can understand why the appellation "the divine" has sometimes been awarded to certain actresses. For the other performers — Ralph Richardson, Jason Robards, Jr., and Dean Stockwell, for the director Sidney Lumet, and for the cinematographer Boris Kaufman, perhaps even a critic may express simple gratitude. To borrow from Nietzsche: "In praise there is often more obtrusiveness than in blame." 1962.

⊙ ⊙ ⊙

Lord Love a Duck. For *Lord Love a Duck,* which is set in a Los Angeles high school but belongs to the genre of college football comedies — even though nobody plays such innocent games in it — George Axelrod draws upon the novel *Candy,* which he is beating to the movie post, as well as *What's New, Pussycat?* and the Richard Lester movies. There is eating à la Tony Richardson, and tidbits from all over, even Fellini's *Nights of Cabiria.* Among other things, this movie is about a girl getting into the movies: the remarkably talented Tuesday Weld is a sort of Candy-Trilby, and she has a blank, childlike quality that is well used. But *Lord Love a Duck* is not really about anything that's been thought through; it's just way-out — and that, finally, is no place.

It's bright and inventive, and it has some very funny things in it. But it's not difficult to make jokes about modern education, psychoanalysis, etc. It's easy if you don't bother trying to work out a structure that they come out of and mean something in, if you just use them as gags, thrown in any old which way, with a genie (Roddy McDowall) to hold them together. Just about all the good effects get killed by overemphasis and excess: Axelrod's work has a way of turning ugly.

Like *The Loved One, Lord Love a Duck* is a new-style hate letter to America. Axelrod selects the easiest, most grotesque targets and keeps screaming at us to enjoy how funny-awful everything is. And then, after we've sat laughing occasionally, but also being rather appalled by this exhibition of lack of control, we are preached at from the screen for our tiny minds and our family spray deodorants. He's like a man sitting in the middle of his gambling casino condemning the kids shooting craps outside. *Lord Love a Duck* even pretends that it's satirizing beach-party movies as an excuse for showing a multitude of wriggling bodies; it's less honest (or more self-deceived) about what it's doing than the movies it claims to satirize.

There are some good performers: Ruth Gordon creates a new kind of dementia (though, unfortunately, she seems better if one does not see her in several roles in a season); Lola Albright once again demonstrates that she is one of the finest wasted actresses in American movies; several of the other performers (Sarah Marshall, Martin West, Max Showalter, etc.) are admirable — until they're made to slaver and shout. This movie probably represents the worst misuse of many talents since *The Loved One,* and in this case, the principal talent, George Axelrod, seems to be the misuser. How can he be so good and so bad? *Lord Love a Duck* is the best American comedy of 1966, and yet it's mostly terrible.

☉   ☉   ☉

The Loved One. What's funny about *The Loved One* (and although it's a bad movie, it *is* funny) is that just about everybody in it seems to be playing satyrs or sissies or faggots. It's like a big movie with W. C. Fields and Grady Sutton and Franklin Pangborn in all the roles. Even badly misused, Jonathan Winters, John Gielgud, Rod Steiger, Robert Morley, Liberace, Lionel Stander, Robert Morse, Margaret Leighton, James Coburn, Milton Berle, Tab Hunter, Roddy McDowall, Anjanette Comer, Ayllene Gibbons, et al., are more fun to watch than most actors, and you keep imagining what they *could* do if only the director knew his business.

Almost incredibly, the director, Tony Richardson, manages to miss one of the biggest targets imaginable: Los Angeles. It's hard to believe the movie was made there. Richardson aims for the bizarre, the strange, the ugly, the unreal. He conveys no sense of L.A., the world of the future, middle-class model — L.A. with its luxurious banality, its science-fiction impersonality, and the chintzy reality of it all.

In 1947 Evelyn Waugh went to Hollywood to clear up censorial objections to the script for his *Brideshead Revisited;* after seven weeks he simply withdrew the book and went back to England. Out of his experiences he wrote the essay *Death in Hollywood* on Forest Lawn Memorial Park, and in 1948, *The Loved One,* a short satirical novel about one of the last outposts of empire, the British colony in the movie business and its renegade poet who goes to work in a cemetery for pets. Bought for the movies, the novel became a Hollywood legend through the efforts of various writers (including Luis Buñuel and Elaine May) to get an acceptable film script out of material that was considered too naughty and macabre for the screen. But movies (and popular culture in general) have been changing so fast that by the time Tony Richardson was scheduled to direct the production, the novel — then being scripted by Christopher Isherwood — was probably considered too tame and limited. Terry Southern was brought in to juice it up. (Waugh tried, but was unable, to withdraw *The Loved One.*)

The movie, advertised as "The motion picture with something to offend everyone," begins and ends with "America the Beautiful" on the sound track. What comes between is a hate letter to America — which is equated with the most grotesque aspect of Los Angeles. But it takes talent to shock. *The Loved One* will seem outrageous only to the kind of people who think the flag is insulted if a kid pops his bubble gum on the Fourth of July. What is offensive about the movie is not the satirical points it makes, but the ones it misses and the miscalculation of our reaction: Richardson and company obviously think they're going to make our hair stand on end. There is something else offensive: the complacent assumption that things badly done are brilliant just because they may give offense. They give offense because they're badly done.

Terry Southern has somehow acquired the reputation of being the ultimate put-on artist: anything he writes is supposed to be the cool beyond cool. He has a modern adolescent's notion of the *enemy:* white Southerners, businessmen, the military, scientists. His types have names that are possibly still funny in the boy-boy world of *Mad* comics; what they say comes out in capital letters in balloons: PINKO PREVERTS, SAN ANTONE, MR. BIG. And he can't let a name, a word, or a joke die a natural, dignified death of overwork and old age. Southern's heavy hand wouldn't stick out so much if the director would only slap it down; instead, Richardson is trying to overreach it. They're competing with each other in how much they can get by with.

Even a chaotic satire like this is cleansing, and it's embarrassing to pan even a bad movie that comes out against God, mother, and country. But to be scathing one must be exact. (To see the difference between art and clumsy intention, one need only compare the dwarf-headmaster of *Zero for Conduct* with the child-scientist of *The Loved One* whose introduction is staged as if for daytime television.) From the look of this movie Richardson wasn't sure what he was doing, shot every plausible idea that came up, and then, as the material was of megalomaniac length and had no flow, no development, he chopped it up and slapped it together hard, trying to use overlapping sound to plug up the holes.

Editing *can* cover up a lot of mistakes, but it shouldn't need to. A good director shoots his film so that the editing will (usually unobtrusively) give his material the rhythm that is best for the story he's telling. Tony Richardson — of necessity — uses the most glaringly obtrusive editing in the business, and this ineptitude is often mistaken for dazzling style and "genius." Fortunately, although the picture has lost its center (the poet has become as quirky and crazy as everybody else), some of the fragments are good and jagged, and Richardson's specialty — using eating as sex — provides an unforgettable climax. A failure in almost all its serious intentions, this botched, patched-together movie is a triumphant disaster — like a sinking ship that makes it to port because everybody aboard is too giddy to panic. They're so high and lucky they just float it in. Perhaps they didn't even notice how low they'd sunk. 1965.

⊙ ⊙ ⊙

Lovers and Thieves (*Assassins et Voleurs*). Just before his death in 1957, Sacha Guitry, then seventy-two, wrote and directed (from a wheelchair!) this sly little detective comedy. The old master of casual, ironic wit had intended to play the leading role himself, but old age had at last caught up with him and he appeared only in a bit part; still true to his reputation as a womanizer, he directed an extended romantic sequence that is one of the most impudent ever filmed.

Magali Noel, the enchantingly stylish murder victim, loathes her husband so much that she and her lover make love all over Paris, so that everyone will know the husband is a cuckold. The lover, who is also the narrator (Jean Poiret), inadvertently commits a murder for which an innocent thief (Michel Serrault) is sent to prison; conscience-stricken, the lover takes over the occupation of the thief. But all this is only the loose framework; Guitry makes a sortie into a great loony bin, provides an exquisitely audacious painting theft, and stops everything while a mad beatnik (Darry Cowl) addresses a courtroom.

In the thirties, Guitry had, in *The Story of a Cheat* and *The Pearls of the Crown,* developed a new approach to the talking picture: the narrator provides a cynical and witty counterpoint to the actions we observe (this technique was to become familiar to a later generation through the English comedy *Kind Hearts and Coronets*). This approach, to which he returned in *Assassins et Voleurs,* permits him to treat the film medium with nonchalant intimacy — there are insolent interruptions, changes of subject and pace. He teases the classic unities as well as the classic virtues: in his fresh, offhand way he seems to say, "Look how easy it is to make a movie — one just begins and then improvises." It's a lovely movie.

⊙ ⊙ ⊙

The Lower Depths (*Les Bas-Fonds*). The bottom drawer of society is represented in a filthy rooming house for transients — a skid row that has the horror and fascination of looking over a cliff. One might, like the gambler baron (Louis Jouvet) or the actor (Robert Le Vigan), fall down there — or one might, like the thief (Jean Gabin), be down there trying to climb up. The cast includes Jany Holt as a prostitute with aspirations toward love with sentiment, Suzy Prim, Vladimir Sokoloff, Junie Astor. These people at the lower depths are not very different from people anywhere, except for the loss of human dignity: in a flophouse, gregariousness is the unspeakably ugly fact of life. Jean Renoir transcribed the Maxim Gorky play so that those two poles of French acting style — Gabin and Jouvet — act magnetically. 1936. (This movie has one of those great moments that people talk about for years afterward: the scene when Jouvet comes away from the gaming tables and cannot light his cigarette. It was, for the thirties, like Belmondo rubbing his lips in *Breathless.*)

⊙ ⊙ ⊙

M. Fritz Lang's first sound film, made in Germany in 1932, has visual excitement, pace, brilliance of surface, and feeling for detail. Above all it has, caught in a manhunt, a small, fat man, sweating in his uncomfortable clothes: the sexual psychopath who murders little girls — interpreted by Peter Lorre with a spark of genius. *M* is based on the actual case of the Düsseldorf murderer: the police, in trying to track him down, disturbed the normal criminal activities of the city, and the underworld organized to find him — so that crime could go on as usual. Lang turns the movie into a melodramatic thriller by centering on this ironic chase, and the film is similar to Pabst's *Three Penny Opera* (made the year before) in its satirical use of the beggars and criminals.

It is Lorre's triumph that he makes us understand the terrified, suffering human being who murders. Trapped by the underworld, he screams, "I can't help myself!" and it is one of the great, unforgettable cries of anguish. So complete is our identification with Lorre as a psychopath (one of the two great performances of his movie career; the other — Raskolnikov in von Sternberg's 1935 Hollywood production of *Crime and Punishment*) that it is almost incredible to learn that while appearing before Fritz Lang's cameras in the daytime, he was, at night, acting as a comedian in a farce.

◎ ◎ ◎

Mademoiselle Gobette. A girl who can't keep her clothes on may seem like a subject for low-grade entertainment, but suppose that her foible is used to satirize the conventions of respectable society? This neat little farce begins with a judge investigating charges that a theatrical performer (Silvana Pampanini) is too scantily dressed; she proceeds to scandalize a number of overdressed people, and ends up happily ensconced with the Minister of Justice. The cast and director (Pietro Germi) are Italian, but the source is a French play (by Maurice Hennequin and Pierre Weber), and the whole thing has somehow gotten itself into French with English subtitles — presumably on the basis that boudoir comedy will sell better in French for American sex-art houses. *Mademoiselle Gobette* is a boudoir comedy, all right, but it isn't low grade — the boudoir is used as a vantage point for social ridicule and some light, deft horseplay. Even the strapping Pampanini shows a relaxed and inventive comedy style. 1955.

◎ ◎ ◎

Maedchen in Uniform. The controversy has never completely subsided since this German film was released in 1932. A sensitive young girl (Herthe Thiele) in a fashionable school is unhappy under the harsh, Prussian discipline; she flowers when a sympathetic, understanding teacher (Dorothea Wieck) gives her special consideration. To American audiences this consideration seems especially special — ambiguous and certainly sensual. The teacher is not viewed as decadent or even naughty; she appears to be on the side of the liberal, humanitarian angels, and yet she seems unmistakably lesbian. The film is already a legend, but for the sake of the record: it was temporarily obstructed by censors, later voted the best film of the year by the New York press, and the New York *World-Telegram,* not content with that, called it "the year's ten best programs rolled into one." It was directed by Leontine Sagen from Christa Winsloe's play *Yesterday and Today* — one of the few occasions in film history when a woman writer's material has also been directed by a woman.

◎ ◎ ◎

The Magician (Ansiktet, which is The Face). I don't think this 1958 film by Ingmar Bergman is a masterwork or even a very good movie, but it is clearly a film made by a master. It has a fairy-tale atmosphere of expectation, like those stories that begin, "We started out to see the king and along the way we met . . . ," but then it becomes confused and we are left with pieces of different stories. But the mysterious images of Max von Sydow as the nineteenth-century mesmerist, Vogler, and Ingrid Thulin as his assistant, Aman, carry so much latent charge of meaning that they dominate the loosely thrown-together material. Bergman labels it a comedy, but audiences may not agree. I thought the low comedy was much too low, the grisly eyeball-hand sequence pretty cheap, and the magic-versus-rationalism (or, if you prefer, faith-versus-scepticism, or art-versus-science, or illusion-versus-reality) struck me as too Gothic and silly to sustain such heavy-breathing dialogue as "I always longed for a knife to cut away my tongue and my sex — to cut away all impurities." There are times when I'd be happy to hand Bergman that knife. The general range of ideas is of the type that we old philosophy majors used to refer to contemptuously as "metaphysical." Bergman conveniently places his story in the nineteenth century, but he retains all the clichés of the twentieth (the Man of Science is cold, sadistic, etc.). Those who worry about the supposed division between emotion and intellect never leave one in doubt about which side they're on. With Gunnar Bjornstrand as Vergerus, Bibi Andersson as Sara, Naima Wifstrand as Grandmother, Bengt Ekerot as Spegel. Photographed by Gunnar Fischer.

◉　◉　◉

The Magnificent Ambersons. Orson Welles's first film, *Citizen Kane,* was a resounding flop; this one, his second (which he was not permitted to complete) lost money more quietly. If people didn't want to see the autopsy of a scandalous public figure, they wanted even less to look inside themselves. Although Welles achieved great sequences, these are intense, harrowing family squabbles that could not help but alienate a forties public committed to the sentimental myths of family life. Tim Holt is the arrogant, mother-fixated son who falls from American aristocracy to working class with a thud; Dolores Costello, the great beauty of the silent screen, is the warm and yielding mother. As the nervous, bitter, hysterical old-maid aunt, Agnes Moorehead just about belts you out of the theatre. (Her performance has been discussed by drama critics everywhere; but in Hollywood, where the very mention of a money-loser like *The Ambersons* is in bad taste, the Academy Awards of 1942 went to Greer Garson and Teresa Wright for the atrocious but profitable *Mrs. Miniver.*) With the amazing old Richard Bennett as the family patriarch, Joseph Cotten, Anne Baxter, Ray Collins. Welles adapted, from Booth Tarkington. Edited by Robert Wise. (Even in the mid-sixties Welles still talked of wanting to make the concluding three reels that he had intended.)

◉　◉　◉

The Maltese Falcon. Humphrey Bogart's most exciting role was Sam Spade — that ambiguous mixture of avarice and honor, sexuality and fear, who gave new dimension to the detective genre. This first film by writer-director John Huston made him famous, and a good many of us think it's still his best. It is an almost perfect visual equivalent of the Dashiell Hammett thriller: Huston used Hammett's plot design and economic dialogue in a hard, precise directorial style that brings out the full viciousness of characters so ruthless and greedy that they become comic. It is — and this is rare in American films — a work of entertainment that is yet so skillfully constructed that after many years and many viewings, it has the same brittle explosiveness — and even some of the same surprise — that it had in 1941. Bogart is backed by an impeccably "right" cast: Sydney Greenstreet as Casper Gutman, Mary Astor as Brigid O'Shaughnessy, Peter Lorre as Joel Cairo, Gladys George as Iva, Elisha Cook, Jr. as Wilmer the gunsel, Jerome Cowan as Miles Archer, Lee Patrick as Effie, and Ward Bond and Barton MacLane as the cops.

Warner Brothers weren't taking too big a chance on Huston: they had already gotten their money's worth out of *The Maltese Falcon,* which they had filmed in 1931 and again in 1936 (as *Satan Met a Lady* with Bette Davis in the Brigid role). Huston was a good enough screenwriter to see that Hammett had already written the scenario, and he had the wit not to soften Sam Spade's character. Bogart played him as written by Hammett, and Hammett was not sentimental about detectives: they were cops who were going it alone, i.e., who had smartened up and become more openly mercenary and crooked. In *The Maltese Falcon* Spade is a loner who uses nice, simple people, a man who is constantly testing himself, who doesn't want to be touched, who enjoys hitting Joel Cairo and humiliating Wilmer, a man who's obsessively anti-homosexual.

A minor flaw: the appalling Warners music, rising and swelling to call our attention to the big "I won't because all of me wants to" speech at the end, almost kills the scene. And a regret: that Huston didn't (or couldn't) retain Hammett's final scene — when Effie realizes what a bastard Spade is. But perhaps the absence of that final scene is part of what made the movie a hit: Huston, by shooting the material from Spade's point of view, makes it possible for the audience to enjoy Spade's petty, sadistic victories and his sense of triumph as he proves he's tougher than anybody. Spade was left a romantic figure, though he's only a few steps away from the psychopathic "Nobody ever put anything over on Fred C. Dobbs" of *The Treasure of Sierra Madre,* which was a box-office failure — perhaps because the audience was forced to see what was inside their hero.

◉   ◉   ◉

A Man Escaped (*Un Condamné à Mort s'est Echappé*). The experience of imprisonment and escape is inevitably closer to Europeans than to Americans, and this film, which has been a great prizewinning critical and popular success in Europe, has been a total failure in the United States. It is not ingratiating: the director, Robert Bresson, is famous for his uncompromising methods, and having been a prisoner of the Nazis himself, he is not disposed to treat his material (André Devigny's account of his escape from the Montluc fortress prison) lightly. In this country, escape is a theme for action movies; the Bresson hero's ascetic, singleminded dedication to escape is almost mystic, and the fortress is as impersonal and isolated a world as Kafka's. The movie was shot at Montluc with fanatic authenticity; the photography by Burel is austerely beautiful. François Leterrier, a Sorbonne philosophy student, is the lead. The music is Mozart's Mass in C minor. I know all this makes it sound terribly pretentious and yet, such is the treacherous power of an artist, that sometimes even the worst ideas are made to work. It's a marvelous movie. Award for Best Direction, Cannes, 1957.

◉　◉　◉

The Man in the White Suit. As a comedian, Alec Guinness has always been best in the role of an ordinary man with an obsession; who, in the modern world, could be so ordinary and so obsessed as a scientist? In an economy based on rapid replacement of consumer goods, Guinness is the quirky idealist fixated on the long-range benefits to humanity of a cloth that will stay clean and last forever. The impersonal, bland monomaniac scientist is beautifully matched with Joan Greenwood — all guile and scorn and perversity, and without any real aim or purpose. Alexander Mackendrick directed this deft social triangle (capital-science-labor) with a good eye for the tragi-comic scientific mentality; the inventor is defeated, not by economic storms, but by a technical flaw. With Cecil Parker, and Ernest Thesiger as the half-dead industrialist. Screenplay by Roger MacDougall, John Dighton, and Mackendrick. (Item for collectors of ghastly movie memorabilia: the gurgling, bubbling squirts and drips of the hero's experimental apparatus were joined to a rhythm and issued by Coral Records as *The White Suit Samba.*) 1951.

◉　◉　◉

Man of Aran. Robert Flaherty gave two years of his life to making *Man of Aran* and left the Aran Islands with a truly exalted work. *Man of Aran,* completed in 1934, is undoubtedly the greatest film tribute to man's struggle against hostile nature. The Atlantic, which sweeps in all the way from America, lashes the cliffs of Aran with an almost malignant ferocity — it is considered the most horrible sea in the world. Only thirty miles from Galway, civilized people live on islands of rock so bare that they must gather seaweed to plant their potatoes in. This rock constitutes their independence but it also enforces an isolation so complete that primitive elements have crept into their thinking. (Boys, for example, wear girls' dresses until they are twelve — this is supposed to fool the sea, which doesn't go out of its way to swallow up girls.) Perhaps because of the mixture of extreme courage and extreme simplicity in the lives of these people, *Man of Aran* achieves a true epic quality, a celebration of heroic traditions — even though we realize that Flaherty has given us not so much a study of Aran in the thirties as Aran (and man) through the ages.

⊙ ⊙ ⊙

Man with a Million (The English title, *The Million Pound Note,* is the title of Mark Twain's story on which the movie is based). There is something wonderfully satisfying about watching a shabby young man dine in a restaurant and then casually hand over a million pound banknote, while murmuring, "I'm awfully sorry, but I don't have anything smaller." Mark Twain's little satire on attitudes toward money and on English mores posits a perfect practical joke: a young American (Gregory Peck), stranded in London, is given an authentic million pound note; but he cannot cash it, he can only flash it. The question is, can a penniless man live for a month by this display? One of the best English comedies of the fifties, *Man with a Million* was a total flop in this country; I suspect that American audiences assumed from the author's name that the film must be a dull classic. The cast includes Jane Griffith, and such distinguished and charming gentlemen as Ronald Squire and A. E. Matthews. Ronald Neame directed from Jill Craigie's screenplay. 1954, color.

⊙ ⊙ ⊙

Marked Woman. As the smart, lively young "clip-joint hostess" who turns informer, Bette Davis in *Marked Woman* is the embodiment of the sensational side of thirties movies. (The closest modern equivalent is Jeanne Moreau in *Bay of the Angels,* but Moreau is different, more purely conceptual; she's never as vibrantly, coarsely *there* as Davis swinging in her beaded fringe dress.) This 1937 racketeering melodrama is based on the career of Lucky Luciano, who lived high at the Waldorf-Astoria on the proceeds of a thousand prostitutes. In the film, Eduardo Ciannelli plays the role, with Humphrey Bogart (never at his best when cast on the side of officialdom — but then, who is?) taking over Thomas E. Dewey's function as prosecutor. One of the prostitutes Dewey persuaded to testify was branded, "marked" as Davis is in the film. Though a new generation may see *Marked Woman* as just a tawdry melodrama — a sleazy exploitation of headline stories — for the moviegoers of the thirties, used to the genre, it appeared to be a small but authentic tragedy of excessive pride, with more impact than most dramas played out in more elevated surroundings. The presence of Allen Jenkins in the cast certified the film as Warners contemporary. Talented, young Jane Bryan is interesting as the heroine's sister, and there are the "hostesses" of the Club Intime — Mayo Methot, Lola Lane, Isabel Jewell, Rosalind Marquis — who negate the euphemism. And when Davis tells Luciano-Ciannelli, "I'll get you if I have to come back from the grave to do it," you believe it. Lloyd Bacon directed; Robert Rossen and Abem Finkel wrote the screenplay.

⊙ ⊙ ⊙

The Medium. Gian-Carlo Menotti, who had already startled musical circles by directing the opera he had written (in English) and composed, went to Rome in 1951 and directed the film version himself. The story is a Grand Guignol thriller about a swindling charlatan of a medium, who, in the middle of a fake seance, feels a ghostly hand on her throat. The roles are expertly handled by the American contralto, Marie Powers, as the shrewd, blowsy brute of a woman, the fourteen-year-old Italian coloratura, Anna Maria Alberghetti, and Leo Coleman as the mute gypsy. This is the only time an opera has been put on film by the composer himself — and the movie doesn't have that deadly air of compromise that poisons attempts to "popularize" opera. *The Medium* was, of course, popular from the start, and never labored under the mixed blessings of greatness.

⊙ ⊙ ⊙

The Member of the Wedding. Carson McCullers's writing is one of the high points of literacy in American films: sharp and full of wit, yet with a lyricism rarely found on the screen. The theme is human isolation and the need to identify with something; the form is a fugue for three voices. No work has ever come so close to being the definitive text of the human comedy, junior division. Miss McCullers had written of her qualms about putting this lyric tragicomedy on the stage: "The funniness and the grief are often coexistent in a single line and I did not know how an audience would respond to this." Stage audiences responded with delight, and the play ran for sixty-two weeks. The film version opened to a different type of audience: in vast movie palaces people were puzzled and suspicious (it is said that in some towns customers couldn't understand the material and thought Frankie was supposed to be a boy) and rejected the work. Columbia cut a crucial twenty-minute section and tossed the movie into the lower half of double bills.

There is no story in the usual sense. Frankie is a motherless, fiercely lonely twelve-year-old tomboy, caught between childhood and adolescence and fighting them both. Berenice, the Negro cook who looks after her, is a woman just past her prime: the one man she really loved has died, but she is still going strong. Owlish little John Henry is Frankie's six-year-old cousin and playmate — her whipping boy and her only friend. The setting is summer in an old house in a small Southern town. During this crucial summer, these three, who cling together for solace and human companionship, are torn apart.

Filmed plays are often subjected to a peculiar kind of criticism: they are attacked for being what they are. Although Fred Zinnemann's direction imparts a fine nervous intensity to the film, the drama is in the dialogue. Unfortunately, audiences have become so accustomed to the flat, contrived language of the movies that the rare work with beautiful dialogue — *The Member of the Wedding* or *A Streetcar Named Desire* — is regarded as having something the matter with it; good writing is considered "artificial." The finest qualities of this film are in its sense of language and in the extraordinary performances. The worst (and the most artificial) passage in the film is the journey through town — a conventionally "cinematic" sequence — which disrupts the flow of language and makes us aware of a mechanically constructed outside world. Another but lesser defect is the melodramatic sequence showing Berenice's relatives trying to escape the law. Sequences like these, obviously designed to provide action or some point considered necessary for the total structure, fail because the intentions are simply too transparent, and the execution too clumsy. It is enough that Berenice will have no place in Frankie's future life; it is insulting to give us melodrama when we already have drama.

The credits list Ethel Waters above Julie Harris and Brandon De Wilde; but though Miss Waters is not much less than magnificent and is certainly a feast for the camera, scrawny, cracked-voice Julie Harris, as the member of the wedding, demonstrates why she was at that time generally regarded as the best young American actress. (She was twenty-four when she created the role on the stage, twenty-six in the film version; it was her first film performance, and it was Ethel Waters's best — but a long road from her first, back in 1929 when she sang "Am I Blue" in *On With the Show*.) 1952.

⊙ ⊙ ⊙

Metropolis. This is one of the greatest insanities ever perpetrated in the world of film — not so great as *Intolerance,* but in some ways even more insane. H. G. Wells called it "quite the silliest film"; Hitler was so impressed by the conception that many years later he tried (unsuccessfully) to persuade Lang to make Nazi movies. Lang moves masses of people in decorative, geometric patterns — like a Marxian Busby Berkeley. His prophetic city of the twenty-first century (suggested by his first view of New York) has two levels: one for the rich and pleasure-loving, another — labyrinthine, underground — for the slaveworkers who tend the machines. A sketch of the plot may provide some notion of the strange ideology: the industrialist-tyrant who runs Metropolis plots to incite riots so that he can crush the workers' rebelliousness. His son has gone down to the workers and fallen in love with saintly Maria (Brigitte Helm), who gives spiritual comfort to the oppressed. The tyrant plots with his inventor, Rotwang (a mad, medieval type like Dr. Caligari and, with his mechanical arm, father to Dr. Strangelove), who, in a fabulous science-fiction laboratory sequence, creates a steel double — the false Maria, who leads the masses to revolt. But the destruction gets out of hand, and all of Metropolis would be destroyed by floods, were it not for the final alliance of the industrialist, his son, the true Maria, and the workers. One of the last examples of the imaginative — but often monstrous — grandeur of the Golden Period of the German film, *Metropolis* is a brilliant piece of expressionist design (grouped human beings are used architecturally), with moments of almost incredible beauty and power (the visionary sequence about the Tower of Babel), absurd ineptitudes (the lovesick hero in his preposterous knickerbockers), and oddities that defy analysis (the robot vamp's bizarre, lewd wink). 1926, silent.

⊙ ⊙ ⊙

Miracle in Milan. Part social satire, part fantasy, this Vittorio De Sica film suggests a childlike view of Dostoyevsky's *The Idiot.* A fun-loving old lady finds a newborn baby in a cabbage patch. The baby becomes Toto the Good, the happy man who loves everyone; when he is frustrated in his desire to help people, the old lady, now an angel, comes down and gives him the power to work miracles. Toto the hero, naïve and full of love, organizes a hobo shantytown into an ideal community; but the social contradictions are ludicrously hopeless — not even magic powers can resolve them. The failure of experience, as in *The Bicycle Thief* and *Umberto D.,* is tragic, but the failure of innocence is touchingly absurd — stylized poetry. Francesco Golissano is perfect as Toto; the heroine, Brunella Bovo, is what Chaplin's heroines should have been but weren't. The film provides a beautiful role for that great, almost legendary lady of the Italian theatre, Emma Gramatica (many, many years ago, she took over Duse's roles and acted under the direction of D'Annunzio); as the supremely silly old woman of De Sica's fairy tale, she is as yielding and permissive as his Umberto D. is proud and stubborn. With Paolo Stoppa as the unhappy man. Cesare Zavattini adapted his own novel, *Toto Il Buono.* Grand Prix, Cannes, 1951.

⊙ ⊙ ⊙

The Mischief-Makers (Les Mistons). Five little French boys seek to become members of a courtship: they follow the lovers (Gérard Blain and Bernadette Lafont), spy on them, jeer at them. François Truffaut's first feature film, *The 400 Blows,* is a child's cry of protest against a world black with adult injustice; the earlier short (twenty-seven minutes) *Les Mistons,* made in 1957, is a poetic reverie: the children look at the adult world greedily but contemptuously, the adult world pays no heed. As an experimental work in the medium, it shows a marvelous command of sensual image and atmosphere (the opening bicycle ride, for example), but to Americans the total conception may seem just too fearfully sensitive, precocious, and precious. French artists are so narcissistic about their lost innocence. The English commentary, in particular, with its high-flown romantic nostalgia toward the first confused stirrings of sexual desire, may make you exclaim, "Oh, the French are at it again!" There is a good deal of "the fate and the privilege of the flesh" sort of thing, with references to mythology, rites, divinity, etc. *Les Mistons,* based on the short story "Virginales" by Maurice Pons, took a grand prize at Brussels.

◉ ◉ ◉

Mon Oncle. One often appreciates what Jacques Tati is trying to do more than what he actually brings off. His target is the depersonalization of modern life — not so much the mechanization that René Clair satirized in À *Nous La Liberté* and Chaplin in *Modern Times,* but the sterile, tasteless tedium that modern hygienic design has produced. There are genuinely inventive moments: the little boys gambling on whether passers-by will fall into their lamp-post trap; the old man directing a chauffeur trying to park an inordinately long car; the willful garage doors; the wonderful use of the modern functional house as a cartooned face, so that heads at the circular windows become eyes looking out. But the moments are intermittent, and a fundamental miscasting confuses the issues: my guess is that the unemotional, gawky, butterfingered Tati should play the plastics manufacturer, not the warm, friendly uncle. Academy Award, Best Foreign Film of 1958. Color.

◉ ◉ ◉

Monsieur Ripois (Knave of Hearts). René Clément's original and amusing study of a compulsive seducer, a Frenchman (Gérard Philipe) at work in London on a succession of English girls, was made in two versions — French and English. *Monsieur Ripois* took First Prize for Direction at Cannes in 1954 and was highly regarded; *Knave of Hearts* so incensed the English that "nasty" and "disgusting" appeared in almost all reviews. (*The Daily Mirror* cried, "a story about a French wolf who comes to prey on our girls.") The reason for this hostility is the satiric treatment of English morals: the shallow French roué has a knack for spotting women's weaknesses, and he seduces the English girls (who take themselves fairly seriously) by appealing to each one's aspirations and fantasies. The English may also have resented the photographic invasion of their urban ugliness by Oswald Morris's concealed cameras — which catch the pubs, restaurants, busses, and rush hours of a gray and grubby city which was not visible in English movies until later films like *Room at the Top, Look Back in Anger,* and *Saturday Night and Sunday Morning* broke down English reserve. Roman Vlad contributes a witty score with a little theme for each mistress (Joan Greenwood, Margaret Johnston, Valerie Hobson, Natasha Perry, et al.). The script (by Raymond Queneau and others) provides some subtle mockery of the Don Juan type: expert at playing roles to please women, the Frenchman cannot win love in his own character. (In the United States the film was cut and released under two titles — *Lovers, Happy Lovers* and *Lover Boy* — and was whisked in and out of a few art houses.)

◉ ◉ ◉

Monsieur Vincent. Pierre Fresnay's performance as the desperately compassionate Vincent de Paul gives extraordinary feeling and depth to Jean Anouilh's sensitive, lucid scenario. Though de Paul's very considerable intellectual gifts are minimized, this diminution is preferable to the usual dreadful solution of having an actor mutter platitudes while the other actors gasp, how brilliant! Although the character is simplified, it is quite possibly the best biographical film ever made: the emotions — the revulsion and horror at poverty, misery, cruelty — come through without mawkishness. Directed by Maurice Cloche, photographed by Claude Renoir. The cast includes Aimé Clariond, Jean Debucourt, Gabrielle Dorziat. Grand Prix and Best Actor Award (Fresnay) at Venice; Grand Prix du Cinema Français; Academy Award, Best Foreign Film of 1948.

◉ ◉ ◉

Mother. Selected at Brussels in 1958 as one of the twelve greatest films of all time, Pudovkin's 1926 masterpiece, based on the Maxim Gorky novel, is a rare work of the revolutionary period — not harsh and intellectual like Eisenstein's films, but poetic and emotional, and yet impressive in its brilliant and varied use of the medium. Pudovkin, himself an actor and the author of *Film Acting,* used actors to extraordinary effect. Vera Baranovskaia plays the mother who is tricked by the police into betraying her son (Nikolai Batalov). Pudovkin is the officer who interrogates her. *Mother* gives an epic sense of the 1905 revolution through the emotions of the participants, and though it is much less overtly political than Eisenstein's work, it sweeps one along by its fervor. It's more *believable.*

◉ ◉ ◉

Mr. Hulot's Holiday (*Les Vacances de Monsieur Hulot*). People are at their most desperate when they are working at enjoying themselves: it is Jacques Tati's peculiar comic triumph to have caught the ghastliness of a summer vacation at the beach. Fortunately his technique is light and dry slapstick: the chronicle of human foibles and frustrations never sinks to the moist or lovable. As director, co-author, and star, Tati is sparse, eccentric, quick. It is not until afterward — with the sweet, nostalgic music lingering

— that these misadventures may take on a certain depth and poignancy. Grand Prix, Cannes, 1953.

⊙ ⊙ ⊙

Murder, My Sweet. The late Raymond Chandler once attacked the intricate jigsaw puzzle style of English whodunits and asserted that Dashiell Hammett "gave murder back to the kind of people who commit it for reasons, not just to provide a corpse; and with the means at hand, not with handwrought dueling pistols, curare and tropical fish." For Chandler, as for Hammett, the background for the outbreak of violence is social corruption. Philip Marlowe, the private eye, the man who seeks the truth, knows the big city but is not part of it; he is, despite appearances, incorruptible. Chandler regarded *Murder, My Sweet,* based on his *Farewell, My Lovely,* as the most successful film adaptation of his novels, and thought that Dick Powell came closest to his conception of Marlowe. The author could be wrong on both counts: the crumminess of the movie can't all be explained by fidelity to the material. Edward Dmytryk directed in the brutal, fast style popular in the war years; the screenplay is by John Paxton. With Claire Trevor, Esther Howard, Otto Kruger, Mike Mazurki, Miles Mander, Ralf Harolde, Anne Shirley. 1944.

⊙ ⊙ ⊙

My Little Chickadee. W. C. Fields and Mae West acted together only once, in 1940, in *My Little Chickadee* — near the end of both of their screen careers.

Fields had made his first movie in 1915 and had worked with D. W. Griffith. But it was in the talkies of the thirties that he became the familiar figure with the assertive drawl, the muttered asides, the grandiose pretensions, and the florid, obsequious flattery that was his own brand of insult. Whether playing con men or harried, hen pecked, lower-middle-class husbands who schemed to escape to the barbershop-poolhall-racetrack-saloon world for a few hours, Fields was shifty, weaseling, mean-spirited, put-upon. His characters never asked for sympathy; they always expected the worst — that they would be found out. His film effusions form one big snarl of contempt for abstinence, truth, honest endeavor, respectability, and human and animal offspring. The great tosspot is essentially a man's comedian, a bulbous fixture of the man's world. Women are not easily won over to his cringing cowardice, his massive pretentiousness, his paranoia, his gloating over his secret knowledge of avarice or sin (Fields, peeking through a keyhole, mutters, "What won't they think of next?"), his vaunted prowess (Fields to Peggy Hopkins Joyce: "I shall dally in the valley and believe me I can dally"), his ambivalence (Fields to Franklin Pangborn: "Young man, if you're not very careful, you're going to lose my trade").

Groucho, with all his affront, has a pixyish charm, but Fields is a dirty, repulsive man — a man without romantic illusions. His world is divided between blue noses and red noses. No maiden escapes his lewd suggestions; no shrew escapes his foul derision; no homosexual escapes his knowing eye. In his top hat and long johns, he is American dada. For women, he is an acquired taste — like sour-mash bourbon. But then, you can't go on sipping daiquiris forever.

Mae West was a wiggling, bosom-heaving combination of permissive mama and shady lady hinting at exotic new tricks. She enraged the respectable women of America by turning sin into a joke ("I used to be Snow White but I drifted"). The primrose path might be thorny but at least it went somewhere; the gin mill might be perdition but it wasn't dull, like your small town. In movies like *She Done Him Wrong, I'm No Angel,* and *Belle of the Nineties,* Mae West celebrated the victory of experience over innocence, of talent over youth. Shifting her white flesh in her corsets, she sang good, dirty blues. And if songs like, "Where Has My Easy Rider Gone?" led to the industry's self-policing Production Code, they were worth it. We enjoyed the crime so much that we could endure even the punishment of family entertainment.

My Little Chickadee is a classic among bad movies: despite the presence of Mae West and W. C. Fields, the satire of Westerns never really gets off the ground. But the ground is such an honest mixture of dirt, manure, and corn that at times it is fairly aromatic. Mae West is rather slowed down by the censors breathing down her decolletage; but even less bawdy, and rather more grotesque than at her best, she is still overwhelming. Fields is in better form: whether cheating at cards, or kissing Miss West's hand ("What symmetrical digits!"), or spending his wedding night with a goat, he remains the scowling, snarling misanthrope. With Joseph Calleia, Margaret Hamilton, Dick Foran. Directed by Edward Cline. Fields and West, who wrote most of their own vehicles, collaborated on the script.

Fields went on a little longer. His last two comedies, *The Bank Dick* (1940) and *Never Give a Sucker an Even Break* (1941), which are just about one-man shows, are often described as "the height of his achievement." Both deal with making a movie. In *The Bank Dick* there are moviemakers and bank robbers and a great chase on a dirt road up a mountain. With Una Merkel, and, of course, Franklin Pangborn and Grady Sutton. In *Never Give a Sucker an Even Break,* the movie Fields wants to make is a large part of the film, and it's set in a kind of cuckoo-cloud Ruritania that's the damnedest thing ever seen. Up there Fields encounters the woman for him: Margaret Dumont. He gets back to some kind of earth for the chase-finale. The film has its horror: an erstwhile ingenue named Gloria Jean; you can't just shut your eyes, because she *sings.* With Leon Errol. Edward Cline directed both.

⊙ ⊙ ⊙

Le Mystère Picasso. Picasso and Clouzot (*The Wages of Fear, Diabolique*) collaborate. The result, *Le Mystère Picasso,* a bone of critical contention abroad, has hardly been nipped on here; a great success when shown at the Museum of Modern Art at ten dollars a ticket, it has been a disastrous failure theatrically. Yet it is one of the most exciting and joyful movies ever made. Picasso seems to take art back to an earlier function, before the centuries of museums and masterpieces; he is the artist as clown, as conjurer, as master funmaker. For most of the film the screen is his paper or canvas, and in seventy-five minutes he draws or paints fifteen pictures. When he complains to Clouzot that the canvas is too small, the screen expands to CinemaScope size. Some sequences use time-lapse photography to compress the working time on a canvas to a few minutes: the changes and developments (when, for example, a goat's head becomes a skull and then a head again) suggest what animation might be but isn't. Photographed in color by Claude Renoir; score by Georges Auric. Special Prize, Cannes, 1956. (Don't be put off by the fatuous narrator who tells us that we will see what is in the mind of a genius at work, and exclaims, "We would give much to know what was in Joyce's mind while he was writing *Ulysses!*")

⊙ ⊙ ⊙

The Naked Night (*Gycklarnas Afton,* which might be translated as Night of the Jesters or Sunset of a Clown; in England the film is known as *Sawdust and Tinsel,* in France as *La Nuit des Forains*). This 1953 Ingmar Bergman film is set in the circus world at the turn of the century. It opens with a flashback, shot on different film stock: a clown's wife — a dumpy, middle-aged woman — bathes exhibitionistically in view of a whole regiment of soldiers; the clown comes and takes her away. From there the story moves to the circus owner, Ake Groenberg, and his mistress, Harriet Andersson; this swinish Circe betrays him, and is in turn betrayed, and they go on together. The atmosphere suggests Jannings's *Variety* but has upsetting qualities all its own. There is an erotic scene between Miss Andersson and Hasse Ekman, as the seducer-actor, that leaves audiences slightly out of breath. *The Naked Night* is one of the blackest of Bergman's films: no one is saved from the total damnation; life is a circus and the people are gross clowns; it is a round of frustration, humiliation, and defeat. Yet it has been extraordinarily popular with college audiences. Heavy, mawkish expressionism circa 1920 may strike them as the latest thing; and if it does, it becomes the latest thing. *The Naked Night* is powerful all right, but I think it's powerfully awful.

⊙ ⊙ ⊙

Nanook of the North. Robert Flaherty, who began as an explorer and anthropologist, once remarked that in the usual travelogue, the film-maker looks down on and never up to his subject. By looking up, Flaherty created a new genre of movies: he began to record the life of a people with a camera, and then, in editing, to distill the meaning of their existence. Instead of going to a culture with a story, he developed his stories out of the life he observed; his films have no human villains, nor even human enemies, yet they have great drama. His study of the Eskimo, Nanook, who lives where nothing grows and who depends on what he can kill, was made in 1920 and 1921. Two years later, while people all over the world were applauding this extraordinary record of a human being in his cold and hostile environment, Flaherty's hero died of starvation.

⊙ ⊙ ⊙

National Velvet. The high point in Elizabeth Taylor's acting career came when she was twelve: under Clarence Brown's direction, she gave her best performance to date as Velvet Brown, the heroine of Enid Bagnold's account of a little girl's sublime folly. Quite possibly the role coincided with the child's own animal-centered universe: she had her own folly, wanting to play the part so badly that she worked out to gain the necessary height (three inches in four months), a process not unlike Velvet's training of The Pie, the horse she wins in a lottery, to ready him for the Grand National Steeplechase. In lots of ways *National Velvet* isn't a very good movie, but it has a rare and memorable quality: it touches areas in our experience that movies rarely touch — the passions and obsessions of childhood. It's one of the most *likable* movies of all time. The cast includes Anne Revere (whose performance as the mother won the Academy Award as Best Supporting Actress of 1945), Mickey Rooney, Jackie "Butch" Jenkins, Donald Crisp, Angela Lansbury, Arthur Treacher. Color.

⊙ ⊙ ⊙

Night and the City. Several years before he made *Rififi,* Jules Dassin directed this less flamboyant thriller, which is much less well known, but, in some ways, better. Dassin's shocking specialty — a kind of stifled violence that one fears will explode — finds the right milieu in the Gerald Kersh novel, a complex view of the underside of London entertainment. An Anglo-American cast is headed by Richard Widmark, who has his best role as Harry Fabian, "the artist without an art," a tout with a creative passion for fantastic, shady schemes. The victims of his double-crossing artistry include Googie Withers, Francis L. Sullivan, Gene Tierney, Herbert Lom, and, as the old-time wrestler pitted against Mike Mazurki — Stanislaus Zbyszko. With Hugh Marlowe. Script by Jo Eisinger. 1950.

⊙ ⊙ ⊙

A Night at the Opera. It is said that the Marx Brothers consider the 1935 *A Night at the Opera* their best film; it isn't, but it was their greatest hit. Two beautifully stuffed American targets — grand opera and high society — are left dismantled, flapping like scarecrows. (If you could ever listen to *Il Trovatore* with a straight face, you can never do so again.) Many writers have tried to analyze Marx Brothers wit, and they come up with little monographs on "dissociated thinking," "disguised social protest," or "commedia dell'arte." Think about it too much and sanity, like a lettuce leaf, begins to wilt and curl at the edges. The Marx Brothers keep turning corners you didn't know were there, and while you're trying to break down the content of lines like Groucho's "You big bully, why are you hitting that little bully?" you miss the series of nonsequiturs that are piling up on top of it. George S. Kaufman and Morrie Ryskind did the script; Sam Wood directed. The cast includes Groucho's perennial grand-dame inamorata, Margaret Dumont, the most stately of stooges (her smirking dowager is rather like a comic derivative of Edna Purviance in Chaplin's movies). There are also the vocalizing lovers, Kitty Carlisle and Allan Jones, that Irving Thalberg, the producer and a master diagnostician of popular taste, put in for people (*what* people?) to "identify with," and the cruel villain, Walter Woolf King. (Incredible as it may seem, the banal romantic melodrama which intermittently wrecks the movie proved sound at the box office.) This comedy has its classic sequence: the stateroom scene, which is widely regarded as the funniest five minutes in screen history. It will sustain you through the dreadful duets.

⊙ ⊙ ⊙

The Night of the Hunter. The week this picture opened in 1955, I saw it in a theater with about two thousand seats, of which perhaps a dozen were occupied. It was not only a financial disaster, it was a critical failure as well; yet this Protestant fable is, despite its peculiar overtones of humor, one of the most frightening movies ever made (and truly frightening movies become classics of a kind). The sex-obsessed, hymn-singing madman (Robert Mitchum) has hypnotic powers not unlike Caligari's (his terrified wife, Shelley Winters, becomes a fervent disciple). But he is something of a Pied Piper in reverse: adults trust him, children try to escape. Their flight from the soul-saver is one of the most strangely dreamlike episodes ever filmed, a deliberately "artistic" nightmare of suspense, broken by the appearance of a Christian variety of fairy godmother (Lillian Gish). The adaptation of Davis Grubb's novel was the last film work of the late James Agee; Charles Laughton never had a chance to direct another movie. With Evelyn Varden and James Gleason.

⊙ ⊙ ⊙

Nights of Cabiria (*Notti di Cabiria*). I think this is Federico Fellini's finest film, and a work in which Giulietta Masina earns the praise she received for *La Strada*. The film is a series of episodes in the life of Cabiria (Masina), a shabby, aging, dreamy little Roman streetwalker — a girl whose hard, knowing air is no protection against her fundamental gullibility which, we finally see, is her humanity and her saving grace. A famous actor (Amedeo Nazzari) picks her up and takes her to his luxurious villa; she goes to a cheap vaudeville show, and when the magician hypnotizes her, the innocent dreams of her adolescence pour out; a young man in the audience (François Périer) meets her and proposes to her, etc. Though the film seems free and almost unplanned, this is art not carelessness, and each seeming irrelevance falls into place. Academy Award, Best Foreign Film of 1957.

⊙ ⊙ ⊙

Ninotchka. "Garbo Laughs," said the original ads in 1939, but there is by now a widespread story that although Garbo could pantomime laughter superbly, no sounds emerged, and these were provided by an anonymous creature in the sound lab. The rest of her performance is her own — and she brings distinction as well as her incredible throaty, sensual abandon to the role of a glum, scientifically-trained Bolshevik envoy who succumbs to Parisian freedom, i.e., champagne. The film includes an historic encounter when the great instinctive artist of the screen meets the great stylist and technician of the stage, Ina Claire: the fur flies exquisitely. Directed by Ernst Lubitsch, this light, satirical comedy has the nonchalance and sophistication which were his trademark — but it also reveals that this time the trade marked him too high. With Melvyn Douglas, Sig Rumann, Felix Bressart, Bela Lugosi, Alexander Granach. Screenplay by Charles Brackett, Billy Wilder, and Walter Reisch.

⊙ ⊙ ⊙

North by Northwest. The title (from Hamlet's "I am but mad north-northwest: when the wind is southerly, I know a hawk from a handsaw") is the clue to the mad geography and improbable plot. The compass seems to be spinning as the action hops all over the country and the wrong people rush about in the wrong directions. It is an amusing Alfred Hitchcock thriller (the crop-dusting sequence ranks with classic early Hitchcock), though he persists in his new worst fault: he makes even a good thing last too long. Cary Grant is the perfect actor for the part (he incarnates the directional confusion of the title — he seems to have gotten younger and better-looking, yet he's probably older than Jessie Royce Landis, who plays his mother). Eva Marie Saint's flat voice and affectless style suggest a midwestern Grace Kelly, and a perverse make-up artist has turned her into an albino African mask. But there is the blue-eyed menace of Martin Landau, and James Mason, Leo G. Carroll, etc. The script, which has a family resemblance to *The Thirty-Nine Steps,* is credited to Ernest Lehman (pieces of it turn up again, transposed only slightly, in his script for Mark Robson's *The Prize*). 1959, color.

◉ ◉ ◉

Nosferatu. Directed by F. W. Murnau, the original, superbly loathsome 1922 German version of Bram Stoker's novel, *Dracula,* is a concentrated essay in horror fantasy, full of weird, macabre camera effects. Though ludicrous at times (every horror film seems to become absurd with the passage of time, and many before — yet the horror remains), this first important film of the vampire genre has more spectral atmosphere, more ingenuity, and more imaginative ghoulish ghastliness than any of its successors. As Murnau concentrates on scenes of suggestive and horrible beauty (the movie often seems more closely related to demonic painting than to the later, rather rigid vampire-movie genre) and doesn't make the narrative line very clear, those who have had little contact with blood-suckers may be helped by a bit of outline. Henrik Galeen's adaptation of the novel changes the setting from Victorian England to Bremen in 1838. A real estate agent in Bremen sends his young, recently married clerk to the Carpathian Woods to settle some property matters at the castle of Nosferatu (Dracula). An emaciated skeleton of a man with a rodent face, Nosferatu spends his days in his coffin, his nights sucking blood. The clerk, weakened by the nightly loss of blood, is saved by telepathy: his wife wakes in Bremen calling her husband's name — and Nosferatu leaves him intact for the moment. The clerk escapes and returns to his wife. But Nosferatu follows: he boards a sailing ship for Bremen and, incarnating and carrying pestilence, he infects the whole crew. The phantom ship reaches Bremen and Nosferatu meets the wife, who, knowing that vampires cannot survive the dawn, surrenders herself to him. As the morning sun breaks into her bedroom, Nosferatu dissolves. With Max Schreck as the vampire. (The influence of this film can be seen in movies as disparate as Bergman's *The Magician* — the opening sequences of the coach — and Godard's *Alphaville* — the use of negative film.)

◉ ◉ ◉

Nothing Sacred. Thirties satires often managed to be romantic comedies. In Ben Hecht's script for *Nothing Sacred* of 1937, the target is what are generally sentimentalized as "the little people." For Hecht they are boobs and lascivious slobs. They drip crocodile tears over a girl they think is dying of radium poisoning, and enjoy every minute of it. While Hecht and the director, William Wellman, jab at just about every sacred cow in the national pasture, the audience may begin to wonder what makes the hero, Fredric March, and the girl, Carole Lombard — who was by that time the national anti-heroine of the era, "the screwball girl," the "Duse of daffy comedy" — any better than anybody else. What makes *their* feelings true? The answer can only be that they, like the author, hate phoniness. Early catchers in the rye, perhaps? This comedy has some classic moments: March's leg being bitten by a small boy; Lombard passing out, while showgirls impersonating the heroines of history parade in her honor; and a great slugging match between March and Lombard. Maxie Rosenbloom, in his acting debut, proved that he didn't need to slug: he could knock words around. Walter Connolly and Charles Winninger give durable performances in the kind of roles so familiar in the thirties: the dyspeptic big-city editor and the alcoholic small-town doctor. Color.

⊙ ⊙ ⊙

Notorious. Alfred Hitchcock's amatory thriller stars Ingrid Bergman as the daughter of a Nazi, a shady lady who trades secrets and all sorts of things with American agent Cary Grant. The suspense is terrific: will suspicious, passive Grant succeed in making Bergman seduce him, or will he take over? The honor of the American male is saved by a hairbreadth, but Bergman is literally ravishing in what is probably her sexiest performance. With Claude Rains, Louis Calhern, Madame Konstantin. Script by Ben Hecht. No awards but lots of box-office. 1946.

⊙ ⊙ ⊙

À Nous La Liberté. Raymond Cordy plays the man who escapes from prison only to build a business that turns into a prison. He and his phonograph industry are modeled on the career of Charles Pathé — the man who could say of his phonograph-cinema empire, "Only the armaments industry made profits like ours." René Clair's 1931 satire on the mechanization of modern life may have acquired the status of a film classic partly because of its use of a soft "little man" lost in the system; I don't think it's as much fun as the earlier *The Italian Straw Hat* or the later *Le Million,* but it's an imaginative social comedy paced to one of the earliest, and best, film scores ever written (by Georges Auric). (*À Nous La Liberté* has obvious, close connections with Chaplin's later *Modern Times,* just as Clair's *Le Million,* also made in 1931, has close ties with the later *A Night at the Opera.*)

⊙ ⊙ ⊙

Occupe-Toi d'Amélie (*Oh, Amelia!,* also *Look After Amelia*). A Parisian cocotte (Danielle Darrieux) agrees to a mock marriage ceremony, is deceived by a genuine ceremony, but manages to outwit the fate worse than death — respectability. Georges Feydeau, "the father of French farce," wrote about forty of these beautifully constructed follies; this is one of his most famous. Claude Autant-Lara's direction is all speed and artifice, a surprising change of pace from his other work (*Devil in the Flesh, The Game of Love*). He emphasizes the stylization by setting the action behind the footlights and moving in and out of the theatre. With Jean Desailly, Carette, and Gregoire Aslan in his best screen role as Le Prince de Palestrie. 1950. (Peter Glenville attempted the same thing with *Hotel Paradiso* in 1967. But a lot of lavish furnishings don't make style. And having the actors rush about to coy, repetitive music destroyed the rhythm and the form of the farce. Confusion is a very low form of comedy unless it's choreographed; it's as if Glenville set out to lampoon Feydeau: he turned a ballet into an elephant stampede.)

◎ ◎ ◎

Odd Man Out. Wounded at noon, the Irish rebel Johnny MacQueen (James Mason) stumbles through the streets of Belfast until midnight — the object of the most complex manhunt ever filmed. The tormented, delirious man, bleeding to death, seeks but does not find refuge on his way to the grave. Those he encounters evade handing him over to the police, but they see him as a man beyond help; his final denunciation of a world without charity is one of the most memorable scenes on film — despite the reservations we may feel about it. Carol Reed, for many years the only English director who attempted contemporary themes, has always been at his best when dealing with outsiders (*The Stars Look Down, The Fallen Idol, The Third Man, An Outcast of the Islands*); in *Odd Man Out,* he handles his theme in its purest expression — and if he doesn't quite succeed in creating a masterpiece (he never does), he gives you an experience you can't shrug off. With Kathleen Ryan, W. G. Fay, Maureen Delany, Denis O'Dea, F. J. McCormick, William Hartnell, Dan O'Herlihy, Fay Compton, Cyril Cusack and, regrettably, Robert Newton in a badly misconceived performance in a badly misconceived role — the mad painter, Lukey. F. L. Green's novel was adapted by Green and R. C. Sherriff. Photographed by Robert Krasker. 1946.

◎ ◎ ◎

Oedipus Rex. Tyrone Guthrie's 1956 film transcribes his famous production of *Oedipus Rex,* as it was performed at the Stratford Shakespearean Festival of Canada in 1954 and 1955. Sophocles' tragedy (fifth century B.C.) is the most famous and most disturbing of all detective dramas: Oedipus, king of Thebes, looks for the source of the misfortunes falling on his people, and discovers that he is the criminal the gods are punishing. Unwittingly, he has killed his father and married his mother. Guthrie uses the W.

B. Yeats translation of the play, and the cast performs in masks. That last innocent little word will either make or break the film for you. Although masks were used in the classic period — because of the great distance separating actors and audience, and presumably also because the actors represented figures larger than life — the camera destroys even ordinary stage distance and brings us smack up against painted, sculpted papier-mâché. Some may argue that the masks now provide another kind of distance, that they separate us from actors whose naked faces would be ludicrous in the throes of superhuman and primordial emotions, but I'd rather risk it — I'd rather watch inept, embarrassed human beings than immobile blanks. I've always loathed puppet and marionette films (I'm not even happy with Orson Welles's false noses), and I was benumbed, looking at the mouth openings for a sign of life underneath (though I'll admit that the hypnotic effect of masks and endlessly moving robed figures begins to suggest a ritual experience). This is a minority opinion: the film has usually been discussed in superlatives. Co-directed by Irving Lerner. With Douglas Campbell. Color.

◉   ◉   ◉

Oliver Twist. In the person of Alec Guinness, Fagin the Viper, the corrupter of youth, has a sly, depraved charm. David Lean directed this phantasmagoric version of the Dickens novel in England in 1948, right after *Great Expectations* (that was Guinness's first film, this is his second), but it ran into some troubles over here: Fagin, the master pickpocket, is Semitic, and pressure groups objected to such a low Semitic character; with seven minutes of the offending close-ups and profiles plucked, a somewhat assimilated Fagin was allowed to enter the country in 1951. Possibly, the group that should have protested was the Mattachine Society: Fagin comes across as a malignant old faggot. The book is, of course, an attack on cruelty, and the movie in its fidelity is sometimes cruel to the audience. Let me admit my cowardice: I would enjoy the picture much more if I didn't know that the terrible moment is coming when Bill Sikes (Robert Newton) will murder his Nancy (Kay Walsh) while that dog scratches at the door. With John Howard Davies as Oliver, Francis L. Sullivan as Bumble, Anthony Newley as The Artful Dodger. Screenplay by Lean and Stanley Haynes. Director of photography, Guy Green; camera operator, Oswald Morris.

◉   ◉   ◉

Los Olvidados (sometimes known as *The Young and the Damned*). Luis Buñuel's almost surgical study of youth, poverty, and corruption is a tragedy set in Mexican squalor. He treats his characters pitilessly, not as ideas, but as morally responsible human beings; there is little of the social workers' cant that makes everyone responsible for juvenile crimes except the juveniles. Buñuel, whose early work fascinated Freud, creates scenes that shock one psychologically, and remain shocking despite one's best efforts to pigeonhole them or explain them away. Among them is the mother-meat dream sequence in *Los Olvidados,* the most brilliantly conceived dream I have ever seen in a film, and a sequence that is disturbing long after the lacerations of the more realistic material have healed. What the film might be like had Buñuel had a completely free hand, one can guess at from his remarks here and there. For example, in the scene in which Jaibo goes to beat up and kill the other boy, the camera reveals in the distance a huge eleven-story building under construction. Buñuel wanted to put an orchestra of a hundred musicians in the building . . . The cast includes Estela Inda, Roberto Cobo; First Prize for Direction at Cannes, 1951, with a First Prize for Photography to Gabriel Figueroa.

◉ ◉ ◉

Olympiad. During the thirties the international press ridiculed Hitler's supposed infatuation for the red-haired dancer-skier-actress turned movie director, Leni Riefenstahl, to whom he had entrusted the production of movies on his political conventions and on the 1936 Olympic Games. Ironically, this beautiful young woman proved herself one of the dozen or so creative geniuses who have ever worked in the film medium. Out of the Nuremberg Rally of 1934, she made the most outrageous political epic of all time, the hypnotic *Triumph of the Will* (the outrage is that she could make a great film of it); out of the Berlin Olympics she made a great lyric spectacle. *Olympiad* is only incidentally a record of the actual games: she selected shots for their beauty rather than for a documentary record. After eighteen months of editing she emerged with over three hours of dazzling quality — a film that moves one kinesthetically in response to physical tension, and psychologically in response to the anguish and strain of men and women desperately competing for a place in history. And despite Hitler's Aryan myth, she knew beauty when she saw it: in the throbbing veins in Jesse Owens's forehead (in her book on *Olympiad,* Leni Riefenstahl has a simple caption for his picture — *"Jesse Owens, der schnellste Mann der Welt"*); in the lean Japanese swimmers; in the divers soaring in flight so continuous that they have no nationality. Now, *Olympiad* is an elegy on the youth of 1936: here they are in their flower, dedicated to the highest ideals of sportsmanship — these young men who were so soon to kill each other.

◉ ◉ ◉

On Approval. Clive Brook, Beatrice Lillie, Roland Culver, and Googie Withers hold to the drawing-room style of Frederick Lonsdale's antique comedy so relentlessly that the old, arch clichés of "daring" dialogue are reactivated. You can't help responding to these old quips when they are delivered with such an exquisite sense of their absurdity. Groomed by Cecil

Beaton, the quartet of players is almost surrealistically elegant. As the shrew, Beatrice Lillie delivers what has been acclaimed as the perfect Lillie line: "You will find the dinghy by the jetty." As the heroine, Googie Withers demonstrates that an actress can be utterly charming even while parodying romantic charm. Everyone who has seen the movie seems to remember the great proposal scene and the great refusal, and Googie Withers asking, "What color are my eyes?" The real star of the piece is the fantastically adroit Clive Brook; his timing is perfection, both in the role of the exhausted, effete Duke, and in the adaptation and direction. 1944.

⊚ ⊚ ⊚

On the Bowery. The derelicts of New York's enormous skid row were persuaded to act out a story that is essentially their own story. This is the technique Flaherty used in *Man of Aran* and *Nanook of the North* — but how different it seemed. The basic truth of this story may be gauged by the fact that the man who plays the derelict hero later refused a Hollywood contract with the words, "I just want to be left alone. . . . There's nothing else in life but the booze." Yet, as it's played, the script seems all wrong, and the work is awkward, hesitant, without the revelations the material cries out for. I wish I could agree with the critics who link this film with Dostoyevsky and Christ, but I don't think it's a very good movie. Produced by Lionel Rogosin. Grand Prix, Venice Documentary Festival, 1956.

⊚ ⊚ ⊚

Open City (*Roma, Città Aperta*). Roberto Rossellini burst upon the world with *Open City,* made in 1944, just after the Allies took Rome. The story is a melodramatic account of the underground resistance to the German occupation, but the film's fame rests on its extraordinary immediacy (and brutality). Many Americans, used to slick war films, reacted as if it were a document, and mistook the magnificent Anna Magnani, Aldo Fabrizi, Maria Michi, and the other actors for nonprofessionals — this despite such theatrical elements as the rapacious lesbian Gestapo agent and the Hollywood-and-Vine type Gestapo chief. Shot on odds and ends of film stock, with fluctuating electricity, showing people who a few weeks before had been part of the events, the movie cut a cross-section of a city under terrible stress. (When the initial twenty-five thousand dollars which Rossellini had raised was used up, he and Magnani sold their clothes; Maria Michi, who had hidden men like Togliatti — and the scriptwriter, Sergio Amidei — in her flat, now provided the flat for some of the sequences.)

⊚ ⊚ ⊚

Operation Mad Ball. From the total Hollywood output in 1957, there are only a handful of films worth seeing; this uninhibited little farce is one of them. The perennial war of enlisted men and officers is joined again, fortunately under the direction of Richard Quine. Jack Lemmon is the buck private hero determined to stage a mad ball for a group of nurses. Ernie Kovacs is the maddeningly unctuous, obnoxious officer determined to thwart him — a barracks Malvolio. Dick York is the liaison man between the two factions, Mickey Rooney the sergeant who pulls together a jazz group for the ball. The four of them are good and occasionally so good they seem inspired. If Arthur O'Connell as the commanding officer, Kathryn Grant, and the French concierge could have been eliminated, this might have been a classic American comedy. Screenplay by Arthur Carter, Jed Harris, and Blake Edwards.

⊙　⊙　⊙

Orchids and Ermine. The best comedienne of the silent flapper period was lively, gifted Colleen Moore — no mere personality girl but a light, unaffected, inventive actress, in style a little like Buster Keaton. *Orchids and Ermine,* made in 1927, is one of her best comedies. The wisecracking titles have a fine patina, and there is nostalgic charm in the sequences shot in and around the Plaza Hotel and on top of a Fifth Avenue bus. Jack Mulhall plays a young millionaire, and Gwen Lee and Sam Hardy are the gold-digger and the valet. There is a sequence at the hotel switchboard when a midget addresses Miss Moore — the "midget" is the first screen appearance of Mickey Rooney. Alfred Santell directed; the script is by Carey Wilson and Mervyn LeRoy.

⊙　⊙　⊙

Ordet (*The Word*). Among the films that have moved me most deeply there are two by Carl Dreyer — *The Passion of Joan of Arc* and *Day of Wrath;* and among the films that have excited me most by their visual and conceptual daring there is Dreyer's *Vampyr.* This is a roundabout approach to *Ordet* — his most widely acclaimed, even revered film — because I'm hesitant to admit that I really don't care for it. I have considered the possibility that the New York critics used all their superlatives as a way of atoning for their scandalous mistreatment of *Day of Wrath,* but the world press seems to agree with them that *Ordet* is a masterpiece.

Kaj Munk, author of the play *Ordet,* was a Danish pastor, famed for such statements as, "It is better that Denmark's relations with Germany should suffer than that her relations with Jesus Christ should suffer." In 1944 the Nazis shot him through the head and tossed him in a ditch. *Ordet,* written on the text, "O ye of little faith," deals with a modern resurrection, and Dreyer treats it literally. I find it difficult to accept the holy madman (driven insane by too close study of Kierkegaard!), and even more difficult to accept Dreyer's use of the home as a stage set for interminable entrances and exits, and impossible to get involved in the factional strife between bright, happy Christianity and dark, gloomy Christianity — represented as they are by people sitting around drinking vast quantities of coffee. Grand Prix, Venice, 1955.

◉   ◉   ◉

Orpheus (Orphée). Jean Cocteau's *Orpheus* is the masterpiece of magical film-making. Though a narrative treatment of the legend of Orpheus in a modern Parisian setting, it is as inventive and enigmatic as a dream. Orpheus wants to get beyond the limits of human experience, he wants to reach the unknowable, and it is death which represents the unknowable — the mystery beyond mortality. Jean Marais is ideally cast as the successful, popular poet who is envied and despised by the younger poets; his conflicts, his desire to renew himself, his feverish listening for signals from the source of mystery, are the substance of the film. Dark, troubled, passionate Maria Casarès is his Death: attended by her roaring motorcyclists — the hooded messengers of death — she is mystery incarnate. Marie Dea is the sickly-sweet Eurydice; François Périer is Heurtebise (part chauffeur, part guardian-angel, he suggests the ferryman Charon); Edouard Dermithe is Cegeste; Juliette Greco is Aglaonice. The music is by Georges Auric. Photography by Nicolas Hayer.

The motorcyclists are part of a new mythology, they suggest images of our time: secret police . . . black heroes . . . the anonymous and impersonal . . . agents of some unknown authority . . . executioners . . . visitors from outer space . . . the irrational. They are the men you can't reach and you can't deal with; they stand for sudden, shockingly accidental death. The trial of Death is like a nightmare of a wartime resistance movement "underground" trial. Cocteau uses emblems and images of the then recent Nazi period and merges them with other, more primitive images of fear — as, indeed, they are merged in the modern consciousness. This gives the violence and mystery of the Orpheus story a kind of contemporaneity that, in other hands, might seem merely chic; but Cocteau's special gift was to raise chic to art.

Who but Cocteau would have had the wit to place Orpheus under attack by modern Bohemians in just the places where poets *are* attacked? And this jazzy modern milieu gives the movie a sense of urgency and excitement. For those interested in the continuity of theatrical and film traditions: Cocteau's death figure and much of the film's imagery derive from the American movie *Death Takes a Holiday* starring Fredric March. (The theme of that 1934 film is also closely related to the way Orpheus' Death takes *her* holiday.) The only new film image of death that, visually and psychologically, stands comparison with the haunting figure of Maria Casarès is in Ingmar Bergman's *The Seventh Seal.* And, of course, Cocteau's glazier in the "zone" (who appeared in the guise of the angel in *Blood of a Poet*) must be a

tribute to (or a memory of?) Chaplin as the angelic glazier of *The Kid*.
1949.

⊙ ⊙ ⊙

Our Man in Havana. Though Alec Guinness's name is Wormold and he
is the Havana representative of a vacuum cleaner company, he is the hero.
This hero, recruited into the British secret service (by dry, hunched Noel
Coward — the mandarin as secret agent), has no idea what is wanted of
him. He must send in reports, however; so he fills them with inventions and
fantasies. This satirical comedy turns into a nightmarish thriller when his
absurd, phony reports precipitate actual reprisals and murders. *Our Man in
Havana* appears to be, like *Beat the Devil,* a travesty of the international
spy story, but Graham Greene likes to have his pinprick of purpose. In this
case, the deep thought that innocence can lead to evil is not likely to keep
one up nights. Carol Reed employs the Cuban locations (photographed by
Oswald Morris) as wittily as the actors — Ralph Richardson, Burl Ives,
Ernie Kovacs, Maureen O'Hara, Gregoire Aslan (he takes Wormold's
washroom spying overtures for an indecent proposition), Jo Morrow, Paul
Rogers, etc. The farce is perhaps too gravely straight-faced, low-keyed, and
tenuous: it needs more insanity and exuberance. One reason it isn't as good
as *Beat the Devil* is that everything is so beautifully held in check — sometimes a worse movie can be a better movie. But this one has some first-rate
sequences and is continuously entertaining. 1960. (It came in just under the
wire, before Castro.)

⊙ ⊙ ⊙

An Outcast of the Islands. One of the most underrated and unattended
of important modern films, *Outcast* (1952) is not only better than any
previous film drawn from Joseph Conrad's work, but also contains some of
the most remarkable sequences ever filmed by the English director, Carol
Reed. The extraordinary cast includes Trevor Howard, Robert Morley,
Wendy Hiller, Ralph Richardson, Kerima, George Coulouris, Wilfred Hyde-
White, Frederick Valk. Trevor Howard is superb as Willems, who makes
himself an outcast first through contemptible irresponsibility and betrayal of
those who trust him, and finally and hopelessly when, against his own will, he
is attracted to the silent, primitive, terrifying Aissa. Willems is wrong in almost everything he does, but he represents a gesture toward life; his enemy,
Almayer (Robert Morley), is so horribly, pathetically stuffy that his family
life (with Wendy Hiller as his wife and Annabel Morley as his child) is a
painfully funny screen experience. There are so many splendid moments in
this film that one regrets that it's uneven (and Richardson's role may be ill-
conceived); but even with its flaws, it's a brilliant work and probably the
only movie that has attempted to treat the civilized man's ambivalence to-

ward the savage. The screenplay is by William Fairchild; photography by John Wilcox.

⊙ ⊙ ⊙

The Ox-Bow Incident. This Western is an attempt at a poetic tragedy of mob violence. It is set in Nevada in 1885; two cowboys (Henry Fonda and Harry Morgan) ride into a small, lonely cattle town and become involved in the hysteria of a lynch mob. Three innocent men (Dana Andrews, Anthony Quinn, and Francis Ford) are hanged, while we see not only their fear and despair, but the varied motives of the members of the posse who take justice into their hands and are left to suffer for their injustice. If you expect too much of this film you may reject it altogether: it's easy to be put off by the studio sets and lighting and the forties approach to a "serious" subject. But William Wellman, a good, under-rated director, has made the characters so vivid that after many years people may still recall Frank Conroy as the sadistic Southern major and the rapid changes of expression of William Eythe as his son. With Harry Davenport as Mr. Davies, Leigh Whipper as Sparks, and Jane Darwell as the raucous old lady who enjoys the excitement. From Walter Van Tilburg Clark's novel; however, Lamar Trotti's script omits some of the more interesting ambiguities in the book. 1943.

⊙ ⊙ ⊙

Panique. Julien Duvivier's 1946 psychological thriller is so well conceived cinematically that whether you like it or not, you may be forced to agree it's a near-perfect movie. Michel Simon plays a stranger in a Paris suburb; Viviane Romance and Paul Bernard are the lovers who frame him for a murder. The movie has some pretensions toward being a parable of human injustice, with a sadistic mob, etc. It's difficult to accept the high purposes or to accept the movie as entertainment on a lower plane, but just as visual story-telling, *Panique* is devastatingly effective. Film students might learn from it. From a Simenon novel.

⊙ ⊙ ⊙

Paradise Lagoon (*The Admirable Crichton*). James M. Barrie's comedy about class distinctions was turned into the epic *Male and Female* by Cecil B. DeMille in 1919 (the shipwrecked Gloria Swanson looked wonderful in wet satin). The best qualities of the 1957 English version derive from Barrie's original — solid construction, a sense of fun, and well-turned phrases at the expense of the English aristocracy (who seem to be more useful to the theatre than to the country). However, the director, Lewis Gilbert, works somewhat heavily and for rather boisterous effects, as if Barrie's gentle, expert style could be updated by noise. Kenneth More is "the perfect butler" — stuffy, tyrannical Crichton, and Cecil Parker is the democratic, liberal Lord Loam. Cast on a desert island where there are no classes, where skill and aptitude count, the servant becomes master, the master servant. This will hold few surprises for audiences; still there's something rather satisfying in the demonstration. *Paradise Lagoon* is an interesting example of the way movies scavenge on themselves and their theatrical ancestors, and an indication of why: there's a solid nugget of entertainment in many of the old repertory items. The cast includes Martita Hunt, Sally Ann Howes, Diane Cilento. Color.

◉ ◉ ◉

Les Parents Terribles (American title, *The Storm Within*). Cocteau, the master of fantasy, demonstrates that when it suits his purposes, he can be a master of realism, using his artistry inconspicuously, with witty thrusts into psychological depths that destroy the realist-surrealist division. He has taken his play about the disorderly, unpredictable parents who cannot accept their son's growing up and re-created it for the screen with such skill and intimacy that a true claustrophobic family atmosphere is achieved. The conventional coincidence-ridden boulevard drama is endowed with magic and lifted to the realm of fable. (The mother screams for the police when she learns her son has a girl — these touches are so appallingly true that the Oedipal meanings are immediately clear.) Yvonne de Bray, Gabrielle Dorziat, Marcel André, Jean Marais, and Josette Day make this one of the greatest examples of group acting ever photographed; Cocteau has said that they ceased to be actors and became a real family. Designed by Christian Bérard, photography by Michel Kelber, music by Georges Auric. 1949.

◉ ◉ ◉

The Passion of Joan of Arc. This is quite simply one of the great films; fear, betrayal, suffering are seen in a new way. The script is based on the trial records; Carl Dreyer has taken this testimony and made it appear to be given for the first time. *The Passion* is a real passion, photographed (by Rudolph Maté) in a style that suggests the Stations of the Cross. As five grueling cross-examinations follow each other, Dreyer turns the camera on the faces of Joan and the judges, and in giant close-ups he reveals his interpretation of their emotions. In this enlargement Joan and her persecutors are shockingly fleshly — isolated with their sweat, warts, spittle, and tears, and (as no one in the film used makeup) with startlingly individual contours, features, and skin. No other film has so subtly linked eroticism with religious persecution. Falconetti's portrayal of Joan is one of the greatest performances ever photographed. Silvain is Cauchon; as Massieu, the young Antonin Artaud is the image of passionate idealism. 1928.

◉ ◉ ◉

Passport to Pimlico. The British satirize the British: in a London shellhole an ancient royal Charter ceding Pimlico to the dukes of Burgundy is unearthed, and the people of Pimlico are "just British enough to fight for our right to be Burgundians." Margaret Rutherford is the historian who gives scholarly sanction to an independent Pimlico; Basil Radford and Naunton Wayne are the protocol-ridden bureaucrats trying to handle the crisis; Stanley Holloway and Hermione Baddeley are shopkeepers. The ingenious author, T.E.B. Clarke, got the idea from a wartime newspaper item: the Canadian government transferred the area of the room in which the exiled Princess Juliana was about to bear a child to the Netherlands; in this way the child could technically be born on Dutch soil and thus be a legal heir to the throne. (Clarke set his land grant in the Middle Ages on the theory that people can accept the peculiarities of their ancestors more readily than those of their own generation.) Henry Cornelius directed. Music by Georges Auric. 1949.

⊙ ⊙ ⊙

Pat and Mike. In 1952 Katharine Hepburn and Spencer Tracy played together so expertly in *Pat and Mike* that some of their previous films seemed almost like warm-ups. The script, by Ruth Gordon and Garson Kanin, isn't up to the best of *Adam's Rib,* but the stars have achieved such teamwork that their sparring is more beautiful than punch lines. Hepburn plays a phenomenal all-around athlete, and in the course of the picture she takes on Gussie Moran, Babe Zaharias, and a series of other professionals, touching off the comic possibilities in various sports with grace and ease. Aldo Ray plays a sulky boxer. George Cukor directed. It's the most perfectly pleasant of the Hepburn-Tracy comedies; some of the better known ones (like *Woman of the Year*) are not really very good, and *Without Love* is pretty bad.

⊙ ⊙ ⊙

The Phantom of the Opera. One of Lon Chaney's successes, this is not so perverse as some of his others, but it is certainly grisly enough, and it has some good scenes — the phantom's kidnapping of the girl, his appearance at the ball, the chase through the studio-built streets of Paris (where quick-eyed observers may detect the set constructed two years earlier for *The Hunchback of Notre Dame*).

Public taste and possibly his own inclinations steered Chaney onto an anomalous theatrical bypath. The man who made over one hundred and fifty silent films (most of them with no horror) began in the theatre at the age of ten, and was skilled as a singer and comedian before he entered the movies, first to play straight parts and then to embark on that grotesque career of playing mutilated, twisted characters — a career which brought him such fabulous popularity that one might be moved to speculate on the peculiar tastes of the mass audiences of the twenties. People nostalgic about old movies often talk about them as if they were sweet and innocent, recalling those pure heroines, the curly-haired models of know-nothingness. They tend to forget that the heroine's purity accentuated the villain's shocking designs on her (who could have "corrupt" designs on Ann-Margret?). In *The Phantom of the Opera,* Mary Philbin is so virtuous that any contact with her suggests rape and carnage. Lon Chaney and his director here, Rupert Julian, were not necessarily innocent in churning up these images from the depths, and the enormous success of this film in 1925 indicates that they knew their audience. With Norman Kerry, Arthur Edmund Carew, Gibson Gowland, Snitz Edwards. Based on Gaston Leroux's novel.

⊚　⊚　⊚

The Pickwick Papers. If I were to pick the most enjoyable of the dozens of films derived from Dickens, this 1953 English production would be among the top three or four. The episodic book almost defies a simple continuity, but the adapter-director, Noel Langley, has been surprisingly successful at cutting through the labyrinth and keeping the enormous collection of characters rattling along. The best is Nigel Patrick's Jingle — swaggering, staccato, outrageously amoral, and finally, because of Patrick's creative characterization, the most sympathetic and most human of the company. As the dueling Winkle, James Donald has moments so ethereally absurd that he seems to have emerged from *A Midsummer Night's Dream.* James Hayter's Pickwick is more of a reasonable facsimile than a person, but the only really bad casting is the lamentably immodest Harry Fowler as Sam Weller. With Donald Wolfit, Hermione Gingold, Joyce Grenfell, etc.

⊚　⊚　⊚

A Place in the Sun. George Stevens's most highly respected work is an almost incredibly painstaking movie derived from Dreiser's *An American Tragedy.* Perhaps because Stevens's methods here are studied, slow, and accumulative (which does suggest a parallel with Dreiser), the work was acclaimed as "realistic" — which it most certainly is not. It is full of meaning-charged details, murky psychological overtones, darkening landscapes, the eerie sounds of a loon, and overlapping dissolves designed to affect you emotionally without your conscious awareness. It is mannered enough for a very fancy Gothic murder mystery, while its sleek capitalists and oppressed workers seem to come out of a Depression cartoon. This version gives the story a modern setting, but the town is an arrangement of symbols of wealth, glamour, and power versus symbols of poor, drab helplessness — an arrangement far more appropriate to the thirties than to the fifties. Stevens and his scriptwriters (Michael Wilson and Harry Brown) pre-interpret everything, turning the rather simple story into something portentous and "deep."

Having expressed rather major reservations, I should point out that this is definitely not the accepted view, and that the movie is almost universally honored as an example of adult cinema, one critic having gone so far as to say: "It will bankrupt the emotions." Whatever one thinks about it, it is a famous and impressive film. The performances by Montgomery Clift, Shelley Winters, and Elizabeth Taylor are good enough (and Clift is almost too good, too sensitive), though they appear to be over-directed pawns. Specifically, one might object to the way the poor girl is not even allowed to be attractive: part of the horror of the thirties version, in which Sylvia Sidney was the victim, was that despite her appeal, her poverty made her, finally, undesirable. If Elizabeth Taylor had played the victim in this production, then the poor could at least be shown to have some natural assets. But Shelley Winters makes the victim so horrifyingly, naggingly pathetic that Clift hardly seems to be contemplating a crime: it's more like euthanasia. A final objection: the conclusion of the film in which the hero (and presumably the audience) is supposed to be convinced that a man should pay with his life for a murder he didn't commit — but wanted to commit — is bizarre. "Who doesn't desire his father's death?" asked Ivan Karamazov. Stevens and company would send us all up for it. Academy Awards of 1951: Best Director, Best Screenplay, Cinematography (William C. Mellor), etc.

⊚　⊚　⊚

Port of Shadows (*Quai des Brumes*). This 1938 film was the first of the three major collaborations of director Marcel Carné and writer Jacques Prévert (followed by the infinitely superior *Daybreak* in 1939 and by *Children of Paradise* in 1944) — the films which helped to create the French cinematic style of poetic fatalism. In *Port of Shadows,* which is a drearily predictable film, the central figure of the French film was, nevertheless, created — the hopelessly rebellious hero, the decent man trapped by society; it was the beginning of the Jean Gabin era. A man (Gabin) is running away from the police; he arrives at a dock-side backstreet looking for a ship in which to escape. He meets a girl, the exquisite, raincoated Michèle Morgan, and tries to free her from her disreputable guardian (Michel Simon) and his crony (Pierre Brasseur). He doesn't escape. *Port of Shadows,* rather like Robert E. Sherwood's *The Petrified Forest,* is gloomy and shallow, but at the time the defeatism of the film was like a breath of fresh air to American filmgoers saturated with empty optimism.

⊚　⊚　⊚

The Postman Always Rings Twice. Hack movie-making of the forties had a hard, glossy patina and, of course, a juicy center. *The Postman Al-*

ways Rings Twice is a fair example of movies as products. The director, Tay Garnett, compromised with the front office and the box office, and still knew enough tricks to keep this shoddy melodrama going. James M. Cain's animals-in-love are played by John Garfield and Lana Turner (her Cora, dressed in impeccable white, as if to conceal her sweaty, murderous impulses, is infantile in a bored, helpless, pre-moral sort of way). I must admit that I've never really understood the logic or the appeal of these postman-fate-retribution systems in which one escapes the crimes one has committed, but is trapped by accidents in which one is innocent; but just as surely as tragic fate is Greek, this cheap little ironic twist is American. With Cecil Kellaway, Hume Cronyn, Leon Ames. 1946.

⊚ ⊚ ⊚

Pot Bouille (literally, the pot boils; sometimes called *Lovers of Paris;* the English title is *The House of Lovers*). Julien Duvivier's 1957 production — a lavish satire on the triumph of business values over bourgeois morals — was only a moderate success in the United States. Perhaps art-house audiences, still recovering from the anguish of *Gervaise,* were reluctant to face more Zola. But, Mendelian that he was, Zola allowed the Rougon-Macquart series one sport: an unscrupulous young fortune hunter from the provinces who climbs to respectability over the beds of satisfied bourgeois ladies. Duvivier's re-creation of Paris in the overstuffed eighties is one of the most extraordinary historical evocations I have ever seen: ugly, ludicrous, conspicuous expenditure dominates the enormous apartment house, the shops, the streets. In the best sequence, a group of merchants gather to discuss a matter of honor and load themselves with food and drink. Duvivier keeps his balance on the tightrope over the dangerous material — human mediocrity, bad taste, the middle-class man as animal — but sometimes you may get the feeling that the tightrope is suspended much too low. Gérard Philipe is the dimply, curly-haired seducer, the man who accepts venality so simply and instinctively that he has no need of hyprocrisy. With Danielle Darrieux, Dany Carrel, Anouk Aimée, Claude Nollier, Henri Vilbert, and Jane Marken.

⊚ ⊚ ⊚

Potemkin (also known as *The Battleship Potemkin*). Voted the greatest film of all time at Brussels in 1958, as it was in 1950, and at just about every other competition, *Potemkin* (Russians and purists pronounce it Po-*tyom*-kin) has achieved such an unholy eminence that critics no longer even dispute its merits. Great as it undoubtedly is, it's not really a likable film; but it has excitement and brilliance that rivet your attention even if you resist its violence and its cartoon message. Sergei Eisenstein opened up a new technique of psychological stimulation by means of rhythmic editing

— "montage." The Odessa Steps sequence, the most celebrated single sequence in film history, is imitated in one way or another in just about every television news program or movie with crowds, and yet the power of the original is undiminished. In this 1925 film, montage is used for revolutionary political purposes; the subject is the 1905 mutiny of the sailors of the battleship *Potemkin,* and the massacre of the people who sympathized with them. But policies in the U.S.S.R. changed: mutiny could no longer be sanctioned, nor could experimental film techniques, and under Stalin, Eisenstein was purged, partially reinstated, and then fell from grace over and over. *Potemkin* looks astonishingly like a newsreel, and the politically naïve have often interpreted it as a "documentary"; the more knowing have a graceful euphemism: Eisenstein, they say, "sacrificed historical facts for dramatic effect."

◉ ◉ ◉

The Prince and the Showgirl. The only non-Shakespearean movie Laurence Olivier has directed, this 1957 Ruritanian romance is slanted to show off the talents of Marilyn Monroe as an innocent abroad. Olivier, perhaps with excess gallantry, makes his prince something of a cold cod; but even in an uningratiating role, Olivier has a high gloss — an irony that shines. Miss Monroe's polymorphous perverse non-acting has its special charm that none of her imitators seems able to capture. With Sybil Thorndike, Richard Wattis, and Daphne Anderson. The drawback to the film is that Terence Rattigan's script, though it improves on his play *The Sleeping Prince,* still lacks invention and wit. Color.

◉ ◉ ◉

The Professionals. This 1966 action-Western — with Burt Lancaster, Lee Marvin, Robert Ryan, Woody Strode, Jack Palance, Claudia Cardinale; adapted and directed by Richard Brooks — has the expertise of a cold old whore with practiced hands and no thoughts of love. There's something to be said for this kind of professionalism: the movie-makers know their business and they work us over. We're not always in the mood for love or for art, and this movie makes no demands, raises no questions, doesn't confuse the emotions. Even the absence of visual beauty or of beauty of language or concept can be something of a relief. The buyer gets exactly what he expects and wants and pays for: manipulation for excitement. We use the movie and the movie uses us.

This shallow movie with its jokes not of the first freshness, and its hard pressing of the Western to squeeze out the last bit of oil is as modern a product as a new car. (It may be no accident that Ryan, the man who loves horses in this Western, is treated as some sort of weakling.) Color.

⊙   ⊙   ⊙

The Promoter. Denry the audacious, the opportunist who rises from washerwoman's son to town mayor through devious and ingenious scheming, is probably Alec Guinness's most winning role — he even gets the girl (Petula Clark, looking very pretty at this stage in her career, though she doesn't sing). His performance is neatly matched against Glynis Johns's portrait of a female opportunist — a babyfaced, husky-voiced dancing teacher who latches on to wealth and a title. Eric Ambler adapted Arnold Bennett's 1911 satire on business methods and class barriers, originally called *The Card;* it makes a blithe, wonderfully satisfying comedy. With Valerie Hobson as the Countess of Chell. Ronald Neame directed. 1952.

⊙   ⊙   ⊙

The Proud and the Beautiful (*Les Orgueilleux* — literally, the proud ones). The China Coast of Sartre's *L'Amour Redempteur* has become Veracruz in Yves Allegret's 1953 film, but the milieu is still the depths: heat, squalor, disease, and desperation, exotic but unbearable. A bored Frenchwoman (Michèle Morgan) searches for a doctor to take care of her dying husband (André Toffel); she finds a drunken derelict (Gérard Philipe) who refuses to treat him. Through founding a plague hospital, the woman and the doctor redeem themselves and, incidentally, find love. Allegret uses this story atmospherically in an effort to approximate the ironies, inconsequences, accidents, and stupidities of life, and the atmosphere *almost* redeems the movie. (Audiences gasp at one shot: the camera watches, intoxicated, as a hypodermic is slowly inserted.)

⊙   ⊙   ⊙

The Puritan. In 1939 Jean-Louis Barrault was not yet an internationally known actor, and those of us who saw this unheralded young man in *The Puritan* experienced a sense of discovery. His bony, thin young face was perfect for Liam O'Flaherty's psychological study of the murderer, Ferriter, a righteous reformer and sexually obsessed religious fanatic. Barrault's acting was so unusually objective that one respected this poor devil even at his most hopelessly self-deceived. The film, condemned by New York's State Board of Censors in toto as "indecent, immoral, sacrilegious, tending to incite to crime and corrupt morals," is in perfectly good taste, but the censors had a reason for their stand: Ferriter is not only conceived as a censor type, he's actually engaged in this work in the film. The production, which also features Pierre Fresnay and Viviane Romance, was made in Paris by the director Jeff Musso for a total cost of twenty-seven thousand dollars.

⊙   ⊙   ⊙

Quality Street. It isn't really so long ago — though it seems like another age — that the heroine of a Hollywood movie could say, "I could bear all the rest, but I've been unladylike," when a film could be set in an English village during the Napoleonic wars and never leave the village to show the slaughter. This 1937 film is about a street where gentlemen are an event, and where the dashing, gallant Franchot Tone devastates the maiden ladies. As in so much of James M. Barrie, the sensitive, all-knowing woman (Katharine Hepburn) gets the vain, infantile male. (Why does she bother? Well, in the Barrie world, that's the only kind of man there is.) Underneath all the propriety, there's a dismaying and rather grim view of human relationships. Unfortunately, the word "quaint" does apply: Barrie is rather like Jane Austen adapted to ladies' luncheon clubs. But fortunately — it is one of those great accidents of nature — Hepburn has such elegance that the material is elevated. George Stevens directed, and the cast includes Cora Witherspoon as the belligerent servant, Fay Bainter, Florence Lake, Helena Grant, Eric Blore, Bonita Granville, and — in a lace cap and tall hat — Estelle Winwood.

◉ ◉ ◉

The Quiet American. This 1958 movie was a commercial failure, and it is also an artistic failure. But its theme and principal characters are of such immediacy and interest that you may find it far more absorbing than successful movies with a more conventional subject matter. Graham Greene's 1956 novel was based on his experiences as a correspondent in Indo-China, and Joseph L. Mankiewicz, who adapted the book and directed the movie, photographed most of it in Vietnam. It is a study of the American (Audie Murphy) as do-gooder and of the harm that innocent and crusading idealism can do, and it is a study of the Englishman (Michael Redgrave) as cynical, convictionless neutralist. There are so many fine things in the film (especially Redgrave's portrait of a man whose cold exterior is just a thin skin over his passionate desperation) that perhaps you can simply put aside the offending compromises of the last reel. With Claude Dauphin and Georgia Moll; photographed by Robert Krasker (which may explain why this Mankiewicz film has some camera movement).

◉ ◉ ◉

The Rainmaker. The lady suffering from drought is Katharine Hepburn, and the con man who delivers the rain is Burt Lancaster. The confidence man needs the confidence he tries to win; he is a poet and dreamer as much as a trickster. Lancaster, as often in athletic roles, is effective: when he can move a lot he can be moving. Hepburn, perfectly cast, is stringy and tomboyish, believably plain yet magnetically beautiful. Although this is a fairy tale (the ugly duckling) dressed up as a bucolic comedy and padded out with metaphysical falsies, it is also genuinely appealing — the sort of fairy tale that people need to see now and then to remind them of what they used to believe in. It is, of course, aimed solidly at the lower-middle-class mind; best evidence: the heroine rejects the poet for deputy sheriff Wendell Corey. No one will film the sequel, where she suffers from the drought in his imagination. Joseph Anthony, who did it on the stage, directed, and though *The Rainmaker* is a just barely adapted play (both play and adaptation by N. Richard Nash), it's enjoyable in a crude, good-spirited way. With Lloyd Bridges, Earl Holliman, Cameron Prud'homme, Wallace Ford. 1956, color.

⊚　⊚　⊚

Rashomon. It is ninth-century Kyoto: a nobleman's bride is raped by a bandit; the nobleman is murdered, or possibly he is a suicide. The double crime is acted out four times, in the versions of the three participants, each giving an account that increases the prestige of his conduct, and in the version of a woodcutter who witnessed the episode. Murder mysteries reconstruct the crime to find the culprit. *Rashomon* continuously reconstructs the crime to demonstrate the terrible unknowability of truth. With barbaric simplicity, it goes to the center of the human mystery — what can one ever be sure of? — and leaves one gasping for the author's own solution (Akutagawa died from an overdose of veronal). The introductory and closing sequences are tedious; the woman's whimpering is almost enough to drive you to the nearest exit. But *Rashomon* is one of the great film experiences — a film one will see again because there are pleasures — as well as pain — in looking into an abyss. Akira Kurosawa directed. With Machiko Kyo, Toshiro Mifune as the bandit, Masayuki Mori as the samurai, Takashi Shimura as the woodcutter. Grand Prix, Venice; Academy Award, Best Foreign Film of 1951.

⊚　⊚　⊚

Razzia (*Razzia sur la Chnouf* — "*Razzia*" means a raid, "*chnouf*" means dope — i.e., raid on the dope ring). America's movie gangsters of the thirties and forties, adored by the French and now imitated by them, come back to us with strange accents, more refined sadistic and erotic habits, and a whole new vocabulary of exotic gangster argot. This cultural crossfertilization produces an amusingly plodding pseudo-documentary like *Razzia*. The French are very serious about vice, and the dedicated authenticity with which director Henri Decoin follows Jean Gabin and his hoods and pushers through dingy waterfront cafés, beat bistros where glistening African bodies writhe in the hashish smoke, gay bars presided over by bass-voiced lesbians, lonely subway stops, and opium dens where the decorator types recline among Orientalia, would probably shock the American directors who, in their innocence, created the genre. As the ring's enforcer, snarling, shiv-eyed Gabin is the familiar, inexorable tough of the French tradition. One may wonder whether the teeth he sinks into Magali Noel's magnificent neck are his own; in the film's final moment, when morality triumphs and the audience is cheated, one knows the answer. With Lila Kedrova. 1957.

⊙ ⊙ ⊙

Red River. In 1948 one of the finest young actors in the country put on cowboy jeans and, overnight, Montgomery Clift became the hottest thing in Hollywood. *Red River* is a magnificent horse opera — one of the more elaborate celebrations of those trail-blazing episodes that Hollywood loves to glorify as "historical events," i.e., the mid-nineteenth-century first cattle drive up the Chisholm Trail. (The cattle in this production are not to be passed over lightly: they are impressive and they were very expensive. Six thousand head were rented at ten dollars a day each — and then it rained and rained while the cattle waited, and the film's cost rose from $1,750,000 to $3,200,000. Figures like that help make a movie an epic.) The director, Howard Hawks, makes the drive an exciting series of stampedes, Indian battles, and gunfights, with the fight between the two principals, John Wayne as the father and Clift as the stepson, as the ferocious climax. *Red River* is not really so "great" as its devotees claim (what Western is?), and a lot of it is just terrible, but Clift — in his most aggressively sexual screen performance — is angular and tense and audacious, and the other actors brawl amusingly in the strong-silent-man tradition. Russell Harlan's photography makes the rolling plains the true hero: the setting, if not the material, has epic grandeur. With Walter Brennan, Harry Carey, John Ireland, and frantic Joanne Dru, who acts as if the Old West were Greenwich Village. Screenplay by Borden Chase and Charles Schnee, from a novel by Chase.

⊙ ⊙ ⊙

Rififi (*Du Rififi Chez les Hommes*). The most talked-about sequence in Jules Dassin's gangster movie is a silent half hour in which four men rob a jewelry store. It is like a highly skillful documentary on how to disconnect a burglar alarm and open a safe, and it is thoroughly engrossing because we see the criminals, not from some outside point of moral reference, but as craftsmen, and we celebrate their teamwork, their finesse, their triumph. Ironically, we find ourselves sympathizing with their honest exhaustion after their dishonest labor. From there on the movie follows the tradition of *Scarface, Public Enemy,* and *The Asphalt Jungle* (and of *Macbeth* before them), and brings the tragic, trapped figures (now symbols of our own anti-social impulses) to a finish so cadaverous that, as one critic remarked, "The lesson that crime doesn't pay is taught so thoroughly that no one in the cast is left alive to profit from it." Along the way Dassin keeps things actively vicious with assorted blackmail, murder, the thrashing of a faithless mistress (stripped), kidnapping, etc. I had the uncomfortable feeling that the movie was directed by a gangster who had been holed up somewhere with early Fritz Lang movies and had decided this was a good way to make money. I can't think of any other reason to make *Rififi*. With Jean Servais, Robert Manuel, Carl Mohner, and Dassin as the four; and Robert Hossein, Marie Sabouret, Magali Noel. 1955.

◉   ◉   ◉

The Rocking Horse Winner. This little-known English production of the D. H. Lawrence story is a demonstration of how good a movie intelligent people can make when they have better-than-intelligent material to work on. Sentimental movies used to dwell on how parents sacrificed themselves for their children; this is a sharp reversal. A child (the marvelous little John Howard Davies who also played Oliver Twist) uses his second sight to rescue his parents; the painful part is that he lacks first sight — the judgment which would enable him to see that they are already destroyed. His performance is matched by that of Valerie Hobson as his mother; in all her long and honorable career as a great beauty, this is her only real acting that comes to mind (scenes like the pawnshop episode are hard to put out of mind). With John Mills and Ronald Squire. Anthony Pelissier directed. 1950.

◉   ◉   ◉

Romeo and Juliet. Renato Castellani literally gives Shakespeare a kingdom for a stage in the 1954 Anglo-Italian color production, photographed by Robert Krasker in the golden remnants of the High Renaissance in Verona, Venice, Siena, and other Italian cities. Leonor Fini's fabulous costume designs are derived from Piero della Francesca, Pisanello, Carpaccio, and Fiorenzo di Lorenzo. Amongst these visual splendors, it seems pointless to worry about the loss of Shakespeare's dramatic rhythm: the film, it is true, is not a great performance of the play — but can there be a great performance of *Romeo and Juliet?* This film provides more sense of what the play is *about* than conventional stage interpretations. You may achingly long to be at the Capulets' ball when the boy sopranos begin to sing and the sensual atmosphere of masks, color, violence, and elegance fatally encompasses the boy and the girl who, all in a moment, meet, love, and quiveringly touch. Laurence Harvey (at twenty-six) is Romeo and his readings are often exciting and alive; the Juliet, twenty-year-old Susan Shentall, is lovely, but lacks voice and presence. There are sudden miracles in this production — like the way Mervyn Johns transforms tiresome old Friar Laurence into a radiant, divinely silly little man; and miracles of sight and sound

— the clanging of the great church doors, the sudden recognition that the servants carrying food are right out of Botticelli, or that, dressed by Fini, a big lug like Bill Travers is a Benvolio that Italian painters might have fought over. This *Romeo and Juliet* is part of a glorious, voluptuous, poisoned age. With Flora Robson as the nurse, Sebastian Cabot as Capulet; John Gielgud is the chorus. Music by Roman Vlad. Grand Prix, Venice. (The 1936 George Cukor–MGM version, with Leslie Howard and Norma Shearer, is expensively devotional, but it, too, has some value: it is partially redeemed by clear, sensible readings, and by John Barrymore as Mercutio and Edna May Oliver as the nurse.)

◉　◉　◉

Rosemary (*Das Mädchen Rosemarie*). From the reviews I had expected a witty, stylized musical satire; it was widely compared to early René Clair — I can only assume by people who hadn't seen much early René Clair. *Rosemary* makes some attempts at musical satire and rhythmic editing — but it's fairly simpleminded stuff. Nine capitalists in their black Homburg hats step out of nine black Mercedes-Benz limousines and snap the doors shut in time to the music — that's about as close to the style of René Clair as the Rockettes at Easter. And as for the critics' enthusiastic idea that *Rosemary* was the *Three Penny Opera* of the fifties, well it's easy enough to see how they got the idea — the score is just a reprise of Kurt Weill's music, and the subject matter is social corruption. But who wants to eat a sausage when he can see what's being ground up into it? Rolf Thiele, the director, and his scenarist, Erich Kuby, are so busy stuffing in irony, horror, songs, and farce that we sit coldly examining the ingredients.

The actual Rosemary Nitribitt was a high-class-call-girl who became a favorite of Frankfurt's postwar industrialists; it was thought that she dabbled in blackmail and sold information — presumably about the industrial manipulations of her clients — and she was found dead in 1957; the case was never solved. Nadja Tiller, who plays the role, is a former Miss Austria; she — or perhaps her publicity agent — felt it necessary to explain that she had accepted the role because the film was not intended simply to show "the tragic fate of a prostitute but rather to produce a critique of our modern times. That takes courage. And since courage seems to be at a premium in our film industry, I felt morally bound to cooperate." The irony is that the best element of the film is precisely Nadja Tiller as a prostitute: she's one of the best whores who ever walked the screen. The critique of our modern times is labored and silly. With the suave Peter Van Eyck, Gert Frobe, Mario Adorf, Werner Peters, Carl Raddatz. 1958. For German self-satire, *Aren't We Wonderful?* (*Wir Wunderkinder*) is considerably better.

◉　◉　◉

Roxie Hart. Roxie (Ginger Rogers) is the 1926 sensation of Chicago —
a flapper on trial for her life who has the time of her life while on trial. She
is coached and defended by Adolphe Menjou — "Roxie's simple, barefoot
mouthpiece" — in what is probably the best courtroom satire on film. Ben
Hecht adapted Maurine Watkins's play *Chicago* in the style of his *Nothing
Sacred* — with a loving look at the speakeasies, floozies, murders, and tab-
loids, the "phony" urban excitement, and a glance at the forsaken rural
boredom (Roxie's farmer-father, summoned to the long distance phone and
informed that she has been arrested on a murder charge, returns to the
rocker on his porch, rocks for a while, and then says to the mother,
"They're going to hang Roxie." The mother nods approvingly, "What did I
tell you?"). William Wellman directed in a faster, broader, more spirited
style than *Nothing Sacred* (though the end is the kind of Hollywood studio
idea of a finish that no director can do anything with). The cast is first-rate:
Iris Adrian as Two-Gun Gertie ("Got a butt, buddy?"); the reporters and
photographers include Lynne Overman (whose vocal inflections could do as
much for dialogue as Lee Tracy's), Phil Silvers, George Montgomery, and
Spring Byington as a sob sister. Sara Allgood is the prison matron, Nigel
Bruce a theatrical agent, and George Chandler is Roxie's husband. Even Jeff
Corey turns up in a bit. The plot of this 1942 picture turns on the death of a
man named Finnegan.

(Lee Tracy himself can be heard at his staccato best in *Bombshell* opposite Harlow, and in Roy Del Ruth's *Blessed Event,* a 1932 film based on the
rise of Walter Winchell. The columnist's pet peeve is a maddeningly sweet
crooner, played disarmingly by a very young, very funny Dick Powell.)

⊚ ⊚ ⊚

The Rules of the Game (*La Règle du Jeu*). Jean Renoir's *The Rules of
the Game* is a love roundelay that accelerates and intensifies until it becomes a rare mingling of lyric poetry and macabre farce. The lyric and the
macabre turn out to be different aspects of the same love game.

What is, at one level, simply a large house party is, at another level, a
tragi-comic world in motion. Ironically, the man who begins at the center of
it all, the romantic aviator-hero, becomes irrelevant and expendable. He is
odd man out on a carousel: when the whole mechanism is spinning he is
flicked off. After observing his courtship rites, we can only accede to his
quick demise: in this whirl, who has patience for his outmoded sense of
honor?

The chase is a combination of two shooting parties. The hunt, the osten-
sible reason for the weekend gathering, serves as a relief from moneyed
boredom. Who cares what you shoot? The beaters precede the guests who
shoot at animals, birds — any living thing that can be shot at. The second
shooting party is not planned: the jealous gamekeeper, a rigid man with an

342 · THE MOVIE PAST

antique morality, runs amuck among the guests who confuse his passion with play-acting. They accept as divertissement the chase of servants and master among them (a later generation would call this "total theatre"). Mechanical toys are in motion, shots are fired; the targets are random — a toy, and then the romantic hero, as surprised by the shot as the rabbit.

In *La Grande Illusion,* made in 1937 but set during World War I, Renoir had dealt with a trio of heroes — the French aristocrat De Boeldieu, the German aristocrat von Rauffenstein, and the French plebeian Maréchal. A fourth character, Rosenthal, played by Dalio, was a rich young Jew from the merchant class. *The Rules of the Game,* Renoir's last prewar French film, is set at the time it was made — at the eve of the outbreak of World War II — and Dalio has become a marquis. But he has not really changed: he is still Rosenthal, or rather Rosenthal's descendant, though socially he has moved into the château and the grounds of a De Boeldieu. The old military aristocracy is dead, as De Boeldieu and von Rauffenstein had predicted it would be; the new aristocracy is based on money and celebrity.

What are "the rules of the game" in this society? They are in flux — nobody knows what they are. The mores are just convenient manners. The aviator and the gamekeeper who *do* live by rules (the rules of an older, more stable society) cannot play the "game"; they upset everything because they can't just relax and adapt to the graceful decay of morals. What are the distinctions that have disappeared or become confused among the house guests? Love is indistinguishable from sexual activity; adultery is an escape from idleness. The concept of honor has disappeared (the honor that meant so much to a von Rauffenstein, a De Boeldieu); dishonor is just another term for indiscretion. Charm is more important than feeling. The marquis and his guests at the château still have some energy and some feeling, but they are becoming enervated; they foreshadow the guests at the big hotel parties in later movies — *La Dolce Vita, L'Avventura,* and *Last Year at Marienbad.* The house party suggests comparison with the house party in Ingmar Bergman's *Smiles of a Summer Night,* which is, however, far less complicated. The way the animals die calls up other film images of death (some, no doubt, inspired by *The Rules of the Game*) — particularly the opening sequence of *Forbidden Games* and Magnani's death in *Open City.* The look of the animals about to die recalls an image from another Renoir film — the frightened eye of the girl in *A Day in the Country* as she is seduced, looking trapped, almost wounded.

Images and ideas that tease the imagination: The marquis's sense of fellowship with the poacher — they're both men of the world, rogues and sly weaklings, and there isn't even much class distinction between them . . . The poacher who poaches rabbits, or with equal ease, the gamekeeper's wife . . . The marquis's distaste for the gamekeeper — who can't keep his own wife from being poached . . . The marquis, who is incapable of conscious cruelty, organizes the slaughter of wild life for the entertainment of his guests; he collects and treasures rare, old mechanical toys . . . It seems right that Renoir himself should be one of the characters. He has never, even in his lesser movies, saved himself from total immersion in the work; here his role, that of Octave, the friendly observer, "the friend of the family" who is suddenly caught up in the game, suggests a parody of the artist as observer. No one in the film — not even its creator — remains aloof from the frenzy. Renoir dresses as a bear for the masquerade — and can't quite shed his animal skin. Is he aligned with the animals hunted down — and with the big shaggy dog-man of *Boudu?*

It would be possible to discuss the film simply in terms of its craftsmanship and the extraordinary editing (particularly in the last sequence); technically, it is breathtaking. But it seems almost an insult to worry over *how* it is done — what is far more exciting is to explore what is in it. Renoir, the great master of French naturalism, and the source of so much of the neorealist movement, is revealed in *The Rules of the Game* as the progenitor also of the trends in film associated with Bergman, Antonioni, Resnais, and others.

With Roland Toutain as the aviator, Carette as the poacher, Gaston Modot as the gamekeeper, Nora Gregor as Christine, Mila Parely as Genevieve, Paulette Dubost as Lisette. Derived from Alfred de Musset's *Les Caprices de Marianne*. Costumes by Chanel. Cinematography by Claude Renoir; Cartier-Bresson served as an assistant director. Released in Paris in 1939 after being cut by the distributors, cut again after violent audience reactions, then banned as demoralizing by the Vichy government and then by the Nazis. The original negative was destroyed when the Allies bombed the studios at Boulogne. Reassembled (from two hundred cans of film and bits of sound track) and restored in the late fifties. Selected in the 1962 international poll of critics as third among the greatest motion pictures of all time. I set that down only for the record: a numbered honor is an insult to the greatest living film artist.

◉ ◉ ◉

The Sandpiper. It's too bad that *The Sandpiper* will probably not seem as funny to future generations — at least not in the same way — but coming when it did, it was probably the greatest movie for audience wisecracks ever made. Martin Ransohoff's name appears on *The Sandpiper* as producer, and as author of the story. He cheated himself, because it's an old Adela Rogers St. John number called *A Free Soul,* which Elizabeth Taylor had already redone as *The Girl Who Had Everything;* and Richard Burton — in his left-over high collar from *The Night of the Iguana* — plays a high-society version of that poor old dear, the Reverend Davidson from Somerset Maugham's *Rain.* As Burton, looking more foreshortened than ever, eyed the portly Taylor in her Irene Sharaff poncho, a man to my left muttered, "It's a pygmy romance," while a voice behind me asked, "Where's the rest of them?"

When a movie has to be set in motion by a gimmick like having a California judge order an atheist mother to send her child to a religious school, it's in trouble from the beginning (and so would the judge be). The plot of *The Sandpiper* thickens inadvertently: somewhere between the interiors (shot in Paris) and the exteriors (shot in the Big Sur area) the continuity seems to have gotten confused. There is no accounting for some of the heroine's irrational outbursts. They seem to come out of nowhere, certainly not out of the previous scenes; the effect is one of hysteria, but the other characters react as if it were normal. There is no doubt, however, about the intentions behind the movie's selling points: the proper clergyman visits our heroine while she is posing nude (from the waist up) for a sculptor. She converses with him, demurely cupping her breasts with her hands — though they seem inadequate to the task.

Listening to lines like "I never knew what love was before" and "I've lost all my sense of sin," it was impossible to separate this unconvincing performance from what we knew about the performers. The whole absurd enterprise up there on the screen seemed to be a vast double-entendre. Burton the clergyman makes high-toned literary remarks to beatnik artist Taylor like "I can't dispel you from my thoughts," and then when he hates himself in the morning, she reassures him with, "Don't you realize what happened between us is *good?*" Someone must have left a copy of Betty Friedan's book on the set, because all of a sudden, for no particular reason, Taylor begins to talk about problems of feminine fulfillment and marriage, which have about as much to do with her character as with a sandpiper's. And we in the audience were dying, United Arab Republic, dying. "Great Lovers" should not be seen, not be heard, only imagined.

At the end Richard Burton, redeemed by contact with atheistic Elizabeth Taylor's spiritual values, cast off the temptations of wealth and worldly success and found his simple faith again. Which, in an MGM production, is high comedy. Martin Ransohoff will surely be the first to take his own advice? As if to parody the Hollywood-style liberalism of the thirties and forties, the script-writers — Dalton Trumbo and Michael Wilson, perhaps in a tired reflex, or the *other* script writers — Irene and Louis Kamp — have added layers of social consciousness to the already rich ($5,300,-000), decaying pastry. The director, Vincente Minnelli, a man with a sophisticated, charming talent, who has in the past made movies about the Hollywood juggernaut, is here crushed under it. With Eva Marie Saint, Charles Bronson. 1965.

⊙ ⊙ ⊙

Saratoga Trunk. A brunette Ingrid Bergman plays the fabulous adventuress Clio Dulaine in this exhilarating travesty of Edna Ferber's costume romance. Flanked by Flora Robson in incredible blackface as the mulatto maid Angelique and Jerry Austin as the dwarf manservant Cupidon, Bergman is a *demi-mondaine* from New Orleans who invades fashionable Saratoga Springs and conquers all, including Gary Cooper, as the gambling Texan Clint Maroon (!). This is a lavish piece of frivolous, ebullient moviemaking — replete with details dear to the readers of tempestuous fiction (i.e., the heroine enjoys champagne with peaches in the afternoon), and those who abandon themselves to it for two hours have a marvelous time. Clio the trollop is Bergman's liveliest, funniest role. Directed by Sam Wood; screenplay by Casey Robinson. Made in 1943, but not released until 1945.

⊙ ⊙ ⊙

The Scarlet Letter. "I wanted to make a film of *The Scarlet Letter* . . . I was asked which director I would like, and I chose Victor Sjostrom, who had arrived at MGM some years earlier from Sweden. I felt that the Swedes were closer to the feelings of New England Puritans than modern Americans." With historic simplicity, Lillian Gish described the background to this 1926 film. She leaves it for us to explain her extraordinary taste and judgment — and her acting genius. Her Hester Prynne is one of the most beautifully sustained performances in screen history — mercurial, delicate, passionate. There isn't an actress on the screen today, and perhaps there never was another, who can move like Lillian Gish: it's as if no bones, no physical barriers, stood between her intuitive understanding of the role and her expression of it. Sjostrom chose the Swedish actor Lars Hanson for Arthur Dimmesdale; Henry B. Walthall plays Prynne. Karl Dane is also in the cast. The photography is by Hendrik Sartov, who had earlier worked with Griffith; the adaptation — or diminution — of Hawthorne is by Frances Marion. Sjostrom presents a heroine struggling against moralistic conventions; his conception is so strong that the coy elements in the scenario and the cloying titles almost disappear from consciousness. He stages Lars Hanson's final revelation scene with a power and conviction that justifies Lillian Gish's hunch: these two Swedes understand Hawthorne's guilt and suffering.

⊙ ⊙ ⊙

The Sea Wall (How Marguerite Duras's *Barrage contre le Pacifique* was turned into *This Angry Age* in the United States, we may never know; the film is called *The Sea Wall* in other English-speaking countries). The novel is a study of decaying colonialism set on the Pacific Coast of Indo-China: a Frenchwoman struggles to keep her rice fields safe, but the Pacific is too strong for the flimsy sea wall she has put up; her son and daughter are too busy with their sexual fantasies to care about the land or the wall. There are a great many cross-currents in the book, and in trying to convey them all, the film turns into a fiasco, but it is in many ways a brilliant fiasco. It has photographic sequences (shot in Thailand) that suggest Renoir's *The River,* and some brother-sister scenes between Tony Perkins and Silvana Mangano that suggest Cocteau. The too-ambitious, too-international project was directed by René Clément, with Jo Van Fleet as the mother, Alida Valli, Nehemiah Persoff, Richard Conte, etc. Screenplay by Irwin Shaw and Clément. 1958. Color, Technirama.

⊙ ⊙ ⊙

The Seventh Seal (*Det Sjunde Inseglet*). Ingmar Bergman's medieval morality play about man in search of the meaning of life is set in fourteenth-century Sweden: a knight (Max von Sydow), tormented and doubting, returns from ten wasted years in the Crusades, and Death (Bengt Ekerot) comes to claim him. Hoping to gain some revelation or obtain some knowledge before he dies, the knight challenges Death to a game of chess. As they play, the knight observes scenes of cruelty, rot, and suffering that suggest the tortures and iniquity Ivan Karamazov described to Alyosha. In the end, the knight tricks Death for the sake of human survival: he saves a family of strolling players — a visionary, innocent, natural man, Joseph (Nils Poppe), his wife (Bibi Andersson), and their infant son. The knight, this sane modern man, asking to believe despite all the evidence of his senses, is childlike compared with his carnal, atheist squire (Gunnar Bjornstrand). The images and the omens are medieval, but the modern erotic and psychological insights add tension, and in some cases, as in the burning of the child-witch (Maud Hansson), excruciation. The actors' faces, the aura of magic, the ambiguities, and the riddle at the heart of the film all contribute to its stature. 1956.

⊙ ⊙ ⊙

The Seventh Veil. In the mid-forties, when the New York critics said a film was for "adult minds" they were referring to something like *The Seventh Veil* — a rich, portentous mixture of Beethoven, Chopin, Kitsch, and Freud. Ann Todd is the shy young pianist obsessed with the idea that she can never hit those keys again, and Heathcliff-Svengali James Mason is the smoldering cause of it all (his fires always seem to be banked). Herbert Lom performs that marvelous forties-movie type of psychoanalytic cure: he discovers which of her suitors the heroine really loves. All this nonsense is highly entertaining: maybe, with a few veils stripped away, most of us have a fantasist inside who gobbles up this sadomasochistic sundae, with its culture sauce. In the late fifties, when I was managing art houses, I was amazed that so many people who phoned to get the starting times for *The Seventh Seal* asked when *The Seventh Veil* was going on: it's probably what they wished they were going to see. Compton-Bennett directed. Academy Award for Best Original Screenplay (Muriel and Sydney Box). 1945.

⊙　⊙　⊙

Shane. Here's Galahad on the range, in one of those elaborately simple epics that important American directors love to make; superficially, this type of film is a Western, and thus salable, but those trained in the New Criticism will recognize it as the creation of a myth. You can start with the way Shane's horse canters or the Agincourt music or the knight's costume or at almost any other detail. The movie-makers put it there and we can find it all right, but it's academic on both sides. It's over-planned and uninspired; the Western was better before it became so self-importantly self-conscious. One trouble with this kind of myth-making is that the myth is ready for the remainder counter by the time Hollywood takes it up. The enigmatic, pure-of-heart hero, Alan Ladd, defeats villains twice his size — e.g., the Prince of Darkness, Jack Palance. Ladd's chivalric purity is his motivation; his fighting technique (a secret weapon?) the enigma. With Van Heflin as the homesteader, Brandon De Wilde as the boy, Jean Arthur (in her last screen appearance to date) as the homesteader's wife, and Elisha Cook, Jr., Edgar Buchanan, etc. Directed by George Stevens. Screenplay by A. B. Guthrie, Jr. Academy Award for Cinematography (Loyal Griggs) — an award that must have seemed like a ghastly joke because Paramount, in order to take advantage of the new fashion for the wide screen, had mutilated the movie by cutting off the top and bottom of the entire picture. 1953, color.

⊙　⊙　⊙

The Sky Above, The Mud Below (*Le Ciel et la Boue*). Although *The Sky Above, The Mud Below* has a rather larger number of unclothed natives than most of these expedition-through-unexplored-areas movies, the New Guinea natives are, as camera subjects, or as anything else, miserably endowed. Apart from this revelation, the film has little to offer. There is the usual self-congratulatory narration about all the hardships and suffering of the expedition, the courage and loyalty of the porters, the height of the mountains to be crossed, the bridges that must be built to cross the swift rivers, the incredible cold and the prostrating heat, the dysentery and malaria and leeches, the jungle that no white men before had ever charted, and the incredible heroism of the intrepid men who made the movie. There's surprisingly little about the Stone Age men, the headhunters whom, presumably, we have come to learn something about.

If the movie were better as an anthropological document, I might be better disposed to hearing about all the ordeals these brave men went through to bring it to us, but one explorer looks very much like another explorer, and their photography of themselves is rarely adventurous. It's a mediocre documentary with a few good sequences showing the natives; the film is clumsily edited and contains some crude, obviously staged and re-enacted sequences. The "poetic" narration is very fancy and may have influenced those who gave this movie an Academy Award. Written and directed by Pierre-Dominique Gaisseau. Made in 1959, released in 1961. Color.

⊚   ⊚   ⊚

Some Like It Hot. It would be easy to provide fairly elaborate explanations of its transvestism, role confusion, and borderline inversion. But it's hilariously innocent, though always on the brink of really disastrous double entendre. Tony Curtis, who had proved he could act in *Sweet Smell of Success* and *Trapeze,* demonstrates a parodistic gift with an imitation of Cary Grant that he's still doing. Jack Lemmon is demoniacally funny; Joe E. Brown is wonderful — so good I remembered how I'd wept from laughter at his last scenes in *A Midsummer Night's Dream.* And, of course, there's Marilyn Monroe (in perhaps her most characteristic role, which means that she's both charming and embarrassing), George Raft, Pat O'Brien, Nehemiah Persoff, etc. Billy Wilder directed (unevenly) and collaborated on the screenplay with I. A. L. Diamond. 1959. (For collectors of useless movie memorabilia: in one of the earlier versions of this material, a German musical film, the orchestra girls were called The Alpine Violets.)

⊚   ⊚   ⊚

Spellbound. The idea is intriguing: a murder mystery set among a group of psychoanalysts, with a solution to be arrived at by clues found in a dream which is analyzed. It was carried out in 1945 by one of the most highly publicized collaborations of all time: Alfred Hitchcock and Salvador Dali. The screenplay was by Ben Hecht and the star was Ingrid Bergman, as an analyst, playing opposite Gregory Peck, her amnesia patient — the murder suspect. With all the obvious ingredients for success, *Spellbound* is a disaster. It's not that Peck's Dali-designed dream life is so bad for Peck, but it's not much for Dali. It was fitting, of course, that the actress who was once described as a "fine, strong, cow-country maiden" should be cast as a good, solid, competent analyst, dispensing cures and murder solutions with the wholesome simplicity of a mother adding wheat germ to the family diet, but Bergman's famous "sincerity" has rarely been so out of place as in this confection whipped up by jaded chefs. Bergman was the great-lady star of the forties; but though she is always a joy to look at and listen to, the sincere apple-checked Bergman is often dull; I prefer the insincere hussy of *Saratoga Trunk* and *Notorious.* With Michael Chekhov, John Emery, Leo G. Carroll. Academy Award for Best Original Score (!) to Miklos Rozsa.

⊙   ⊙   ⊙

The Spiral Staircase. In this one the physically afflicted person is the victim of the terror. Robert Siodmak directed this modern horror classic in 1946; it has all the trappings of the genre — a stormy night and a collection of psychopaths in an old house — but the psychopaths are quite presentable people and this, plus the skillful, swift direction, makes the terror convincing. Dorothy McGuire is excellent as the threatened mute servant. With Ethel Barrymore, George Brent, Kent Smith, Sara Allgood, Elsa Lanchester, Rhonda Fleming.

⊙   ⊙   ⊙

Stalag 17. In this rowdy prisoner-of-war comedy, William Holden is the cynical heel (the audience identifies with) who turns into a hero. Though you probably wouldn't guess that anybody connected with this production had ever so much as seen a German, the director, Billy Wilder, is one (sort of), and the authors of the original play (Donald Devan and Edmund Trycinski) are ex-G.I.s who were interned in the real Stalag 17. It's a safe bet that someone connected with the movie had had a long look at *La Grande Illusion.* The melodramatics of the plot are simply corny, but perhaps the horseplay and the gallows humor are, for Americans, as genuine a response to adversity as the fiery mystique of *A Man Escaped* is for a European (and former prisoner) like Robert Bresson. Holden took the Academy Award for Best Actor. It was overdue. Holden, an excellent actor who had begun in movies as *Golden Boy* in 1939, became so popular as a result of this film, however, that he became a big box-office star and has appeared mostly in big clinkers since. With Don Taylor, Robert Strauss, Sig Rumann, and Otto Preminger (who seems to have made an acting career out of playing Erich von Stroheim). 1953.

⊙   ⊙   ⊙

The Stars Look Down. Looking at this 1939 film by Carol Reed — until the sixties one of the rare English films with strong contemporary subject matter — is rather like reading a Thomas Hardy novel: the story unfolds with authority and control; we are told everything we need to know, so that we believe in what happens to the characters, we believe even in the accidents. It's a story about life in a Welsh mining town, and one sequence is almost pure Hardy: a group of men are trapped in a mine; the mine owner, on his way to the rescue squad with the plans that will save the men, has a fatal stroke; the plans fall from his hand and the trapped men die. We experience the same mixture of fury and belief that we do when Tess's letter slides under the rug — and her marriage to Angel Clare is doomed. There are few artists who can achieve this kind of effect.

The hero (Michael Redgrave) is a frustrated idealist not unlike Hardy's Jude; Redgrave was new to the movies: he had previously made only *The Lady Vanishes* and *Stolen Life,* in both of which he was rather an undistinguished juvenile — and this performance was the first film evidence that he was to become an important actor. Reed was only thirty-three when he made this work and he had not yet acquired the technical virtuosity of his later style, but this straightforward film may just possibly be his best. I think it is better than most of the over-praised English social films of the sixties. *The Stars Look Down* has nothing as brilliant as the first sequences of *Odd Man Out* when the Irish conspirators stage their robbery, and lose their leader in the get-away. But it has an understanding, an achieved beauty, that Carol Reed was never again able to sustain. (*Odd Man Out* almost had it — but Reed was trying for too much that time, and Robert Newton and a faulty script pulled the film down.) With Emlyn Williams, Margaret Lockwood (this English star, so mediocre in dozens of films, is excellent in the role of a stupid, vulgar, unhappy girl; we see her destroy the hero and we cannot despise her for it), Nancy Price as the mother, Edward Rigby as the father, and a cast including Desmond Tester, Ivor Barnard, and Cecil Parker. From the novel by A. J. Cronin.

Few people in this country have seen *The Stars Look Down:* Hollywood made *How Green Was My Valley* during the same period. The American film had a similar subject matter, and the more sentimental American treatment was much easier for audiences to take. Also, Reed's film met with a hostile reaction from unions, and — like David Lean's *Oliver Twist,* which was regarded with disfavor by Jewish groups — it did not get extensive bookings.

It's perfectly true that in *The Stars Look Down* the miners are seen to be contemptuous of their own union, and the early strike sequence of the film is a wildcat strike. Nor does the film indulge in those glorifications of unions and working men which literate film audiences so often seem to think necessary (*On the Waterfront* has almost destroyed Kazan's reputation — not because of what was dramatically false in it but because of what was sociologically *true*). Yet it's probably because *The Stars Look Down* does not sentimentalize the characters of the working-class community that they have a classic dignity completely unlike workers in American films. The hero's mother as played by Nancy Price is an embodiment of David Riesman's tradition-directed type: she believes in authority and she doesn't believe the men have the right to strike against the employer. Another miner's wife doesn't want her child exposed to ideas. It is in dealing with such conflicts within a working-class group that the film gains stature; it does not try to make us believe that workers are all on the side of humanity and progress and a free and noble life. To many of us *The Grapes of Wrath* was a rather maudlin, embarrassing film — and not because we were opposed to working people or because we didn't know working people. It wasn't that we did not know the Joads; to some degree we were the Joads, and that's why we couldn't accept the glorification of the common man. When *The Stars Look Down* appeared, this propagandistic sentimentality was at its height — and a film in which workers were no better than other people could be attacked as an anti-labor film.

◎ ◎ ◎

Stella. There is the archaic row of young male Greek dancers in the sunlight; there are the dark café songs heard beneath the high-pitched, almost metallic bouzoukia orchestra; there is the solemn, solitary man who dances in front of the orchestra. The images and sounds are much more memorable than the story of the young Greek writer-director Michael Cacoyannis's crude, vigorous 1956 film. The story is rather like Camille crossed with Carmen — an overcharged melodrama about a fiery young woman (the handsome, blonde Greek stage actress, Melina Mercouri, whose leonine head is set on magnificent shoulders) and her uncompromising determination to be emotionally independent of her lovers. She refuses to marry the weak, insomniac aristocrat (Aleko Alexandrakis), outrages his condescending relatives, and drives him to his death; she falls in love with a young peasant athlete (George Foundas), but she stands him up at the altar, and he kills her. *Stella* doesn't have the grace of Cacoyannis's later, more subdued *A Girl in Black,* but it has exciting locale — the streets and bistros of Athens — and it is a triumph of temperament. It's been a long time since an American movie had this kind of turbulence and vitality.

◎ ◎ ◎

La Strada (literally, The Road). Federico Fellini's spiritual fable has captured over fifty awards in at least nine countries. The theme — that everyone has a purpose in the universe — is acted out by three symbolic characters: soul (innocence, spirit, dreams), Giulietta Masina; body (physical, brute strength, man as animal), Anthony Quinn; mind (the artist-fool), Richard Basehart. Though the background of the film is neo-realist poverty, it is transformed by the romanticism of the conception. Giulietta Masina's performance has by now been compared variously to Chaplin, Harry Langdon, Stan Laurel, Barrault, Marceau; and the comparisons are just — maybe too just. I would rather single out Basehart's fool — which is not like anything else I've seen. The strange thing about this movie is that even if one rejects its concepts — and I do reject them—the mood and details of scenes stay with one; suddenly a year or two later, a gesture or a situation brings it all back. Academy Award, Best Foreign Film of 1956.

◎ ◎ ◎

Strangers on a Train. A pretty good case could be made for Alfred Hitchcock as the master entertainer of the movie medium: from the 1930s to the 1960s his films have been a source of perverse pleasure. My favorite among his American films is this bizarre, malicious comedy of 1951, in which the late Robert Walker brought sportive originality to the role of the chilling wit, dear degenerate Bruno. The murder plot is so universally practical that any man may adapt it to his needs: Bruno perceives that though he cannot murder his father with impunity, someone else could; when he meets the unhappily married tennis player Guy (Farley Granger), he murders Guy's wife for him and expects Guy to return the favor. Technically, the climax of the film is the celebrated runaway merry-go-round, but the high point of excitement and amusement is Bruno trying to recover his cigarette lighter while Guy plays a fantastically nerve-wracking tennis match. Even this high point isn't what we remember best from *Strangers on a Train:* it's Robert Walker. It isn't often that we think about a performance in a Hitchcock movie; usually what we recall are bits of "business" — the stump finger in *The Thirty-Nine Steps,* the windmill turning the wrong way in *Foreign Correspondent,* etc. But Walker's performance is what gives this movie much of its character and its peculiar charm.

It is typical of Hollywood's own brand of perversity that Raymond Chandler was never hired to adapt any of his own novels for the screen; he was, however, employed on *Double Indemnity* and *Strangers on a Train* (which is based on a novel by Patricia Highsmith). Chandler (or someone?) provided Hitchcock with some of the best dialogue that ever graced a thriller. With Marion Lorne as Bruno's doting, dotty mother, and Leo G. Carroll, Ruth Roman, Patricia Hitchcock, Laura Elliott.

⊚ ⊚ ⊚

A Streetcar Named Desire. Vivien Leigh gives one of those rare performances that can truly be said to evoke pity and terror. As Blanche, she looks and acts like a destroyed Dresden shepherdess. No one since the early Lillian Gish and the almost unknown, exquisite Nadia Sibirskaya of *Menilmontant* has had this quality of hopeless, feminine frailty; Shakespeare might have had women like this in mind when he conceived Ophelia. Blanche's plea, "I don't want realism . . . I want magic!" is central to *Streetcar.* When Marlon Brando, as the realist Kowalski, shatters her system of illusions, she disintegrates. And he is revealed as a man without compassion — both infant and brute. Elia Kazan's direction is often stagey, the sets and arrangements of actors are frequently too transparently "worked out"; but who cares when you're looking at just about the best feminine performance you're ever going to see, as well as an interpretation by Brando that is just about perfection. This film has some of the best dialogue ever written by an American: when Vivien Leigh says, "The Tarantula Arms!" or "It's Della Robbia blue," you know how good Tennessee Williams can be. Academy Awards of 1951: Best Actress, Supporting Actress (Kim Hunter), Supporting Actor (Karl Malden), etc. But at the time, theatre managers complained that more customers left than came in.

⊚ ⊚ ⊚

Summer Interlude (*Sommarlek,* literally Summerplay). In *Sommarlek* (1951) Ingmar Bergman found his style, and the film is regarded by cinema historians not only as Bergman's breakthrough but also as the beginning of "a new, great epoch in Swedish films." Many of the themes (whatever one thinks of them —) that Bergman later expanded are here: the artists who have lost their identities, the faces that have become masks, the mirrors that reflect death at work. But this movie also has a lighter side — the rapture, the elegance and poetry of the ruined love affair suggest his exquisite erotic tragicomedy, *Smiles of a Summer Night. Sommarlek* is about the loss of love: a tired ballerina of twenty-eight (Maj-Britt Nilsson), who has ceased to feel or care, is suddenly caught up by the memory of the summer when her life ended. We see her then as a fresh, eager fifteen-year-old, in love with a frightened, uncertain student (beautifully played by Birger Malmsten), and we watch the delicate shades of their "summerplay," interrupted by glances at adult relatives, as Bergman contrasts decadence and youth, corruption and beauty. It is the highly personal work of a young director, a work with elegiac charm and sweetness, qualities which are disappearing from his later films. With Alf Kjellin as the suitor, Stig Olin as the ballet master, George Funkquist as the lecherous uncle. Photographed by Gunnar Fischer.

⊚ ⊚ ⊚

Summertime. Katharine Hepburn is probably the greatest actress of the sound era. Her career spans talkies almost from the beginning, and the transformations that have taken place in her, the way she has embodied new tastes in heroines, make her career an index of American changes. There were actresses who were career women types, others proud heiresses, others madcap comediennes, others sufferers for humanity, others defiant modernists. Hepburn has been all of them — rich girls, poor girls, pioneers, decadents. In the late thirties, after her brief period as "box-office poison," modern comedies had so completely restored her to public favor that even her poisonous performances in such poisonous pictures as *Song of Love, Dragon Seed,* and *Undercurrent* did not tarnish her name. Hepburn began — when she was close to fifty — to play "plain Janes." It may be relevant that Hepburn rarely played a woman with a child; she was almost invariably the modern woman, the career girl, the bachelor girl. By 1955, in *Summer-*

time, she was at the end point of that tradition — as the aging virgin, an innocent abroad in corrupt, sensual Venice. Prim and gaunt, withering in her loneliness, she is the female Yankee, the archetype of a Henry James heroine grown old. There is an element of embarrassment in this kind of role, but she is so good at it that she almost — though not quite — kills the embarrassment.

Here again David Lean tends to repeat *Brief Encounter,* and Hepburn's affair with the married Venetian art dealer (Rossano Brazzi) has its overwrought, understated emotions. This is one of those romantic movies that people love and remember, even though it's hard to believe that the coming together of a middle-aged roué and a puritanical spinster would light up the sky with the glittering display of fireworks that Lean provides. Or was it the producer who shot the works in order to justify the outlandish publicity campaign? — "It happens to Hepburn, it happens in Venice. All the pent-up passion of her life explodes one night in the splendor of the world's most fabulous city." Venice, according to *Variety,* "emerges as a great set for sheer eyeball appeal." With Isa Miranda, Darren McGavin. From Arthur Laurents's play *The Time of the Cuckoo.* Art director, Vincent Korda; cinematographer, Jack Hildyard. Color.

◎ ◎ ◎

Sunset Boulevard. A young scriptwriter (William Holden) speeding away from the finance-company men who have come to repossess his car (it is Los Angeles, where a man can get along without his honor, but not without his car) turns into a driveway on Sunset Boulevard and finds himself in the fantastic, decaying mansion of the once-great silent screen star, Norma Desmond (Gloria Swanson). Attended by her butler (Erich von Stroheim), who was once her husband and her director, she lives among the mementos of her past and plots her comeback in her own adaptation of *Salome.* The rapacious old vamp persuades the young man to stay and work with her on the script: he becomes her kept man, her lover, her victim.

The details of the film are baroque and glittering: the rats in the empty swimming pool; the wind moaning in the organ pipes; the midnight burial scene, when the star and her butler put a pet chimpanzee in the garden — with full honors; a grisly weekly bridge party, with a table of phantoms — Buster Keaton, H. B. Warner, and Anna Q. Nilsson. The whole enterprise exudes decadence like a stale, exotic perfume. You might not want to smell it every day, but then in 1950 you didn't get the chance: it was certainly a change from oceans of rosewater, lilies of the San Fernando Valley, and the scrubbed, healthy look.

The film is almost too clever — yet it is at its best in this cleverness, and is much less interesting when it deals with normal human beings (the sequences involving Nancy Olson and modern Hollywood). Charles Brackett, who wrote and produced, and Billy Wilder, who wrote and directed, have helped to create modern Hollywood; their pictures — some of the best of what are now called "product" — have no sweetness, no simplicity, no spontaneity. Even to them, at the top, this modern, wisecracking, anxious, realistic businessman's community fades into insignificance when contrasted with Norma Desmond's leopardskin past. The opulence, the grandeur, the primitivism, the extravagance, the glamour and insanity of those days when movies were new and already corrupt — these are the heart of *Sunset Boulevard,* a bizarre and bitter tribute to vanished glory. "I am big," says Norma Desmond, "it's the pictures that got smaller." (When an older, but still monocled, Erich von Stroheim flew from Paris to Hollywood, scene of his splendors and defeats as a director, to appear in *Sunset Boulevard,* he was greeted by Billy Wilder: "We are honored to have you with us . . . I have always admired your great films. You were ten years ahead of your time." "You are wrong — twenty years.")

Glint-eyed Swanson clutches at her comeback role almost as if it were *Salome.* William Holden gives the finest performance in the film; his writer — decent, charming, casually cynical — is trapped at first by curiosity and fascination, then by his weakness, and finally by his humanity (he tries to leave but Norma attempts suicide). When, in a mixture of pity and guilt, he makes love to the crazy, demanding old woman, he expresses a nausea so acute that we can almost forgive Holden his career during the last decade: this man knows the full self-disgust of prostitution. With Cecil B. DeMille, Hedda Hopper, Jack Webb, Fred Clark, Lloyd Gough. Academy Award for Best Story and Screenplay (Brackett, Wilder, and D. M. Marshman, Jr.).

⊙   ⊙   ⊙

Svengali. John Barrymore's love of bizarre roles and outré makeup (no man had less reason to cover his face) led him in 1931 to take on George Du Maurier's wonderful hokum about the sinister, strange-eyed musician who hypnotizes beautiful, blue-eyed little Trilby (Marian Marsh) into becoming a great singer. Some of the sequences are startling: Svengali, his eyes a blank white, stands at the window and casts his spell over the rooftops to the room where Trilby lives; and there are affecting moments, like the failure of Trilby's voice when Svengali's influence wanes. Barrymore, of course, never needed occult powers to be magnetic; Marian Marsh, on the other hand, physically perfect for Trilby, is generally considered the classic example of type-casting. Archie Mayo's direction occasionally suggests the German expressionist films of the preceding decade. With Bramwell Fletcher, Donald Crisp (ubiquitous and eternal), Lumsden Hare, Carmel Myers. (Barrymore always managed to do interesting things with warhorse roles; even his 1933 *Topaze* has nice touches, like the way the shabby, unworldly teacher, handed his first martini, gulps the olive with the liquid.)

⊙ ⊙ ⊙

Sweet Smell of Success. For several years a young clod named Tony Curtis had been a virtual guarantor of box-office success, and the locations for this film were invaded by thousands of teen-agers who broke through police barricades to get at their idol. But these throngs ignored the completed picture, in which Curtis grew up into an actor and gave the best performance of his career. Even the presence of that other box-office guarantor, Burt Lancaster, did not lift the picture from the red ink. This is understandable, for the movie is a sweet slice of perversity, a study of dollar and power worship, with Lancaster as a Broadway gossip columnist and Curtis as an ingratiating, blackmailing press agent. It's seasoned with Clifford Odets's peculiar idiom and served up crisp by director Alexander Mackendrick. The production is shaped by a zest for the corrupt milieu, the pulsating big city life (what used to be called "the symphony of a city") — the streets, the nightclubs, the cynical types, the noise and desperation. There's more vitality in this decadence than most of us care to admit. The weakest part is in the contrasting sweetness and light of the young lovers, Martin Milner and Susan Harrison. This film may be synthetic and melodramatically plotted, but it has more body and flavor than many a more highly regarded work. With Barbara Nichols, Sam Levene. From a short story by Ernest Lehman. Photographed by James Wong Howe. 1957.

⊙ ⊙ ⊙

Symphonie Pastorale. Under André Gide's supervision, his early, subtly disquieting novel about good and evil was transferred to the screen by Jean Delannoy. Pierre Blanchar gives an extraordinary performance as the Swiss pastor who finds a blind girl, teaches and trains her to live without sight, becoming himself involved blindly in a passion for her that destroys the lives of his wife and household; and Michèle Morgan has the role of her career (it won her the Best Actress Award at Cannes in 1947) as the sensitive blind girl who becomes tormented and withdrawn when she gains sight (and insight). Blindness in the film is a touchstone for the spiritual and psychological blindness people cannot overcome. With Jean Desailly and Line Noro. Other awards at Cannes: Best French Film, Best Musical Score (Georges Auric). (Truffaut later did homage to this film in the death scene of Marie Dubois in *Shoot the Piano Player;* Desailly appears as the central figure in *Le Peau Douce.*)

⊙ ⊙ ⊙

Tabu. When two great directors whose approaches to film are very different decide to collaborate, the worst may be expected. Film historians usually discuss this 1930 collaboration between F. W. Murnau (*Nosferatu,*

Faust, The Last Laugh, Sunrise) and Robert Flaherty (*Nanook of The North, Moana, Man of Aran, Louisiana Story*) from the point of view of Flaherty, who quit, sold his interest in the production to Murnau, and left the South Seas. (Murnau himself was killed in an auto accident in 1931, before the opening of *Tabu*.)

It is something like heresy to the generations who revere (rightly) the Flaherty tradition to suggest that the corrupted *Tabu* is a far greater film than Flaherty's uncorrupted *Moana*. *Tabu* has some of the worst scenes that have ever been part of a work of screen art — cavorting natives and a creaking plot, and a heroine with plucked eyebrows for purists to complain about — and its musical score is a classic of kitsch (plaintive, moaning choirs, bits of Schubert and The Moldau), but it also has some of the most exciting sequences ever filmed. The dancing is superlative — indeed, you may cry out in rage at the editor who keeps cutting away from it to a "cute" little boy — and there are sophisticated pictorial effects that must be the work of Murnau. German mysticism may be alien to the islands, but it does wonders for the movie: the old chieftain of the village becomes as chilly a figure of doom as the emaciated vampire of *Nosferatu,* and at the end the ghostly little boat does not seem to be sailing like an ordinary boat . . . It is headed for nothing so commonplace as land. Academy Award for Cinematography to Floyd Crosby.

◉　◉　◉

Tarnished Angels. Rock Hudson said this movie was not like his others, that he disapproved of it, and that such nasty stories shouldn't be presented to the American public. The nasty material is, of course, William Faulkner's *Pylon*. Set in New Orleans in 1931, this 1957 movie attempts to re-create Faulkner's hectic, feverish atmosphere and heroes — the ex-war pilots who will do anything to sustain the thrill of flying. The daredevils are played by Robert Stack, Dorothy Malone as his parachutist wife, and Jack Carson; Hudson, limp as ever, is the newspaperman. This movie would be better — in its odd, neo-thirties sort of way — if the last quarter hour had been left out. It's the kind of bad movie that you know is bad — and yet you're held by it. Douglas Sirk directed. CinemaScope.

◉　◉　◉

Ten Days That Shook the World (known abroad as *October*). Eisenstein followed *Potemkin* with another epic, this 1927 celebration of the ten days in 1917 during which the Bolsheviks overthrew the Kerensky government. This work continues his striking experimental methods — the violent juxtapositions, the use of visual symbols to communicate abstract ideas, and the concept of masses as hero. The movie also has a niche in the history of political falsification: the Soviet government commissioned the film for the tenth anniversary of the Revolution, but it was not shown. Trotsky was one of the main characters in Eisenstein's original version and Trotsky at the time was organizing demonstrations against the Communist Party; Eisenstein had to spend five months re-editing the work to dislodge Trotsky from his place in the making of the Revolution. Even this edited version was later banned, as "formalist." I'm a little cold about this film (one can't really be cold to *Potemkin*) — its satire is heavyhanded, its visual puns too simpleminded. The brutal, bloody *Strike* — his 1924 film — has a charge, a sense of a new direction. *Ten Days* seems already the end.

◉ ◉ ◉

The Thin Man. Alexander Woollcott had called Dashiell Hammett's novel "the best detective story yet written in America," but no one foresaw the success it would have on the screen. Adapted by Albert Hackett and Frances Goodrich, and directed by W. S. Van Dyke in 1934, it took just sixteen days to film. But it turned out to be one of the most popular comedies ever made. It started a new cycle in screen entertainment by demonstrating that a murder mystery could also be a sophisticated comedy. As Nick and Nora Charles, William Powell and Myrna Loy shocked and delighted the country by indicating that a married couple didn't have to suffer and adjust and learn to live with each other. These two drank cocktails, exchanged insolent remarks, and got along fine. (*The Thin Man* has one of the classic moments of thirties comedy: William Powell taking the gun his complaisant wife has just given him for Christmas and shooting the ornaments off the tree.) This is the kind of commercially successful movie that new audiences can't enjoy as audiences of the time did, because new audiences aren't fed up, as the public in 1934 was, with what *The Thin Man* was breaking away from.

◉ ◉ ◉

The Third Man. The most famous collaboration of Carol Reed and Graham Greene has the structure of a good suspense thriller. The simple American, Joseph Cotten, arrives in postwar Vienna to meet an old friend, only to be told that the friend has been killed in an accident. In trying to discover the facts, Cotten learns so much about his friend that when he finally finds him alive, he kills him. Orson Welles's portrait of the friend, Harry Lime, is a brilliant study of corruption — evil, witty, unreachable; it is balanced against Trevor Howard's quietly elegant underplaying of the army officer who teaches the American some of the uglier facts of life. There is a fascinating ambiguity about our relation to the Cotten character: he is alone against the forces of the city and, in a final, devastating stroke, he is even robbed of the illusion that the girl (Alida Valli) is interested in him, but his illusions are so commonplace that his disillusion does not strike us deeply.

Greene has made him a shallow, ineffectual, well-meaning American. *The Third Man* has a peculiar atmosphere: the sardonic world-weary people, the sound of the zither, the baroque statues in the chic ruins, the tawdriness, are rotten but glamorous; Welles's monster is attractively macabre. But the ghastly hospital sequence (which is based on facts) seems a little unfair: we've been enjoying all this decadence and stylish acting and these people living on their nerves, and then we're forced to take evil seriously. Robert Krasker's photography won the Academy Award. The zither music is by Anton Karas. 1949. (According to Welles, the producer, Alexander Korda, provided the conception of the movie — both the story and the setting.)

⊙　⊙　⊙

The Thirty-Nine Steps. In 1935 Alfred Hitchcock explained the point of view behind *The Thirty-Nine Steps:* "I am out to give the public good, healthy, mental shake-ups. Civilization has become so screening and sheltering that we cannot experience sufficient thrills at first hand. Therefore, to prevent our becoming sluggish and jellified, we have to experience them artificially." What fun to make a movie in an era when people still needed a bit of a jolt! Even now, oddly enough, these little jolts are more surprising — and certainly more satisfying — than most of the shocks engineered to stun modern audiences. *The Thirty-Nine Steps* is a suave, amusing spy melodrama, directed with so sure a touch that the suspense is charged with wit; it's one of the three or four best things Hitchcock has ever done. The lead, Robert Donat, was that rarity among English actors: a performer with both personal warmth and professional skill. The heroine is Madeleine Carroll. Hitchcock paired them off by the mischievous use of a gimmick: a man and a woman who detest each other are handcuffed together; as day wears into night, they fall in love. The movie thus contains an extra — implicit, as it were — element of suspense, and theatre employees reported a sharp rise in the use of washroom facilities. Among Hitchcock's pleasing perversities was the casting of Godfrey Tearle, who looked astonishingly like Franklin Delano Roosevelt, as the chief enemy agent. The film also has one of his rare emotionally felt sequences: the brief, chilling scenes between Peggy Ashcroft and John Laurie as a mismated couple, joined together by real chains. John Buchan's novel was adapted by Charles Bennett, Ian Hay, and Alma Reville.

⊙　⊙　⊙

To Have and Have Not. In 1944 Humphrey Bogart, the greatest cynical hero of them all, found himself in Martinique, where a beautiful big cat of a girl named Lauren Bacall slouched across the screen for the first time and managed to make the question, "Anybody got a match?" sound like the most insolent and insinuating of demands. Howard Hawks directed this thoroughly enjoyable entertainment from what the Warner Brothers advertised as Ernest Hemingway's novel, with William Faulkner listed as co-author (with Jules Furthman) of the screenplay — which makes this the only movie I know of with two Nobel Prize-winning authors. Don't let this mislead you: it's the Warners mixture as before — sex and politics — but better this time.

Some years ago François Truffaut and Jacques Rivette, then young critics for *Cahiers du Cinema,* interviewed Howard Hawks, whom they considered a genius. They asked him about *To Have and Have Not,* and he replied that once when he and Ernest Hemingway were hunting together, he had claimed that he could take Hemingway's worst story and make a movie of it. Hemingway asked which was his worst, and Hawks said *To Have and Have Not.* According to Hawks, Hemingway then explained that he had written it in one sitting when he needed money. Hawks made a good movie but he and the screenwriters cheated a bit: the movie deals with what may have occurred in the lives of the characters before the novel begins. (Footnotes for somebody's Ph.D. thesis on "Novel into Film": the novel's ending was used to polish off John Huston's film version of Maxwell Anderson's dreary play *Key Largo;* the novel's plot was used for another movie, *The Breaking Point,* directed by Michael Curtiz in 1950; and the short story "One Trip Across" which Hemingway had expanded into *To Have and Have Not* was used for an Audie Murphy movie, *The Gun Runners,* directed by Don Siegel in 1958. An additional irony: the Hawks version no doubt altered the Hemingway original in order to combine elements that had made big box office of Curtiz's *Casablanca.*)

Viewed today, the simple-mindedness and the slick professionalism of a film like *To Have and Have Not* are so refreshing that the tawdry forties may seem like a golden age. They weren't, but the characters were defined: if a man was perverse, you knew he was a Nazi. A movie like this one seemed quite daring in those days when daring meant sexy. A writer said of Lauren Bacall that her "husky, underslung voice, which is ideal for the double entendre, makes even her simplest remarks sound like jungle mating cries." Hoagy Carmichael provides the music and accompaniment for Miss Bacall's facial exercises; the singing voice is that of Andy Williams and it never sounded sexier than when coming out of her. Lauren Bacall's debut had, in a sense, been pre-tested: Jules Furthman had worked out that good-bad girl act for Betty Compson in *Docks of New York* and perfected it on Marlene Dietrich in *Morocco.* With Walter Brennan, Marcel Dalio, and Dan Seymour (literally, the heavy).

◉　◉　◉

Touch of Evil. Marlene Dietrich (done up in her Gypsy makeup from *Golden Earrings* of 1947), greets the grotesquely oversized, padded, false-nosed Orson Welles with a glorious understatement — "You're a mess, honey. You've been eating too much candy." When the final bullet punctures him and he is floating in the water like a dead whale, she eulogizes — "What can you say about anybody? He was some kind of a man . . ." That may be the worst line ever written or a sly parody of modern bad writing, e.g., the funeral scene in *Death of a Salesman*. *Touch of Evil*, in 1958, Welles's first American production in a decade, is a garish, flamboyant thriller which has something, but not very much, to do with drugs and police corruption in a border town. What it really has to do with is love of the film medium and all its stylistic possibilities; and if Welles can't resist the candy of shadows and angles and baroque décor, he turns it into stronger fare than most directors' solemn meat-and-potatoes. Despite early charges that the producers had re-edited parts of *Touch of Evil*, Welles says that it has been mutilated less than most of his pictures, and that the changes were less than a tenth of what has been done to some of them. One obvious offense was superimposing the titles over the opening sequence — one of the most brilliantly entertaining film openings of all time (and, incidentally, the key to the mystery). The cast, assembled as perversely as in a nightmare, includes Dietrich as the madam of a Mexican bordello, Charlton Heston, Joseph Calleia, Akim Tamiroff, Joseph Cotten, Zsa Zsa Gabor, Mercedes McCambridge, and Janet Leigh. Photographed in the nightmare city, Venice, California. Welles wrote the script, but not the original story, nor the preposterous title. *Touch of Evil* won the Critics' Prize for the Best Film at the Brussels Fair; in the United States the distributing company had so little confidence in it that it was released in most areas without any press showings.

◉　◉　◉

The Treasure of Sierra Madre. In a brilliant characterization, Humphrey Bogart takes the tough-guy role to its psychological limits: the man who stands alone goes from depravity through paranoia to total disintegration. (Almost incredibly, *The Treasure of Sierra Madre* was a box-office flop; apparently audiences resented Bogart's departure from the immensely popular *Casablanca* stereotype.) Three Americans stranded in Mexico strike it rich, and the director, John Huston, "looks on," as he says, and "lets them stew in their own juice." Bogart's companions are a toothless Walter Huston as a shrewd old prospector, and Tim Holt as a blunt, honest young man. Bogart's character (Fred C. Dobbs) is enough fate for anyone, but it has its outward representative in Alfonso Bedoya as a primitive bandit (if you've never appreciated civilization, the encounter with Bedoya may change your outlook). With Bruce Bennett, Barton MacLane, and John Huston as the victim of Bogart's cadging. Ted McCord gets the credit for the photography, Max Steiner the blame for the music, and somebody should be slapped hard for the intrusion of that loving-wife's letter. But all in all, this adaptation of the B. Traven novel is one of the strongest of all American movies. Academy Awards for 1948: Best Direction, Screenplay, Supporting Actor (Walter Huston).

⊙   ⊙   ⊙

Twentieth Century. In no other period or place in movie history has satirical farce flourished as it did in Hollywood in the thirties. Sound had brought in the wisecrack, and in the Depression little was sacrosanct. Everybody knew that money and fame were ludicrous and transitory; racial humor was still gross, but usually affectionate and corny; even religion could be kidded. In our comedies now there is nothing like the careless irreverence of *Twentieth Century* — produced in those days when Hollywood was not yet subservient to the image-conscious pressure groups who have now made it almost impossible for a joke to have a butt, for satire to have a target, for wit to contain any truth.

Twentieth Century of 1934 is a first-rate farce about theatrical personalities, and John Barrymore was perhaps the greatest of the farceurs. Great romantic actors are rarely great comedians; in our day Laurence Olivier is almost the only example. Barrymore, a Shakespearean actor and then a romantic movie idol, reveled in satire of the theatre. He makes the egomaniac producer Oscar Jaffe a roaring caricature of theatrical drive and temperament. He is assisted by Carole Lombard as his protegée, Lily Garland née Mildred Plotka. Lombard's talents were not of the highest, but her spirits were, and in her skin-tight satins she incarnates the giddy, absurd glamour of thirties comedy. Most of the action takes place on the "crack" train of the title, the "Twentieth Century," going from Chicago to New York; in the thirties, the "Twentieth Century" represented the latest thing in speed and luxury.

The director, Howard Hawks, represents the American commercial film at its best — fast, unpretentious, entertaining, with a sophisticated and "hardboiled" attitude toward sex and money. In *Twentieth Century* he worked with a fine collection of character actors, faces that were as familiar as the faces with great names: Walter Connolly as Oliver; Roscoe Karns as Owen; Charles Levison as Max Jacobs; Etienne Giradot as Clark, the religious zealot; Edgar Kennedy as Mr. McGonigle; Edward Gargan as the sheriff; Herman Bing as the bearded Passion Play actor; et al. Ben Hecht and Charles MacArthur adapted the play by Bruce Millholland. Barrymore appeared in other successful thirties comedies; he was with Lombard again in *True Confession* (she was a compulsive liar in this one), and he performed charmingly with Claudette Colbert in the romantic comedy *Midnight.* The genre of sophisticated romantic comedy, which also flourished in the thirties, produced some of the best entertainments of the period, such as

The Greeks Had a Word for Them with Ina Claire, Joan Blondell, and Madge Evans; *The Richest Girl in the World* with Miriam Hopkins and Joel McCrea; Lubitsch's *Trouble in Paradise; The Moon's Our Home* with Margaret Sullavan and Henry Fonda; *Topper* with Constance Bennett, Cary Grant, and Roland Young; *He Married His Wife* with Nancy Kelly, Joel McCrea, and Mary Boland; *Easy Living* with Jean Arthur, from a Preston Sturges script. There were still occasional examples of this genre in the early forties, such as *The Lady Eve* with Barbara Stanwyck and Henry Fonda and *The Palm Beach Story* with Claudette Colbert and Joel McCrea, both written and directed by Preston Sturges; but, somehow, the genre didn't survive the war. Most of those lovely comediennes survived, but as "stars" — and their pictures were neither romantic nor sophisticated.

⊙   ⊙   ⊙

Two Weeks in Another Town. In *Two Weeks in Another Town* five men who had earlier worked together on *The Bad and the Beautiful* — the producer John Houseman, the director Vincente Minnelli, the screenwriter Charles Schnee, the composer David Raksin, and the star Kirk Douglas — hold up *The Bad and the Beautiful* as the model of a great film. They run scenes from it and discuss it as the example of what they once did when they were really creative (it's as if they'd been reading Albert Johnson and believed him). They actually run sequences of Lana Turner in that film as examples of great screen acting. Now truly, sentiment can go only so far; artists must be tough-minded. *The Bad and the Beautiful* was a glossy, entertaining, novelettish movie, punctuated with some flashy hysterical scenes. In *Two Weeks in Another Town* the hysteria is predominant, and money and craftsmanship are lavished on a maudlin form of cynicism. This movie resembles the Norman Maine side of *A Star is Born*. The thematic material about shooting a film in Rome is, peculiarly, a fantasy, and the characters are seen at a time of extreme strain and extravagant disorder. Hollywood's infatuation with its own wickedness begins to seem ridiculous in this overheated atmosphere.

The movie is accoutered with swank and sophistication (it includes orgies designed to out-do *La Dolce Vita,* and Cyd Charisse done-up like the heroine of *Marienbad*); the compositions are fancy and stylized. And, once again, what passes for screenwriting are a series of clinkers:

On a beach where, presumably, people speak the truth, the young "fresh" heroine (Daliah Lavi) asks the tired ex-star (Douglas) what he was like when he was a star. "Lonely", he answers. "So famous and alone?" she asks. "Everybody's alone. Actors more so." "Why would anyone want to be an actor?" And Kirk Douglas replies with a straight face, "That's a good question. To hide from the world. What's the audience doing there but hiding . . . trading their problems for mine on the screen."

Douglas meets this girl in the screening room after the showing of an old film of his (in both senses): "I thought everybody had gone," he says. "Everybody has", she replies. "What's your name?" "Veronica." "Veronica what?" "Veronica what's-the-difference." In this way does the script writer establish (a) that the girl is not famous, and (b) that she doesn't care about fame. And how do we know that she's really a sweet and sympathetic character? When Douglas kisses her, she touches the scar on his face, thus demonstrating that it is the hurt man rather than the famous man that she cares about.

Is it impossible for the Hollywood studios to find (and trust) writers? Minnelli movies are beginning to resemble the worst of von Sternberg: *Two Weeks in Another Town* is to *The Bad and the Beautiful* as *Shanghai Gesture* is to *Shanghai Express*. And Minnelli's pictorial imagination is just too pretty — the sumptuous gorgeousness turns into slop. In the circumstances, some of the performers — Kirk Douglas and Edward G. Robinson — are surprisingly good. With George Hamilton, Claire Trevor, James Gregory, Rosanna Schiaffino. Based on the novel by Irwin Shaw. 1962, color.

⊚ ⊚ ⊚

Umberto D. Vittorio De Sica's Umberto D. is a stubborn old gentleman with bourgeois standards and no means, isolated in an impersonal modern city, unable to communicate with anyone. His alienation has such pride and spirit that he is not unworthy to stand as a symbol of man's fate. But men do not necessarily want to view their fate: this great, pure, and compassionate work has been seen by only a few thousand people. Yet for those few — and their numbers grow each year — it may be a rare, transforming experience. Script by Cesare Zavattini. 1952.

⊚ ⊚ ⊚

Unfaithfully Yours. The hero is Rex Harrison in a sensational parody of Sir Thomas Beecham; he disposes of his wife (Linda Darnell) in three different ways, to the music of Rossini, Wagner, and Tchaikovsky. What more can one ask of a movie? This late (1948) work written and directed by Preston Sturges is one of the best comedies ever made in this country (though, for reasons I can't fathom, it got very bad reviews). Harrison gives perhaps his most amusing screen performance since Carol Reed's 1940 thriller *Night Train* — and *Unfaithfully Yours* gives him a much better role. (Harrison's best "serious" performance is probably in Joseph L. Mankiewicz's neglected *Escape,* also in 1948.) It's all been downhill since . . . With Edgar Kennedy, Rudy Vallee, Lionel Stander, Kurt Kreuger, Barbara Lawrence. Writers and directors have been stealing from this movie for years, most recently in *Gambit.*

⊙ ⊙ ⊙

Vampyr. Carl Dreyer's *Vampyr* can scarcely be discussed in the context of vampire movies. With the exception of Murnau's *Nosferatu,* the other works in the genre are mostly silly, meretricious, obvious. Dreyer seems to prey upon our subconscious, our unformulated fears: the mood is evocative, dreamy, spectral. Psychological surprise, dread, and obsession are the substance of the film; death hovers over everyone.

Many years later, in Hollywood, Val Lewton was to employ suggestion in that horror series that started with *The Cat People,* but the suggestions were banal compared with Dreyer's murky, ambiguous trances and terrors. For a more startling contrast in method, it is fascinating to compare this great 1932 classic of the supernatural with a recent exercise in supernatural chic — Roger Vadim's *Blood and Roses,* which is based on the same story by Sheridan Le Fanu.

The cast of *Vampyr* is headed by Julian West (the movie name of Nicolas de Gunzburg), with Henriette Gerard as the blood-sucker, Reva Mandel and Sybille Schmitz as her potential victims. The incomparable photographic effects are, of course, the work of Rudolph Maté. (Lovers of film will cherish what appears to be Dreyer's homage to Cocteau — the use of the little heart from *Blood of a Poet.*)

⊙ ⊙ ⊙

Variety Lights (*Luci del Varieta*). In 1949 Federico Fellini, who had been a scriptwriter on about a dozen films, directed his first picture (working with Alberto Lattuada as co-director). *Variety Lights* is a "backstage" story (with a theme he returned to later in the big trashy phantasmagoria, *Juliet of the Spirits*). Giulietta Masina plays the aging mistress of the head of a touring company; he goes off with a younger woman, then returns to her. It's a very simple and in some ways tawdry film, but Fellini shows his extraordinary talent for the dejected setting, the shabby performer, the fat old chorine, the singer who will never hit the high notes. Though he always deals with "artists," he never deals with talent or artistry (not even in *La Dolce Vita* or *8½*). His specialty is revealing the shoddiness of theatrical life. For Fellini, the magic of show business (and this is the magic of his films) is in self-delusion. The most memorable moments of a Fellini film are likely to be images of defeat, nostalgia, forlorn hopes, dismal theatrical routines; in *Variety Lights* there is the troupe on a back country road at night, and the satirical "glorification" of a sex goddess. The failure — the dreamer fooled by dreams — is the poetic center of Fellini's films. He has a special feeling for the beauty in a desolate human landscape, for the cheaters who are so transparently losers, for the indestructible dreamers. With Peppino de Filippo, Carla del Poggio, Folco Lulli, John Kitzmiller.

◉ ◉ ◉

I Vitelloni (released in the United States as *The Young and the Passionate;* the French title was *Les Inutiles;* a literal translation of the Italian would be "the big calves", i.e., the sucklings — which, rendered idiomatically, would be something like "adolescent slobs"). Frustrated small-town boys with big ideas, these sons of indulgent, middle-class families cadge off their parents, loaf, and dream of women, riches, and glory. Their energies are wasted in idiotic pursuits; whatever dreams or ideals they have are pathetically childish or rotten. Fellini, who wrote and directed this film in 1953, has an altogether different approach to the subject from, say, the Hollywood attitude as revealed in *The Wild One.* His treatment is ambiguous — a fusion of acid satire and warm acceptance. He never suggests that these men should adjust to anything; he observes the farce of their aimless lives without condescension.

Americans have argued that the actors are too old for their roles; Europeans reply that this misses the point of the film, that it is not the actors but the characters they portray who are indeed too old for the parasitical lives they lead. (The Italian film historian, Mario Gromo, described them as "eternal adolescents, even though approaching thirty — and when they reach it, it makes them more slothful.") The young heroes suggest an American wolf pack. There is Fausto the flirt (Franco Fabrizi), who will become another unhappy, middle-class family man; plump, ludicrous Alberto the buffoon (Alberto Sordi, Fellini's "White Sheik" of the previous year, and before that a music hall actor who first achieved recognition as the dubbed voice of Oliver Hardy); Leopoldo the poet (Leopoldo Trieste), whose naïve artistic illusions wilt when he is propositioned by an ancient homosexual actor; and there is Moraldo (Franco Interlenghi, who a few years earlier had been one of De Sica's two great child stars in *Shoeshine*), the Fellini figure, the autobiographical hero, the only one who finds the guts to say goodbye to all this futile provincial life. In 1953 there was no indication in Fellini's work that the road his hero takes out of the provinces will lead to the urban corruption of *La Dolce Vita.* (Incidentally, *I Vitelloni* provides a perfect rebuttal to the eminent American judge who proposed as a solution to our juvenile delinquency the restoration of the father's authority as he observed it during a trip to Italy.)

◉ ◉ ◉

Viva Zapata! Before the rifles of that infamous concealed regiment get poor Zapata (Marlon Brando), John Steinbeck's script has thoroughly done him in. Land and liberty, the simple slogans of the Mexican civil wars of 1911–19, are transformed into the American liberal clichés of 1952, and phrased in that slurpy imitation of simplicity and grandeur which high school English teachers call "poetry." The virtues of the production are in Elia Kazan's slam-bang direction: some of the scenes have startling immediacy; the fighting is first-rate; even the phony folklore is continuously interesting; there is a reminiscence of Malraux's *L'Espoir*. And the actors are fun to watch: there's the magnetic young Brando (age twenty-seven) impersonating a great revolutionary leader — an illiterate young titan, a peasant and thinker (and in the time-worn actor-peasant tradition, he screws up his face when he has to think — as if thinking were heavy labor, like hod-carrying). And there are Anthony Quinn (his performance took the Academy Award for Best Supporting Actor) as Zapata's older brother; Jean Peters as Josefa; Joseph Wiseman (later to be Dr. No) as Fernando the journalist, acting like some sinister mixture of Judas Iscariot and a junkie; Alan Reed as Pancho Villa; Lou Gilbert as Pablo; Margo (I'd almost thought they'd shriveled her up for good in *Lost Horizon*) as Soldadera; Harold Gordon as Madero; Frank Silvera as Huerta; and Mildred Dunnock, Arnold Moss, etc. The film includes Steinbeck's folly: the famous, supposedly terribly touching wedding night scene in which Zapata asks Josefa to teach him to read. (To deflower his virgin mind?)

◎   ◎   ◎

Waxworks (*Das Wachsfigurenkabinett*). Conrad Veidt, Emil Jannings, and Werner (*Dr. Caligari*) Krauss are the three villains of this German horror fantasy of 1924; they play, respectively, Ivan the Terrible, Haroun-al-Raschid (one of Jannings's rare comic performances), and Jack the Ripper. The Veidt-Ivan sequence has ingenious sadistic touches: Ivan enjoys poisoning people and presenting them with hourglasses timed for the precise moment of their deaths; one fine day, he discovers an hourglass labeled "Ivan." The director, Paul Leni, a former Max Reinhardt collaborator, was an extraordinary scenic artist whose influence may be guessed at in Eisenstein's *Ivan;* his work on the macabre, expressionistic décor for the Jack-the-Ripper sequence — which is made entirely from sheets of painted paper — may have (directly or indirectly) influenced the sequence in *Modesty Blaise* in which Tina Marquand is murdered. With William Dieterle.

◎   ◎   ◎

Where's Charley? Ray Bolger's earlier screen roles never gave him a full-scale opportunity; *Where's Charley?* transfers one of his most famous Broadway performances to film record, capturing the airy grace of the greatest comic dancer this country has produced. The plot is sturdy old *Charley's Aunt,* and Bolger is Oxford's favorite female impersonator. He has a charming partner in Allyn McLerie as Amy, as well as a suitor in Horace Cooper as Mr. Spettigue. There are a pair of lovers — Robert Shackleton and Mary Germaine — but you can find some excuse to step oustide during their duet. Frank Loesser contributed the music (which includes "Make a Miracle" and "Once in Love with Amy"). David Butler directed. 1952, color.

⊚ ⊚ ⊚

The White Sheik (*Lo Sceicco Bianco*). This 1952 social comedy is perhaps the most gentle and naturalistic of Federico Fellini's films, but it was not a success: perhaps because it is a little flat in places (Fellini is still clumsy and the story-telling is rather drawn-out) or perhaps because the target of the affectionate satire on glamour and delusion is precisely the kind of people who go to the movies. The heroine, Brunella Bovo (also the heroine of De Sica's *Miracle in Milan*) has come to Rome for her honeymoon, but the devotion of the groom (Leopoldo Trieste) is much less important to her than her infatuation for the "White Shiek" — the hero of a photographic comic strip. She rushes off to find her ideal, and the poor wretch of a vulgar actor (Alberto Sordi) tries to rise above himself to the level of her fantasies. The White Shiek, it turns out, is far more a creature of self-delusion than the star-struck bride. The groom, deserted, sad, and anxious, wandering at night in the piazza, finds solace in conversation with a lively, friendly little prostitute (Giuletta Masina; Fellini later developed this episode into *Nights of Cabiria*). Among those who worked on the story and script were Fellini, Ennio Flaiano, Tullio Pinelli, and Michelangelo Antonioni. Music by Nino Rota.

⊚ ⊚ ⊚

The Whole Town's Talking. In 1935 John Ford directed this comedy-melodrama about a gentle clerk, his gangster double (Edward G. Robinson in a dual role), and the hard-boiled girl, Bill, that the clerk adores. Bill is Jean Arthur, the charming and astonishingly durable comedienne. In 1923 Ford directed her in a John Gilbert vehicle, *Cameo Kirby,* and during the silent period she was a popular leading lady. Talkies made her a star; her distinctive, wistful-husky voice was one of the best sounds in romantic comedies of the thirties and forties. In 1953 Miss Arthur was the heroine of *Shane;* her thirty years as the heroine is an almost incredible record. *The Whole Town's Talking,* adapted from a W. R. Burnett story, is a gangster comedy-thriller with a humane outlook: its lack of violence stands in almost poignant contrast to the thrillers of later decades.

⊚ ⊚ ⊚

Wild Strawberries (*Smultronstallet*). After an opening that excited expectations (although it bore a startling resemblance to the "room for one more" nightmare in *Dead of Night* and to passages in Dreyer's *Vampyr*), I found Ingmar Bergman's *Wild Strawberries* a rather lumpy Odyssey. What might have been a complex, serene contemplation of a man's life is too tricked up with effects and contrasts and peculiarly unconvincing flashbacks. The dialogue is over-explicit; the representatives of youth are incredibly callow; Gunnar Bjornstrand as the son is much too rigid; Bibi Andersson, who was so magical in *The Seventh Seal,* is disappointingly vacuous as the two Saras; Naima Wifstrand as the ancient mother is rather expendable. But I don't expect that I will ever forget Victor Sjostrom's image; nor the vicious, bickering couple who rasp at each other in the back seat of the car; nor the large-scale mask of the beautiful Ingrid Thulin as the daughter-in-law. And how many movies give us even one memorable moment? 1957.

⊚ ⊚ ⊚

Winterset. Maxwell Anderson's most famous verse drama came out of the Depression years. It is a blend of *Romeo and Juliet* with the Sacco-Vanzetti case, and in 1936 it was widely held to be the supremely-eloquent-last-word-on-the-unconquerable-soul-of-man. Burgess Meredith, who mastered the cadences for Broadway, made his first screen appearance as Mio, giving fine voice and excellent interpretation to the soaring banalities that one might — in a romantic mood — mistake for poetry. The work does have some quality, but I hesitate to name it. With Margo as Miriamne ("Is it better to tell a lie — and live?"!), Edward Ellis as Judge Gaunt, Eduardo Ciannelli in his most memorable screen performance as Trock Estrella, Stanley Ridges as Shadow, Maurice Moscovitch as Esdras, Paul Guilfoyle as Garth Esdras. Alfred Santell directed.

⊚ ⊚ ⊚

Woman in a Dressing Gown. Yvonne Mitchell is an extraordinary English actress whose best performances are usually in films that nobody in the United States goes to see. Her role here as the desperately disorganized wife of a neat, rising office worker (Anthony Quayle) took the Best Actress Award at Berlin in 1957; she achieves an unusual balance of sensitivity and insensitivity, the painful and the absurd. The movie is well written (by Ted Willis) in the semi-angry mode and well directed by J. Lee Thompson; it deserves a wider audience, though it carries unpretentiousness to a fault. With Sylvia Syms, Andrew Ray.

⊚ ⊚ ⊚

The Young in Heart. The title is sickening, and the movie does have a mushy messagey side, but the story about a family-style confidence gang (Roland Young and Billie Burke are the parents; Douglas Fairbanks, Jr. and Janet Gaynor are the children) has some good bright moments. There is the posh automobile, the "Flying Wombat," and the marvelous sequence in which Fairbanks and Young set out to look for work and pause to watch the honest labor of hod carriers as if they were observing a strange kind of insect activity. I've never been addicted to Miss Gaynor's peculiarly saccharine charms, but Paulette Goddard is in it too, and she's shiny and attractive. With Richard Carlson and Minnie Dupree. Richard Wallace directed. 1938.

◉ ◉ ◉

Zazie. Movies are said to be an international language, but sometimes a film that is popular in one country finds only a small audience in another. This anarchistic, impudent comedy (from Raymond Queneau's novel *Zazie dans le Metro*), a great success in France in 1960, has hardly even been heard of in the United States. There is perhaps some major national difference in reactions to slapstick and wit: the film, which is like a Mack Sennett two-reeler running wild, has been peculiarly disturbing for American critics and audiences alike. To Americans, *Zazie* seems to go too far, to be almost demonic in its inventiveness, like a joke that gets so complicated you can't time your laughs comfortably. The editing, which is very fast, may be too clever: audiences here can't quite keep up. Some critics have suggested that, for Americans, this comedy turns into some kind of freakish, fantastic anxiety. Putting it as squarely as possible, Bosley Crowther wrote in the New York *Times:* "There is something not quite innocent or healthy about this film." Yet the film is like *Alice in Wonderland:* Zazie (Catherine Demongeot) is a foul-mouthed little cynic, age eleven, who comes to Paris for a weekend with her uncle (Philippe Noiret), a female impersonator, and nobody and nothing are quite what they seem. Louis Malle, who directed, includes satirical allusions to *La Dolce Vita* and other films, and a parody of his own *The Lovers.* Many of the latest styles in film editing, which are generally said to derive from Alain Resnais or Richard Lester, have an earlier source in *Zazie.* Color.

Index